Divining Victory
Airpower in the 2006 Israel-Hezbollah War

WILLIAM M. ARKIN

Maxwell Air Force Base, Alabama

August 2007

Disclaimer

Opinions, conclusions, and recommendations expressed or implied within are solely those of the author and do not necessarily represent the views of Air University, the United States Air Force, the Department of Defense, or any other US government agency. Cleared for public release: distribution unlimited.

Published by Books Express Publishing

Copyright © Books Express, 2010

ISBN 978-1-907521-11-9

To purchase copies at discounted prices please contact info@books-express.com

As far as the Lebanese situation is concerned, the main problem is how do we consider what has happened and how matters have ended up? Do we consider it a victory or a defeat? If we consider it a victory, what are the limits and value of this victory so that we can compare the victory with the sacrifices that have been made? It is then that we can say if the sacrifices have detracted from this victory or not. This is the key to the discussion of every question.

—Hezbollah secretary-general Hassan Nasrallah
As-Safir, 6 September 2006

Nobody can impose terms on us, or commit us to anything we do not believe in. Let me be clear: Israel won't get through politics what it didn't get through war, even if the UN resolution gave this to Israel . . . What they couldn't do through war, they want to do by peaceful means? It doesn't work like that.

—Hezbollah deputy secretary-general Naim Qassem
Al-Manar television, 15 August 2006

Hezbollah is trying to say it won but in fact, according to the facts, the guerrilla group took a big hit with the destruction of major infrastructure in southern Lebanon and our achievements are significant. . . . We have to focus on the facts. We are ready in a different way in the North than we were before the war. We have succeeded in lowering the dangers there and have increased our readiness.

—Israeli minister of defense Amir Peretz
The Jerusalem Post, 1 October 2006

We must read the picture and learn our lessons. But we must arrive at a situation in which we do not miss the forests due to the trees.

—Lt Gen Dan Halutz
Israeli Defense Force chief of staff
20 September 2006

I don't want to get into an argument about the meaning of victory, but I ask: Were we in such a state of defeat before July 12 that we needed such a "great" and "strategic" victory following July 12? . . . If "strategic victory" refers to our bombing of Haifa . . . Saddam Hussein attacked Tel Aviv with Scud missiles—was that a strategic victory as well? . . . You hear people say: He entered the battlefield, fought like a brave hero, and then was martyred. Is that really our goal? . . . I don't understand how anyone can claim that one side was defeated, without losing lives or suffering destruction, while the other side has won, with all this destruction and loss of lives. How can one be called a victory and the other a defeat?

—Sheik Ali Al-Amin
Shi'a Mufti of Tyre, 26 August 2006

Contents

Illustrations

Figure		*Page*

About
the Author

Author William M. Arkin in Aiyt a-Shab, at a village
along the Lebanese-Israeli border in September 2006.

William M. Arkin is an independent military analyst, journalist, and author. He writes the "Early Warning" column for
washingtonpost.com (where he previously wrote the "DOT.MIL"
column from 1998 to 2003) and is a longtime NBC News military analyst. During the writing of this study in early 2007, he
was National Security and Human Rights Fellow at the Carr
Center for Human Rights Policy at the John F. Kennedy School
of Government at Harvard University. He is currently working on an empirical study with Matthew McKinzie for the Carr
Center, using data from Iraq, Yugoslavia, and Afghanistan to
answer the question "Why Civilians Die."

Arkin is also an adjunct at the School of Advanced Air and
Space Studies, Air University, Maxwell AFB, Alabama. He previously served as Senior Military Adviser to Human Rights
Watch, the largest international human rights and law organization in the United States.

Since 1991 Arkin has also participated in or conducted on-
the-ground assessments of the effects of military conflict in
Iraq, Lebanon, the former Yugoslavia, Afghanistan, and Eritrea.
He is well known as a pioneer in the method of independent
fieldwork and research to investigate the effects of weapons
and warfare on civilian populations and has visited more than
1,000 targets that have been the subject of aerial attack.

Arkin headed Greenpeace International's war response team in the Persian Gulf during Operation Desert Storm, and co-authored *On Impact—Modern Warfare and the Environment: A Case of the Gulf War*, the first comprehensive study of the civilian and environmental effects of the war. In 1991 he visited Iraq to evaluate civilian damage as part of the International Study Team, conducting one of the most methodical on-the-ground bomb damage assessments. On subsequent visits to Iraq, he evaluated the effects of the bombing of electrical power and the use of cluster bombs. He visited Lebanon after Operation Grapes of Wrath, Serbia after Operation Allied Force, and Afghanistan after Operation Enduring Freedom for Human Rights Watch to evaluate civilian casualties and the impact of those conflicts. Arkin subsequently served as a consultant on Iraq to the office of the secretary-general of the United Nations during Operation Desert Fox. He served as military advisor to a UN fact-finding mission in Israel and Lebanon in 2006.

Arkin has briefed the findings of his investigations before dozens of government and nongovernmental audiences at the headquarters level and to various "lesson learned" projects (the *Gulf War Air Power Survey*, the Air War over Serbia project, the Center for Naval Analysis, Operation Enduring Look, Defense Science Board). He has authored or coauthored several books and over 500 articles and conference papers on military affairs as well as chapters in more than two dozen edited books. Arkin served in the US Army as an intelligence analyst in West Berlin from 1974 to 1978.

Acknowledgments

This study would not have been possible without the support of Lt Gen Stephen Lorenz, commander of Air University, Maxwell AFB, Alabama. He instantly recognized the importance of an independent quick-look study of the role of airpower in the 2006 Israel-Hezbollah war and arranged for the College of Aerospace Doctrine, Research and Education/Airpower Research Institute (CADRE/ARI) to shepherd this study into existence as part of a new initiative. Dr. Daniel R. Mortensen, chief of research at CADRE/ARI, cheerfully and unswervingly maneuvered the study to completion. Col Steven Carey, commander of CADRE, cleared the way. Col Michael Davis, director of the Airpower Research Institute and by my good luck a Middle East expert, provided detailed comments and piled on constant additional research materials. Jerry L. Gantt at Air University Press took on the burden of coordinating the editing of a complex manuscript.

I was in residence at the Carr Center for Human Rights Policy at the John F. Kennedy School of Government at Harvard University during completion of the manuscript. My good friend Sarah Sewall, director of the center, deserves credit not only for opening the door at Harvard but also for enduring neglect of other responsibilities while the author obsessed. The staff and interns at the center provided essential help, noise, and diversion. Ken Roth, director of Human Rights Watch, provided important comments and food for debate.

I would also like express my gratitude to the following persons at Air University for their comments, support and assistance in making this study possible: Dr. Mark Conversino, associate dean of Academic Programs, Air War College; Stan Norris, research and publications support, Air War College; Dr. Robert C. DiPrizio, course director, International Security Studies, Air Command and Staff College; Lt Col Barak Carlson, director Research and Publications, Air Command and Staff College; and Dr. David R. Mets, Robyn Read, and John Conway, military analysts at CADRE/ARI. Steven V. Borders of ARI translated valuable primary source material from Arabic. Additional help came from the Air University Press Team: Tammi Long and Lula

Barnes, technical editors; L. Susan Fair, illustrator; Vivian D. O'Neal, print specialist; and Mary Moore, quality review.

My old friend Gen John D. W. Corley, USAF vice chief of staff at the time I was working on this manuscript, and Lt Gen David Deptula, deputy chief of staff for Intelligence, Headquarters US Air Force, provided their own top cover and insights. Others in the Air Force and the intelligence community assisted and commented and have to accept my thanks. The Air Force may be courageous enough to support a study by one of its fiercest critics, but physics have not changed: people still have to be concerned about their careers. It is not just a military reality or US government sickness: The United Nations personnel and officials who invited me to Lebanon and Israel in the first place as military advisor to a time-sensitive fact-finding mission have also requested anonymity.

I would particularly like to recognize Dr. Stephen D. Chiabotti, vice commander of the School of Advanced Air and Space Studies, Air University, for his unceasing support. Steve has been there with me through thick and thin over the years and has, in his uniquely entrepreneurial way, helped to navigate me through the Air Force system. My research partner, Matthew McKinzie, once again came through with GIS and mapping support, procuring commercial satellite imagery and help to build databases and ArcView projects.

Finally, thanks to my wife Nanc and to my daughters Rikki and Hannah. Yes, I am finished now.

Introduction

Air warfare is inherently a difficult to imagine activity, and images of urban devastation, carpet bombing, and mass civilian casualties dominate public discourse. With the emergence of 24/7 television and the Internet in the 1990s—a period that also coincided with the maturation of precision weapons and airpower as the dominant component of strategic warfare—the challenge of "seeing" airpower ironically magnified even more. Air warfare "statistics" and gun camera video accumulated, but they communicated video game heartlessness and suggested perfection while emphasizing the almost industrial nature of the air warfare enterprise (airmen even spoke of the "production" of sorties). Habitual operational security and the sensitivity of operating from foreign bases, together with the internal challenges of jointness, further constrained the telling of the airpower story.

Airpower's inherent quality and these constraints have made destruction the most accessible and visible element of the enterprise. Airpower and its targets have become intrinsically subject to greater review and audit because of the very economy of effort and the triumph of discrimination. The airpower story then, located almost always in "enemy" territory, has naturally become one-dimensional. The friendly briefing and public relations function has largely been reduced to one of incident management of the occasional, though highly magnified, mistake (i.e., industrial accident).

Israel faced all of these problems and more in 2006. Even ignoring the bigger question of prejudice against the Israeli state, Israel followed all of the self-defeating patterns of conveying the modern air war story. What is more, it operated with even more obsessive security classification and information control than the United States, making even the statistics of IDF activity sparing and inconsistent. Hezbollah, on the other hand, practiced not only consummate operational security but also mounted an extremely skillful and centralized information war, practicing admirable and strict message discipline. Hezbollah was further aided by a government of Lebanon that filled emotional, disorganized, and inaccurate space that let the terrorist organization bask as a seemingly passive bystander.

When I went to Lebanon and Israel in September 2006, I knew that telling the story of the air war, whatever I would find, would be difficult. So many minds had already been made up about Israel, about the destruction it caused, and about the failure of airpower. I was well aware that although a truth-telling effort was first needed to sort out what had actually happened from the false images and propaganda, I also was mindful that images of bomb damage and enumerations of a relentless effort could also end up conveying exactly the opposite of the actual meaning. The task at hand then is to tell the story of an airpower-dominated campaign, one that was deeply flawed in its design yet impressive in its efficiency, without being either pedantically fault-finding or apologetic about a modern instrument that is still little understood, even by its practitioners.

Methodology

This quick-look study is based upon visits to damaged sites, villages, towns, and cities; discussions with government and military officials; and experience of having evaluated airpower and its effects in Afghanistan, Iraq, and the former Yugoslavia (and previously in Lebanon). Months of follow-up research included interaction and exchanges with Israeli, Lebanese, Hezbollah, and US experts.

In order to understand (divine) IDF and Hezbollah actions and reactions, I compiled what eventually became a 900-page chronology of the 34-day war. Because of the transparent nature of Israeli and Lebanese society, there was an abundance of raw data from which to work.

The wire services (AP, AFP, DPA, IRIN, Reuters, ReliefWeb), the Israeli news media (*Haaretz*, *The Jerusalem Post*, *YnetNews .com*, etc.), and even the international press, all had reporters on the ground and filed voluminous dispatches and took many photographs. The Lebanese press was a little trickier; free, yet largely aligned with different political and religious factions. But one feature of the energy unleashed by the war was an attempt on the part of different Lebanese news media organizations, Lebanese political factions, and NGOs to record what was happening. This contemporaneous record, broadcast over the Internet, provided the basis for an almost minute-by-minute record and included, most centrally:

- Lebanon News Live, which compiled minute-by-minute reports of events and attacks, http://lebanonnewslive .com/;

- Lebanon News by *tayyar.org*, "the official site of the Free Patriotic Movement (FPM) led by General [Michel] Aoun" that compiled minute-by-minute events of the 34-day war, http://www.tayyar.org/;

- Al Mashriq, "July War 2006 major incidents," compiled on the campus of the University of Beirut and including chronologies and Google Earth maps, http://almashriq.hiof .no/lebanon/300/350/355/july-war/index.html;

- *As-Safir* newspaper (translated courtesy of Lebanese contacts), associated with *tayyar.org* of General Aoun, http:// www.assafir.com/;

- "Samidoun Day-by-Day," a Web site and monitoring service run by a grassroots Lebanese NGO coalition that compiled day-to-day chronologies and maps of Israeli attacks, http://www.samidoun.org; and

- "Updates on the Aggression Against Lebanon," "news updates . . . from NewTV, one of the main Lebanese television stations," another minute-by-minute reporter of events, http://lebanonupdates.blogspot.com/.[1]

Hundreds of hours were then spent harmonizing place names and prospective targets—no meager task given the peculiarities of Arabic to English spellings and transliteration, peculiar local names, nicknames, and even nonstandard spellings of well-known places (e.g., Baalbek, Ba'albak, Baalbeck). The georeferencing of the final list of locations required both standard geographic information systems (GIS) methodologies and lots of detective work. The georeferenced gazetteer of locations and

---

[1] Some of these Web sites have since disappeared, but all of the material quoted was captured in its original form.

targets (Appendix C) was then converted into an ArcView GIS project to allow geospatial visualization and analysis of military targets and civilian damage. This in itself required extensive map study and imagery analysis to find the minutest of villages and to trace and understand roads and terrain. In this endeavor, I was assisted ably by Matthew McKinzie, who developed the Access database of Hezbollah actions and IDF attacks, georeferencing and converting the now two-dimensional chronology into an overall ArcView project.

Finally, analysis was immeasurably aided by commercial satellite imagery of Lebanon that allowed in-depth analysis of Beirut and certain southern villages. Matthew McKinzie obtained DigitalGlobe public domain imagery and prepared ArcView projects to superimpose various data layers. DigitalGlobe imagery from the QuickBird satellite, with its 70-centimeter resolution, allows analysis of individual houses, some of which do not measure more than dozens of pixels, a vast improvement over the one-meter-resolution Ikonos imagery utilized by the United Nations. QuickBird satellite imagery of the southern Beirut suburbs provided a unique window into the destructive power of the Israeli Defense Forces (IDF). Finally, the GIS effort benefited enormously from the collaborative tool of Google Earth and from Lebanese citizens who posted information as Google Earth files, thus allowing a common geospatial reference point.

The Israeli and Lebanese governments, the IDF themselves, and their various entities, issued regular statements regarding their activities. The IDF, the Israeli Ministry of Foreign Affairs (MFA), and the office of the Prime Minister all established special Web sites to post press materials, daily briefings, and fact sheets. Most of this material, frankly, was incomplete and extremely random. After the war, the Israeli MFA provided CD-ROMs with photographs and documents about the war.

The government of Lebanon, particularly the Higher Relief Commission, monitored civilian casualties and war damage, particularly later in the conflict, and issued daily situation reports. These were useful to track what the Beirut government and its entities were thinking, but they were also highly unreliable. After the war, additional information was obtained from the Ministry of Health, Ministry of Education, Ministry of Environment, Ministry of Culture, Ministry of Defense, Ministry of Economy and Trade, Ministry of Agriculture, the Ministry of Social Affairs, as well as by a number of municipalities. The Lebanese Presidency press office, the Lebanese General Staff, and the Lebanese Embassy in Washington also provided photographs and documents.

The United Nations and the various international organizations also closely tracked the conflict (and its aftermath). Within the parameters of its missions, the United Nations Interim Forces in Lebanon (UNIFIL) situation reports and press releases were most useful, but other UN bodies, particularly OCHA, FAO, UNICEF, UNWRA, and WHO also released valuable material during the war. Numerous postwar surveys were also done by international organizations, some of which were quite good. UN mapping was incomparable as a source of information, and the UN Mine Action Coordination Center (UN-MACC) provided a georeferenced spreadsheet of unexploded submunitions in Lebanon.

After the conflict, UNOSAT (UN operational satellite program) also compiled a series of photo-interpretation products based upon Ikonos satellite imagery, which was used to identify individual locations and types of damage to buildings, bridges, and roads. These graphics include:

- Damage summary in region of Tyre, Lebanon (August 2006).
- Satellite Identification of Damage in Region of Baalbek, Lebanon (September 2006).
- Satellite Identification of Damage in Beirut, Lebanon (October 2006).
- Satellite Identification of Damage in Beirut, Lebanon— Version 1.0 (September 2006).
- Satellite Identification of Damage in Bent Jbail [Bint Jbeil], Lebanon, Overview map (October 2006).
- Satellite Identification of Damage in Region of El Khiam [Al-Khiyam], Lebanon (September 2006).
- Satellite Identification of Damage in Region of Majdel Zoun [Madjal Zoun], Lebanon (October 2006).

- Satellite Identification of Damage in the Region of Rmaysh [Rmeish], Lebanon (October 2006).

- Satellite Identification of Damage in Nabatiye [Nabatiyeh] Lebanon (October 2006).

- Situation Along the Border of Lebanon and Israel—Version 2.2 (14 August 2006).

- Situation Map: Middle East Crisis—Version 1.9 (12 July–14 August 2006).

Despite all of the research effort that went into understanding the flow and physical geography of the conflict, this study is still quite flawed. The study is weakened by the fact that Israel was extremely sparse in divulging details of either its air campaign or its ground activity. Hezbollah was even more secretive. Absent accurate data on Israeli strikes, weapons expended, or the Israeli side of the story as to what was being attacked daily and for what reason, we are consigned to the empirical task of divining Israeli and Hezbollah intent through examining destruction on the ground. It is the very task that can, if one is not careful, convey a much distorted picture.

This is a "quick" look, and in that regard, it values timeliness over comprehensiveness or exactness. The intent is to have an airpower-oriented narrative that will enhance both professional military education and planning, both inside and outside the military. Perhaps despite the obvious flaws, and the inevitable tendency of some to dismiss the information and analysis because it is in the unclassified domain, others will see that the effort proves that there could be a better way to "tell" a coherent airpower story in the future.

Overview

In the summer of 2006, Israel fought an intense 34-day war with Hezbollah, the first sustained modern air campaign conducted by a country other than the United States. As soon as the fighting was under way, many were declaring airpower oversold and inadequate. Commentators clamored for more-decisive ground action, asserting that only ground forces could defeat Hezbollah rocket fire, that the ground alternative would produce a "cleaner" and less tangled outcome, bring about different political realities, reduce civilian casualties and damage, and make greater gains in the battle for hearts and minds. When the Israeli government itself seemingly expressed its frustration with airpower and escalated ground fighting well into the second week of the campaign, airpower critics felt vindicated. The antiairpower view could not help but further echo with all of the stark images of Beirut, with the cavalcade of statistics of civilian deaths and destruction, and the fact that barely six months after the initial Hezbollah incursion across the Israeli border, the air force general who served as the chief of staff of Israeli Defense Forces—the first air force officer ever to command Israel's military—was gone. What is more, despite all of the claimed Israeli military accomplishments, Hezbollah was declared as strong as ever. The war itself has thus been labeled a failure by many, and many of the war's ills are blamed on airpower.

It is precisely because the 2006 Israel-Hezbollah war was not fought by the United States, because it was an intense and technologically complex irregular conflict fought between a nation-state and a terrorist organization, and because it involved difficult questions of civilian protection and modern information warfare that the US Air Force and the US military should examine it closely. Analysis that does not assume fault or fall prey to biased anti-Israeli, antiairpower, or antiwar assumptions opens the way for better military doctrine and plans; for a deeper understanding of the issues associated with so-called "effects-based operations" and the battle for hearts and minds; for the achievement of maximized civilian protections; and, dare I say, even for better military command and political direction and expectations in the future.

Last September—barely a month after Israel and Hezbollah implemented a UN-brokered cease-fire—I arrived at Beirut International Airport as military advisor to a UN fact-finding mission. Having previously been involved in postwar evaluations of air campaigns in Afghanistan, Iraq, the former Yugoslavia, and even in Lebanon, I was fully prepared to find much to be desired in the conventional narrative of damage and destruction, as well as much to criticize in the claims of military achievement and/or failure. Lebanon did not disappoint.

On the one hand, I arrived on a regularly scheduled airline at the ultramodern Beirut International Airport, took a taxi to a five-star hotel, and hooked up to a high-speed Internet connection. Here in the heart of Lebanon's capital, the "destroyed" airport was already back in operation; the electric power grid—reportedly also bombed—was operating as it had been prewar; everyone seemed permanently attached to their cell phones, habitually talking and texting: the city was abuzz with life. It was immediately clear, at least to me, that Israel had exercised some degree of discrimination: right or wrong, it had made choices of what to bomb and what not to bomb.

Yet, just a short drive from Beirut's swank downtown was the utter ruin of *dahiye*—the southern Shi'a neighborhoods of mostly illegal apartment blocks, once home to hundreds of thousands of Lebanon's poorest, and the center for Hezbollah. Here is how one observer described the area midwar: "block after block of extraordinary canyons of devastation . . . multi-storey [*sic*] tenements collapsed or eviscerated, their domestic interiors spilled in mountainous waves of rubble across the streets."[2] I saw the same: well over 100 high-rise buildings completely destroyed and a similar number badly damaged and burned. Irrespective of the causes of the conflict and the military justification or lack thereof for Israel to attack each individual building, Beirut's southern suburbs suffered a level of damage unmatched by any other example of bombing in the precision era. In southern Lebanon, hundreds of towns and villages and thousands upon thousands of homes showed similar levels of severe destruction. The frontline villages that were fought over nearest the border were the most devastated, and dozens of bridges and miles of roads were damaged and destroyed.

---

[2] Richard Pendlebury, "Southern Beirut: Only the dead or insane remain," *Daily Mail* (UK), 20 July 2006. See also Nick Parker, "Tour of terror in Beirut," *The Sun* (UK), 26 July 2006, http://www.thesun.co.uk/article/0,,2-2006330627,00.html: "The scale of the destruction was truly incredible. One bunker-buster seemed to have wiped out at least four nine-storey [*sic*] blocks in a high-rise estate. Only a 30 ft pile of smoking concrete remained with layers of furniture, clothes and belongings squashed between collapsed floors. The muffled shriek of a car alarm in a vehicle entombed beneath the smashed buildings filled the smoky air. Curtains waved like banners from the broken windows of blackened apartment blocks as far as the eye could see."

The picture in Beirut and the south, and the dominant international narrative of Israel's wholesale destruction of Lebanon's infrastructure and economy—of rampant civilian casualties, of hundreds upon hundreds of schools, mosques, hospitals, and factories destroyed and of unexploded ordnance littering the countryside—suggests excess, indiscriminate bombing and intentional and malicious destruction.

But is any of the evidence true; and death and damage compared to what? Virtually absent from this picture for many in the international community and the Arab world is Hezbollah, an organization that managed to fire over 4,000 rockets and projectiles at 160 Israeli settlements, towns, and cities (and over 1,000 powerful antitank missiles inside Lebanon!), mounting an organized and capable defense against what would eventually be 30,000 Israeli troops fighting in some 16 enclaves in the south. Despite Israeli efforts, Hezbollah rocket fire was never subdued, and the organization's military operations were never fully suppressed, demonstrating just how prepared Hezbollah was and how entrenched the fighting force was in the country's civilian fabric. And yet when human rights organizations and much of the international community showed up or commented, they seemed to act as if the force Israel was battling was nonexistent. As for the critique of airpower, the connotation was that somehow a full-fledged ground war with the same mission against this same tricky and dug-in force would have been both more successful and less destructive.

The level of destruction in southern Beirut and south Lebanon certainly suggests a very different kind of campaign waged by Israel. Israel chose to go to war over the kidnapping of two Israeli soldiers, seemingly choosing as well to disregard the central American tenet of precision—that fewer weapons and less physical destruction can achieve desired effects with far less "collateral" damage, human and political. But Israel is also a country that pursued its war from a different political reality. The United States may have conducted a half-dozen air campaigns in the precision era, but it has never had to fight an enemy on its borders, nor has it had to make the tough decision of exacting as much damage as possible on a mortal enemy regardless of the political consequences.

None of this is to excuse any actual Israeli excesses. Israel's military strategy was indeed deeply flawed. Israel bombed too much and bombed the wrong targets, falling back upon cookie-cutter conventional targeting in attacking traditional military objects. Individual elements of each target group might have been justified, but Israel also undertook an intentionally punishing and destructive air campaign against the people and government of Lebanon. All the while, the IDF seemed to satisfy itself with conventional measures of "success"—accumulating statistics of Hezbollah launchers and rockets hit, dead fighters, and destroyed Hezbollah "structures." Israel may have satisfied itself that every building and structure it was attacking in Beirut and every civilian home in the south was associated with Hezbollah, but the cumulative impact was far less impressive militarily and far more politically damaging than the planners and commanders projected.

As the conflict escalated, destruction in Beirut and the south accumulated, as did overall damage to the Lebanese civilian infrastructure. There is no question that the IDF was intensely focused on destroying rockets and launch sites, killing Hezbollah fighters, destroying weapons storage, bunkers, and other strictly military objects. But hundreds if not thousands of civilian buildings were also promiscuously labeled Hezbollah "structures" and attacked in the name of degrading or destroying that organization. The argument we hear from the Israeli government is that it had no alternative—that these otherwise civilian homes and buildings had to be attacked because of the nature of Hezbollah and its use of Lebanese society as a "shield."

If this is true, is there a different strategy Israel could have pursued against Hezbollah to achieve its objectives with less political fallout? In order to answer that question one needs to be honest about the actual record of Israeli attacks, not some hyperbolic description of destruction. Lebanon was not systematically destroyed, an objective certainly within Israel's reach. Gross destruction was visited upon Hezbollah's stronghold in south Beirut, but that destruction was still undertaken with precision, as is evidenced by its coexistence with vast untouched areas of the city. Israel indeed made decisions and took steps to limit civilian harm. Israel made a decision at an extremely high political level not to attack Lebanon's electric power grid (as it had done in 1996) and not to attack any water-related targets. It did not "attack" hospitals, or schools, or mosques, or Lebanon's "refinery," though all were reported as such. Israel indeed showed initial restraint on the ground, a decision that could and should be interpreted not as some air-power daydream or a lack in "understanding" ground war but as a desire to avoid a protracted battle, an occupation, and all of the subsequent killing and destruction that would follow. As part of its preplanned retaliation for the kidnapping, Israel also did not initially attack any targets in south Beirut, even Hezbollah leadership, despite the fact that a surprise attack might have achieved decapitation.

As the war quickly escalated, Israel never realized much benefit from these sound decisions. Frustrated by its inability to stem rocket attacks on Israeli soil, Israel expanded its attacks on civilian targets to exact punishment on Hezbollah supporters and the government and people of Lebanon. Israel doggedly explained its action by reiterating again and again that Hezbollah fighters were "terrorists" and that Hezbollah was ultimately responsible for any damage caused, but outside of a small circle of supporters, Israel increasingly was objectified as the aggressor.

Hezbollah's resilience demonstrated that the organization had deep roots and enormous popular support in Lebanon, and yet Israeli political and military leaders seemed to believe their own propaganda that Hezbollah had no Lebanese support, was weak, and was losing. From this stemmed a wholly conventional measure of success that Israel seemed content to apply: Hezbollah's six years of investment and effort to build up infrastructure in Lebanon were gone, the routes of Syrian and Iranian resupply were disrupted, 70–80 percent of the long-range and 50 percent of the short-range launchers were destroyed, half of the stock of actual rockets and missiles was destroyed or expended, and more than 600 Hezbollah fighters were dead. Destruction of the organization's support infrastructure—roads and bridges, fuel, communications, media, even financial institutions—accumulated. The facts were all valid, but Israel just could not make a holistic analysis of the military benefit relative to the human (and political) impact.

Some commentators and observers seem content to chalk up any conceded failures on Israel's part to intelligence failure: Hezbollah, they say, possessed sophisticated Syrian and Iranian arms, "surprising" and abundant technology, and was not some lightly armed militia but a professional fighting force. This argument seems particularly weak: first, because Israeli intelligence knew enough about what Hezbollah was and possessed; and second, because it was Israel's very stubbornness in seeing Hezbollah as a conventional military force—armed with 12,000 rockets and missiles and other weapons—that influenced pursuit of a conventional military strategy in the first place. If anything, the IDF would have preferred an even more-conventional battle. After all, that is what the IDF is best at and would provide the clearest outcome.

As Hezbollah's secretary-general Sayyed Hassan Nasrallah said in a televised address during the conflict though, "We are not a regular army and we will not fight like a regular army." Hezbollah was morally and politically strengthened in the face of the Israeli military—with celebrations rippling through the Arab world that Israel was thwarted (just as the United States has been in Iraq)—because the only damage done to the organization indeed was "conventional." Here is the narrative that is heard from the Arab "street" and from huge segments of the Arab population that extend far beyond the Hezbollah faithful: Israel and the United States use their technology and their conventional might to bomb the Arab people back to the stone age, showing no regard for civilians, destroying homes and mosques and schools and bridges and factories and even gas stations. Given that "they" don't have F-16s to fight with, they are reduced to using rockets or airliners or suicide bombers and IEDs (improvised explosive devices) to strike back.

Hezbollah may not have defeated Israel on the battlefield, but the organization won the hearts and minds of many. Hezbollah's own narrative as it moves forward is that it survived the best that Israel could throw at it, that only a few of its fighters were killed (in other words, that only Lebanese civilians were hit), that only it stood up to Israel and was victorious.

Lining the Beirut International Airport access road just days after the cease-fire were a freshly erected set of billboards. "Divine Victory," they proclaim, with various photographs of uniformed and civilian-clad Hezbollah fighters loading Soviet-style Katyusha rocket launchers. "A Victory from God," alternating signs exclaim over the faces of Lebanese children and celebrating civilians. In all, the billboard displays along Lebanon's main roads develop three key themes: Hezbollah courage, Lebanon's resilience, and defeat of the "invincible" Israeli army.

So Israel is stuck, as is the United States, with the conundrum of modern conventional military power in the fight against terrorism. Both countries intone that they are fighting a "new" enemy, but neither seems able to modify its conventional military approach and get away from fighting in old ways. Israel and the United States can win all of the conventional battles and accumulate statistical successes to no political avail and to future detriment. It is clear that an alternative is needed, but the dominant alternative postulated by pundits and experts is that Israel just needed to be more aggressive on the ground in gaining control of southern Lebanon to stem the firing of rockets. Israel, this line of argument goes, placed too much faith on airpower, failing to launch a broad enough ground offensive until it was too late. Blinded by the false promise of winning "on the cheap," Israel failed to learn the US lesson from Iraq: committing too few troops. What is more, Israel "lost" the information war, outsmarted by a clever and duplicitous practitioner of political theater who ensured that Israel had to inflict civilian harm in order to fight it.

Many in the Israeli government and IDF defend the war's achievements, however seemingly modest militarily—damage to Hezbollah's fighting capability, expulsion of the organization from its sanctuary on the Israeli border, a message of Israeli willingness to use great force in response to provocations—as not only notable but also better than the alternatives of either inaction or even greater overreaction and a quagmire. Airpower of course facilitated these achievements by uniquely allowing rapid "strategic" attacks and disengagement. None of this is to say that how airpower was applied was particularly imaginative or forward-looking, but there is no question that airpower was the tool and the enabler.

More troops and a massive ground invasion would indeed have produced a different outcome, but the notion that somehow that effort would have resulted in a more decisive victory over Hezbollah, fewer political problems, and less destruction and fewer civilian casualties, has no basis in historical example or logic. There has to have been a different course to follow. Airpower as it was employed is not that alternative, but lost in the shuffle of the unresolved ground versus air rivalry and the intense emotional and political issues regarding Israel and Hezbollah are the most interesting questions as to how the most modern and flexible instrument could best be employed in the future.

Chapter 1

Escalation

At around 9:05 a.m. on Wednesday, 12 July 2006, Hezbollah initiated "True Promise," a meticulously planned and coordinated operation involving rocket, antitank missile, mortar, and sniper fire intended to mask a raid to kidnap Israeli soldiers. Katyusha rockets and mortars rained down on Israeli Defense Force (IDF) border posts and villages at multiple points from Zar'it to Dovev in the central sector. Within sight of the hilltop village of Aiyt a-Shab across from Border Mark 105, about 20 Hezbollah fighters attacked a pair of patrolling Division 91 Humvees. One Humvee was destroyed by a long-range antitank missile, and three soldiers were killed; a second Humvee was hit with rocket-propelled grenade (RPG) fire, and two reserve soldiers—Ehud Goldwasser and Eldad Regev—were captured.[1]

The incursion precipitated Israeli emergency "Hannibal" procedures and retaliatory strikes on Hezbollah border observation posts and positions opposite Zar'it. An exchange of fire

---

[1] United Nations, "Report of the Secretary-General on the United Nations Interim Force in Lebanon (For the period from 21 January 2006 to 18 July 2006)," S/2006/560, 21 July 2006; and British Broadcasting Corporation (BBC) Worldwide Monitoring, "Israeli general says 'this is war;' pledges 'forceful' response to Lebanon," live news conference with Maj Gen Udi Adam, commander of the IDF's Northern Command, site unknown, on Israeli Channel 2 TV on 12 July, 1512 Greenwich Mean Time (GMT). See also Israeli Ministry of Foreign Affairs (MFA), "IDF Spokesman: Hezbollah attack on northern border and IDF response," 12 July 2006, http://www.mfa.gov.il/MFA/Terro rism+Obstacle+to+Peace/Terrorism+from+Lebanon+Hizbullah/Hizbullah+attack+on+ northern+border+and+IDF+response+12-Jul-2006.htm; IDF, Intelligence and Terrorism Information Center (ITIC) at the Center for Special Studies (CSS), Hezbollah's use of Lebanese civilians as human shields: the extensive military infrastructure positioned and hidden in populated areas. Part Three: Israel Population Centers as Targets for Hezbollah Rocket Fire, November 2006, 150–ff; Grigory Asmolov, "We Are Ready for the Next War," *Kommersant* (Russia), 9 November 2006, http://www.kommersant.com/ p719977/r_527/Israel_Lebanon_Syria_Hizballah/; Yaakov Katz, "Eyeballing different Lebanese at the kidnapping site," *Jerusalem Post*, 10 December 2006. http://www .jpost.com/servlet/Satellite?cid=1164881865641&pagename=JPost%2FJPArticle%2F ShowFull; *Deutsche Presse-Agentur (DPA)*, "Two projectiles fired from Lebanon land in northern Israel," 12 July 2006, 0712 [GMT]; BBC Worldwide Monitoring, "Israel bombs Lebanese villages, Hezbollah shells targets—TV," reporting Al-Arabiya TV in Arabic, 12 July 2006, 0718 GMT; *Deutsche Presse-Agentur* (DPA), "Two projectiles fired from Lebanon land in northern Israel," 12 July 2006, 0722 [GMT]; and Reuters (Beirut), "UPDATE 3-Hezbollah says seizes Israeli soldiers in border raid (Recasts with Hezbollah saying captured Israeli soldier)," 12 July 2006, 6:32:39 a.m. (0932 GMT).

between the IDF and Hezbollah gunners then ensued across much of the entire Blue Line, with heavy bombardment also occurring in the areas around Bint Jbeil and in the Shebaa Farms area of the Golan Heights. For the first time in six years, IDF conventional forces entered southern Lebanon in pursuit of the kidnappers.[2] The platoon-sized force met with intense small arms and antitank missile fire, walking into an obvious trap: a pre-positioned explosive just over the border was detonated under a pursuing Israeli Merkava tank at about 11 a.m., killing four additional soldiers.[3]

Within an hour of the initial clash, Al-Manar, the Hezbollah-owned and run television network in Beirut, was reporting that the Islamic Resistance, the military arm of Hezbollah, had captured two Israeli soldiers and that Israeli artillery was "pounding" the fringes of Aiyt a-Shab, nearby Ramiya, and Yaroun.[4] At 10 a.m., Hezbollah secretary-general Sayyed Hassan Nasrallah held a rare press conference, confirming that his organization had indeed kidnapped the Israeli soldiers, saying that they were in a "safe and far" away place and that they would only be released as part of a swap.[5] "No military operation will return them," Nasrallah said. "The prisoners will not be returned except through one way: indirect negotiations and a trade."[6] Con-

---

[2] "Fighting on two fronts," *Jerusalem Post*, 13 July 2006, 1.

[3] An eighth Israeli soldier was later killed on the ground inside Lebanon in the afternoon. The eight soldiers killed made up the single highest number of Israeli military casualties since the IDF's offensive in Jenin on 9 April 2002, which left 14 soldiers dead. The Israeli press reported that "dozens" of ground troops entered southwestern Lebanon on 12 July. See also MFA, "IDF Spokesman: Hezbollah attack on northern border and IDF response."

[4] Associated Press (AP) Beirut— "Hezbollah and Israeli forces clash across the border in southern Lebanon," 12 July 2006, 0735 GMT; AP, "Heavy clashes in southern Lebanon as Hezbollah TV announces capture of two Israeli soldiers," 12 July 2006, 0813 GMT.

[5] "Operation True Promise" had as its declared aim obtaining the release of Lebanese and other Arab prisoners held in Israel by exchanging them for captured Israeli soldiers—as "promised" by Nasrallah.

[6] A written statement by Hezbollah issued Wednesday morning said: "Implementing our promise to release the Arab prisoners in Israeli jails, our strugglers have captured at 9:05 am (0605 GMT) two Israeli soldiers in southern Lebanon. . . . The two soldiers have already been moved to a safe place." See also AP (Gaza City), "Nine Palestinians killed in Israeli airstrike [sic], Hezbollah claims to kidnap two Israeli soldiers," 12 July 2006, 0920 GMT; and AP (Beirut), "Hezbollah captures two Israeli soldiers, sparking Israeli bombardment in south Lebanon," 12 July 2006, 1546 GMT.

gratulating the Hezbollah kidnappers and fighters, Nasrallah said the organization had so far exercised "self-restraint" in its operations. "We have no intention to escalate or to start a war. But if the enemy seeks that they will pay a price," he said. "We are ready for a confrontation to the extreme." Nasrallah also called on all Lebanese to come together in a "national front" against Israel.[7] As news of the kidnapping emerged, Hezbollah supporters took to the streets of south Beirut, firing guns in the air and setting off firecrackers to celebrate. "God is great . . . our prisoners will be out soon," the media reported them chanting.[8]

At about 10:20 a.m., Israel initiated a wave of preplanned air strikes in southern Lebanon,[9] initially attacking 17 Hez-

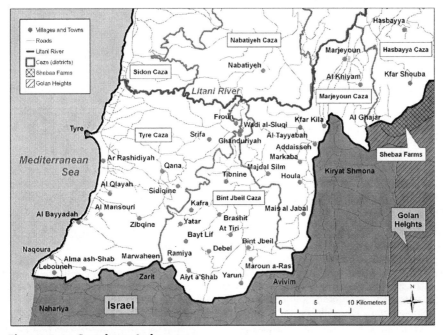

Figure 1.1: Southern Lebanon

[7] AP (Sam F. Ghattas, Beirut), "Israel bombs southern Lebanon after Hezbollah fighters snatch 2 Israeli soldiers," 12 July 2006, 1948 GMT; and United Press International (UPI), Beirut, "Analysis: Iran, Syria use Lebanese militia," 12 July 2006, 1646 GMT.

[8] DPA, "Israeli troops enter Lebanon in hunt after soldiers," 12 July 2006, 1050 GMT; and AP (Beirut), "Heavy clashes in southern Lebanon as Hezbollah announces capture of two Israeli soldiers," 12 July 2006, 1435 GMT.

[9] UN, Identical letters dated 17 July 2006 from the chargé d'affaires of the Permanent Mission of Lebanon to the United Nations addressed to the secretary-general and the president of the Security Council, A/60/942–S/2006/531, 17 July 2006.

bollah command posts and bases, as well as three southern bridges over the Litani River.[10] Lebanese government "security" officials commented on the Israeli strikes at about 11:00 a.m., saying that bridges, roads, and Hezbollah positions had been attacked. The Israeli objective, these Lebanese officials opined, was "to block any escape route for the guerrillas" which might then prevent an Israeli rescue mission.[11]

At midday, Israeli prime minister Ehud Olmert appeared before the news media as part of a photo opportunity associated with a previously scheduled meeting with the Japanese prime minister, who was in Jerusalem. Olmert called the attacks and kidnapping "an act of war" and held the Lebanese government responsible for Hezbollah's behavior. "I want to make it clear, the events of this morning are not a terror attack but an act by a sovereign state which attacked the state of Israel without reason or provocation," Olmert said. He vowed that the Israeli response would be "restrained, but very, very, very painful."[12] Israeli TV also reported that IDF chief of staff Lt Gen Dan Halutz warned that the Israeli assault would "turn

---

[10] IDF, "Attacks on Israel from Lebanese Territory," Wednesday, 12 July 2006, 1202 GMT. http://www1.idf.il/DOVER/site/mainpage.asp?sl=EN&id=7&docid=54183.EN.

[11] AP, "Heavy clashes in southern Lebanon as Hezbollah TV announces capture of two Israeli soldiers," 12 July 2006, 0813 GMT; and Reuters (Beirut), "UPDATE 3—Hezbollah says seizes Israeli soldiers in border raid (Recasts with Hezbollah saying captured Israeli soldier)," 12 July 2006, 6:32:39 AM (0932 GMT). Israel confirmed that it was attacking "a number of bridges and roads . . . in order to prevent Hezbollah from transferring the abducted soldiers" and also targeting "Hezbollah bases"; and MFA, "IDF Spokesman: Hezbollah attack on northern border and IDF response."

[12] AP (Beirut), "Hezbollah captures two Israeli soldiers, sparking Israeli bombardment in south Lebanon," 12 July 2006, 1546 GMT; and Yaakov Katz, "IDF set for massive assault on Lebanon. Eight soldiers killed two kidnapped in Hizbullah attack on northern border," *Jerusalem Post*, 13 July 2006, 1. http://www.jpost.com/servlet/Satellite?cid=1150885985413&pagename=JPost%2FJPArticle%2FPrinter. "Lebanon will bear the consequences of its actions," Olmert said. AP (Beirut), "Heavy clashes in southern Lebanon." For the text of Olmert's initial statement, see also http://www.mfa.gov.il/MFA/Government/Communiques/2006/PM+Olmert+Lebanon+is+responsible+and+will+bear+the+consequences+12-Jul-2006.htm.

Israeli Justice Minister Haim Ramon said, "The Lebanese government, which allowed Hezbollah to commit an act of war against Israel, will pay a heavy price. The rules of the game have changed; "and *Agence France-Presse* (AFP) Beirut, "Israel bombs Beirut airport, 27 killed in raids," 13 July 2006, 0614 GMT.

back the clock in Lebanon by 20 years" if the soldiers were not returned.[13]

Lebanese prime minister Fouad Siniora phoned UN secretary-general Kofi Annan soon after the kidnappings to ask that the UN "prevent Israeli aggression" against Lebanon. Meeting in Rome with Italian premier Romano Prodi, Annan publicly called for the immediate release of the kidnapped Israeli soldiers and condemned Israel's retaliation. "I condemn without reservations the attack in southern Lebanon, and demand that Israeli troops be released immediately," he said.[14]

Siniora also summoned an aide to Nasrallah to his office in downtown Beirut to ask what Hezbollah had done. Just a few days earlier Nasrallah had assured the Lebanese government that it would be a calm summer and a successful tourist season, and that Hezbollah rockets "deterred" Israel from attacking. "It will calm down in 24 to 48 hours," the aide assured the Lebanese prime minister.[15] "The government was not aware of and does not take responsibility for, nor endorse what happened on the international border," Siniora told the news media.[16]

At about 6 p.m., Maj Gen Udi Adam, commander of the Northern Command responsible for Lebanon, spoke to the press from his headquarters in northern Israel. He said Israel was responding "very forcefully in the air, sea, and land, and is readying for a mighty response later. . . . As to where to attack, everything is legitimate . . . not just southern Lebanon and Hezbollah's border positions."[17]

---

[13] CBS News, "Israel Bombs Foreign Ministry in Gaza," 12 July 2006; Donald Macintyre, "Israel launches ferocious assault on Lebanon after capture of troops," *The Independent* (United Kingdom [UK]), 13 July 2006, 4; and AP (Beirut), "Heavy clashes in southern Lebanon as Hezbollah announces capture of two Israeli soldiers," 12 July 2006, 1435 GMT.

[14] Ynetnews, "Annan condemns Israel attack in Lebanon," *Ynetnews.com*, 12 July 2006, 18:03. http://www.ynetnews.com/Ext/Comp/ArticleLayout/CdaArticlePrintPreview/1,2506,L-3274607,00.html.

[15] Anthony Shadid, "Inside Hezbollah, Big Miscalculations; Militia Leaders Caught Off Guard by Scope of Israel's Response in War," *Washington Post*, 8 October 2006, A1.

[16] BBC, "Hezbollah warns Israel over raids," 12 July 2006. http://news.bbc.co.uk/1/hi/world/middle_east/5173078.stm. See also AP (Sam F. Ghattas, Beirut), "Israel bombs southern Lebanon after Hezbollah fighters snatch 2 Israeli soldiers," 12 July 2006, 1948 GMT.

[17] BBC Worldwide Monitoring, "Israeli general says 'this is war'."

Adam reiterated Olmert's and Halutz's warnings that Israel held the Lebanese government accountable. "The moment a state is responsible, we will realize and demand this responsibility," Adam said. Though he demurred in elaborating about what he called "wide-ranging and comprehensive" IDF operational plans, he said that the Israeli objective would be to destroy Hezbollah's military capabilities and push the organization "away from the border."[18]

While Adam was speaking, the Israeli Security Cabinet was convening in emergency session. Olmert says he was in contact with Halutz and Minister of Defense Amir Peretz from the first moments of the border incident. "I have issued instructions to the security establishment," he said; "I have coordinated with Defense Minister Peretz, naturally."[19] Now the Cabinet was formally meeting to hear briefings from IDF representatives and the General Staff and receive the recommendations of Halutz as to possible responses. After the meeting, a Cabinet communiqué was issued, which read in part:

> Israel views the sovereign Lebanese Government as responsible for the action that originated on its soil and for the return of the abducted soldiers to Israel. Israel demands that the Lebanese Government implement UN Security Council Resolution #1559. . . .
>
> Israel will respond aggressively and harshly to those who carried out, and are responsible for, today's action, and will work to foil actions and efforts directed against it. . . . Israel must respond with the necessary severity to this act of aggression and it will indeed do so.[20]

Throughout the afternoon and night of 12 July, Hezbollah and Israel traded rocket, artillery, mortar, and small arms fire over the border. On the ground, Hezbollah attempted two additional infiltrations in the central sector, and fighters armed with RPG launchers and antitank missiles battled IDF rescuers

---

[18] Ibid. See also Nicholas Blanford, Ian MacKinnon, and Stephen Farrell, "How Israel was pulled back into the peril of Lebanon," *The Times* (London), 13 July 2006, 4.

[19] Office of the Prime Minister, transcript, "PM Olmert's remarks at his press conference with Japanese PM Junichiro Koizum," 12 July 2006.

[20] Israel, Cabinet Communiqué, 12 July 2006. http://www.mfa.gov.il/MFA/Government/Communiques/2006/Special+Cabinet+Communique+Hizbullah+attack+12-Jul-2006.htm. See also AP (Ravi Nessman, Jerusalem), "Israeli troops raid Lebanon after Islamic militants capture two soldiers in cross-border raid," 12 July 2006, 2227 GMT.

who crossed into Lebanon. Hezbollah rocket attacks continued into Israel against border villages and the area of Mount Meron, and snipers fired on the Israeli town of Rosh Hanikra on the coast.[21] An Israeli army spokesman said it was an "unprecedented attack" in terms of the number of Israeli villages targeted and the depth of the rocket strikes.[22] In the first 24 hours, Hezbollah launched some 60 rockets into Israel, as well as dozens of mortars and other projectiles.

Photo courtesy Government of Lebanon

The Damour old bridge, just south of metropolitan Beirut, was attacked 12 July. The old bridge had become a secondary route with the building of the north-south coastal highway. Though the bridge was destroyed in the initial attack, follow-on attacks on the Damour main bridge (Oceana bridge) and three highway interchanges were needed to stop traffic between Beirut and the south.

Israel maintained its own artillery and rocket fire against Hezbollah positions throughout the day and night, attacking targets along the entire breadth of the Lebanese border from Naqoura on the coast to Kfar Shouba, less than 10 km from

---

[21] One Hezbollah fighter was shot and killed trying to infiltrate the IDF's Oranit outpost and another was killed trying to infiltrate the Biranit base. AP (Ghattas), "Israel bombs southern Lebanon"; "Fighting on two fronts," *Jerusalem Post*, 13 July 2006, 1; and MFA, "IDF Spokesman: Hezbollah attack on northern border and IDF response."

[22] DPA (Beirut/Tel Aviv), "7TH LEAD: Israel strikes Beirut airport, suburbs; at least 31 killed," 13 July 2006, 1004 GMT.

the Syrian border. A second wave of air strikes occurred in the afternoon, and another 40 targets were attacked by air and naval fire overnight. In the first 24 hours, the IDF had carried out over 100 "aerial" attacks, the IDF said.[23] An Israeli army statement said more than 30 targets associated with preventing the transfer of the abducted soldiers, including the main bridges over the Litani and Zahrani rivers and the north-south coastal road, had been attacked.[24] A senior IDF officer said that dozens of Katyusha launching sites were attacked, with approximately 40 destroyed. The IDF also said that approximately 30 Hezbollah fighters were killed in the first 24 hours.[25]

When Major General Adam appeared before the news media barely nine hours into the operation on 12 July, he was prepared to give a glowing assessment. "We are in control," the combatant commander said of Israeli forces. "We have destroyed *all* the Hezbollah outposts in the border and we are now continuing to operate in depth, mainly from sea and air" (emphasis added).[26] Given the official pronouncement of Adam and others, Israeli media followed with its own glowing assessment. With reports of an attack on Beirut's international airport, Israeli radio reported early Thursday that "southern Lebanon *has been cut off* from the rest of the country after our aircraft, helicopters, and naval vessels bombed dozens of targets, including about

---

[23] MFA, "IDF Spokesman: Hezbollah attack on northern border and IDF response." Lebanese "security officials" also said that a Palestinian base 10 miles south of Beirut was bombed; and Chris McGreal in Jerusalem, "Capture of soldiers was 'act of war' says Israel," *The Guardian* (UK) 13 July 2006, http://www.guardian.co.uk/israel/Story/0,,1819123,00.html.

[24] According to the author's research, the bridges attacked on 12 July included: the Damour old bridge, south of Beirut; the old and new bridges over the Zahrani, south of Sidon; the coastal Qasimiyeh main bridge, north of Tyre; the coastal Awali and Wadi al-Zaynah bridges, north of Sidon; the Tayr Filsay-al-Zrariyeh bridge, between Tyre and Nabatiyeh; the al-Mahmoudiyeh/Dimashqiyeh bridge, near Marjeyoun; and the al-Qa'qa'iyah al-Jisr bridge, over the Zahrani river in Nabatiyeh. According to the AP, some bridges were attacked several times to ensure they were destroyed to cut off movement between the south and the rest of the country. AP (Beirut), "Heavy clashes in southern Lebanon as Hezbollah announces capture of two Israeli soldiers," 12 July 2006, 1435 GMT; and AP (Sam F. Ghattas, Beirut), "Israel bombs southern Lebanon after Hezbollah fighters snatch 2 Israeli soldiers," 12 July 2006, 1948 GMT.

[25] BBC Worldwide Monitoring, "Israeli officials vow to remove Hezbollah from border," Voice of Israel, Jerusalem, in Hebrew, 13 July 2006, 0905 GMT.

[26] BBC Worldwide Monitoring, "Israeli general says 'this is war.'" See also Blanford et al., "How Israel was pulled back into the peril of Lebanon."

20 bridges, the roads of southern Lebanon and other parts of the country" (emphasis added).[27] "*All* the bridges" between the Israeli border and Beirut on the coastal road had been bombed, Voice of Israel said (emphasis added).[28]

Certainly the most visible and symbolic Israeli target in the first 24 hours—and the northernmost strike—was Beirut's Rafiq Hariri International Airport. At 4 a.m. on 13 July, aircraft placed four 2,000 lb. laser-guided bombs with BLU-109 hard-target warheads on runway intersections to shut down airport operations (see fig. 1.2).[29] Though some Israeli spokesmen described the airport as a transportation node in the same category with bridges, justifying the attack as impeding export of the abducted soldiers, an Israeli army spokesman said that "the reason for the attack is that the airport is used as a central hub for the transfer of weapons and supplies to the Hezbollah terror organization."[30] Acting Lebanese minister of the Interior Ahmed Fatfat opined that the airport attack had nothing to do with Hezbollah but was instead an attack against Lebanon's "economic interests," especially its summer tourism industry.[31]

By the afternoon of 13 July, the Beirut airport attack was the only significant strike the IDF had mounted beyond southern Lebanon and, other than attacks on bridges, it was the only "civilian infrastructure" attack. The wire services, nevertheless, were describing significant destruction to the country of Lebanon overall and saying that as many as 52 civilians had been

---

[27] BBC Worldwide Monitoring, "Israel Air Force bombs Beirut airport, isolates South Lebanon [Studio talk between correspondent Miki Gurdus and Ya'aqov Ahime'ir - live]," 13 July 2006, Excerpt from report by Israel radio on 13 July, 0405 GMT.

[28] BBC Worldwide Monitoring, "Israeli officials vow to remove Hezbollah from border."

[29] Information provided to the author by the Lebanese army and by the author's own observations.

[30] AFP (Jerusalem), "Israel bombed Beirut airport to halt Hezbollah arms: army," 13 July 2006, 0510 GMT.

[31] Japan Economic Newswire, "Israeli bombs Beirut airport, imposes sea, air blockade," 13 July 2006, 1116 GMT.

Damage to runways at Beirut International Airport. Israel attacked critical nodes at the intersections of runways and taxiways to disable the airport but did not initially attack other airport facilities, such as terminal buildings and air traffic control radars. Later, as part of an escalatory move, Israel attacked fuel storage tanks at the airport. Limited air traffic resumed at Beirut International even before the 14 August cease-fire, and regularly scheduled airline traffic resumed within a week of the cease-fire.

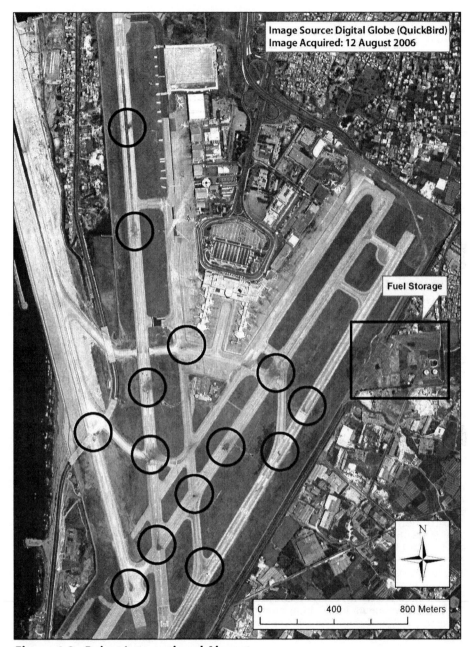

Image Source: Digital Globe (QuickBird)
Image Acquired: 12 August 2006

Fuel Storage

N

0   400   800 Meters

Figure 1.2: Beirut International Airport

killed in air strikes, with another 100 wounded.[32] "They are killing civilians because they cannot kill Hezbollah militants," a Lebanese man was quoted as saying. "They want to bring us back to the occupation era. . . . Will the world continue to watch them kill children without doing anything?"[33]

Before it was clear how many civilians indeed had been killed or under what circumstances, an Israeli spokeswoman expressed regret, saying the IDF had "no intention whatsoever to harm innocent civilians."[34] Israeli Air Force (IAF) chief Brig Gen Amir Eshel explained, "Hezbollah has established its infrastructure in the heart of a peaceful civilian population and our challenge is to attempt to target this infrastructure accurately while exerting the greatest efforts to avoid harming non-combatants."[35]

Hezbollah had fired rockets and artillery into Israel and was continuing to do so, it had kidnapped Israeli soldiers, and it was exacting Israeli civilian deaths and injuries. But barely 24 hours into the crisis—despite Israel's actual attacks—and despite Israeli statements of regret and caution, France, Russia, Italy, and others condemned Israel's actions as "disproportion-

---

[32] For reporting on a variety of numbers, see DPA, "2ND ROUNDUP: Israel strikes Beirut airport, suburbs; over 40 killed," 13 July 2006, 1438 GMT; AFP (Jihad Siqlawa, Tyre, Lebanon), "Gruesome scenes after Israeli air raids on south Lebanon," 13 July 2006, 1158 GMT; AFP (Beirut), "Israel strikes Lebanon over seized soldiers, dozens killed," 13 July 2006, 1133 GMT; and DPA (Beirut/Tel Aviv), "7TH LEAD: Israel strikes Beirut airport, suburbs; at least 31 killed," 13 July 2006, 1004 GMT. See also Reuters (Beirut), "Israel kills 52 civilians, including more than 15 children, in Lebanon," 13 July 2006, http://www.dawn.com/2006/07/13/welcome.htm; and DPA (Beirut/Tel Aviv), "5TH LEAD: Israeli airstrikes [sic] hit Beirut airport, suburbs; 27 killed," 13 July 2006, 0542 GMT; Reuters, "Chronology-Six months of rising Mideast tensions," 13 July 2006, 09:44:18; Daily Star (Lebanon) July War 2006 Timeline, http://www.daily star.com.lb/July_War06.asp; and BBC News, "Day-by-day: Lebanon crisis—week one," http://news.bbc.co.uk/2/hi/middle_east/5179434.stm. After the initial strikes of 12 July, the news media in Lebanon reported only two Lebanese civilians killed. AP (Jerusalem, Ravi Nessman), "Israeli Cabinet approves strikes in Lebanon after Hezbollah captures two soldiers in raid," 13 July 2006, 0354 GMT.

[33] AFP (Jihad Siqlawa, Tyre, Lebanon), "Gruesome scenes after Israeli air raids on south Lebanon," 13 July 2006, 1158 GMT.

[34] DPA (Beirut/Tel Aviv), "5TH LEAD: Israeli airstrikes hit Beirut airport, suburbs; 27 killed," 13 July 2006, 0542 GMT.

[35] BBC Worldwide Monitoring, "Israeli officials vow to remove Hezbollah from border."

ate."[36] Kofi Annan's personal representative to Lebanon, Gier Pederson, said he was "highly alarmed by Israel's *heavy attacks and escalation*" (emphasis added).[37] Amnesty International called for a cessation of Israeli attacks on Lebanese civilian infrastructure, citing the supposed attack on Lebanese electrical power.[38] The Arab League called an emergency meeting.

Could it be the criticism had nothing to do with Israel's actual conduct? After all, though there were news media reports that Israel had struck an electrical power plant in southern Lebanon, there was actually no such attack on the first day.[39] Media reporting about attacks into Beirut were also exaggerated and erroneous. At first, the wire services quoted Al-Jazeera television as saying that 26 civilians had been killed in the Beirut airport attack.[40] Later reports that same day mentioned three dead at the airport; evidently Al-Jazeera was reporting a total of 26 civilians killed overall in southern Lebanon.[41] Lebanese

---

[36] 6 AFP (Beirut), "28 killed as Israel pounds Lebanon in soldier crisis," 13 July 2006, 0851 GMT; AFP (Beirut), "Israel strikes Lebanon over seized soldiers, dozens killed," 13 July 2006, 1133 GMT; and AFP (Beirut), "Dozens killed as Israel bombs Lebanon over seized soldiers," 13 July 2006, 0203 GMT.

"This is a disproportionate response to what has happened and if both sides are going to drive each other into a tight corner then I think that all this will develop in a very dramatic and tragic way," the Russian news agency Interfax quoted Foreign Minister Sergei Lavrov as saying.

"We have the impression that this is a disproportionate and dangerous reaction in view of the consequences it could have," Italian foreign minister Massimo D'Alema said.

[37] AFP (Beirut), "Dozens killed as Israel bombs Lebanon," 13 July 2006, 2258 GMT.

[38] Amnesty International, "Israel/Lebanon: End immediately attacks against civilians," press release, 13 July 2006.

[39] An electrical power station was reported attacked in Wadi Jilo east of Tyre (See Xinhua News Service, "Israeli forces, Hizbollah [sic] clash, two Israeli soldiers feared kidnapped," 12 July 2006; and Bahrain News Agency [Al-Arabiya TV, Dubai, in Arabic], "Two civilians killed in South Lebanon," 12 July 2006, 1351 GMT), but there was no such attack.

[40] Xinhua General News Service (Beirut), "Update: Israeli warplanes bomb Beirut airport," 13 July 2006, 0301 GMT.

[41] BBC Worldwide Monitoring, "Israel Air Force bombs Beirut airport." See also BBC Worldwide Monitoring, "(Correction) Israel bombs Beirut airport; twenty-six Lebanese killed—Al-Jazeera," 13 July 2006, 0420 GMT. Initial reports stated that Al-Jazeera reported 26 killed at the airport. The screen caption actually read: "Al-Jazeera's correspondent: 26 Lebanese civilians were killed and the runway of Beirut Airport was destroyed in an Israeli bombardment."

police later told *Agence France-Presse* (AFP), the French news agency, that no civilians had indeed been killed in the attack on the airport, but that 27 Lebanese civilians, "including 10 children," had been killed overall.[42]

Disproportionate or not, Hezbollah responsibility or not, the conflict clearly had a different character than the dozens of other Israeli-Hezbollah incidents that had occurred since the Israeli withdrawal from southern Lebanon in 2000—escalation was in the air. On the morning of 13 July, the leading Israeli newspaper *Haaretz* reported that Israel would target Hezbollah in Beirut in response to any attacks on northern Israeli cities; Hezbollah responded by threatening to attack the northern port city of Haifa if Israel attacked Beirut.[43] A senior IDF officer was quoted on Israeli radio as threatening "grave harm to Lebanese civilian infrastructures . . . linked to Hezbollah" if the organization escalated its attacks.[44] General Halutz, who the previous day warned that Israeli bombing would turn back the Lebanese clock 20 years, said on 13 July that "nothing" was safe in the country.[45] "It is impossible that we will continue to be in a situation where in Beirut people are sleeping peacefully, while people in northern Israel are sitting in bomb shelters," Silvan Shalom, a Likud member of the Knesset, said.[46]

As evening approached on Thursday, 13 July, Hezbollah rockets hit the Stella Maris neighborhood of Haifa, the furthest south that rockets fired from Lebanon had ever hit.[47] Hezbol-

---

[42] AFP (Beirut), "Israeli aircraft bomb Beirut international airport," 13 July 2006, 0418 GMT; and AP (Sam F. Ghattas, Beirut), "Israel attacks Beirut international airport runways, airport closed; Civilians killed in south Lebanon," 13 July 2006, 0522 GMT.

[43] UPI (Jerusalem), "Hezbollah, Israel trade bombing threats," 13 July 2006, 1036 GMT.

[44] BBC Worldwide Monitoring, "Israeli officials vow to remove Hezbollah from border."

[45] Stephen Farrell, "Our aim is to win—nothing is safe, Israeli chiefs declare," *The Times* (UK), 14 July 2006, 1.

[46] "Interview with Silvan Shalom, Former Israeli Finance Minister and Member of The Knesset's Subcommittee for Intelligence And Secret Services, Discussing the Need to Act Decisively in Damascus and Beirut Following Hezbollah's Attack on Northern Israel (Iba Reshet Bet Radio, 12:44 (GMT+3)," Federal News Service, 13 July 2006, 0944 GMT.

[47] AP (Nahariya, Israel), "Rockets hit northern city of Haifa, causing no injuries," 13 July 2006, 1740 GMT.

lah initially denied that it had attacked Haifa, hoping, it seems, to save the escalatory move if Israel indeed attacked Hezbollah targets in south Beirut. "Bombing Haifa would be linked to any bombing of Beirut and its suburbs," Sheikh Naim Qassem, Hezbollah deputy secretary-general, told Al-Jazeera television. "It would be . . . a reaction and not preemptive."[48] Hezbollah secretary-general Nasrallah, for his part, claimed to Al-Jazeera television that it was not Hezbollah which escalated:

> We were not the ones who began the war or the ones who launched a large-scale war. . . . It is not from the first moment after we captured two soldiers that we began to shell Nahariya, Haifa, Tiberias and Zefat and launched war. No. Even in advancing, the Israelis were much faster than us. We were patient in the hope that things would stop at this point because we don't want to take our country to war.[49]

Israel's ambassador to the United States, Daniel Ayalon, immediately called the attack on Haifa "a major, major escalation."[50] Soon after the strike, four Israeli attack helicopters were back at the international airport, shooting air-to-surface missiles at airport fuel tanks, setting them on fire, and lighting up the Beirut night sky. Defense Minister Peretz said that Israel would now "break" Hezbollah.[51]

Before the Haifa attack, though, Israel had already dropped leaflets over south Beirut warning residents to stay away from Hezbollah strongholds:

> To the Inhabitants of Lebanon
>
> Due to the terrorist activities carried out by Hezbollah which destroys the effort to find a brighter future for Lebanon. The Israeli Army will continue its work within Lebanon for as long as it deems fit to protect the citizens of the State of Israel.

---

[48] AFP (Beirut), "Hezbollah denies firing rockets on Israel's Haifa," 13 July 2006, 1752 GMT.

[49] Transcript of interview with Hassan Nasrallah on Al-Jazeera, 20 July 2006.

[50] AP (Beirut, Sam F. Ghattas), "Israel blasts Beirut's airport as guerilla rockets hit Israel's third largest city in escalating battle," 13 July 2006, 1943 GMT.

[51] DPA, "4TH ROUNDUP: Israel strikes Beirut airport, rockets land in Haifa," 13 July 2006, 2110 GMT.

> For your own safety and because we do not wish to cause any more civilian deaths, you are advised to avoid all places frequented by Hezbollah.
>
> You should know that the continuation of terrorist activities against the State of Israel will be considered a double-edged sword for you and Lebanon.
>
> The State of Israel[52]

Now as part of its escalation for Hezbollah attacks on Haifa, the IDF implemented what its spokesmen labeled "deterrence" strikes; reaching into south Beirut to attack buildings in the main Hezbollah headquarters complex, the home of Secretary-General Nasrallah, and the headquarters of Hezbollah's Al-Manar television. But as part of its punishment strategy against the government of Lebanon, Israeli aircraft also attacked two Lebanese military airfields—Qulayaat near Tripoli and Riyaq in the north Bekaa Valley—a reminder as well to the Lebanese military to stay out of the fight after it fired on Israeli aircraft overflying Sidon.[53] A handful of television and radio transmission and relay stations were also added to the target list.

Probably everything that there is to be said about the Israeli-Hezbollah war of 2006 can be traced to these first 48 hours: each side firmly believing that they were taking the action that was necessary for their security and standing; each convinced that they could control their actions, their opponent's reactions, and the effects; believing as well that they could precisely signal their intentions. The two sides implemented their "plans," suggesting deliberation and a thorough understanding of their objectives and of the enemy. Yet neither side really could anticipate how the conflict would unfold, nor did they properly assess the capabilities or actions of the other. Neither side really believed that there was ultimately a "military" solution that they could pursue to achieve victory over the other, yet they succumbed to the inexorable drag of war.

From the very beginning of the 2006 conflict, information warfare and propaganda played a prominent role. The "IDF

---

[52] Information provided by the IDF.

[53] AP (Ghattas), "Israel bombs southern Lebanon."

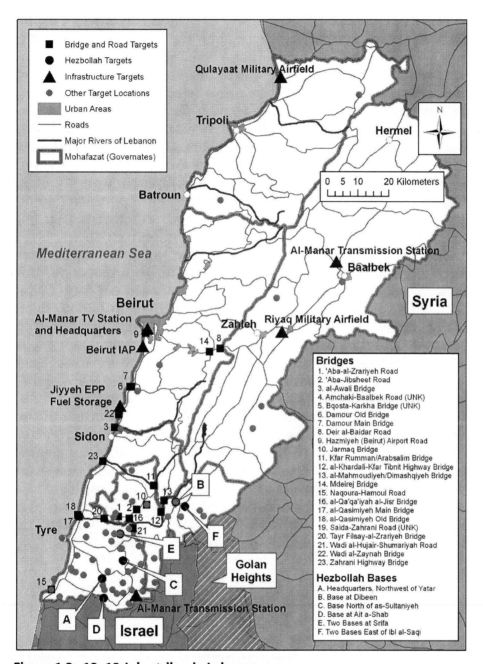

Figure 1.3: 12–13 July strikes in Lebanon

will continue to operate decisively to defend the citizens of the State of Israel against terror originating from Lebanese territory and to bring about conditions leading to the safe return of the two kidnapped soldiers," the Israeli government stated and then reiterated every day in its press releases. The responsibility for any civilian deaths rests with Hezbollah, IDF spokesmen repeated again and again. The news media were filled with stories—many demonstrably false—about Israeli conspiracies and misdeeds, about "illegal" weapons being used in Lebanon, about massive civilian casualties and infrastructure damage, and yet it seemed all the Israeli information apparatus could do in response was to mechanically make statements that left Hezbollah firmly in control of the information battlefield.

Obviously any conflict involving Israel and an Islamic terrorist organization is guaranteed to incite deep passions, but even the most dispassionate of observers could not help being buffeted and confused as the war of narratives unfolded. Even under the best of circumstances, an air campaign is difficult to describe, and the narrative lacks the kind of personal story-telling and frontline heroics so characteristic of ground war. Add to all of this the excessive secrecy practiced by the IDF regarding the basic facts of its actions, and even of its military units, and no wonder the international community and much of the news media jumped to conclusions. Though Israel and Hezbollah (and Lebanon) were fighting a ferocious battle for hearts and minds, what was crystal clear from 12 July was that even in the transparent Internet era, even in a conflict involving two countries with wide-open news environments, there was not only an absence of consensus about what was really going on, but there was also widespread misunderstanding.

Chapter 2

Hezbollah

Hezbollah ("Party of God") is a terrorist organization that is one of the most powerful and significant independent militant movements in the Middle East, if not the world.[1] It is also the dominant Shi'a political and social organization in Lebanon, a recognized political party, and a major nongovernmental factor in Lebanese society with an extensive social development program.[2]

Hezbollah originated in the Bekaa Valley as a merger of several groups associated in opposition to the Israeli June 1982 invasion and occupation.[3] Hezbollah was founded with the assistance of the Iranian Revolutionary Guards and, over the years, received most of its external monetary and material support from Iran. Though Hezbollah has advocated the elimination of Israel and the liberation of Jerusalem, as well as the establishment of Islamic rule in Lebanon, the organization gained political power in the 1990s through its Lebanese national "resistance" agenda: resistance to Israeli occupation, release of

---

[1] Hezbollah has been designated by the US government under three different counterterrorism authorities as a Foreign Terrorist Organization, a Specially Designated Terrorist, and a Specially Designated Global Terrorist. Other groups in Lebanon also designated as terrorist groups include Palestinian Islamic Jihad (PIJ), the Popular Front for the Liberation of Palestine-General Command (PFLP-GC), the Abu Nidal organization (ANO), and Hamas.

[2] Socially, Hezbollah provides substantial medical, educational, and other services to Lebanon's people, particularly the traditionally marginalized Shi'a Muslim population, who are also the poorest segment of Lebanese society.

[3] The Lebanese civil war goes back to 1975, if not earlier, with fighting between Christian groups and a coalition of Lebanese Druze and Muslim militias and dislocated Palestinian forces (expelled from Jordan). Syria intervened, initially to prevent a Christian defeat and later as an Arab League force, but fighting continued through 1982, during which some 10 percent of the Lebanese population was reportedly killed or wounded. In June 1982, Israel launched a ground invasion of Lebanon, occupying parts of Beirut by September of that year. A US, French, and Italian peacekeeping contingent deployed that month. In May 1983, Israel and Lebanon signed an agreement on Israeli withdrawal, ending hostilities and establishing a security region in southern Lebanon. On 23 October 1983, 241 US Marines and 56 French paratroopers were killed in two bomb explosions in Beirut; responsibility was claimed by two Shi'a groups, including Hezbollah.

Lebanese prisoners in Israeli detention, and "return" of the occupied Shebaa Farms area.[4]

From its founding, Hezbollah has extensively used terrorism, both inside Lebanon and in other parts of the world. Inside Lebanon, the organization made its mark though suicide truck bombings of the US Embassy and Marine barracks in Beirut in 1983 and the US Embassy annex in 1984. There is no question that these attacks were decisive in Pres. Ronald Reagan's decision to withdraw US forces from Lebanon. After the US withdrawal, Hezbollah conducted or participated in a number of high-profile terrorist attacks outside Lebanon (e.g., the hijacking of TWA flight 847 in 1985, the bombing of the Israeli Embassy in Argentina in 1992, and the attack on the Khobar Towers in Saudi Arabia in 1996).

When Israeli forces partially withdrew from southern Lebanon in 1985, Hezbollah focused its military effort on battling the pro-Israeli South Lebanon Army (SLA). In the late 1980s, civil war continued inside Lebanon, with Muslim and Christian factions defending their own enclaves, and with Syrian forces supporting the Christian government.[5] Though the 1989 Taif Agreement of national reconciliation ordered the dissolution of all militias, Hezbollah was allowed to remain active.[6] The SLA also refused to disband, extending fighting in southern Lebanon into the 1990s even as most of the rest of the country entered a period of relative calm.

------

[4] After the 2000 Israeli withdrawal, Hezbollah continued to claim that Israel still occupied Lebanese territory at Shebaa Farms, saying also that it would not stop its operations against Israel until it and the rest of "occupied Palestine" were liberated. Iranian support for Hezbollah continued and Syrian support significantly increased. Israel is holding more than 8,000 Palestinian prisoners, but only three Lebanese. It released more than 400 Lebanese detainees in return for an Israeli businessman and the bodies of three soldiers in a high-profile prisoner swap in January 2004, brokered by German mediators. Shebaa Farms is officially regarded by the United Nations and the United States as part of the Israeli-occupied Syrian territory of the Golan Heights and not Lebanese territory. Hezbollah regards the area as part of Lebanese territory, and Syria and Lebanon maintain that it is Lebanese territory from which Israel failed to withdraw when it withdrew from southern Lebanon in 2000.

[5] Significantly, in late 1990, Syria was granted additional freedoms to operate in the country following its commitment of forces to the US grand coalition against Iraq.

[6] Hezbollah, for its part, also later refused to disarm in accordance with *UNSCR 1559* (2004), saying it is a "resistance movement" and not a militia, the term used by the United Nations.

Throughout the late 1980s and 1990s, Hezbollah and Israel continued to battle. Hezbollah harassed IDF forces and citizens on the northern border, firing weapons into Israel and making occasional forays on the ground. On 16 February 1992, Israeli attack helicopters killed Sheikh Abbas al-Musawi, secretary-general of Hezbollah, while he and his family were traveling on a road near Jibsheet southwest of Nabatiyeh. Israel further launched Operation Accountability in July 1993, attacking Hezbollah and Popular Front for the Liberation of Palestine–General Command (PFLP–GC) capabilities in southern Lebanon. On 11 April 1996, Israel undertook Operation Grapes of Wrath, an intense bombing campaign ranging deep into Beirut and the Bekaa Valley. But in 2000, with the final collapse of the SLA, Israeli prime minister Ehud Barak decided to withdraw all remaining IDF units in Lebanon behind the Blue Line. Though the Lebanese government deployed some 1,000 policemen and soldiers to the former Israeli security zone, it made no other attempt to disarm or interfere with the Hezbollah buildup in the south, eventually abandoning responsibility for areas dominated by Hezbollah, including southern Beirut and parts of the Bekaa Valley.

With the passage of *UN Security Council Resolution 1559 (UNSCR 1559)* on 2 September 2004, the government of Lebanon again pledged to disarm Hezbollah (and other militias), and Syria was ordered to withdraw its forces from the country. That withdrawal did not occur until May 2005, when the assassination of former Prime Minister Rafik Hariri provoked the so-called Cedars Revolution, a series of popular demonstrations against Syria and the pro-Syrian Lebanese government. An anti-Syrian alliance won control of parliament, choosing Hariri ally Fouad Siniora as the new prime minister. With the Cedars Revolution, Hezbollah became an active participant in Lebanese political life, when along with rival Shi'a organization Amal, it won seats in the National Assembly as part of the Resistance and Development Bloc. At the outbreak of war in July 2006, Hezbollah had two ministers serving in the Lebanese cabinet and held 14 seats in the parliament.

Even after the Israeli withdrawal, Israel and Hezbollah continued their low-level war. Hezbollah took advantage of the Israeli withdrawal (and Lebanese government weakness) to build up military capabilities in the south, formalizing a military structure and preparing a military command, offensive capabilities, and defenses. With funding and support from Iran and Syria, Hezbollah was transformed from a loose militia possessing small arms and a few mainly short-range Katyusha rockets into a highly organized force possessing a diverse Russian-, Chinese-, Syrian-, and Iranian-made arsenal of short- and medium-range rockets and missiles, antiship and antitank missiles, and even long-range unmanned drones.

According to Israel's Ministry of Foreign Affairs, between the 2000 IDF withdrawal and 12 July 2006, Hezbollah conducted 183 rocket and mortar attacks across the northern border, killing several Israeli soldiers. There were also multiple incursions and kidnapping attempts, beginning in October 2000, when three IDF soldiers were abducted at Shebaa Farms. United Nations Interim Forces in Lebanon (UNIFIL) and other international agencies reported increased Hezbollah activity and an arms buildup throughout 2005 and early 2006. Hezbollah's continued refusal to disarm paralyzed the Lebanese government for months in early 2006; the organization pledged to eventually lay down its arms in the "next round" of national dialogue talks. Renewed fighting in the Gaza strip with the Hamas electoral victory in January 2006 added increased pressures.[7] More than a year before hostilities escalated in July 2006, Israel began dropping psychological operations (PSYOPS) leaflets on the south, attempting to split the local population from the organization and labeling Hezbollah a tool of Syria and Iran.

Organization

The Majlis al-Shura, or Consultative Council, is Hezbollah's highest governing body and has been led by Secretary-General Hassan Nasrallah since 1992.[8] Nasrallah is chairman of the

---

[7] In March 2004, Hezbollah and Hamas signed an agreement to increase joint efforts to perpetrate attacks against Israel.

[8] Information on Hezbollah structure was provided by Israeli intelligence, by Hezbollah operatives and experts, and observers on the ground in Lebanon, as well as other confidential sources.

Consultative Council and chairman of the Jihad Council, the organization's military decision-making body.[9]

Hezbollah's command structure in Lebanon covers four territorial subdivisions: a Beirut headquarters and high command, with some subordinate special units; a southern command (Nasr command), operating from south of the Litani River; a rear area and coastal command (Badr command), operating north of the Litani and south of Beirut; and a Bekaa command, concentrating

Legend
1. Hassan Nasrallah's house
2. Hezbollah base
3. Hezbollah base
4. Fadlallah Center, Hezbollah's office building
5. Hezbollah base
6. Hezbollah headquarters complex
7. Hezbollah base for terrorist activity
8. Buildings housing Hezbollah offices
9. Hezbollah's security center
10. Al Manar television station

Figure 2.1: Hezbollah leadership and command in Haret Hreik, Beirut (Adapted from IDF information.)

---

[9] Sheikh Naim Qassem is Hezbollah deputy secretary-general. Hashem Safi al-Din is chairman of the Executive Council. Hajj 'Imad Fayez Mughniyah is military deputy to Nasrallah and deputy chairman of the Jihad Council. Sheikh Nabil Qawouk (Qaouq) is head of the southern region under the Executive Council.

predominantly on training and logistics. "Strategic" (long-range) surface-to-surface rocket units were directly subordinate to the high command, as were Hezbollah's unmanned aerial vehicle (UAV) unit, air defense elements, and a naval unit.

Hezbollah headquarters prior to the 2006 war was located in *dahiye*[10] of south Beirut. Its headquarters, bases, and main offices were situated in the Haret Hreik district and, to a lesser extent, in nearby districts of Bir al-Abd and Al-Ruwis. A "restricted area" of Haret Hreik, the IDF says, contained Hezbollah headquarters alongside its military, administrative, and civilian infrastructures. These included "the main operations room, general staff functions (logistics, manpower, intelligence, and security), propaganda apparatuses (Al-Manar television and Al-Nour radio), logistics sites, workshops, and apartments of the organization's leaders and operatives. Also situated in these districts are the offices of the Iranian Revolutionary Guards, which support Hezbollah."[11]

The southern Nasr ("Victory") command, responsible for the area south of the Litani River, was organized into direct-reporting functional battalions, Eastern and Western commands, subordinate territorial subdivisions, and geographic sectors.[12] Functional battalions included communications and intelligence, rocket and antiarmor units, explosives (demolition) units, and "special forces."[13] Sector "battalions" were further divided into

---

[10] Beirut's southern suburbs, literally *dahiye* in Arabic, constitute a variety of neighborhoods generally under the control of Hezbollah. It is not particularly one place, and there are distinct neighborhoods that make up the area.

[11] IDF, ITIC/CSS, Hezbollah's use of Lebanese civilians as human shields: the extensive military infrastructure positioned and hidden in populated areas; Part Two: Documentation; Hezbollah's Military Infrastructure and Operational Activities Carried Out from Within the Civilian Population, November 2006, 63. There were reports during the war of Iranian Revolutionary Guard Corps personnel active on the ground in Lebanon, providing training and technical support, but they do not appear to have played any major role in the 2006 war.

[12] The Second Territorial Subdivision, for instance, was headquartered in Ya'atar. A territorial subdivision headquarters was located near the village of Aitit. The eastern sector of the Fifth Territorial Subdivision, for example, extended from Dibeen to Kfar Kila.

[13] "Special forces" elements were additionally deployed to key villages and choke points and operated some of the newer and better equipment. According to one report, special forces operated the more advanced antitank missiles (e.g., Kornet and Metis-M) and had both night-vision equipment and flak vests. David Makovsky and Jeffrey White, "Lessons and Implications of the Israel-Hezbollah War: A Preliminary Assessment," Washington Institute for Near East Policy, October 2006, 36.

semiautonomous units of a few to several dozen fighters. The cellular structure worked to increase security and success in guerilla war, magnifying the small number of fighters actually "stationed" in the villages. For instance, about 100–150 regular and reserve operatives fought in the Bint Jbeil-Ainata region.[14]

Overall, Nasr command (south Lebanon) was made up of a core of about 1,000 regular soldiers, supplemented by some 3,000 "reservists" and a few hundred special forces. The reservists, though relatively unskilled, were nevertheless drawn from home villages, kept their weapons at home, and were relied upon for their intimate knowledge of the territory.[15] As Hassan Nasrallah himself said in May 2006, "[The organization's operatives] live in their houses, in their schools, in their mosques, in their churches, in their fields, in their farms, and in their factories. You can't destroy them in the same way you would destroy an army."[16] Supplementing the reservists were additional local militia fighters from Amal and the Lebanese Communist Party, fighters who may of may not have been under Hezbollah's direct operational control.[17]

As Israeli ground forces crossed into the south and stayed, and as it became clear what specific Israeli objectives were, the Hezbollah command was also able to reinforce specific villages, choke points, and avenues of approach. Forces from the Nasr command itself were moved around under the cover of darkness to reinforce weak points. Some 1,000 additional soldiers were redeployed from Badr command north of the Litani River to augment losses and reinforce southern defenses.[18] Hezbollah special forces units were additionally concentrated at key nodes and geographically important villages.[19] Hezbollah also

---

[14] IDF, ITIC/CSS, Part Two, 76.

[15] Information provided by Israeli intelligence. See also Anthony Shadid, "Inside Hezbollah, Big Miscalculations; Militia Leaders Caught off Guard by Scope of Israel's Response in War," *Washington Post*, 8 October 2006, A1.

[16] Hassan Nasrallah, interview on Al-Manar television, 27 May 2006.

[17] UN General Assembly, Human Rights Council, Report of the Commission of Inquiry on Lebanon pursuant to Human Rights Council resolution S-2/1, A/HRC/3/2, 23 November 2006, 31.

[18] IDF, ITIC/CSS, Part One, 30.

[19] For instance, about 40 Special Force operatives were stationed in the Bint Jbeil-Ainata region, according to the IDF. IDF, ITIC/CSS, Part Two, 76.

maintained listening posts, reportedly with trained Hebrew speakers, and employed commercial scanners to monitor Israeli radio communications.[20]

Beginning with the Israeli withdrawal from southern Lebanon in 2000, Hezbollah launched an extensive program of building a command structure, military positions, and a logistics support system to sustain its southern forces. Infrastructure included underground command and control centers, observation posts, and surveillance sites; fighter hide-sites and presurveyed rocket launch positions; border defenses; minefields; and other obstacles, as well as arms caches and supply and support bases dispersed down to the house level.[21] UNIFIL in 2006 reported Hezbollah "permanent observation posts, temporary checkpoints and patrols" and "intensive construction works," including the construction of new access roads all along the Blue Line (the Lebanon-Israel border) to fortify its positions.[22]

According to Israeli intelligence, prior to the July hostilities Hezbollah "bases" were spread out over some 130 villages in southern Lebanon. At the village level, Israeli intelligence identified specific Hezbollah headquarters, bases, and storehouses: 26, for instance, in and around Bint Jbeil, 10 in Aiyt

---

[20] Mohamad Bazzi, "Hezbollah cracked Israeli radio code during war," Yalibnan.com, 21 September 2006, http://yalibnan.com/site/archives/2006/09/Hezbollah_crack.php.

[21] According to one report, "most of Hizbullah's [sic] construction activities were shrouded in secrecy and kept to remoter tracts of the border when the group established mini security zones, off-limits to the general public. There were persistent reports over those six years of residents of villages in remote areas of the border being kept awake at night by distant explosions as Hizbullah [sic] dynamited new bunkers and positions. The extent and thoroughness of this military infrastructure was underestimated by observers and by the IDF, despite the latter enjoying extensive reconnaissance capabilities through overflights by jets and drones as well as possible assets on the ground in south Lebanon. Israeli troops came across some of these bunkers during the war, finding spacious well-equipped rooms 25 feet underground with side tunnels, storage chambers and TV cameras mounted at the entrances for security;" Nicholas Blanford, "Hizbullah [sic] and the IDF: Accepting New Realities Along the Blue Line," *The MIT Electronic Journal of Middle East Studies*, Summer 2006. Hezbollah was shown as well to have sophisticated observation devices, including night-vision systems and remote-controlled cameras. David A Fulghum, "Israel examines its military during Lebanon fighting lull," *Aerospace Daily and Defense Report*, 21 August 2006, 4. See also Yaakov Katz, "IDF report card," *Jerusalem Post Magazine*, 24 August 2006, http://www.jpost.com/servlet/Satellite?cid=1154525936817&pagename=JPost/JPArticle/ShowFull.

[22] UN, Report of the Secretary-General on the United Nations Interim Force in Lebanon (For the period from 21 January 2006 to 18 July 2006), S/2006/560, 21 July 2006.

Lebanese armed forces recover a stash of Hezbollah rockets from a natural cave in the Bekaa Valley. Much of Hezbollah's short-range rocket supply, and one out of every ten rockets fired upon Israel, came from north of the Litani River.

a-Shab, eight in Sultaniyeh, and six in Ghandouriyeh.[23] Just as the term *Hezbollah rocket launchers* led to confusing images suggesting large trucks and specialized launch vehicles, *bases* equally connotes traditional military objects. In Hezbollah's case, though, the base structure was almost exclusively and intrinsically integrated into otherwise normal civilian homes and structures. In Beirut, Hezbollah commandeered entire civilian neighborhoods and built military and political offices and bases in and amongst civilian buildings.[24] In the south, Hezbollah's military infrastructure was intentionally situated in and around densely populated areas. Through the use of civilian structures, much of Hezbollah's base structure was also highly clandestine. For instance, much of its underground capability, even that close to the border, was only discovered by Israeli intelligence and the IDF after ground forces occupied the south. One such bunker complex was described as "built 40 m underground and covered an area of 2 km. It included firing positions, operations rooms, connecting tunnels, medical facilities, ammunition and weapons stockpiles, ventilation and air conditioning, bathrooms with hot and cold running water and dormitories—enough to keep a large number of fighters underground without requiring re-supply for many weeks."[25]

Hezbollah's Arsenal

Hezbollah's military arsenal prior to the 2006 war included offensive rockets and missiles of a wide variety and ranges, as well as other types of ordnance, including a significant and unexpected arsenal of modern antitank missiles. The categories included:

- surface-to-surface rockets and missiles of up to 210 km range;
- antitank missiles with ranges up to 4 km, including modern laser-guided varieties;

---

[23] IDF, ITIC/CSS, Part Two, 76, 83, 90, 118.

[24] Ibid., 63.

[25] Nicholas Blanford, "Deconstructing Hizbullah's [*sic*] surprise military prowess," *Jane's Intelligence Review*, November 2006.

- 60, 81, 120, and 160 mm mortars with maximum ranges of 3,000, 5,700, and 8,000 m respectively;[26]
- recoilless guns with maximum ranges of 1,300 m;
- antiaircraft guns (and perhaps SA-7 shoulder-fired surface-to-air missiles);
- RPG launchers, including modern types with sophisticated warheads; and
- the full panoply of small arms.

Hezbollah also possessed the "Noor" (C-802) Chinese-designed and Iranian-supplied antiship missile, which was successfully employed to strike an Israeli naval vessel on 14 July, killing four.[27] It launched three Iranian-made Mirsad-1 UAVs, both reconnaissance and armed versions. Two were intercepted by the Israeli Air Force; one had a technical failure and crashed into the sea.[28] Finally, Hezbollah had an extensive demolitions and mining effort, preparing booby traps and explosives in Lebanese villages, planting explosive devices

---

[26] Unexploded ordnance (UXO) specialists of the Israeli police were able to identify 81 mm, 120 mm, and 160 mm high explosive shells on the ground in Israel. IDF, ITIC/CSS, Part Three, 152. It is believed that Hezbollah also possesses several Israeli-made self-propelled mortars captured from the SLA. While Hezbollah is credited with having 122 mm, 130 mm, and 155 mm towed artillery guns, there is no evidence that any conventional artillery was fired on Israel during the 2006 war. The reports of their possession are therefore probably wrong.

[27] At least two FL-10 missiles were fired from Beirut; one hit and sank a merchant ship. The turbojet-powered C-802 has a range of up to 120 km (74.5 mi) and carries a 155 kg (341 lb) blast-fragmentation warhead. See David A. Fulghum and Douglas Barrie, "The Iranian Connection: New operations, advanced weapons, Iranian advisers are influencing the course of Lebanon/Israel conflict," *Aviation Week & Space Technology*, 14 August 2006, 20. *Jane's Intelligence Review* raises the possibility that the Hezbollah missile fired was a smaller, television-guided C-701. Blanford, "Deconstructing."

[28] Information provided by Israeli intelligence sources. Mirsad-1 is the Hezbollah name for the "Ababil" (Swallow) UAV. Hezbollah sent reconnaissance UAVs into Israel a number of times before the 2006 war. The IDF says that a drone shot on 7 August was recovered in Israel and had 10 kg of explosive ball-bearings packed inside the warhead. The Ababil-T/Ababil-3 (Swallow) UAV is manufactured by the Iran Aircraft Manufacturing Industries (HESA). See also "Iranian-made Hezbollah UAV shot down by Israeli fighter," *Flight International*, 15 August 2006; and Fulghum and Barrie, "The Iranian Connection," 20.

on roads leading to southern villages, and making extensive use of shaped charges or explosively formed penetrators.[29]

Hezbollah's arsenal was made up of weapons from many different sources, including Chinese, Russian, US, and European designs, as well as various production models and indigenous designs from Iran, Syria, and North Korea. Contrary to the notion that Hezbollah is solely or primarily a patron of Iran, the rocket and missile arsenal was found to have been predominantly supplied and supported by Syria.[30] The diversity of Hezbollah's support and the degree of its prewar build-up and preparations can be seen in the types of weapons it is known to possess: at least 11 types of surface-to-surface rockets and missiles and 10 types of antitank missiles.

The actual size of Hezbollah's pre- and postwar arsenal is virtually impossible to determine. Israeli intelligence says that it was aware of all of the weapons Hezbollah possessed but was itself surprised by the numbers. As the war unfolded, Hezbollah was shown to have a seemingly endless supply of rocket launchers, though the image of a traditional Scud-type launcher on a large truck is somewhat misleading. In most cases, the firings of Katyusha rockets (more than 90 percent of the total; see chap. 4) were much improvised; the launchers were often little more than tripod mounts or single tubes positioned facing Israel. Others were multiple tubes (four to six) lashed together and placed inside buildings or on the backs of small trucks. Only a few score of the 4,000 rockets fired were larger weapons launched from traditional multiple-rocket launchers on large vehicles. Some other types of larger rockets (of the Fajr type; see below) were actually tied to fixed launchers and were not mobile at all.

---

[29] The IDF assessed that four Israeli tanks hit large land mines. Three of the tanks, which lacked underbelly protective armor, lost all 12 crew members. The fourth had underbelly protective armor; of its six crew members, only one died. Ze'ev Schiff, "The War's Surprises," *Haaretz*, 19 August 2006, http://www.haaretz.com/hasen/pages/ShArt.jhtml?itemNo=751958.

[30] Maj Gen Amos Yadlin, director of IDF intelligence, told the Knesset Foreign Affairs and Defense Committee on 24 August 2007 that most of the rockets fired on Israel were of Syrian origin. There have been reports that some of the recovered Fajr-3 rockets appear to be Iranian in origin. The long-range Zelzal rockets were also of Iranian origin, but none were successfully launched against Israel.

Photo courtesy of Israeli Defense Forces

This mobile Katyusha launcher was detected and attacked in southern Lebanon on 23 July 2006. The four-tube truck-mounted launcher was typical of Hezbollah's arsenal and far more easily concealed than mobile rocket launchers typically used by conventional militaries. Hezbollah also used remote controls to fire rockets, thereby protecting the rocketeers from counterbattery fire.

Surface-to-Surface Rockets and Missiles

Israeli intelligence estimated that Hezbollah had an arsenal of more than 20,000 rockets of varying ranges (from short-range to long-range rockets capable of reaching northern and central Israel).[31]

---

[31] IDF, ITIC/CSS, Part One, 28. During the war itself, most reports placed Hezbollah's arsenal at about 12,000–13,000 rockets and missiles. "There is no agreement as to the number of short-range rockets the Hezbollah had when the war began, or how many survive. Israeli officials offered pre-conflict estimates of more than 10,000–16,000 regular and extended range Katyushas, with a nominal total of 13,000. Errors of 5,000 rockets are easily possible, compounded by the ongoing supply just before the war and the discovery that Syria had supplied more such rockets than Israel initially estimated." Anthony H. Cordesman, "Preliminary 'Lessons' of the Israeli-Hezbollah War," CSIS working draft, 17 August 2006, 4.

Name	Caliber	Range (km)	Warhead Size (kg)	Number Available	Number Fired	Country of Origin
Type 63 (Fajr 1)	107 mm	6–8.5	5–7	Scores	Very few	China or N. Korea
Katyusha	122 mm	11–40	10–30	Thousands of all types	~3,800 of all types	Russia, via Iran/Syria
Syrian 220mm (Uragan)	220 mm	10–35	280	Dozens	~200–300	Russia, via Syria
Fajr-3 (Ra'ad or Khaibar)	240 mm	17–45	45	Scores	Tens	Iran/Syria
Falaq	240 mm/ 333 mm	10–11	111–120	Dozens	Less than 10	Iran
Syrian 302 mm (possibly WS-1)	302 mm	40–110+	100–150	Dozens	Scores to over 100	China, via Syria
Fajr-5 (Ra'ad or Khaibar-1)	333 mm	75	90	Scores	Tens	Iran
Zelzal-2	610 mm	200	600	Few dozen	None	Iran

Figure 2.2: Hezbollah surface-to-surface rockets

Compiled from Israeli and US intelligence; IDF, Intelligence and Terrorism Information Center at the Center for Special Studies (ITIC/CSS), "Hezbollah as a strategic arm of Iran," 8 September 2006; International Institute for Strategic Studies; Jamestown Foundation Terrorism Monitor; and Yiftah Shapir, "Artillery Rockets: Should Means of Interception be Developed?" *Strategic Assessment* (Jaffee Center for Strategic Studies) 9, no 2 (August 2006).

From shortest to longest range, Hezbollah rockets used during the 2006 war included:

- Type-63 107 mm rockets with a maximum range of 8.5 km and a 5–7 kg warhead. None or very few of these rockets were used. The Chinese-made systems were originally truck towable, but it is believed that Hezbollah reconfigured North Korean–made versions to fire individually.

- Falaq demolition rockets of Iranian manufacture with "intensified warheads."[32] The 240 mm Falaq-1 has a maximum range of 10–11 km (6 mi) and carries a 50 kg high-explosive fragmentation warhead. A Falaq-1 was accidentally fired by Hezbollah on Israel on 25 August 2005.[33]

- Katyusha *Grad*-type, Soviet-designed 122 mm rockets. The Katyushas used by Hezbollah included:

---

[32] IDF, ITIC/CSS, Part Three, 139–40.

[33] A 333 mm Falaq-2 also has a maximum range of 10.8 km and carries a 120 kg warhead.

o The original models (Type 9M22) of Iranian/Syrian, Chinese, Russian, and Bulgarian origin with an effective range of about 11 km and a maximum range of about 21 km with a warhead of approximately 10 kg.

o An "improved" and extended-range model (Type 9M17/9M18) of Russian, Chinese, Iranian, and Bulgarian origin with a range of 20–40 km and a larger warhead (60 kg?).

o A rocket of Chinese origin (received from Iran and Syria) that carried 6 mm (1/4-inch) antipersonnel ball bearings.[34]

o A rocket of Chinese origin (received from Iran and Syria) with an antitank/antipersonnel submunition (cluster bomb) warhead and a shell casing carrying ball bearings 3.5 mm (about 1/8-inch) in diameter.[35]

Israeli intelligence spotted military-style truck-mounted Katyusha launchers in Hezbollah possession in 2001, but the majority of the Katyushas fired were individually packaged and fired from improvised trucks and preplanned positions. The flight duration of the rockets is relatively short, about a minute or two, out to maximum range. Under the best of conditions, the rockets have an accuracy of 300–400 m at maximum range.

• 220 mm rockets of Syrian manufacture with a maximum range of 70 km (43 mi) and a 100–280 kg warhead, depending on type. The Russian versions (Uragan/Ouragan "Hurricanes") were originally designed to carry an antitank mine submunition warhead, and some of the Hezbollah rockets were modified to carry thousands of 6 mm (1/4-inch) diameter ball bearings.[36] Mobile launchers seen in Lebanon differed from the Soviet design with only one layer of four tubes rather than the standard three layers—two with six tubes and one with four. Israeli intelligence sus-

---

[34] IDF, ITIC/CSS, Part Three, 139–42.

[35] Ibid.

[36] Ibid.

Photo courtesy of Israeli Defense Forces

Syrian-supplied 220 mm rockets were found in a civilian house in southern Lebanon.

pects that the change was made to accommodate a lighter and more maneuverable vehicle.[37]

- Fajr-3 (Ra'ad or Khaibar-1) 240 mm rockets designed by Iran's military industry but possibly also manufactured by Syria and North Korea. The Fajr-3 has a maximum range of 43 km (27 mi) and a warhead of approximately 90 kg. Initially Israeli intelligence believed that the Fajr-3 rockets were pre-positioned and not mobile and that most had been destroyed in the first two days of the war. Later in the war, though, mobile Iranian versions with 14 launch tubes emerged, and Fajr-3's were then detected in large numbers.[38]

---

[37] Robert Wall, Paris; David A. Fulghum, Washington; and Douglas Barrie, London, "Israel Tries to Identify Latest Hezbollah Rocket Threat" and "Harsh Trajectories: Israel continues to attack Hezbollah's rocket arsenal, but larger and more destructive threats loom," *Aviation Week & Space Technology*, 7 August 2006, 28.

[38] Fulghum, "Israel examines its military," 4.

- Fajr-5 (Ra'ad or Khaibar-2) 330 mm rockets designed by Iran's military industry but possibly also manufactured by Syria and North Korea. The Fajr-5 had a maximum range of 75 km (47 mi) and a warhead of approximately 45 kg.[39] Like the Fajr-3s, Israeli intelligence initially believed that the Fajr-5s were pre-positioned. The mobile Fajr-5 versions ended up having up to four rockets per launcher.[40] The IAF was convinced that it had destroyed the majority of the fixed Fajr-5 launchers on the first or second night of the war, but later realized not only that there were additional mobile launchers, but there were 302 mm Syrian rockets of similar attributes that had not been detected before the war.[41]

- B-302 mobile 302 mm rockets of Syrian manufacture or origin with a maximum range of 100 km (62 mi) and a warhead weight of 175 kg. There have been reports that this weapon is associated with or based upon the Chinese WS-1 multiple rocket launchers, also exported to Iran. However, the Hezbollah launchers have been modified to carry six tubes in two rows of three tubes each, a configuration that does not appear in the Chinese or Iranian system.[42] The warheads for this rocket have also evidently been modified to carry thousands of 16 mm (about 2/3-inch) square-shaped antipersonnel fragments.[43]

- Zelzal (Earthquake in Farsi) rockets/missiles of Iranian manufacture or origin. Hezbollah was believed to possess three variants of the Zelzal: 1, 2, and 3. Ranges were model- and payload-dependent from 125 km up to 210 km (78–137 mi) with a warhead as large as 600 kg (the Zelzal-1 has a range of 125 km and the Zelzal-2 has a range of 210

---

[39] Some reports say the Fajr-5 rockets had a warhead as large as 175 kg, but this seems unlikely.

[40] Cordesman, "Preliminary 'Lessons,'" 17.

[41] IDF, ITIC/CSS, "Hezbollah as a strategic arm of Iran," 8 September 2006, http://www.intelligence.org.il/eng/eng_n/html/iran_Hezbollah_e1b.htm.

[42] Wall et al., "Israel Tries To Identify Latest Hezbollah Rocket Threat," 28; and Wall, et al., "Harsh Trajectories," 28.

[43] IDF, ITIC/CSS, Part Three, 139–42.

km). The Zelzal-1 and 2 are described as artillery rockets and the Zelzal-3 as a ballistic missile with considerable accuracy. The Zelzal-2 is assessed as capable of reaching Israeli targets south of Askhelon; the Zelzal-3 can reach targets south of Tel Aviv. The Zelzal is derived from the Soviet-era FROG 7 rocket; it requires a large transporter-erector-launcher (TEL) and has a large radar and infrared signature.[44]

A number of additional rockets were also reported in the Hezbollah inventory, but there is no sign that they were used in the 2006 war: Fatah 110,[45] Nazc'at,[46] Oghab, and Shahin-1/2.

Antitank Weapons

Most of Hezbollah's antitank missiles were of Russian design and Iranian and Syrian origin.[47] Antitank missiles in the Hezbollah arsenal included:

- Metis-M (AT-13 or 9M131) optically tracked antitank missiles of Russian origin and Syrian and Iranian supply.[48]
- Kornet-E (AT-14 or 9P133) heat-seeking antitank missiles of Russian origin and supplied by Syria,[49] Hezbollah's longest range antitank weapon, the Kornet-E has a powerful tandem-type warhead that offers a "double punch" effective against explosive reactive armor, bunkers, and hardened buildings.[50]

---

[44] Cordesman, "Preliminary 'Lessons'," 17.

[45] The Fatah 110 has a range reportedly up to 220 km.

[46] The various models in Hezbollah possession (Naze'at 4–10) were 356–450 mm in diameter and varied in range from 80–140 km, with 240–430 kg warheads. None were used in the 2006 war. See IDF, ITIC/CSS, "Hezbollah as a strategic arm of Iran"; and IDF, ITIC/CSS, Part Three, 139–40.

[47] IDF, ITIC/CSS, "Hezbollah as a strategic arm of Iran."

[48] "Israel encounters top-line Russian weaponry in Lebanon," *Aerospace Daily and Defense Report*, 5 September 2006, 1; Fulghum, "Israel examines its military," 4; and Cordesman, "Preliminary 'Lessons'," 17.

[49] IDF, ITIC/CSS, Part Two, 93. Some reports additionally say that the Kornet was supplied by Iran, but there is no evidence of that.

[50] Blanford, "Deconstructing"; "Israel encounters top-line Russian weaponry," 1; Fulghum, "Israel examines its military," 4; and Cordesman, "Preliminary 'Lessons'," 17.

- Konkurs (Tousans or 9K113) antitank guided missiles of Russian design and Iranian manufacture.[51]

- Sagger (AT-3) wire-guided antitank missiles of Russian origin. The Sagger is considered the Hezbollah workhorse and is the easiest of the older antitank missiles to fire.

- Fagot (AT-4 or 9K111) wire-guided antitank missiles of Russian origin.[52]

- Spandrel (AT-5) Russian-designed, Iranian- and Russian-produced wire-guided antitank missiles with shaped-charge warheads.[53]

- Raad antitank guided missiles of Russian origin and Iranian manufacture. The Raad is an Iranian version of the Sagger, with a range of 3 km and the ability to penetrate 400 mm of armor with its double tandem-type warhead.[54]

- Milan wire-guided missiles of Franco-German origin.

- TOW (tube-launched optically sighted wire-guided) missiles, some purloined from Lebanese armed forces and some originally supplied to Iran and built under license as the Toophan. The Toophan has a range of up to 3.75 km and can penetrate 550 mm of steel armor.[55] Iran and Syria delivered the advanced antitank missile to Hezbollah. They were used with a high degree of skill day and night, hitting dozens of armored IDF vehicles in south Lebanon.[56]

- Dragon antitank missiles of US origin but reverse-engineered and built in Iran.[57]

---

[51] IDF, ITIC/CSS, Part Two, 81.

[52] Fulghum, "Israel examines its military," 4.

[53] Blanford, "Deconstructing"; and Fulghum, "Israel examines its military," 4.

[54] IDF, ITIC/CSS, "Hezbollah as a strategic arm of Iran."

[55] Ibid. See also Barbara Opall-Rome, "Did Hezbollah Fire U.S. Missiles at Israeli Tanks?" *Defense News*, September 2006, 1.

[56] IDF, ITIC/CSS, "Hezbollah as a strategic arm of Iran."

[57] Greg Grant, "Hezbollah Missile Swarms Pounded Armor, Infantry," *Defense News*, August 2006, 8.

Hezbollah also employed two types of RPG launchers—the venerable RPG-7 (Shager) of Russian design and Iranian manufacture and the newer RPG-29 Vampyr of Russian origin and Syrian supply. The 105.2 mm RPG-29 is a much heavier system than previous designs. The two-man-crew weapon has a 450 m range and an advanced 4.5 kg grenade that can be used to attack both armor and bunkers. Some versions were reportedly equipped with night sights.[58] The RPG-29 was first used by Hezbollah in November 2005 when it launched a coordinated, but unsuccessful, kidnapping attempt on the IDF position at Ghajar.[59]

---

[58] Cordesman, "Preliminary 'Lessons,'" 17.

[59] Blanford, "Hizbullah [sic] and the IDF."

Chapter 3

The War

On 12 July, when Israel decided to respond to the Hezbollah attacks, incursion, and kidnapping with a major military operation, the government of Ehud Olmert laid out a set of four objectives for the IDF to guide its operations:

- return of the two abducted soldiers,
- imposition of a new order in Lebanon, particularly in southern Lebanon,
- the strengthening of Israel's deterrent against external attack, and
- the crushing of Hezbollah.

The Cabinet stated in its first communiqué that Israel would "respond aggressively and harshly to those who carried out, and are responsible for, today's action."[1] Though some in the Cabinet favored broader objectives, including attacking Lebanese infrastructure beyond bridges and roads, attacking Syria directly, and seeking the elimination of Hezbollah as an explicit objective of the campaign, military sources say that the IDF argued that these were not feasible objectives.[2]

The first three objectives were as much political as military in nature. Though Israel subsequently undertook military and special operations to rescue its soldiers, its long history with kidnappings and back-channel negotiations with Hezbollah consigned the problem to the political and clandestine world.

---

[1] Israeli MFA, Cabinet Communiqué, 12 July 2006.

[2] Background interviews with Israeli government spokesmen and participants, September 2006. The shrewd military observer Anthony Cordesman agrees, writing that the IDF had an "understanding that [Hezbollah] could not be destroyed as a military force and would continue to be a major political actor in Lebanon." Cordesman, "Preliminary 'Lessons'," 3. Lt Gen Dan Halutz, the IDF chief of staff, says that three options were discussed: "We go for Hezbollah alone; we go for Hezbollah and Lebanon; or for Hezbollah, Lebanon and Syria. I believed that we should go for the second option, Hezbollah and Lebanon. I was opposed to the third option: not to attack Syria because of the kidnapping of the two soldiers." Nahum Barnea and Shimon Schiffer, "What Would Halutz Say," *Yediot Aharonot* (Tel Aviv), 25 August 2006.

The second objective sought Lebanese implementation of *UN-SCR 1559*, which demanded that the central government exercise sovereignty over southern Lebanon and disband independent militias.[3] Israel hoped to end Hezbollah's status as a permissible state within a state, but it was again as much a political objective as a military one. At least initially, the Israeli government did not pursue ground operations to physically eject the organization from the border area or to disarm it.[4] The third objective was political as well. Some felt that Israel needed to project a stronger image against Hezbollah and the Palestinians after the 2000 withdrawal from southern Lebanon and the 2005 withdrawal from Gaza to prevent future attacks. Others felt that Israel's deterrence target was actually Iran (and the build-up of Iran's so-called Western Command in Lebanon),[5] while others saw the target as both Iran and Syria.

The final objective of crushing Hezbollah was the purely military one, though what exactly the government asked the IDF to do—weaken, cripple, annihilate—represents potentially different approaches and levels of effort along a spectrum of destruction. According to IDF and Israeli government officials, the operation did have specific quantitative military objectives: x percent of weapons destroyed, x percent of long-range launchers depleted, x percent of Hezbollah leadership and fighters killed, and so forth, but the percentages are unknown. "I said from day one, and all the way through, that the purpose was not to destroy Hizbullah [*sic*]," Prime Minister Olmert later responded to war critics who claimed that the government ordered the IDF to indeed "destroy" the organization:

---

[3] *UNSCR 1559*, 2 September 2004. The resolution called for the withdrawal of all remaining foreign forces from Lebanon; the "disbanding and disarmament of all Lebanese and non-Lebanese militias"; and extension of Lebanese government control over southern Lebanon.

[4] "We have no intention of permitting Hezbollah to redeploy along the international border in southern Lebanon," Defense Minister Amir Peretz told the Knesset's Foreign Affairs and Defense Committee on 13 July, "I state this unequivocally. The Lebanese Army should operate there and the Lebanese government is the only party that will be allowed to deploy forces along the border. If the Lebanese government refrains from deploying its forces, as is expected from a sovereign government, then we will not allow Hezbollah to deploy along Israel's border fences." BBC Worldwide Monitoring, "Israeli officials vow to remove Hezbollah."

[5] Cordesman, "Preliminary 'Lessons'," 3.

The purpose was not to destroy every launcher. The ambition was not to catch every Hizbullah [sic] fighter. The purpose was to impose a new order on Lebanon that would remove to a large degree . . . the threat to the state of Israel that was built up over the last 6 or 7 years to an intolerable degree. I never said we would destroy Hizbullah [sic]. What I said was that we had to create a new order on the basis of implementation of [UNSCR] 1559, and the deployment of the Lebanese army in the south of Lebanon, and so on. How to do it? Not by catching every launcher.[6]

General Halutz told the Cabinet that the IDF would require nine to ten weeks to carry out the assigned objectives: two weeks focused on counterbattery fire to silence Hezbollah rockets and mortars, followed by a six- to eight-week ground operation. Maj Gen Benjamin Gantz, the ground forces commander, said he thought that the IDF "would take control of the area in a week and a half, during which time enemy launch capability would be dramatically degraded. Between week two and week nine, we wouldn't have faced significant warfare on our home front, which would have allowed us to focus on eradicating Hezbollah's efforts to threaten Israel. It also would have provided a week or two for a proper disengagement and return to the border area."[7]

"We said that Katyushas would fall on Israel up to the last day," Halutz said of the Cabinet discussions. "Our assessment was that the fighting would stop earlier because of international intervention."[8]

The Cabinet instructed the IDF to impose a complete air, sea, and land blockade on Lebanon and approved a series of targets for attack. Authority was given to attack Hezbollah headquarters, bases, and tactical positions in the south, and the Cabinet approved limited attacks on Beirut's international airport and Lebanese transportation to put pressure on the government of

---

[6] "Israel's Olmert Talks on Lebanon War, Iran, Prisoner Swap, Qadima Party Survival," interview with Prime Minister Ehud Olmert in his Jerusalem office by Herb Keinon and David Horovitz, n.d.; and "I Had No Illusions about This Job," *Jerusalem Post*, 29 September 2006.

[7] "Interview: Maj Gen Benjamin Gantz, commander, Israel Defense Force's Army Headquarters," *Defense News*, August 2006, 38. Some media reports say Halutz told the Cabinet that the IDF would require six to eight weeks, but this is not confirmed by Israeli officials, even those critical of Halutz.

[8] Barnea and Schiffer, "What Would Halutz Say."

Lebanon and weaken Hezbollah's popular support base.[9] Prime Minister Olmert was reportedly skeptical of attacks on infrastructure beyond bridges, fearing that such a move would have the opposite effect and unite the Lebanese around Hezbollah.[10] What exact instructions the Cabinet initially gave to the IDF regarding attacks on Hezbollah's headquarters and support base in south Beirut is unclear. Israeli ministers would later say that the Cabinet agreed that there would be no attacks on electrical power or water-related installations, a departure from previous Israeli practice in its 1996 campaign. This was a decision taken specifically to spare the civilian population the secondary effects of the loss of modern life-support systems and avoid the negative political and international fallout associated with "attacks" on civilians.[11]

However Hezbollah was to be crushed, the mission had to be accomplished in such a way that it would not undermine larger political and strategic objectives for Israel—not just to buy additional security and increase international support for its existence and right to self-defense, but also to weaken Hezbollah's status in Lebanon and in the Arab world. Finally, as a component of a global "war" against terrorism, Israel's actions against Hezbollah sought concrete and physical achievements that were not at the same time undermined by a sense of victimization or immoral defeat that merely strengthened a future enemy.

Attack and Escalation

Though Israel was well aware of Hezbollah's build-up in southern Lebanon and even forecast that a military confrontation with Hezbollah was inevitable, given the organization's acquisition of a more and more effective offensive arsenal, when Hezbollah attacked on 12 July, the operation seemed to have

---

[9] Report by Israel's Channel 10 television; and DPA, "Israel retaliates with Lebanon attacks; Gaza targeted," 13 July 2006, 12:54 a.m. EST.

[10] Makovsky and White, "Lessons and Implications," 13.

[11] Senior Israeli government official and cabinet member, background interview by author, September 2006.

come as a surprise.[12] The day before Hezbollah's incursion, IDF chief Lt Gen Dan Halutz reportedly made a reservation to vacation with his family in northern Israel.[13] On the day of the attack, Prime Minister Olmert maintained a regular schedule, ironically meeting with the family of another kidnapped soldier, Galid Shalit, and then meeting with Japanese prime minister Junichiro Koizumi.[14]

At the local military level, three days before the Hezbollah attack, Maj Gen Udi Adam, commander of the IDF's Northern Command, lowered the alert level along the northern border. Israeli intelligence provided his command "no early warning, period," Adam says.[15] The commander of Division 91, the higher command for the ambushed patrol, also says Israeli intelligence failed to provide him or his staff with early warning as to Hezbollah plans to carry out the 12 July raid.[16] An official postwar review of the kidnapping incident concluded that the ambushed patrol operated as if it were "out on a trip rather than on an operative mission." The reserve unit evidently had

---

[12] Military intelligence had issued a "strategic warning" in December 2005 predicting Hezbollah operations on the northern border, including the kidnapping of Israeli soldiers and rocket attacks on Haifa. The assessment, according to *Haaretz*, warned that Israel would face a considerable challenge because Hezbollah was a "well-established guerrilla force equipped with advanced anti-tank weapons and well-entrenched in southern Lebanon's nature preserves." Ari Shavit, "Six months of failures," *Haaretz*, 17 November 2006.

[13] Yaakov Katz, "IDF report card," *Jerusalem Post Magazine*. There is, nonetheless, one significant contradiction to this information: claims that Halutz also sold his stock portfolio on 12 July. See Makovsky and White, "Lessons and Implications," 23.

[14] Galid Shalit was kidnapped on the Gaza border on 25 June 2006. AP (Jerusalem), "Japan's Koizumi urges Israel to show restraint, not seek 'eye for eye'," 12 July 2006, 1146 GMT. "I respect his decision to meet with me at such a time," Koizumi said of Olmert after the meeting. "Israel's crisis management is very solid."

[15] BBC Worldwide Monitoring, "Israeli general says 'this is war'."

[16] Nir Hasson, "Gal Hirsch: MI warning would have prevented soldiers' abduction," *Haaretz*, 15 November 2006. Though Israeli intelligence may have known more, no specific warning was transmitted to those who needed it. *Haaretz* also reported that Israeli intelligence tipped off Division 91 at 2 a.m. on 12 July that the border fence had been cut and some 20 Hezbollah fighters had infiltrated into Israel. Amir Oren, "Analysis: In Lebanon, government hamstrung troubled division," *Haaretz*, 15 October 2006, http://www.haaretz.com/hasen/spages/774974.html.

not been given any proper orders in its entire three weeks of border duty.[17]

An Israeli Air Force (IAF) F-16 pilot further describes his surprise on 12 July when, upon returning to base at about 10 a.m. from a routine training flight, he saw aircraft taking off to implement emergency procedures:

> By the time I get out of the plane, I hear the roar of the heavy takeoffs . . . and then another roar, and another. There is something different in the sound of a combat takeoff with a full load of bombs: the takeoff is long, the planes are heavy, the afterburner is used longer—not the light and quick training takeoffs. Something is definitely happening.[18]

And though the 12 July operation was meticulously planned by Hezbollah, Hassan Nasrallah himself claims that he was surprised with the Israeli government's response to the kidnapping, indicating more Israeli improvisation than preparation.[19] After all, there had been other incidents along the border during 2005 and 2006, and as General Adam reminded the media on 12 July, the IDF had deflected them or dealt with them without escalating.[20]

Hezbollah political leaders and operatives in Beirut were also unaware of the operation, making no changes to their day-to-day security procedures or movements. Even after the kidnapping, Hezbollah political leaders had no sense or warning that Israel would respond as they did, particularly in Beirut.[21] The Lebanese government was unaware of Hezbollah's actions on 12

---

[17] Hanan Greenberg, "Almog: Kidnappings could have been avoided," *Ynetnews* .com, 12 November 2006, http://www.ynetnews.com/articles/0,7340,L-3327332,00 .html.

[18] "In the cockpit, by MAJOR 'Y'," *Jerusalem Post*, 18 July 2006, 1524 (updated 19 July 2006, 0819), http://www.jpost.com/servlet/Satellite?cid=1150886035223&page name=JPost/JPArticle/ShowFull.

[19] Transcript, interview with Hassan Nasrallah on Al-Jazeera, 20 July 2006; and transcript, interview with Hassan Nasrallah on Lebanese NTV, 27 August 2006.

[20] BBC Worldwide Monitoring, "Israeli general says 'this is war.'" The kidnapping of three soldiers in 2000, as well as the attempted kidnapping in December 2005, all went unanswered by Israel. Hezbollah was also allowed to maintain outposts on the northern border through July 2006. The turning of the other cheek was referred to in Israel as the "Zimmer Policy": Israel would tolerate Hezbollah as long as the zimmers and hotels in the North were full. Katz, "IDF report card."

[21] Shadid, "Inside Hezbollah," A1.

July and went about its business without any advance warning of the Hezbollah attack.[22] And once the attack unfolded, the Beirut government was vociferous in its position that it was neither responsible for Hezbollah's actions nor did it endorse them.[23]

On the second day of the conflict, after Hezbollah attacked Haifa, Israel escalated its attacks to include the runways at Rafiq Hariri International Airport and Hezbollah's Al-Manar television station in Beirut.[24] After Israel returned to the Beirut airport to attack fuel storage tanks on the evening of 13 July, it also attacked fuel storage tanks at the Jiyyeh electric power plant south of the capital. Finally, on the evening of 13 July, the IAF began attacks on Hezbollah headquarters and "security command" targets in the southern Shi'a neighborhoods of Beirut, beginning its campaign to eradicate the Hezbollah-dominated areas of the Lebanese capital. "You wanted an open war, and we are heading for an open war," Hassan Nasrallah responded to the south Beirut attacks. "We are ready for it." Nasrallah also vowed that Israeli military action would never win the release of the two soldiers, saying that the two IDF soldiers had been moved to a safe place far from the border. Nasrallah further threatened that if Israel escalated, Hezbollah would respond strongly and that Israel "should be ready for surprises."

By the end of the first 24 hours, Hezbollah had fired 125 Katyushas into Israel. By 14 July, the number reached 185. On 14 July, 103 Hezbollah rockets were fired, followed by 100 on the 15th. Israel might have thought that its air attacks were having an impact when the number of rocket firings declined to 43 on 16 July and 92 on the 17th, but by 18 July, the number

---

[22] In mid-2005, UNIFIL commander Maj Gen Alain Pellegrini was reportedly told by a senior IDF officer during a meeting in Jerusalem that if Hezbollah staged another kidnapping, the Israelis would "burn Beirut." Pellegrini says he relayed the warning to the Lebanese government. See Blanford, "Deconstructing."

[23] The Lebanese prime minister stated on 15 July that "the Lebanese government announced from the first instance when the events broke, that it had no prior knowledge of what happened. Nor did it endorse the operation carried out by Hezbollah, which led to the abduction of the two Israeli soldiers." Address to the Lebanese People of Prime Minister Fouad Siniora, 15 July 2006.

[24] Two Lebanese military airfields were also attacked. A handful of television and radio transmission and relay stations in southern Lebanon and the Bekaa Valley was also attacked, but not in any methodical way.

was again above 100, and there was little evidence, as Hezbollah mobilized in the south, that air attacks alone were having the effect of stemming the rocket fire into Israel. What is more, after the initial attack on Haifa on 13 July, Hezbollah continued its long-range attacks on Israeli cities, attacking Tiberias (25 mi from the Lebanese border) on 15 July, and the Galilee town of Afula (31 mi south of the Lebanese border) on 17 July. Afula was the furthest south a rocket fired from Lebanon had ever landed inside Israel. Hezbollah also hit Haifa on 16 July with an Iranian Fajr rocket, killing eight railroad workers and injuring another 50. Haifa and Tiberias were hit again on 17 July. Despite extensive Israeli bombing, Hezbollah had managed to fire more than 500 rockets in the first seven days.

Israel's initial ground operations against Hezbollah were limited to a half-hearted rescue attempt and commando and reconnaissance missions. By the end of the third day, IDF ground forces had crossed the border at a number of points from Ras al-Naqoura along the coast, all the way to al-Majidiyah north of the Golan Heights in the west, but these were all temporary

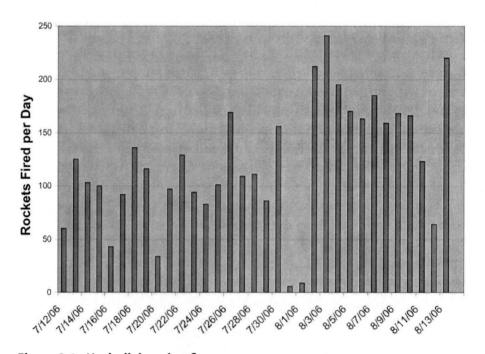

Figure 3.1: Hezbollah rocket fire

incursions. Israeli armored vehicles entered approximately one kilometer inside Lebanese territory, demolishing Hezbollah outposts, setting up cement block barriers, and exchanging fire with Hezbollah forces.[25]

It was not until 18 July—six days after the kidnapping—that Israeli ground forces made a major assault deep into Lebanese territory, initially focused on Maroun a-Ras as a stepping-stone to its assault on the Hezbollah center at Bint Jbeil just to its north.

Reality Sets In

Hezbollah forces in southern Lebanon were placed on full alert within minutes of the 12 July kidnapping, as the organization implemented plans to continue rocket attacks into Israel and defend its forces in Lebanon. Hezbollah had carefully studied its terrain and the supporting transportation and communication systems, as well as Israeli capabilities and deployments, allowing it to sustain rocket fire under attack and allowing it to concentrate forces at critical points, prepare optimum defenses, and streamline its logistical needs. From the border, where it was able to predict where Israel would cross, to the approaches into villages, where it was able to lay mines and explosives, to villages themselves, where it was able to establish firing positions and set booby traps, Hezbollah mounted an effective and economical defense.[26]

As the IDF attacked or made advances on the ground, most Hezbollah fighters withdrew from fixed border posts and prepared fire sites to positions closer to or inside villages and towns, where they either made use of prepared infrastructure or commandeered new civilian assets.[27] Organizationally, Hezbollah was also prepared to mount a stubborn "veneer" defense—wide and thin—and its forces and supplies were widely dispersed and organized to reinforce the weakest sectors. In just one village around Naqoura, a small fishing village on the Mediterranean coast just two kilometers from the Israeli border, Hezbollah de-

---

[25] UNIFIL press release PR02, 18 July 2006.

[26] Shadid, "Inside Hezbollah," A1; and IDF, ITIC/CSS, Part One, 46.

[27] Ibid.

ployed 10–15 squads that could shuttle amongst various pre-pared defenses. In the rocky, uninhabited hillside running along the border nearby, Hezbollah had closed off civilian traffic for over three years, building a "formidable network of tunnels, bunkers and weapons depots" where fighters were able to survive over the month of pounding by Israeli aircraft and artillery.[28]

Photo courtesy of Israeli Defense Forces

Hezbollah antitank missiles were found in the back of a van on the grounds of a mosque in Marwaheen, in the eastern sector near the Israel-Lebanon border.

---

[28] Blanford, "Hizbullah [*sic*] and the IDF."

In the built-up areas and inside the villages, Hezbollah had the advantages of civilian cover against attack, time to prepare for any Israeli advance, and an urban setting from which to ambush IDF forces and conduct guerrilla warfare once Israeli ground forces advanced. Hezbollah prepared hundreds of firing positions on the outskirts of villages and later booby-trapped civilian houses and buildings where it assumed the IDF would operate.[29] As IDF forces approached Lebanese villages, they were met by both gunfire and antitank fire from inside civilian houses. Hezbollah also used short-range rockets and mortars to fire on IDF forces maneuvering in Lebanese territory and on IDF concentrations that had occupied southern villages.[30]

Hezbollah rocket-firing positions were predominantly set up along paved roads, enabling easy access from weapon stockpiles located inside the villages.[31] Even under Israeli air attack—and as ground forces advanced into Lebanon—Hezbollah managed to conduct extensive logistical activities, making use of the pre-positioned materiel as well as moving arms to supply the fighters, albeit in small quantities, which are all highly needed.[32] For instance, antitank missiles were moved around the south inside backpacks carried by Hezbollah operatives dressed in civilian clothes, often riding motorcycles and carrying white flags, according to Israeli intelligence.[33] Israeli intelligence also alleged that Hezbollah used ambulances and other rescue vehicles for cover in its movements. According to the IDF:

> During the war, Hezbollah made use of vehicles designed for humanitarian purposes, knowing they would not be targeted by the IDF. Thus, there were numerous incidents reported of the use of ambulances, Red Cross vehicles, and the Lebanese government's civilian defense vehicles to transfer operatives, arms and ammunition, and equipment. In other incidents, Hezbollah's civilian vehicles closely followed Red Cross and other humanitarian convoys to minimize risk.[34]

---

[29] IDF, ITIC/CSS, Part One, 49.

[30] Ibid., 50.

[31] Ibid.

[32] IDF, ITIC/CSS, Part Two, 79.

[33] Ibid., 88.

[34] IDF, ITIC/CSS, Part One, 45.

When the Israeli ground offensive finally began in earnest on 19 July, Israeli forces proceeded into Lebanon, mostly taking to the roads, moving slowly, and controlling territory only in a piecemeal fashion in southern Lebanon; Hezbollah seemed far more ready than the IDF.[35] With no established front and no clear line of separation between forces, the IDF faced fire—particularly deadly antitank fire—from all directions. IDF forces took refuge in abandoned Lebanese homes and buildings, becoming prey to the capable multikilometer-range antitank missiles. In the village of Debel, west of Bint Jbeil, Hezbollah fired on civilian structures that IDF reservists were using for shelter during daylight hours; nine Israeli soldiers from a demolition company were killed, and 31 more were wounded.[36] Antitank squads armed with advanced Kornet missiles were mobilized in the Froun-Ghandouriyeh area at the end of the war.[37] Division 162, which fought the battle of the Wadi Saluki at the end of the war near these villages, suffered considerable casualties when they were ambushed by Hezbollah antitank squads.[38]

Israeli tanks entered the area southeast of Bint Jbeil and Maroun a-Ras on 19 July, and the first major ground battle raged at Maroun a-Ras through 24 July.[39] Hezbollah was able to properly read that Bint Jbeil was the ultimate target, and it reinforced the town with "dozens of skilled operatives as well as Special Force operatives in sabotage, anti-tank, and antiaircraft warfare," according to Israeli intelligence.[40] Beginning on

---

[35] Along some parts of the border, for instance, IDF forces mounted temporary ground incursions through 20 July, withdrawing to Israel by nightfall. On 19 July UNIFIL reported, "Two IDF ground incursions inside Lebanese territory were reported today. In the early morning, six tanks, one bulldozer, and two graders moved into the area south of the village of Alma Ash Shab, close to the Mediterranean coast, and withdrew to the Israeli side after a couple of hours." UNIFIL press release PR03, 19 July 2006.

[36] Josh Brannon and jpost.com staff, "Halutz slammed for promoting generals," *Jerusalem Post*, 30 October 2006, http://www.jpost.com/servlet/Satellite?cid=11618 11237367&pagename=JPost%2FJPArticle%2FShowFull.

[37] IDF, ITIC/CSS, Part Two, 91–92.

[38] Amos Harel and Gideon Alon, "Defense sources: Winograd war probe to last at least a year," *Haaretz*, 23 October 2006; and Brannon et al., "Halutz slammed for promoting generals."

[39] UNIFIL press release PR03, 19 July 2006; and UNIFIL press release PR04, 20 July 2006.

[40] IDF, ITIC/CSS, Part Two, 78. As many as 150 civilian-clothed Hezbollah fighters concentrated in Bint Jbeil for the 25-26 July battle, maintaining a low profile and blending in with the local population.

19 July, ground exchanges also took place along the coast and around Marwaheen, where IDF tanks and bulldozers moved into Lebanese territory (though they retreated back into Israel on 21 July).[41] On 24 July, the frustrating and deadly battle of Bint Jbeil began, and on 30 July, the battle of Aiyt a-Shab opened a central front. The ground war slowly and rather ineffectively took on its own momentum, not relevant to stemming the continuing rocket attacks on Israel, while also building up domestic expectations of eventual success.

Israel would mount three more offensives before the end: opening a fourth eastern axis at Kfar Kila on 30 July; undertaking an expansion of ground operations after a Cabinet directive on 1 August; and then mounting a final drive for the Litani River after yet another Cabinet directive on 9 August. Thousands of IDF reservists were eventually called up for operations in southern Lebanon. By 9 August, IDF forces had made their way to Debel in the central sector (4.5 km from the border) and near Qantara in the east (7 km from the border). In the last battle to take place as the IDF drove for the Litani before the cease-fire, ground forces made it 12 kilometers into Lebanon to Ghandouriyeh, a village astride the Wadi Saluki. When the cease-fire went into effect, the IDF occupied 16 pockets/sectors in southern Lebanon.[42]

The final Cabinet decision, nevertheless, came well after an internationally brokered cease-fire was already looming. The government of Lebanon pledged on 27 July that it would once again extend its authority over its territory in an effort to ensure that there would not be any weapons or military other than that of the Lebanese state. A seven-point Lebanese plan to expand UNIFIL and extend Lebanese army control into the south was introduced on 7 August. On 11 August, the UN Security Coun-

---

[41] UNIFIL press release PR04, 20 July 2006. UNIFIL had observed Hezbollah firing rockets from the vicinity of Marwaheen on 16–17 July. UNIFIL press release PR01, 17 July 2006.

[42] UN, Report of the Secretary-General. According to Israeli and UN records, this included Dhaira, Majdal Zoun, Marwaheen, Rajmin, Shama, Shiheen, and Tayr Harfa near the coast; Aiyt a-Shab, Bint Jbeil, Maroun a-Ras, Ramiya, and Yaroun in the central sector; Froun and Ghandouriyeh in the interior; and al-Adayseh, Blida, Deir Mimas, Houla, Kfar Kila, Mais al-Jabel, Markaba, Muhaybib, Rab al-Thalathine, Sarda, and Taybeh in the east.

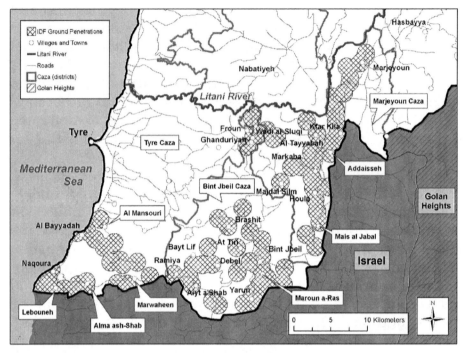

Figure 3.2: IDF ground positions as of the cease-fire

cil unanimously approved *UNSCR 1701* (2006), which additionally called for disarmament of Hezbollah. Lebanon, Hezbollah,
and Israel all accepted the terms, and the cease-fire was to take
effect at 8:00 a.m. local (0500 GMT) on 14 August.[43]

As the cease-fire loomed, both Israel and Hezbollah accelerated their strikes to cause maximum damage to the other. Hezbollah increased its rate of long-range rocket fire, culminating
with 220 rockets launched into Israel on 13 August, its second
highest daily total. Israel picked up the pace of its operations,
expanding air attacks and nearly tripling the number of troops
in southern Lebanon in the final few days of the conflict. Israel, by all evidence, also employed a significant numbers of
air- and ground-delivered cluster bombs in the last 72 hours
of the campaign, ostensibly to stem the rocket attacks and

---

[43] Lebanese army units began deploying to southern Lebanon on 17 August. The
blockade was lifted on 8 September. By 1 October, the IDF had withdrawn from
Lebanon.

cause havoc to movements should the cease-fire collapse, but also seemingly content to leave hundreds of thousands of unexploded bomblets to impede postwar civilian movements and recovery in the south—a reality that it should have anticipated given the record of US cluster bomb use and the IDF's selection of older weapons with higher dud rates.

From the beginning of the 2006 war, it is clear that the Israeli government was intent not to become embroiled in another ground occupation in southern Lebanon. Though there was hope on the part of many that a strong and extensive bombing campaign would eradicate Hezbollah's long-range threat to Israel, when Hezbollah showed itself to be more skilled and resilient than Israel anticipated, domestic pressures inside Israel mounted for an expansion of ground operations.

Some say that the ground forces themselves dawdled in anticipation that the 2006 war indeed could be won from the air, seeking to avoid the casualties that guerrilla operations and occupation would entail.[44] When ground forces were finally ordered into Lebanon on 19 July, there seemed to be great confusion with regard to missions and objectives; units were advanced and withdrawn, and even in the case of forces that went on the offensive, little momentum was maintained. The armor-heavy, road-bound conventional force proved unable to keep in contact with their Hezbollah opponents. Many observers claim that these missteps were due to political and high command indecision; that ground forces were "frozen in place," making them more vulnerable. But others point to a lack of preparedness and training, and a focus away from conventional combat (and the northern theater) by the IDF itself after the 2000 withdrawal.[45] The need for accountability themselves can be seen in their final deployments inside Lebanon. When the war was over, the IDF was deployed mainly in a series of hilltop locations, lacking control of surrounding territory and even lacking

---

[44] Abraham Rabinovich, "Retired Israeli generals vent," *Washington Times*, 27 September 2006, http://washingtontimes.com/world/20060926-105117-2517r.htm.

[45] As postwar reviews showed, Division 91 and Northern Command ground forces were not prepared on 12 July to lead any kind of instant ground retaliation or to assume responsibility for another protracted war and occupation.

control of the terrain between forward positions and the Israeli border.[46]

The conventional description of the 2006 Hezbollah war is that having an IAF officer in charge of the General Staff[47] and naïve reliance on airpower by an inexperienced government resulted in Israeli failure.[48] The IAF, the arm of the Israeli military that had once destroyed whole air forces in a few days, not only proved unable to stop Hezbollah rocket strikes but even to do enough damage to prevent Hezbollah's rapid recovery. The failure is not airpower's alone; Israeli intelligence and ground forces equally focused on stopping the rocket fire, but clearly Israel overestimated the purity of its intelligence and the efficacy of its strategy and technology and underestimated Hezbollah's skill and resilience.[49]

---

[46] As one observer says, "On the first day of the ceasefire [sic], it was possible to reach Bint Jbeil and Aitta Shaab [Aiyt a-Shab] in the western sector of the border district—which lay behind the IDF's frontline positions in Haddatha, Rashaf and Yatar —without even seeing a single IDF soldier." Blanford, "Hizbullah [sic] and the IDF."

[47] Halutz, a fighter pilot who shot down five Arab planes in the Yom Kippur War in 1973, was the first IAF officer ever appointed head of the IDF. He was selected by Prime Minister Ariel Sharon.

[48] See, for example, Shai Feldman, "The Hezbollah-Israel War: A Preliminary Assessment," Middle East Brief, Crown Center for Middle East Studies, Brandeis University, September 2006: "By the end of the first week of fighting, it had become clear that suppressing Hezbollah's attacks exclusively through the use of airpower would not be possible."

[49] The commander of the IDF army headquarters, Maj Gen Benjamin Gantz, said that, "Here we had an enemy armed with the latest weaponry and technology; learned our air operations and our methods of fighting; and mastered the principles of stealth. He burrowed down and concealed himself, and this was a tremendous advantage that we gradually learned to overcome in the course of fighting." *Defense News*, August 2006, 38.

Chapter 4

By the Numbers

From 12 July to 14 August, Hezbollah sustained a steady rate of rocket fire on Israeli territory, mounting as well a surprisingly effective and technologically sophisticated conventional defense of southern Lebanon. Through the creation of a highly dispersed infrastructure, decentralized command and control, and a solid reading of Israeli capabilities and tactics, Hezbollah was able to continue operations under intense fire, concentrating its small force on the necessary points to thwart Israeli land operations. Israel, for its part, conducted a day-and-night bombing campaign of unprecedented intensity and complexity. Israeli air, naval, and ground forces exacted a heavy toll on Hezbollah, destroying much of its fixed infrastructure; destroying military assets, particularly longer-range rockets; and killing a substantial number of Hezbollah fighters.

Through the end of July, Hezbollah rocket attacks averaged about 100 per day, fluctuating between a low of 34 on 20 July and a high of 169 on 26 July. Hezbollah continued to increase its daily rate of fire after 2 August despite Israeli attacks. In the first week of August, the daily average climbed to 200 rocket attacks, and Hezbollah fired 241 rockets on 3 August, its highest daily total. Thereafter, from 7 August through the cease-fire on the 13th, there was a decline to an average of about 150–60 rocket launches daily. But on 13 August, the final day of the conflict, Hezbollah fired 220 rockets, demonstrating its continued capability (see fig. 3.1).

Surprisingly—given Israeli records—the precise total number of Hezbollah rockets that actually reached Israel remains unclear. The Ministry of Foreign Affairs stated on 14 August that the number of rockets hitting Israel was 3,970.[1] Israeli

---

[1] Israeli MFA, "Hezbollah attacks northern Israel and Israel's response," http://www.mfa.gov.il/MFA/Terrorism+Obstacle+to+Peace/Terrorism+from+Lebanon+Hizbullah/Hizbullah+attack+in+northern+Israel+and+Israels+response+12-Jul-2006.htm (accessed 14 August 2006).

Police later reported that 4,228 rockets had impacted on Israel.[2] What is more, Israeli spokesmen and politicians regularly refer to 4,500 "rocket" attacks by Hezbollah. One explanation of the differences in these numbers may indeed be in identifying some of the objects impacting in Israel. It is known that Hezbollah also fired mortars and antitank missiles onto Israeli territory. The differences also exemplify a fundamental problem with making a full assessment of the 2006 war: There is little official public Israeli data, either on Hezbollah's actions overall or Israel's strikes, weapons expended, or targeting emphasis.

The vast majority of Hezbollah projectiles landing on Israel during the war were 122 mm Katyusha rockets. Explosive ordnance disposal experts of the Israeli Police identified 1,381 specific rockets and mortars of six different weapon types impacting in Israel, 85 percent of which were Katyushas:

- 1,200 122 mm Katyushas (859 high-explosive, fragmentation-warhead, short-range rockets; 228 expanded-range rockets; and 113 submunition-carrying rockets),
- 86 220 mm Syrian rockets,
- 30 302 mm Syrian rockets,
- six 240 mm Fajr-3 rockets,
- five 240 mm Falaq rockets,
- one 107 mm North Korean rocket,
- 33 unidentifiable rockets (observed by security forces but located in inaccessible places), and
- 20 81, 120, and 160 mm high-explosive mortar shells.[3]

Israeli officials say overall that of the 4,000 or so rockets that hit Israel, about 90 percent were 122 mm Katyushas.[4] Pre-

---

[2] Information provided by the Israeli government to the author. See also Uzi Rubin, "Hezbollah's Rocket Campaign against Northern Israel: A Preliminary Report," *Jerusalem Issue Brief* 6, no.10 (31 August 2006), Institute for Contemporary Affairs.

[3] IDF, ITIC/CSS, Part Three, 152.

[4] Information provided by Israeli intelligence sources. See also Wall et al., "Harsh Trajectories," 28; and UPI (Joshua Brilliant), "Analysis: Hezbollah's Recovery Timetable," 6 September 2006, http://www.upi.com/InternationalIntelligence/view.php?StoryID=20060906-045027-8532r.

war Israeli intelligence was fixated on the longer-range Iranian Fajr-3 and Fajr-5 rockets, which were believed to be installed at permanent launch sites; and on the even longer-range Zelzal rockets, believed to be in the Beirut area and the Bekaa Valley. The Fajr-3/5 missiles ended up being used "infrequently," according to Israeli intelligence; those that were employed were shot at Haifa and its outskirts.[5] Later in the conflict, mobile versions of the Fajr-3 that had evaded detection and destruction were subsequently fired from north of the Litani River, and very small numbers of Fajr-5 rockets were used to attack Afula (none of the longer-range, mobile Zelzal rockets were ever fired).[6] However, the preponderance of rockets employed other than the 122 mm Katyushas were not the feared Iranian rockets but Syrian-supplied 220 mm and 302 mm models. Syrian 220 mm rockets, many with ball-bearing warheads, proved to be the most deadly Hezbollah weapons; well over 200 were fired.[7] It is unclear whether Israeli intelligence failed to detect or properly assess the quantities of these rockets, or whether they indeed were transported into Lebanon during the fighting.

About 900 of the 4,000 Hezbollah rockets fired (some 25 percent) hit built-up areas in Israel, that is, populated villages, towns, and cities; while the remainder landed in "open areas," according to Israeli government sources.[8] The (estimated) distribution of 3,566 Hezbollah rocket impacts by Israeli area, according to IDF statistics, is

- Kiryat Shmona   876
- Ma'alot   810
- Nahariya   740
- Safed (Tzfat)   442

---

[5] IDF, ITIC/CSS, "Hezbollah as a strategic arm of Iran."

[6] IDF, ITIC/CSS, Part Two, 135.

[7] The 220 mm rockets were responsible for the 16 July deaths at the Haifa railroad yard and for civilian deaths in Tiberias.

[8] Reports on the number that landed in urban areas vary from 901 to 972. The differences could be attributed to counting mortars landing in the border areas (and around Kiryat Shmona) as rockets.

- Carmiel   277
- Haifa   206
- Tiberias   123
- Acre (Akko)   71
- Afula   21[9]

According to Israeli intelligence, 27 percent of Hezbollah rockets were fired at 1–10 km range, 47 percent at 10–20 km range, 15 percent at 20–30 km, and 11 percent at over 30 km.[10] The longest firing reportedly covered about 100 km (62 mi), originating from Lebanon's Bekaa Valley (See fig. 4.1).[11]

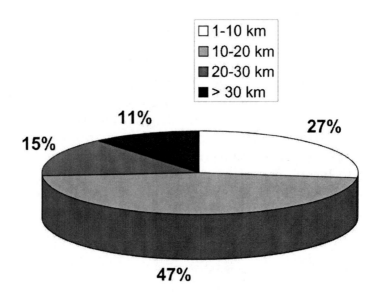

Figure 4.1: Distribution of Hezbollah rocket fire by range

[9] Kiryat Shmona and its surrounding communities were subject to 1,012 impacts of all types. Eli Ashkenazi et al., "The Day After/The War Numbers—4,000 Katyushas, 42 civilians killed," *Haaretz*, 15 August 2006; and "Preparing to rebuild the north," *YnetNews.com*, 14 August 2006.

[10] IDF, ITIC/CSS, Part Three, 140.

[11] Wall et al., "Harsh Trajectories," 28.

Even though the sources of rocket and mortar fire were spread out over some 180 separate firing areas (see fig. 4.2), there were several distinct concentrations of fire (according to Israeli radar tracking): the Bint Jbeil-Maroun a-Ras region (source of rocket and mortar fire), the Sidiqine-Zibqine-Qana region (including 220 mm Syrian rockets), the Srifa-Ghandouriyeh region, the Adayseh-Taybeh region, and the Hosh–Bazouriyeh region (including 220 mm Syrian rockets).[12] Rocket fire from the region north of the Litani River did not begin until well into the fighting, and its relative share was low (less than 20 percent of the total) but still far more significant than many in the international community believe. The largest concentration of rockets originating from north of the river was launched from the areas of Nabatiyeh, Aadshit, and al-Aaishiyeh.[13]

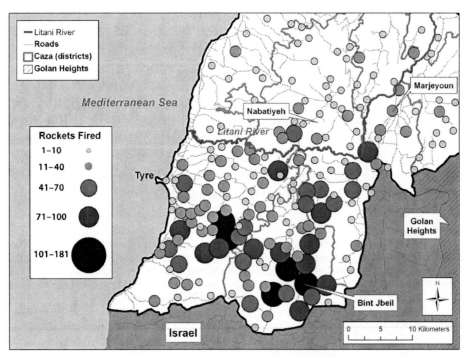

Figure 4.2: Distribution of Hezbollah rocket fire by origin in Lebanon

---

[12] IDF, ITIC/CSS, Part Two, 113.

[13] Ibid., 135.

Magen David Adom (MDA, Israeli "Red Cross") statistics indicate that 43 Israeli civilians were killed, including seven children, from Hezbollah rocket and mortar fire. One-third of those killed were Arab Israelis. Seventy-five civilians were seriously injured, 115 suffered moderate wounds, and 807 suffered light wounds.[14] The MDA reported that its personnel had been called to a total of 1,477 incidents where death or injury had occurred as a result of rocket and mortar fire in Israel.[15]

In Israel, Hezbollah rockets damaged or destroyed 6,000 homes, damaged hospitals and various businesses, and burned farmland and forests.[16] Overall, some 7,600 civilian damage claims were filed with Israeli authorities.[17] As many as 300,000 Israelis were displaced from the north as a result of the rocket fire, and many more were forced to live for some time in shelters during the fighting.[18]

Hezbollah claimed that it initially attempted to hit Israeli "military bases" but that it soon escalated because of Israeli attacks on Lebanese civilians.[19] Though there is no doubt that Hezbollah sought to intentionally attack civilian targets in Israel, rocket fire did exact some toll on the IDF. In a single attack with a 220 mm rocket (or a similar 302 mm rocket with ball bearings) on 6 August, an IDF reserve encampment near the border in northeastern Israel near the Kfar Giladi Kibbutz was hit, and 12 soldiers were killed. Rockets also reportedly caused damage at the IAF regional air operations center at Meron, 20 km inside Israel, and hit a nearby intelligence monitoring station,

---

[14] UN, "Mission to Lebanon," 5; and UN, "Report of the Commission of Inquiry," 26.

[15] MDA removed 134 bodies in Israel, including 42 civilians and 92 soldiers. Information provided by Israeli government sources. See also MDA, "MDA Daily Report—Emergency Urgency," http://www.ukmda.org; and International Committee of the Red Cross, "Lebanon/Israel—ICRC Bulletin No. 11/2006," 11 August 2006.

[16] A total of 6,178 acres of grazing land and 618 acres of forest was reported burned. See Embassy of Israel Backgrounder, "Israel's War with Hezbollah: Facts and Figures," 15 August 2006; and Israeli MFA, "Hezbollah attacks northern Israel."

[17] Embassy of Israel Backgrounder, "Israel's War with Hezbollah."

[18] UN, "Mission to Lebanon," 5; and UN, "Report of the Commission," 26.

[19] Hezbollah leader Nasrallah reportedly stated about the period of 12–14 July: "In the beginning, we started to act calmly, we focused on Israeli military bases and we didn't attack any settlement. . . . However, since the first day, the enemy attacked Lebanese towns and murdered civilians." See "Hezbollah leader promises enemy 'more surprises'," *Daily Star* (Lebanon), 17 July 2006, http://www.freerepublic.com/focus/f-news/1666790/posts.

code-named Apollo. Hezbollah rocket attacks also reportedly affected IAF AH-64 Apache and AH-1 Cobra attack helicopter operations due to their Israeli bases being within rocket range. The IAF reportedly moved its helicopter maintenance and logistics center from northern Israel to a base in the Negev.[20]

Though the Israeli-Hezbollah war of 2006 will always be known as the Katyusha war, a surprisingly large and diverse arsenal of Hezbollah antitank missiles proved as deadly and destructive, if not more so, particularly against the IDF. Because of their large warheads and stand-off ranges (as much as 5 km for the newest Kornet-Es), antitank missiles were effectively used against Israeli armored vehicles and against infantry units, particularly in destructive attacks on Lebanese civilian homes and structures being used by Israeli forces for billeting, cover, or refuge.[21] The newer antitank missile designs in Hezbollah possession were also easier to operate and, with optical tracking, allowed fighters to merely track the target rather than "steer," as they had to do with the older wire-guided missiles. As the combat waged in and around Bint Jbeil on 25–26 July, for instance, Hezbollah extensively employed antitank weapons of various kinds (including recoilless guns and the newer antitank rockets), and the use of these antitank weapons contributed greatly to the high number of IDF casualties.[22] At least 50 of the IDF's 118 fatalities were as a result of antitank missile fire; 30 tank crew members were killed by Hezbollah fire.[23]

Israeli intelligence estimates that Hezbollah fired more than 1,000 antitank missiles at Israeli tanks, vehicles, and soldiers.[24] The missiles struck 46 tanks and 14 other armored

---

[20] Clive Jones, "Israeli offensive may not meet long-term objectives," *Jane's Intelligence Review*, 9 September 2006; and Andrew Brookes, "Air War over Lebanon," International Institute for Strategic Studies, 8 August 2006.

[21] Greg Grant, "Hezbollah Missile Swarms," 8. An antitank missile was also responsible for an attack on an Israeli helicopter at the end of the war, though the helicopter was on ground when it was hit, having just disembarked 30 IDF soldiers minutes earlier. Blanford, "Hezbollah and the IDF."

[22] IDF, ITIC/CSS, Part Two, 79. Another report says that "thousands of antitank missiles" were used, but this does not seem accurate. Katz, "IDF report card."

[23] Ze'ev Schiff, "The War's Surprises," *Haaretz*, 19 August 2006. http://www.haaretz.com/hasen/pages/ShArt.jhtml?itemNo=751958; and Katz, "IDF Report Card."

[24] Information provided by Israeli intelligence sources. See also UPI (Joshua Brilliant), "Analysis."

vehicles, penetrating the armor of 20, thus causing damage to more than 10 percent of the 400 or so tanks that operated inside Lebanese territory by the end of the conflict.[25]

Israeli Strikes and Weapons

During the 34-day Operation Change of Direction, the IDF undertook two parallel efforts: an "air war" involving attacks on Hezbollah fixed and mobile targets (forces, rockets, and movements), Lebanese civil infrastructure, and to some degree, the Lebanese military; and a "ground war" involving special operations and a belated invasion into Lebanon. The air war was conducted day and night and involved preplanned and time-sensitive strikes on mobile and emerging targets. For the IAF, the 2006 war was the first sustained, around-the-clock air campaign; more than 50 percent of the missions were flown at night.[26] Because of the small distances involved and the Lebanese geography, these strikes were mounted not only by IAF F-15 and F-16 fighters, but also by attack helicopters, and were extensively supported by naval ship gunfire and long-range ground forces rocket fire.

Though the air and ground wars were two distinct efforts and the Israeli General Staff even retained control of targeting north of the Litani River, to properly tell the story of Israel attacks, it is necessary to treat the two efforts as one.[27] Aircraft and attack helicopters equally provided support to the counterbattery and tactical ground war effort, even against border targets. Army multiple launch rocket systems (MLRS) and artillery provided "bombing" support against fixed and mobile targets and nearly interchangeably against targets within range, particularly toward the end of the war.

---

[25] Katz, "IDF report card."

[26] Operation Grapes of Wrath (1996) lasted 17 days. Operation Accountability (1993) ended within a week. Both campaigns involved a high preponderance of daylight strikes. On night operations, see Wall et al., "Harsh Trajectories," 28.

[27] "A commander of an MLRS battery said it had fired many rockets against targets north of the Litani River and that those targets had been described as 'General Staff targets'." Nir Hasson and Meron Rappaport, "IDF admits targeting civilian areas in Lebanon with cluster bombs," *Haaretz*, 6 December 2006, http://www.haaretz.com/hasen/spages/789876.html.

The IDF states that fixed-wing aircraft and helicopters conducted 15,500 sorties over Lebanon, including:

- more than 10,000 "combat" missions,

- 2,000 helicopter "combat" missions,

- 1,000 helicopter search-and-rescue missions,

- 1,200 transport missions, and

- over 1,300 reconnaissance missions.

About 100 F-15I, F-16D, and F-16I aircraft[28] and some 48 AH-1 Cobra and AH-64 Apache helicopters[29] flew the 12,000 "combat" missions (an average of some 350 per day). The IDF also made extensive use of unmanned aerial vehicles for reconnaissance, and to a more limited extent, for attack. The Searcher 2 and Hermes 450 transmitted real-time targeting data to fighter cockpits as well as to AH-64 Apache attack helicopters.[30]

By the best estimate, aircraft conducted over 5,000 strike missions where ordnance was delivered—predominantly F-16 missions—with another 700 or so attack helicopter missions involving delivery of ordnance.[31] Naval ships added some 2,500 individual bombardment missions, and artillery and MLRS units fired another 140,000 indirect fire weapons.

---

[28] The IAF possesses some 25 F-15I *Ra'am* (Thunder) aircraft and around 20 F-16I Block 50 *Sufa* (Storm) fighters. As further F-16Is are only being delivered at a rate of two per month, the bulk of the IAF ground-attack effort into Lebanon was conducted by the fleet of 126 older multirole F-16Cs and Ds. Brookes, "Air War over Lebanon." At least one squadron of F-15Is was involved in bombing, and at least some large bunker-busting bombs were expended by the F-15s against underground targets.

[29] One report says that attack helicopters played a limited role apparently due to the potential threat of infrared antiaircraft capabilities. Blanford, "Deconstructing."

[30] The UAVs employed included the Searcher 2, Hermes 450, Heron 1/Eagle 1, "Harpy," and Skylark platforms. At least two of those platforms, the Heron and Harpy were employed for the first time or in experimental roles. On 31 July, according to one report, a Harpy fired a missile at a Hezbollah checkpoint and a truck suspected of supplying Syrian weapons. Brookes, "Air War over Lebanon." See "Israel praises UAV abilities," *Flight International,* 29 August 2006; David A. Fulghum and Robert Wall, "Lebanon Intermission; Israel starts examining the military's roles, missions and technology during lull in Lebanon fighting," *Aviation Week & Space Technology,* 21 August 2006, 32; and David A Fulghum, "Israel's military changes to fight after a nuclear attack," *Aerospace Daily & Defense Report,* 12 September 2006, 5.

[31] Brookes, "Air War over Lebanon."

A total of some 162,000 Israeli weapons are estimated to have been delivered and fired in the 34-day Lebanon war (or some 4,800 weapons per day).[32] The actual number of weapons expended has not been officially divulged by Israel, but a nominal accounting is as follows:

- Aircraft and attack helicopters are estimated to have delivered some 12,000 weapons, including laser-guided bombs (including the hard target BLU-109); JDAM (joint direct attack munitions) satellite-guided bombs; Israeli-made "Spice" electro-optically guided 1,000 and 2,000 lb munitions;[33] Israeli-made Delilah electro-optically guided air-to-surface standoff missiles;[34] CBU-58/71 cluster bombs; nonguided bombs; fighter- and helicopter-fired Hellfire missiles (AGM-114F/K); and possibly the US laser-guided GBU-28 earth-penetration weapon.[35]

- Israeli naval vessels conducted over 2,500 "bombardments" of targets, delivering some 10,000 weapons, primarily 76 mm artillery shells and possibly some Harpoon missiles.[36]

- Israeli ground forces delivered over 140,000 indirect fire weapons—predominantly 155 mm artillery and 227 mm multiple-launch rocket systems, but also other artillery rockets, projectiles, and mortars.[37] Well over 120,000

---

[32] The UNIFIL estimates that Israel dropped 5,000 "bombs" per day on the country or 170,000 weapons in all. According to assessments by the UN Mine Action Coordination Centre (UNMACC) in Lebanon, Israeli aerial and ground strikes during the first weeks of the war expended up to 3,000 bombs, rockets, and artillery rounds daily, with the number rising to 6,000 toward the end of the war. OCHA Situation Report No. 35, 31 August 2006, http://iys.cidi.org/humanitarian/hsr/ixl79.html.

[33] Wall et al., "Harsh Trajectories," 28.

[34] UPI (Tel Aviv), "Israel used Delilah missile in Lebanon," 21 November 2006, http://www.upi.com/SecurityTerrorism/view.php?StoryID=20061120-120755-2918r.

[35] After one of Hezbollah's heavily reinforced bunkers in south Beirut reportedly survived an attack, including a strike in which IAF F-16s dropped 23 tons of bombs on the target almost simultaneously, Israel reportedly took accelerated delivery of GBU-28 bunker-busting bombs ordered in 2005 under a $30 million deal to equip its F-15Is. Arie Egozi, "Israeli air power falls short," *Flight International*, 1 August 2006.

[36] The Israeli 76 mm automatic gun could fire both high-explosive ammunition and semiarmor-piercing extended-range ammunition up to 20 km.

[37] Barbara Opall-Rome, "IMI Shows Signs of Recovery; Israeli Firm Reshapes Portfolio to Heed Lebanon War Lessons," *Defense News*, 4 December 2006, says 200,000 indirect-fire weapons were expended by Israeli ground forces, but this estimate seems high.

artillery projectiles were fired[38] and some 20,000 short-range rockets were launched[39] including some 1,800 MLRS rockets.[40]

Photo by author

Artillery damage in Aiyt a-Shab village in the central border area was extensive. Israel fired some 120,000 artillery shells in the 34-day conflict. Much of the damage to civilian structures in the southern villages was as a result of this artillery fire.

---

[38] On Day 12 of the conflict (23 July), the IDF stated that it had expended "upwards" of 25,000 artillery shells (2,083 per day). On Day 15 (26 July), the IDF stated that it had expended "upwards" of 45,000 artillery shells (3,000 per day). A sustained average of 3,000 shells daily suggests 100,000 weapons expended (102,000 to be precise) assuming a steady rate from the beginning of the conflict. There was, however, a significant acceleration toward the end of the conflict and particularly in the last three or so days. Assuming an increase to 4,500 rounds in the final Israeli ground war push (8–11 August) and a doubling of the rate of fire to 6,000 rounds (11–14 August), the total number fired would be some 123,000 shells.

[39] "The IDF evidently fired well over 20,000 artillery rockets, targeting interchangeably with air strikes." Cordesman, "Preliminary 'Lessons'," 22.

[40] Tony Capaccio, Timothy R. Homan, and Jonathan Ferziger, "Israel, Hezbollah Assess Arsenal, Consider Lessons as War Halts," *Bloomberg News*, 16 August 2006, http://www.bloomberg.com/apps/news?pid=20601070&sid=aJZ6iLvFjso0&refer=home. Quoting his battalion commander, one IDF soldier said the IDF fired some 1,800 cluster rockets on Lebanon during the war and they contained over 1.2 million cluster bombs. Meron Rappaport, "When rockets and phosphorous cluster," *Haaretz*, 30 September 2006, http://www.haaretz.com/hasen/spages/761910.html; and Rappaport, "Israeli Defense Forces commander: We fired more than a million cluster bombs in Lebanon," *Haaretz*, 12 September 2006. One reputable source makes reference to "several thousand" MLRS rockets with cluster munitions being fired, "most during the last three days of the fighting." Alon Ben-David (Tel Aviv), "Israel probes use of cluster munitions in Lebanon," *Jane's Defence Weekly*, 6 December 2006. The Israeli Army possessed older, US-made MLRS rocket launchers as well as newer 12-tube "Destroyer" systems.

Israeli ground forces additionally fired hundreds of tank shells, antitank missiles, and other shoulder-fired weapons, mortars, and small arms. Figure 4.3 compares weapons expended by Israel in the 2006 war with those expended by the United States in Iraq. The comparison is imperfect at best because of enormous variations in the size of the US force compared to Israel, in the size and scope of the opposing force (Iraqi conventional armed forces versus Hezbollah), and in the evolution of precision which has increased the "efficiency" of attacks and thus reduced the number of weapons needed to destroy the same force or the same targets even in comparable cases. To create as comparable a picture as possible, weapons expended here include air- and sea-launched cruise missiles as well as air-delivered weapons for US campaigns but not attack helicopters, artillery, or MLRS, which were largely not employed for "strategic" or fixed target attack. In the case of Israel, naval artillery and Hellfire missiles delivered by attack helicopters are included, as well as MLRS missiles (but not short-range rockets). These weapons were all used interchangeably to attack fixed targets.

	Desert Storm (1991)	Iraqi Freedom (2003)	Change of Direction (2006)
Number of Days	43	22	34
Total "air" weapons expended	250,000	29,500	24,000
Weapons expended per day	5,800	1,340	705

Figure 4.3: Comparison of weapons expended by the United States and Israel in Iraq and Lebanon

Submunition-carrying "cluster bombs"—155 mm DPICM (dual-purpose improved conventional munitions) artillery, MLRS rockets, and air-delivered weapons—proved to be the most controversial weapons employed;[41] Israel is estimated to

---

[41] There have also been claims in both the news media and in international NGO literature to suggest that phosphorous was intentionally used in order to cause fires in southern Lebanon. Rappaport, "Israeli Defense Forces commander," said that phosphorous was "widely forbidden by international law." The IDF spokesman's office responded to *Haaretz* stating: "The convention on conventional weaponry does not declare a prohibition on [phosphorous], rather, on principles regulating the use of such weapons." The UN Commission of Inquiry also highlighted the use of certain "new weapons," which it defined as including depleted uranium and phosphorous, though it did not label either in violation of International Humanitarian Law. See UN, "Report of the Commission of Inquiry," 8.

have expended an estimated 2.7 million bomblets.[42] According to on-the-ground assessments and UN mapping of sites where unexploded submunitions were discovered, cluster bomb use was concentrated in two bands easily within range of both artillery and MLRS and largely away from the border area (where IDF ground forces were or could be anticipated to operate): from southeast of Rashidiyah on the coast (south of Tyre) to northeast of Tyre; and from southwest of Brashit and south of Tibnine extending northwards through Qabrikha into the Bekaa Valley to the west of Marjeyoun.[43] Figure 4.4 shows the general areas of Israeli submunition use (based upon the locations of postwar unexploded bomblets) superimposed on the major areas where Hezbollah rocket fire originated.

---

[42] The total number of bomblets can only be determined based on the types of weapons Israel expended. Some 1,800 227 mm US-model MLRS rockets were expended, all with submunitions. The number of air-delivered cluster bombs and submunition-carrying artillery projectiles employed is unknown. Further complicating the calculation, each rocket on the MLRS contains 644 bomblets. The CBU-58 air-delivered bomb dispenses 650 bomblets. The predominant 155 mm DPICM artillery projectile used by Israel carries 88 bomblets.

As of September 2006, when precise data was made available to the author, UN-MACC had evaluated 457 sites in Lebanon containing unexploded submunitions. Deminers on the ground were able to make a partial or full identification of the weapon types observed at 217 of the sites (some 50 percent): 133 sites contained M42 bomblets (associated with 155 mm artillery), 40 sites contained air-delivered bomblets, 22 contained M85 bomblets (newer self-destruct versions of the bomblet on MLRS), and 22 contained M77 bomblets (nonself-destruct versions of the bomblet on the MLRS). It is not unreasonable to estimate, based on this partial data, that 60 percent of the cluster bombs used overall were thus 155 mm artillery, 20 percent were MLRS rockets, and 20 percent were air-delivered. The calculation of 2.7 million is thus based upon 1,800 MRLS x 644 bomblets; 1,800 aerial bombs x 650 bomblets; and 5,400 155 mm DPICM x 88 bomblets.

UNMACC, on the other hand, reported as of 12 September the destruction of 4,626 bomblets on the ground, distributed as 57 percent MLRS, 40 percent artillery, and 3 percent air-delivered. The suggestion is a greater percentage of MLRS rockets used, but it could also suggest that the MLRS experienced a higher dud rate (with air-delivered cluster bombs having the lowest dud rate overall). Using these proportions (60 percent MLRS and bombs multiplied by 644–50 bomblets and 40 percent artillery multiplied by 88 bomblets), the number of submunitions would be higher than the 2.7 million expended overall. The total number expended obviously relates to the percentage of duds. Since most sources are using 1.2 million as the total number of submunitions expended, the difference in estimating the dud rate could be off by more than half.

[43] The only significant uses in the border zone were in the Yaroun area south of Bint Jbeil and opposite (west of) the Israeli town of Metula.

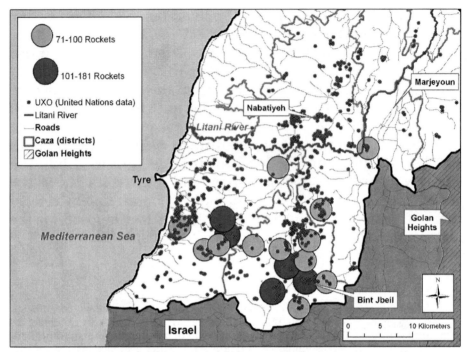

Figure 4.4: Submunition fire against Hezbollah targets (Unexploded ordnance (UXO) data from the United Nations and Hezbollah rocket-fire data from the IDF)

Not only were large numbers of submunitions found in and around Lebanese villages after the war,[44] provoking an outcry from the international human rights community, but UN de-miners and workers on the ground claim that the majority of Israeli submunitions expended—some say as much as 90 percent of the total—was fired by the IDF during the last 72 hours of the conflict.[45] Israel says that it used cluster bombs lawfully

---

[44] During parts of six days immediately following the cease-fire, Human Rights Watch (HRW) researchers documented approximately 50 Israeli cluster strikes, including strikes in about 30 towns and villages. Many strikes hit in the middle of and throughout these urban areas, indicating, HRW said, deliberate targeting of the areas. Large urban areas such as Tibnine and Nabatiyah were hit. The town of Yahmor was hit especially hard, as were Tibnine, Ain Ibel, Yaroun, Bint Jbeil, and Kfar Tibnit. See HRW, "Convention on Conventional Weapons (CCW): First Look at Israel's Use of Cluster Munitions in Lebanon in July–August 2006," briefing delivered by Steve Goose, director of Human Rights Watch Arms Division, at the 15th Meeting of the Group of Governmental Experts, Geneva, Switzerland, 30 August 2006.

[45] UN, "Report of the Commission of Inquiry," 59.

in antipersonnel missions, in area attack counterbattery fire, and in pursuit of mobile launchers and military-related traffic. The IDF Spokesman's Office says, "The use of cluster munitions against built-up areas was done only against military targets where rocket launches against Israel were identified and after taking steps to warn the civilian population."[46]

Photo courtesy of United Nations

An unexploded M42 Israeli artillery submunition stuck on a fence near Hineyeh, south of Tyre along the Lebanese coast. Israel is estimated to have fired over 5,000 "cluster-bomb"–carrying artillery projectiles, as well as MLRS rockets and air-delivered cluster bombs. After the cease-fire, the UN identified over 700 locations containing unexploded cluster-bomb submunitions and other UXOs.

The United Nations and others have speculated that the true explanation behind the use of such a large number of cluster bombs—with known "high" dud rates and the consequent virtual minefields created—was to cause long-term pain for Lebanon's civilian population, either through impeding their return

---

[46] Hasson and Rappaport, "IDF admits targeting civilian areas."

or disrupting cultivation and harvesting once they did return. "The use of cluster bombs suggests a degree of vindictiveness and an effort to punish the population as a whole, including those returning to town," the UN commission of inquiry concluded in November 2006.[47] The commission particularly questioned the concentration of cluster attacks north of the Litani River in the last 72 hours, remarking that since this was out of Katyusha range for targets in Israel but a rich agricultural area, Israel must have been intending to do civilian harm.[48] As figure 4.2 attests, the United Nations was wrong in its view as to where Hezbollah rocket fire originated from, and there is ample evidence that rocket fire from north of the river indeed was initiated even later in the conflict, perhaps, at least in the Israeli mind, justifying an increase in submunitions use. Nonetheless, this does not excuse the excesses associated with Israeli use of submunitions late in the war after the cease-fire was concluded, particularly by Israeli ground forces.

In fact, Israeli military figures have themselves questioned this practice with regard to artillery bombardment and cluster bomb use. Press reporting in Israel suggests indiscriminate artillery bombardment; "We fired like madmen," one artillery officer is quoted as saying.[49] Retired Maj Gen Yoram Yair, who investigated the performance of Division 91, said that Israel's firing of nearly 200,000 artillery shells during the war was "excessive and wasteful . . . and failed to supply meaningful results." Yair questioned the "tremendous damage to its reputation as a result of the large number of Lebanese civilians killed and wounded by the shelling."[50] Another observer said, "Certain Israeli actions were serious mistakes, including the massive use of inaccurate cluster bombs . . . that were largely

---

[47] UN, "Report of the Commission of Inquiry," 32.

[48] Ibid., 59, 75.

[49] Amnesty International reported that an IDF officer told them that his artillery unit was given target coordinates in early August commensurate with "flooding"—dense shelling—of a number of Lebanese villages. See Amnesty International, Israel/Lebanon, "Out of all proportion—civilians bear the brunt of the war," MDE 02/033/2006, 21 November 2006.

[50] Opall-Rome, "IMI Shows Signs of Recovery."

ineffective and counterproductive . . . in a war where public opinion counts as much as actual military maneuvers.[51]

Israeli Targeting

The IDF says that Israeli aircraft and helicopters attacked about 2,700 targets comprised of more than 7,000 individual aim points. Aircraft, naval gunfire, artillery, and MLRS attacked Hezbollah forces and targets located in more than 130 villages and geographic areas south and north of the Litani River and extensively attacked other targets in the Bekaa Valley, Beirut area, and even in northern Lebanon (see fig. 4.5). Air attacks were mounted against targets of all categories: airports, bridges, and roads; Hezbollah command, military forces, and infrastructure; fuel depots and gas stations; and communications and radar sites (see chap. 5). Naval strikes were mostly conducted against targets along the Lebanese coast and included rocket launch sites, launchers, weapons storage sites, roads, radar installations, fuel depots and gas stations, and other Hezbollah "infrastructure." The IDF says that ground forces carried out broad artillery attacks against rocket launching sites, against "squads of Hezbollah terrorists," and structures and "strongholds" along the border.

The 2,700 targets struck, according to various accounts and Israeli data, include:

- 300+ "headquarters" and other command buildings, predominantly in Beirut, but also in Sidon, Tyre, Baalbek, and other locales in the south;

- 1,800 associated "structures," predominantly in the southern villages;

- 70+ weapons storage sites;

- seven training camps, predominantly in the Bekaa Valley;

- 60–100 bunkers and tunnel openings, predominantly in the border area and in the rear areas in the eastern sector;

---

[51] Joshua L. Gleis, "A Disproportionate Response? The Case of Israel and Hezbollah," Jerusalem Center for Public Affairs, December 2006, http://www.jcpa.org/JCPA/Templates/ShowPage.asp?DBID=1&LNGID=1&TMID=111&FID=442&PID=0&IID=1456.

- 100+ rocket launchers;
- 100+ suspect vehicles "seen fleeing the sites of missile launches"; and
- 100+ bridges, overpasses, and roads.[52]

Israel estimates that of some 1,000–1,500 total Hezbollah launchers, it destroyed about 150 short-range and 150 medium- and long-range rocket launchers (fixed and truck-mounted) in 34 days.[53] It estimates that it destroyed more than 1,600 missiles in air attacks,[54] and that some 5,000 rockets remained after the war.[55]

Hezbollah rockets and structures associated with active fighter movements and weapons storage, servicing, and delivery remained the dominant target set throughout the conflict. There is, nonetheless, a conventional image of rocket fire that distorts an accurate picture both of the IDF targeting emphasis and its accomplishments.[56] In the news media, rockets were commonly described as being fired from large mobile launchers, generating a great deal of fire and smoke, or of having clear and identifiable electronic signatures making them (and the

---

[52] One account says 300 Hezbollah headquarters, bases, and rocket launchers; 1,800 Hezbollah associated "structures;" 270 Hezbollah associated vehicles; and 350 roads and bridges. Makovsky and White, "Lessons and Implications," 50. On Day 22, the IDF announced that the IAF had attacked more than 4,600 targets, including 260+ Hezbollah headquarters and other buildings, 60+ Hezbollah bunkers and tunnel openings, 90+ missile launchers and truck-mounted missile launchers, 100+ suspect vehicles seen fleeing the sites of missile launches, 70+ weapons storage sites, seven Hezbollah terror training camps, and 50+ bridges and access roads. Another report says 1,800 buildings used by Hezbollah, 309 rocket launchers, and 33 tunnels were destroyed by Israeli forces. AFP, "The heavy human and economic cost of Lebanon war," 14 August 2006.

[53] Information provided by Israeli government sources. See also Fulghum and Barrie, "The Iranian Connection," 20; and UPI (Brilliant), "Analysis."

[54] The IDF assessed that it destroyed some 1,600 Hezbollah missiles by 11 August. Cordesman, "Preliminary 'Lessons'," 4.

[55] Amir Oren, "IDF preparing for another conflict by next summer," *Haaretz*, 6 November 2006, http://www.haaretz.com/hasen/objects/pages/PrintArticleEn.jhtml?itemNo=784074.

[56] The conventional description did not just appear in the popular press. *Flight International*, for instance, talks of camouflaged Hezbollah rocket launchers and the use of special "carpets" that absorbed the sun's heat and radiated it at night to affect the efficiency of Israeli thermal sensors, suggesting that the challenge was technological. "Israel praises UAV abilities," *Flight International*, 29 August 2006.

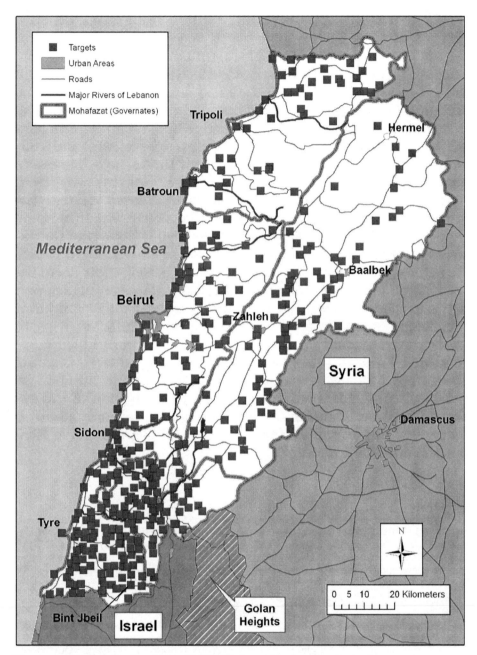

Figure 4.5: Israeli attacks on Hezbollah and Lebanese targets

rocketeers) vulnerable to counterbattery firing. This description might have been applicable to Second World War "Stalin organs" or conventional truck-mounted MLRS-type systems, but not to the preponderance of Hezbollah's assets. Hezbollah tended to fire its 122 mm Katyushas singly or in small salvos and used both improvised fixed installations and normal trucks to transport and fire them. It positioned single-barrel launchers at hide sites—including inside buildings, apartments, and individual homes—and then often operated the rockets by remote control, timers, or a delayed-action fuse.[57] In this way, even "successful" counterbattery fire merely achieved destruction of an already expended launcher—a launcher which in some cases was little more than a metal tube on a tripod—and the associated "structure." Such descriptions of conventional rocket launchers, moreover, not only make the Israeli effort seem incompetent, but also suggest that civilian damage in Lebanon was superfluous to Israel's authentic counterfire effort and that the civilian damage was thereby intentionally inflicted.

In air and ground operations, Israel says that it killed more than 650 (and as many as 750) Hezbollah fighters, tracking them meticulously by name, address, cell phone number, or radio call sign.[58] If true, this constitutes about half of the assessed "regular" fighting force in the south, but only about 5 percent of the overall 15,000-strong regular and reserve Hezbollah combatant force.

---

[57] Presentation of Israel before the UN Security Council's 5508th meeting, 8 August 2006 (S/PV.5508); Hannah Greenberg, "Most Long, Medium-Range Rockets Destroyed," *YnetNews.com*, 31 July 2006, http://www.ynetnews.com/articles/0,7340 ,L-3284302,00.html; and Yiftah Shapir, "Artillery Rockets: Should Means of Interception be Developed?" *Strategic Assessment* 9, no. 2 (August 2006), Jaffee Center for Strategic Studies.

[58] At one point, Israel even began dropping leaflets on Sidon and Tyre listing by name the Hezbollah combatants killed. In September, Halutz said that the IDF was aware of 650 Hezbollah fighters killed during the fighting. See Hanan Greenberg, "Halutz: I don't need a lawyer," *Ynetnews.com*, 20 September 2006, http://www.ynetnews.com/Ext/ Comp/ArticleLayout/CdaArticlePrintPreview/1,2506,L-3306396,00.html. One press report at the same time stated that Israel had the names of 532 Hezbollah fighters killed and estimates that perhaps 200 more were slain. Rabinovich, "Retired Israeli generals vent." This is the same information provided to the author in September 2006 by Israeli and US sources in Israel. Hezbollah has announced the death of 74 combatants. The Amal Shi'a movement has announced it lost 17 militants. The pro-Syrian PFLP-GC said two of its militants were killed.

Chapter 5

Civilian Damage in Lebanon

By the Lebanese government's accounting, Israeli attacks during the 34-day war resulted in $2 billion worth of damage to
airports, ports, utilities, TV stations, broadcasting antennas, gas
stations, bridges, roads, factories, homes, and villages. The government of Lebanon has stated, and the United Nations has accepted, that 32 "vital points" were destroyed, including water and
sewage treatment facilities and electric power plants.[1] In total,
Lebanon says, 15 electric power "plants," 331 water distribution
facilities (dams, reservoirs, pumping stations), and 159 sewage
and wastewater treatment facilities were damaged.[2] The government of Lebanon, as well as specialist international organizations,
states that 142 industrial enterprises suffered complete and/or
partial destruction, and that over 900 medium-sized enterprises
(including "factories" and "farms") and 2,800 small enterprises
suffered extensive damage. Of these, at least 31 major "factories"
in south Lebanon, the Bekaa Valley, and the Beirut suburbs are
reported as having been completely or partially destroyed.[3]

Throughout the 2006 war, the Lebanese news media reported,
and the international news media largely repeated, that Israel
was attacking hospitals, health care facilities, and ambulances;[4]

---

[1] UN, "Report of the Commission of Inquiry," 26.

[2] UN Development Programme (UNDP), "Lebanon: Rapid Environmental Assessment for
Greening, Recovery, Reconstruction and Reform 2006," March 2007.

[3] International Labor Organization (ILO), "An ILO Post Conflict Decent Work Programme
for Lebanon," Report of the September 2006 Multidisciplinary Mission to Lebanon, 8.

[4] On 25 July, for instance, media reports stated that the Lebanese Red Cross in Tyre said
that five of its volunteers and three patients were wounded when Israeli aircraft attacked
two ambulances on Sunday night, 23 July. The attack supposedly took place near Qana
when an ambulance from Tyre arrived to evacuate three patients from the border town of
Tibnine. See "Ambulances fired on by Israel, says Red Cross," *Sunday Morning Herald*, 25
July 2006, www.smh.com.au; Suzanne Goldenberg, "Red Cross ambulances destroyed in
Israeli air strike on rescue mission, *The Guardian* (UK), 25 July 2006. Lebanese NGO's later
said that "photos of this incident have largely circulated and showed that the attack can
be intentional and may qualify as a war crime"; and Nouveaux Droits de l'Homme (NDH,
New Human Rights, Lebanon) and l'Association Libanaise pour l'Education et la Formation
(ALEF, Lebanese Association for Education and Training), "International Humanitarian Law
violations in the July–August 2006 conflict opposing Hezbollah (Lebanon) to the State of
Israel," third report, 4 September 2006.

schools, mosques, and churches; village community centers (*husayniyas*); Lebanese government buildings; even "grain silos" and a "lighthouse" in Beirut. There has been discussion of grave environmental damage caused by attacks on factories and on the coastal fuel storage tanks at Jiyyeh.[5] The prominent international human rights organizations which investigated damage to the civilian infrastructure in Lebanon further reported that they found little or no evidence of previous Hezbollah presence where attacks took place, suggesting Israeli intent to destroy Lebanon's infrastructure and economy as well as gross neglect and lack of discrimination in attacks, even against legitimate targets.[6]

The problem with this dominant and conventional accounting of damage is that most of it is grossly exaggerated, misleading, or patently false. Based upon on-the-ground inspections, discussions with Israeli and Lebanese officials, imagery analysis, and a close reading of government and international organization materials, a good majority of the reports of damage in Lebanon are incorrect or downright fraudulent. There is no evidence that Israel intentionally attacked any proscribed medi-

---

[5] NDH and ALEF, "International Humanitarian Law violations" second report, 14 August 2006.

[6] Amnesty International reported: "In the overwhelming majority of destroyed or damaged buildings it examined, Amnesty International found no evidence to indicate that the buildings were being used by Hizbullah [*sic*] fighters as hide-outs or to store weapons. In most cases, the pattern of destruction suggested that the properties had been targeted to put them out of use rather than to kill individual fighters or destroy weapons stored there. The pattern of damage caused to buildings by this artillery barrage would not usually have impeded the retrieval by Hizbullah [*sic*] of weapons if they had been kept there. In the many buildings surveyed, Amnesty International delegates did not observe conflagrations that would have resulted if a munitions dump had been struck, even when fires had resulted from the use of incendiary projectiles or other factors." See Amnesty International, "Israel/Lebanon; Out of all proportion—civilians bear the brunt of the war," MDE 02/033/2006, 21 November 2006.

Human Rights Watch reported that there were "no cases in which Hezbollah deliberately used civilians as shields to protect them from retaliatory IDF attack. . . . In none of the cases of civilian deaths documented in this report is there evidence to suggest that Hezbollah forces or weapons were in or near the area that the IDF targeted during or just prior to the attack." See Human Rights Watch, "Fatal Strikes, Israel's Indiscriminate Attacks against Civilians in Lebanon," http://hrw.org/reports/2006/lebanon0806/lebanon0806web.pdf.

cal facilities,[7] no real proof that it "targeted" ambulances (and certainly not because they were ambulances engaged in protected activity), no evidence that it targeted mosques or other religious structures, and there were no intentional attacks on schools. The Qreitem "Old Lighthouse" in Beirut was attacked because it housed radar and observation posts used to target Israeli ships. Grain silos were hit incidental to attacking a naval base exclusively used by Hezbollah. Even in cases where Israel did attack or damage many objects, the Lebanese government, news media, and many nongovernmental organizations (NGO) consistently described things as having been "destroyed" when they were not destroyed or only peripherally damaged.[8]

Yet, in an environment where scores of high-rise buildings *were* indeed intentionally attacked in south Beirut and thousands of structures were attacked and damaged in over 100 villages and towns in southern Lebanon, it is hard not to see Israeli excess or to indeed conclude and interpret Israel's intention to punish Lebanon, to coerce the government of Lebanon, and to threaten the possibility of doing even more damage. Attacks on Beirut International Airport, on fuel storage at the airport, and at the Jiyyeh power plant are examples of punishing coercive attacks intended not only to pressure Beirut but also to signal what could happen. The accumulation of damage to the transportation infrastructure also signaled a surreptitious objective to impede Lebanon's recovery.

---

[7] Examination of photographs of damage to hospitals and health facilities in Bint Jbeil, Mais al-Jebel, and Marjeyoun, for instance, clearly indicates that the objects were the subject of collateral damage and that there was no intentional Israeli attacks on these or other prohibited fixed medical facilities.

[8] Of the 199 transformers that were reported damaged, the UN reported the damage to the transmission and distribution networks was "indirect" and involved only shrapnel damage to transformers. UNDP, "Lebanon: Rapid Environmental Assessment," 4–7, 8. This type of exaggerated reporting also occurred particularly in reports of attacks on thousands of industrial facilities and commercial enterprises (see below).

Figure 5.1 summarizes the best information regarding Lebanese civilian objects destroyed or damaged in the 2006 war, both intentionally and unintentionally.

Objects[9]	Targeted	Collateral Damage	Total Destroyed or Damaged
Residential Structures			
Beirut buildings	178	540	718
Homes and apartment units	~8,000	122,000	130,000
Transportation Infrastructure			
Airports	3	0	3
Ports	4	0	4
Bridges and overpasses	107	107	107
Roads (sections)	151	151	151
Public Infrastructure			
Electrical power	1	14	15
Water distribution	0	331	331
Sewage treatment	0	159	159
Government buildings[10]	0	66	66

---

[9] In each category, there are significant questions associated with definitions and numbers. The UN commission of inquiry, for example, cites 15,000 housing units (homes and apartments) destroyed and 55,000 damaged—a significant difference from the 130,000 units in the best estimate done by UN and local authorities on the ground. It cites 78 health care facilities (dispensaries and health centers) destroyed or damaged—20 more than the most comprehensive survey. UN, "Report of the Commission of Inquiry," 47–48.

On the other hand, the most comprehensive survey cites 22 gas stations destroyed or damaged, while the government of Lebanon says 25 gas stations (Government of Lebanon Fact Sheet, "Rebuilding Lebanon Together . . . 4 months after," 15 December 2006), and local authorities report more than double that number destroyed or damaged in the south alone. Though the Higher Relief Commission reported a total of 22 stations partially or completely damaged, local authorities in Bint Jbeil, Marjeyoun, and Tyre provided the UNDP with a list of 47 gas stations that sustained damage. UNDP, "Lebanon: Rapid Environmental Assessment," 4–9.

[10] Government buildings include structures belonging to the Ministries of Economy and Trade, Culture (Baalbek Museum), Justice, Labor, and Agriculture; structures of the National Social Security Fund; community development centers of the Ministry of Social Affairs; and building of Lebanese civil defense.

Objects	Targeted	Collateral Damage	Total Destroyed or Damaged
Schools	0	350	350
Commercial Enterprises			
Factories	~10	21	31
Medium-size enterprises (farms, stores)	~10	890	900
Small-size enterprises	0	2,800	2,800
Gas stations	22	0	22
Health Infrastructure			
Hospitals	0	3	3
Primary and secondary care facilities	0	50	50

Figure 5.1: Summary of claimed Lebanese civilian damage (Data from Lebanon Higher Relief Commission; Lebanon Council for Development and Reconstruction; UN Operational Satellite Applications Programme [UNOSAT]; Economic Research Center; and UN Development Programme [UNDP], "Lebanon: Rapid Environmental Assessment.")

The actual scale of damage in Lebanon though can clearly be seen in the state of civilian homes (apartments and individual homes), both in south Beirut and in southern Lebanon. The Lebanese government has variously stated that anywhere from 15,000–70,000 housing units were damaged or destroyed throughout Lebanon,[11] while the most comprehensive survey puts destruction and damage at 130,000 dwelling units.[12]

---

[11] The Lebanon Higher Relief Commission, as of 15 August 2006, cited 15,000 "private houses/apartments" destroyed (http://www.lebanonundersiege.gov.lb/english/F/Info/Page.asp?PageID=130). Later, a Lebanon Higher Relief Commission fact sheet cited 30,000 "homes" destroyed (http://www.lebanonundersiege.gov.lb/english/F/Main/index.asp?). A Government of Lebanon FAQ, Presidency of the Council of Ministers Communication Unit, n.d. (January 2007) cites 70,000 housing units "affected" (http://www.rebuildlebanon.gov.lb/english/f/Page.asp?PageID=46): "Early preliminary assessments undertaken by the government estimate that a total of more than 70,000 housing units have been affected. Severity factors range from totally destroyed (7,500+ units), to a similar number of partially destroyed units, severely damaged (15,000+ units) and partially damaged (38,000+ units)." The Lebanese Higher Relief Commission, 31 August 2006, stated that 15,500 "homes" had been destroyed (http://www.lebanonundersiege.gov.lb/english/F/Main/index.asp?).

[12] UNDP, "Lebanon: Rapid Environmental Assessment," 2-1.

The most visible and stark damage occurred in predominantly Shi'a south Beirut (*dahiye*), particularly the Haret Hreik municipality, an area made up of 6–10 story apartment buildings, where the ground floor levels generally house retail shops and other small-scale commercial enterprises such as automobile repair shops (see fig. 5.2). Some 150–200 buildings were directly attacked in Haret Hreik—UNOSAT counts 178 buildings in satellite imagery—with a total of some 718 buildings damaged overall. According to the best UN calculation, the damaged 200 by 240-meter area centered on Haret Hreik contained an estimated 5,000–6,000 housing units (30 dwelling units per building).[13] Overall in Beirut, most sources cite as many as 326 "residential buildings" damaged or destroyed, reporting that far more than half of these buildings were completely destroyed.[14]

The number of buildings estimated destroyed varies based on definitions—what is a building, what constitutes destruction, how much is from attacks on adjacent buildings, how much destruction is visible and when was it visible (given that buildings have been demolished over time). Still, a UN commission of inquiry formed by the Human Rights Council accurately described the devastation in their final report:

> The devastation in *Dahiyeh* [sic] was extensive. The area had been subjected to very heavy aerial bombardment from apparently precision-guided bombs. Whole buildings of 10 or more floors had completely collapsed. The bomb craters witnessed by the Commis-

---

[13] Defined as structures located within a 100-meter radius of the point of impact of "destroyed" buildings, based upon imagery analysis by UNOSAT. See UNDP, "Lebanon: Rapid Environmental Assessment," 2-3, 2-5.

[14] The most methodical early assessment found 326 residential buildings and 333 total buildings damaged, with 195 residential buildings and 201 total buildings destroyed, comprising 5,000 apartments. European Commission Joint Research Centre (JRC) and European Satellite Centre (EUSC), "Rapid preliminary damage assessment—Beirut and S Lebanon: Joint JRC and EUSC assessment of damage caused by the recent conflict in view of the Stockholm Donor conference (31st August) and reconstruction efforts," version 3, 30 August 2006.

Some 150 buildings were damaged and a similar number destroyed, according to UN General Assembly, Human Rights Council, "Mission to Lebanon and Israel (7–14 September 2006)," A/HRC/2/7, 2 October 2006, 11.

Amnesty International reported that some 250 multistory buildings containing some 4,000 apartments were damaged or destroyed in Beirut. Amnesty International, Israel/Lebanon, "Out of all proportion."

sion were enormous, indicating the use of very heavy ordnance. There were still unexploded bombs in some buildings. There was a pattern in the bombing and some buildings had been hit several times. Three hundred twenty-six residential buildings were either damaged or destroyed in the southern suburbs.[15]

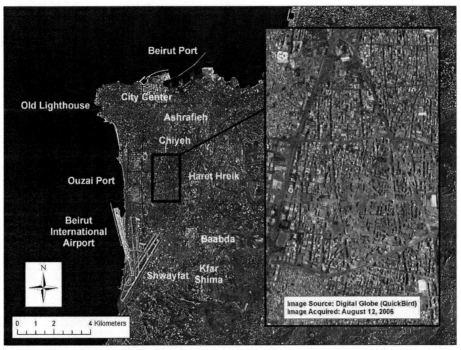

Figure 5.2: Beirut

The government of Lebanon says that some 7,500 housing units were destroyed, and another 20,000 were damaged in southern Lebanon.[16] The most authoritative assessment concludes 5,877 housing units destroyed and 5,500 damaged in the south, with a whopping total of 45,490 "impacted" buildings in southern Lebanon and the Bekaa Valley (see fig. 5.3).

---

[15] UN General Assembly, "Implementation of General Assembly Resolution 60/251 of 15 March 2006 Entitled 'Human Rights Council' "; and "Report of the Commission of Inquiry," 33–34.

[16] Information provided by the government of Lebanon and UN authorities. See also Government of Lebanon, "Damage to Infrastructure" (last updated on 15 August 2006). http://www.lebanonundersiege.gov.lb/english/F/Info/Page.asp?PageID=130. The most methodical assessment of areas of southern Lebanon, based on satellite photography, found 1,489 buildings, 535 road sections, and 545 cultivated fields destroyed or damaged. JRC and EUSC, "Rapid preliminary damage assessment."

District	Housing Units Destroyed	Housing Units Damaged	Total Buildings Impacted	% of Buildings in District[17]
South of Litani River				
Bint Jbeil	2,512	1,908	14,799	87.1
Marjeyoun	1,318	1,676	10,927	80.6
Tyre	1,601	1,322	15,472	46.6
Sub-total	**5,431**	**4,906**	**41,198**	**NA**
Bekaa	333	469	804	NA
Nabatiyeh	113	125	3,488	14.1
Total	**5,877**	**5,500**	**45,490**	

Figure 5.3: Damage to housing and structures in southern Lebanon and the Bekaa Valley (Data from UNDP, "Lebanon: Rapid Environmental Assessment 2-7.)

The damage in southern Lebanon, both inside villages where Israeli and Hezbollah ground forces fought, as well as outside of the areas where the IDF operated, is as stark as Beirut. According to one report by Amnesty International,

> In village after village the pattern was similar: the streets, especially main streets, were scarred with artillery craters along their length. . . . Houses were singled out for precision-guided missile attack and were destroyed, totally or partially. . . . Business premises such as supermarkets or food stores and auto service stations and petrol stations were targeted, often with precision-guided munitions and artillery that started fires and destroyed their contents.[18]

In some towns, particularly where IDF and Hezbollah fighters were engaged on the ground—Aitraroun, Aiyt a-Shab, Bint Jbeil, Khiyam—very heavy damage affected as much as 50 percent of all structures; in others, specific structures were destroyed while others were not, still connoting specific targeting of homes and structures (see fig. 5.4).[19]

---

[17] The total number of buildings by district is 16,988 in Bint Jbeil; 13,565 in Marjeyoun; 24,806 in Nabatiyeh; and 33,170 in Tyre.

[18] Amnesty International, "Israel/Lebanon: Deliberate destruction or 'collateral damage'? Israeli attacks on civilian infrastructure," MDE 18/007/2006, August 2006, 3.

[19] Save the Children, "Rapid Livelihoods Assessment in Southern Lebanon: Tyre Caza (South Lebanon) and Bint Jbeil Caza (Nabatiyeh)," Final Report Date: 29 August 2006.

	Housing Units Destroyed	Housing Units Damaged
Baalbek	250	400
Bint Jbeil district		
Ainata	100	50
Aitaroun	300	1,200
Aiyt a-Shab	450	100
Bayt Lif	90	30
Bint Jbeil	375	500
Bra'shit	172	170
Froun	80	90
Ghandouriyeh	82	35
Jmayjmeh	115	50
Kafra	40	35
Maroun a-Ras	23	30
Shaqra	125	25
Yater	180	150
Marjeyoun district		
Houla	35	0
Khiyam	580	708
Mais al-Jabal	39	60
Majdal Silm	145	140
Marjeyoun	30	100
Markaba	55	0
Qantara	25	100
Talouseh	15	10
al-Taybeh	136	100
Nabatiyeh district		
Aadshit	21	15
Jba'a	25	25
al-Qa'qa'iyah al-Jisr	20	15
Tyre district		
al-Abbasiyeh	100	35
Jabal al-Butm	75	100
Ma'aroub	150	50
Mansouri	100	50
Sidiqine	150	50
Srifa	250	100
Zibqine	150	50

Figure 5.4: Town and village damage in southern Lebanon (Data from UNDP, "Lebanon: Rapid Environmental Assessment"; JRC and EUSC, "Rapid preliminary damage assessment; UN, "Report of the Secretary-General on the implementation of resolution 1701"; UN, "Report of the Commission of Inquiry"; USAID Disaster Assistance daily situation reports; UNIFIL surveys; and UNICEF Situation Report—Lebanon, 30–31 August 2006; and OCHA, Situation Report —Lebanon response, No. 23, 15 August 2006.)

Destruction in one of the most heavily damaged villages, Aiyt a-Shab, is further discussed in the following sidebar.

Photos by author

Damage was extensive in the *dahiye* section of south Beirut, where 178 buildings were destroyed and 540 were damaged. Hezbollah had established its headquarters and military, political, and media centers in this area, taking control of entire neighborhoods and essentially restricting access.

* * *

The Battle of Aiyt a-Shab

Hezbollah's 12 July incursion and kidnapping originated in Aiyt a-Shab (pop. 5,000), a hilltop village within sight of the Israeli border. Once hostilities began, Israeli intelligence estimated that about 30 squads of no more than 200 fighters operated from the village. The presence included specialized antitank missile, RPG launcher, and reconnaissance units. According to a captured Hezbollah soldier, about 25 regular antitank specialists resided in the village; the remaining fighters were mobilized from Hezbollah's regular forces or special units.[20] Israeli intelligence also identified 10 Hezbollah "headquarters, bases and storehouses" in and around the village (see fig. 2.1).[21]

Targets in Aiyt a-Shab were hit almost daily with air raids or artillery attacks; mostly by air at first, soon thereafter by artillery, and then additionally by attack helicopters operating in support of Israeli ground forces. Starting in the afternoon of 14 July, the IDF began warning residents via loudspeaker to evacuate the town, precipitating a large-scale exodus according to UNIFIL observers. Two civilians were killed in the evacuation when a weapon hit their car, according to the AP.[22]

For the next 96 hours, access roads and targets on the outskirts of the village were attacked, as the IDF sought to degrade Hezbollah's capabilities and isolate the village from the outside world. There were some reports of Israeli probes on the ground around Aiyt a-Shab, but air and artillery strikes predominated through most of the month of July, as Lebanese humanitarian groups and the international community increasingly became agitated over residents—many old and infirm—who were isolated along the border with diminishing food and medicines. A second wave of civilians left Aiyt a-Shab and other border villages on 29 July.

On 31 July, IDF ground forces began their assault on the village, took up position in the area of the village, and, Hezbollah claimed through Al-Manar and Lebanese media, that it thwarted an IDF incursion. The IDF and Hezbollah exchanged heavy fire through the morning hours of 1 August.[23] On that day, an IDF officer and two enlisted men of Battalion 101 of the Paratrooper Brigade were killed and 25 were injured in the first major operation into the

---

[20] IDF, ITIC/CSS, Part Two, 85–86.

[21] Ibid., 76, 83, 90, 118.

[22] AP (Kathy Gannon, Tyre, Lebanon), "Lebanese complain Israelis using banned weapons," 25 July 2006, http://www.hamiltonspectator.com/NASApp/cs/ContentServer?pagename=hamilton/Layout/Article_Type1&c=Article&cid=1153779011113&call_pageid=1020420665036&col=111210166267.

[23] Israel MFA, Summary of IDF operations against Hezbollah in Lebanon, 2 August 2006, http://www.mfa.gov.il/MFA/Terrorism+Obstacle+to+Peace/Terrorism+from+Lebanon+Hezbollah/Summary+of+IDF+operations+against+Hezbollah+in+Lebanon+2-Aug-2006.htm.

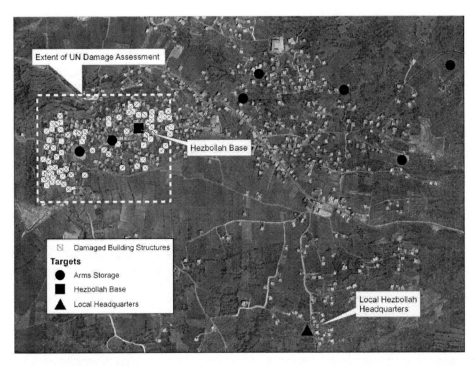

Extent of UN Damage Assessment

Hezbollah Base

Damaged Building Structures

Targets

● Arms Storage

■ Hezbollah Base

▲ Local Headquarters

Local Hezbollah
Headquarters

Damage in Aiyt a-Shab

town, almost all killed by intense Hezbollah antitank rocket fire carried out in the narrow roads and alleyways of the village. The IDF said it killed more than 15 Hezbollah fighters; village targets were intensely attacked by supporting Apache attack helicopters and 155 mm artillery.[24] On 2 August, the IDF announced that its forces were operating in the village, destroying "terror infrastructure" before moving on to the next village, Debel to the north.[25] UNIFIL reported heavy ground fighting, and Hezbollah claimed "house-to-house" fighting in Aiyt a-Shab.[26]

On 4 August, the Lebanese news media reported 10 civilians killed in Aiyt a-Shab after a residential home was attacked. "Corpses remained under the rubble for a while," the government of Lebanon later said.[27] On 5 August, an IDF reservist from Brigade 2 was killed and 21 soldiers were injured when another antitank missile hit a civilian building they were using in the village.[28]

Fighting continued in and around the village through the end of the war (the IDF claimed another 25 Hezbollah deaths through the cease-fire). On 13 August, four IDF soldiers were killed and 14 were injured when yet another antitank missile hit a reserve infantry unit on Abu Tawil hill, just north of the main village.[29] As the cease-fire loomed, the IDF announced that Israeli forces uncovered a Hezbollah bunker containing weaponry and communications, a ready-to-launch "Fagot" antitank missile, and an eight-barrel emplaced Katyusha launcher in Aiyt a-Shab.[30] IDF engineering and demolitions units destroyed some 20 structures in the village that had been used to hide weapons.[31]

---

[24] IDF War Log, "August 1st 2006;" and Yaakov Katz, "3 soldiers killed in Hezbollah ambush; 5 brigades battle village by village in S. Lebanon," *Jerusalem Post*, 2 August 2006, http://info.jpost.com/C002/Supplements/CasualtiesOfWar/2006_08_02.html.

[25] Israeli MFA, "Summary of IDF operations against Hezbollah in Lebanon," 2 August 2006, http://www.mfa.gov.il/MFA/Terrorism+Obstacle+to+Peace/Terrorism+from+Lebanon+Hezbollah/Summary+of+IDF+operations+against+Hezbollah+in+Lebanon+2-Aug-2006.htm; and Yaakov Katz, "IDF soldier killed in battle with Hezbollah in Aita a-Sha'ab [Aiyt a-Shab]," *Jerusalem Post*, 2 August 2006, http://info.jpost.com/C002/Supplements/CasualtiesOfWar/2006_08_03.html.

[26] AFP (Tyre), "Battles rage in Lebanon," 1 August 2006; and AP (Bourj Al-Mulouk, Lebanon), "Heavy fighting rages inside Lebanese border; 35 Israeli killed or wounded," 1 August 2006.

[27] "List of collective massacres perpetrated by Israeli Army in its attack against Lebanon in summer 2006," contained in Annex VI, *Report of the Commission of Inquiry on Lebanon pursuant to Human Rights Council Resolution S-2/1*, Advanced Unedited Version, 10 November 2006.

[28] IDF War Log, "August 5th 2006"; and Yaakov Katz, "Two reserve soldiers were killed," *Jerusalem Post*, 5 August 2006, http://info.jpost.com/C002/Supplements/CasualtiesOfWar/2006_08_06.upd.html.

[29] IDF War Log, "August 13th 2006."

[30] Israeli MFA, "Summary of IDF operations against Hezbollah in Lebanon," 13 August 2006, http://www.mfa.gov.il/MFA/Terrorism+Obstacle+to+Peace/Terrorism+from+Lebanon+Hezbollah/Summary+of+IDF+operations+against+Hezbollah+in+Lebanon+13-Aug-2006.htm.

[31] IDF War Log, "August 13th 2006."

After the war, the UN found 450 houses and structures destroyed in Aiyt a-Shab and another 100 houses and structures damaged.[32] Only Al-Khiyam in the eastern zone along the border received a greater amount of destruction. The IDF says that between 41–70 rockets were fired from Aiyt a-Shab and its surrounding. Overall, the IDF lost seven soldiers in Aiyt a-Shab battles, and suffered 60 injuries, battling Hezbollah on the ground. It claimed to have killed 40 Hezbollah fighters. When the author visited the village a month after the cease-fire, Hezbollah flags flew from the majority of village homes, even destroyed and damaged homes, which were omnipresent. The damage was indeed stark, but life was returning to normal, with clean-up and reconstruction already underway. Twelve civilians were killed in the crossfire.

* * *

Overall, some 400 houses were destroyed, 850 partially damaged, and 4,100 damaged in the Bekaa Valley region (including Baalbek)—the vast majority in and around Baalbek and the villages of Brital, Mashgara, and Nabbi Sheet.[33] An additional smaller number of houses were destroyed and damaged in the north.[34]

As to medical facilities, Lebanon reports three hospitals—Bint Jbeil, Marjeyoun, and Nabatiyeh—and 78 health care facilities (dispensaries and health centers) destroyed or damaged.[35] The most comprehensive survey cites 50 health care facilities destroyed or damaged (not including the three hospitals).[36] The damage in this sector, in many cases, was not as great as reported. The fine print of the UN commission of inquiry report, for instance, describes only one of three hospitals sustaining severe damage. A World Health Organization (WHO) health fa-

---

[32] UNDP, "Lebanon: Rapid Environmental Assessment"; JRC and EUSC, "Rapid preliminary damage assessment; USAID Disaster Assistance daily situation reports; UNIFIL surveys; UNICEF Situation Report—Lebanon, 30–31 August 2006; OCHA, Situation Report—Lebanon response, No. 23, 15 August 2006.

[33] Information provided by the government of Lebanon and UN authorities. See also Government of Lebanon, Damage to Infrastructure.

[34] Ibid.

[35] Ministry of Health and WHO, Lebanon crisis: Service Availability Assessment, 29 August 2006.

[36] UNDP, "Lebanon: Rapid Environmental Assessment."

cility assessment showed 50 percent of the primary health care facilities in Bint Jbeil and 30 percent in Marjeyoun "completely destroyed," while secondary health facilities received far less damage.[37]

In the case of the 900 commercial-sector enterprises (factories, markets, etc.) that Lebanon reported as destroyed, most were very small enterprises and some were individual stores or farms.[38] The 2,800 "small-size enterprises" reported as destroyed or damaged were almost all individual stores or businesses, many damaged because of their locations on the ground floors of south Beirut buildings.

In addition to these various enterprises that sustained damage, the Lebanese Ministry of Industry compiled a list of 127 major "factories" that suffered damaged. Even of the 127 listed, 63 are various minor enterprises located in the bombed neighborhoods of south Beirut; 30 are located in southern Lebanon. Of the 30 in the south, only five have more than 20 employees, according to the Ministry's data.[39]

The Lebanese government and the International Labor Organization (ILO) describe 31 major "factories" in Lebanon as

---

[37] In the case of health care, for example, the UN commission of inquiry said that "An assessment by the WHO and the Lebanese Ministry of Public Health on the damage inflicted on primary health care centres and hospitals shows that 50 percent of outpatient facilities were either completely destroyed or severely damaged, while one of the region's three hospitals sustained severe damage." UN, "Implementation of General Assembly Resolution 60/251"; and UN, "Report of the Commission of Inquiry," 42. See also page 26.

Health centers were indeed damaged as part of the general fighting, but the WHO reported separately that 33 percent of primary health care centers in southern Tyre were damaged, while in Marjeyoun and Bint Jbeil districts, the damage was 22 percent. "Secondary health care facilities were in a better position than the Primary Health Centres (PHC)." See WHO and Government of Lebanon Ministry of Public Health, Lebanon Crisis Service Availability Assessment, 29 August 2006, 32.

[38] Government of Lebanon, Damage to Infrastructure; and UN, "Report of the Commission of Inquiry," 26.

[39] Ministry of Industry, Report of Damaged Factories, n.d. (2007); and UN, "Report of the Commission of Inquiry." 38.

Photos courtesy of Government of Lebanon

Damage to rural roads in the Bekaa Valley illustrates not only how far ranging Israeli attacks were in attempting to cut off transportation routes to stem rocket firings and resupply, but also how difficult it is to shut down road traffic. There is no evidence that the attack itself was directed at a Hezbollah rocket launcher. More likely, the "access" road was attacked to limit the movement of Hezbollah rocketeers in the area as part of the counterbattery effort.

having been damaged or destroyed.[40] The most comprehensive UN survey found that of the 31 reported as completely or partially destroyed, after physical inspection, many were dismissed as having sustained little or no damage. Nine sites were considered significantly damaged. They include:

- Al Arz textile factory, Manara, Bekaa Valley,

- Ghabris detergent factory, Burj Chamali outside Tyre, Tyre district,

- Saffieddine Plasti-med (a.k.a. Sada al-Din plastics factory), Burj Chamali,

- Lamartine food industry, Taanayel, Bekaa Valley,

- the Maliban Sal glass works, the second largest glassworks in the Middle East, in Taanayel, in the Bekaa Valley;

- the Liban Lait dairy production plant, Lebanon's largest, near Baalbek, Bekaa Valley,

- Transmed SAL food and paper goods storage warehouse, Shwayfat, southeast of Beirut International Airport,

- Fine tissue factory/paper mill, Kfar Jarrah, east of Sidon, and

- Lebanese company for Catron Mince and Industry, Shwayfat.[41]

---

[40] The ILO, for instance, reported 142 industrial enterprises suffering complete and/or partial damage and over 900 medium-sized enterprises (including factories, markets, and farms) and 2,800 small enterprises having suffered extensive damage. It described 31 "factories" in South Lebanon, the Bekaa Valley, and Beirut as having been completely or partially destroyed. See ILO, "An ILO Post Conflict Decent Work Programme for Lebanon," Report of the September 2006 Multidisciplinary Mission to Lebanon, 8.

The Lebanese government states that 31 factories were destroyed; other reports say that 23 "large" factories were attacked. Government of Lebanon, "Setting the stage for long term reconstruction: The national early recovery process," Stockholm Conference for Lebanon's Early Recovery, 31 August 2006.

[41] UNDP, "Lebanon: Rapid Environmental Assessment," 5-1.

Photo courtesy of United Nations

The fine tissue factory/paper mill in Kfar Jarrah, east of Sidon was among Israeli targets considered "severely damaged." The factory was a total loss, according to UN surveyors, though Israel's objective in the attack is unknown. Was Hezbollah using the site to launch rockets, was the factory part of Hezbollah's financial network, or did it end up being attacked as part of a "signaling" effort to the Lebanese government?

Interestingly, three factories prominently mentioned in press reports and in Lebanese government materials were not considered of high enough priority or of sufficient damage to be included in the UN's final list of destroyed industrial facilities.[42]

In other words, though Lebanon says that 900 commercial-sector enterprises were deliberately attacked, very few if any "factories" were actually attacked because they were factories. In the few cases where factories were actually attacked, Israel

---

[42] These include the Dalal Steel Industries factory (prefabricated house manufacture) in Taanayel; the Tabara pharmaceutical factory in Shwayfat, south of Beirut; and the Snow lumber mill in Shwayfat.

indeed seems able to justify the targeting because the facilities were actively being used for the storage or hiding of military goods or forces.[43] There is also the possibility of "crony" targeting against Hezbollah or related facilities. A number of financial institutions were explicitly attacked because they were owned by Hezbollah individuals or connected to that organization.[44]

As for attacks on Lebanese "ports," Israel did attack four port facilities—two in Beirut, in Tripoli, and "Jamil Gemayel"—as well as numerous radars along the coast, particularly after the 14 July attack on the Israeli naval vessel *Hanit*.[45] In the attacks on one of the ports, at Ouzai near the Beirut International Airport, Israel has specifically identified the Hezbollah navy unit being housed there.[46] Damage to the area, nonetheless, was reported as, and was indeed, extensive.[47]

---

[43] Information provided to the author, September 2006. Attacks on factories, such as they were conducted, probably cannot be seen as classic military industry attacks but more similar to "crony" targeting conducted by NATO in the 1999 Kosovo war. Though some commentators have stated that it is not proven that these factories had "been diverted from their civilian use," thus making them legitimate military objectives—See NDH and ALEF, "International Humanitarian Law violations," second report, 14 August 2006—each individual factory probably requires an analysis in terms of military necessity.

[44] IDF, ITIC/CSS, "The IDF-Hezbollah confrontation (Updated on the morning of Thursday, July 20)," 20 July 2006.

[45] The IDF concluded that Hezbollah had received targeting data from a Lebanese naval radar in Beirut for the 14 July attack. Arie Egozi, "Israeli air power falls short." The other radars either were or could have been passing additional targeting information to Hezbollah.

[46] According to the IDF, "the organization has a naval unit deployed along the shoreline, notably in the Shi'ite district of Ouzai, which is integrated into the organization's defensive and offensive plans." See IDF, ITIC/CSS, Part Two, 64.

[47] An IAF attack on 4 August, according to Amnesty International, "destroyed" the Ouzai port in Beirut:

> Fishermen told Amnesty International that between 300 and 400 boats, each worth between US$5,000 and US$50,000, were badly damaged or destroyed in repeated air raids. The fishermen's Co-op offices, the cafe, the steel repair garage, carpentry workshop, net repair workshop and market—as well as a three-storey [sic] Lebanese army building—were also all destroyed. Jamal 'Allama, Head of the Co-op, said that Hezbollah combatants could not have been using the port given the sensitive and well-monitored location—just metres from the perimeter fence of Beirut's international airport and with an army checkpoint to pass through to enter the port.

> Amnesty International, Israel/Lebanon, "Out of all proportion."

Similarly, although Lebanon's list of "vital" installations de-stroyed includes water and sewage treatment facilities and electric power plants, Israel did not "target" any of these types of installations. One of the reasons for the confusion about at-tacks on electric power is that early press reports stated outright that electric power installations were attacked.[48] The *Jerusalem Post*, moreover, quoted a high-ranking IDF officer threatening that Israel would destroy Lebanese power plants if Hezbollah fired long-range rockets and missiles at strategic installations in northern Israel.[49] And even after the war, dispassionate ob-servers still referred to electricity plants as destroyed or badly damaged.[50] The UN commission of inquiry formed by the Hu-man Rights Council also stated in their final report that Israel had destroyed "water and sewage treatment plants [and] electri-cal facilities,"[51] as if these attacks were intentional or targeted.

Israel did attack two fuel storage tanks at the Jiyyeh electric power plant, 30 km south of Beirut.[52] Though Israel never pro-vided a suitable military explanation for its attack, the govern-ment of Lebanon reported after the war that electric power gen-eration had indeed never been bombed, enumerating the $114 million worth of damage to the electricity sector as including mostly damage to fuel storage at the Jiyyeh power plant south of Beirut; the rest of the damage was incidental damage to over-head transmission lines, distribution networks, transformers, and equipment.[53] In this case, it appears that Israel chose to

---

[48] An electric power station was reported attacked in Wadi Jilo east of Tyre on the first night, for instance. Bahrain News Agency (Al-Arabiya TV, Dubai, in Arabic), "Two civilians killed in South Lebanon," 12 July 2006, 1351 GMT.

[49] "IAF continues attack on Lebanon," *Jerusalem Post*, 17 July 2006.

[50] See Gregory Katz, "Bint Jbeil bears the scars of weeks of fighting with Israeli forces, but many regard Hezbollah's charge to battle as a point of pride; A war-torn Lebanese city in ruin," *Houston Chronicle*, 23 September 2006, http://www.chron.com/disp/story.mpl/headline/world/4209972.html.

[51] UN, "Report of the Commission of Inquiry," 26.

[52] UNDP, "Lebanon: Rapid Environmental Assessment," 4-1.

[53] The Government of Lebanon, "Setting the stage." Information provided to the au-thor by Electricite du Liban (EDL) further substantiates that Israel did not attack any electric power generators or substations.

Israel attacked fuel storage tanks at the Jiyyeh electric power plant on the coast south of Beirut on 13 and 15 July, creating a significant oil slick in the Mediterranean Sea. The Israeli Cabinet decided not to attack Lebanon's national electric power grid, as it had done in 1996, but the attack on the Jiyyeh plant's fuel not only signaled the possibility of such an attack but also caused sufficient disruption of electricity production that rolling black-outs were instituted in the Beirut area, and power was essentially disrupted in south Lebanon.

Photo by author

The evening attack on a six-story apartment building on Al Assad Street in the "Chiyeh" section of Beirut on 7 August resulted in the death of as many as 40 civilians, according to local documentation. It was the first time that the district of Beirut had been attacked. Many of those killed were internally displaced persons who had fled from southern Lebanon and from the _dahiye_ Hezbollah area, who considered Chiyeh to be a safe area.

do just enough damage to punish Lebanon and threaten more to come while sparing long-term damage to the power plant itself.

As for attacks on water and sewage facilities, there was damage to water storage tanks and towers in various villages in southern Lebanon—some by direct tank fire—and damage to water pumping facilities.[54] But there is no evidence that Israel indeed mounted any methodical effort to "target" Lebanon's water or sewage. (Attacks on transportation will be discussed more extensively in chap. 6).

---

[54] UN, "Report of the Commission of Inquiry," 37.

97

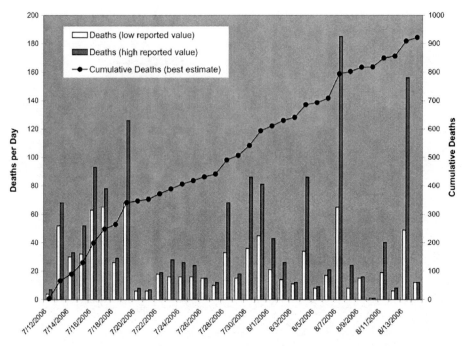

Figure 5.5: Distribution of Lebanese "civilian" deaths, by day

And what about the human cost? From the very beginning of the 2006 war, Israel was condemned for its attacks on Lebanese civilians, for its "indiscriminate" bombing, and for its "disproportionate" response to Hezbollah attacks. The government of Lebanon says that some 1,190 civilians were killed and some 4,000–4,400 were injured,[55] though it remains unclear how many of those killed were Hezbollah fighters.[56] Figure 5.5 portrays the

---

[55] UNICEF, Lebanese Situation Report for 1–8 September 2006; and UN, "Mission to Lebanon and Israel," 4, says that 1,191 civilians were killed and 4,405 injured. Government of Lebanon Fact Sheet, "Rebuilding Lebanon Together," says that 1,200 "martyrs" were killed and 4,400 were injured, including 15 percent disabled. The Lebanese Higher Relief Commission stated that 1,187 civilians had died and 4,092 were injured. Lebanese Higher Relief Commission, 31 August 2006, http://www.lebanonundersiege .gov.lb/english/F/Main/index.asp? The Lebanese government told the US Embassy in Beirut that 1,198 civilians had died and 4,399 were injured. Katz, "Bint Jbeil bears the scars."

[56] UN, "Mission to Lebanon and Israel," 11.

best overall estimate, based upon a database of 352 incidents involving reported civilian deaths, of the low and high estimates of actual deaths and the distribution of deaths by day during the conflict.

The conventional narrative is that 30 percent of those killed were children under the age of 12.[57] On the surface, this seems significant, yet the number pretty much matches the percent of children in the Lebanese population at large.[58]

Overall, one cannot help but conclude that the number of civilian casualties, given the level of damage in Beirut and southern villages, is relatively low. More than 950,000 Lebanese fled their homes as a result of the war, a number that is on the one hand significant but on the other partially explains how so much damage could occur with so few casualties.[59] Because of Israeli warnings (and because of Hezbollah organization and preparation), even attacks or urban Beirut took place mostly against unoccupied multistory buildings. Israeli bombing destroyed almost 200 apartment buildings and damaged hundreds of others. But the buildings, which normally house between 30,000 and 60,000 persons, had been almost entirely evacuated before they were struck, limiting the loss of life.[60] Even according to the UN commission of inquiry, a hypercritical panel:

> The total figures of those killed or injured were . . . comparatively low in relation to the utter destruction of the area, because after the second day of the conflict a large portion of the population had vacated the area. The total of those killed [in Beirut] is estimated at around 110 with another 300 people injured.[61]

---

[57] UNICEF, Lebanese Situation Report for 1-8 September 2006; UN, "Mission to Lebanon and Israel," 5; and UN, "Report of the Commission of Inquiry," 4.

[58] CIA, *World Factbook 2007*, "Lebanon" entry (Age Structure), https://www.cia.gov/cia/publications/factbook/geos/le.html#People.

[59] "According to official government figures, 974,184 persons were displaced by the conflict, an estimated 128,760 of whom were accommodated in schools and other public buildings. An estimated 220,000 fled to the Syrian Arab Republic and other countries while the rest remained in Lebanon. A total of 128,760 IDPs were accommodated in schools or with families or friends and 200,000 remain displaced because Israeli military operations damaged or destroyed their homes." See UN, "Mission to Lebanon and Israel," 15.

[60] UN, "Mission to Lebanon and Israel," 11.

[61] UN, "Report of the Commission of Inquiry," 34. By the author's preliminary calculations, some 79 Lebanese "civilians" died in all of Beirut.

Finally, there is the universal view that all of the civilian damage (and casualties) in Lebanon is Israel's direct responsibility even though there is abundant evidence that Hezbollah was responsible for a significant amount. Hezbollah used Lebanese civil society as a "shield" against attack and was condemned for its "war crimes" in doing so.[62] As figs. 5.6 and 5.7 attest, Israel has also substantiated significant Hezbollah rocket fire from Lebanese civilian areas. UNIFIL reported regular Hezbollah

Village/town	Launches from civilian structures	Launches w/in 200 m of village center	Launches w/in 500 m of village center
Aitaroun	18	23	54
Baflay	13	19	20
Bint Jbeil	87	109	136
Blida	0	0	1
Houla	2	3	4
Kafra	17	36	61
Al-Mansouri	6	11	23
Marjeyoun	7	11	11
Marwaheen	0	0	1
Qana	3	36	106
Srifa	0	1	7
Talouseh	0	4	24
Tyre	1	1	1
Zibqine	2	7	23
Total	**156**	**261**	**472**

Information provided by the IDF, as tracked by IDF radar.

Figure 5.6: Hezbollah rocket launches from in and around towns and villages in southern Lebanon

---

[62] Amnesty International, "Israel/Lebanon: Hezbollah's deliberate attacks on Israeli civilians," MDE 02/026/2006, 14 September 2006, http://web.amnesty.org/library/Index/ENGMDE020262006?open&of=ENG-2D2; and Human Rights Watch, "Hezbollah Must End Attacks on Civilians," 5 August 2006.

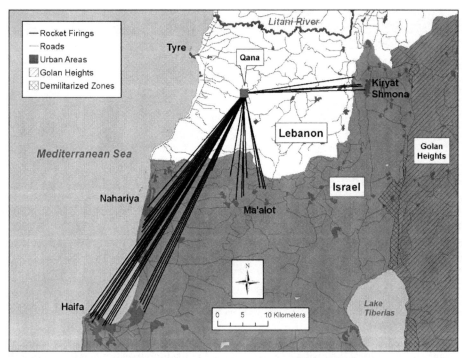

Figure 5.7: Hezbollah rocket fire from the vicinity of Qana

See: Israel MFA, "Incident in Kfar Qana, Israeli cities on which rockets were fired from Qana," 30 July 2006, http://www.mfa.gov.il/MFA/Government/Communiques/2006/Incident+in+Qana+IDF+Spokesman+30-Jul-2006.htm.

rocket fire from the vicinity of UN positions as well as Hezbollah fighters firing upon UN and civilian convoys.[63]

---

[63] See, for example:

- On 27 July, UNIFIL reported that Hezbollah fired from the vicinity of four UN positions at Marwahin, Alma Ash Shab, Brashit, and At Tiri. UNIFIL Press release PR11, 27 July 2006.

- On 28 July, UNIFIL reported that Hezbollah fired from the vicinity of five UN positions at Alma Ash Shab, At Tiri, Bayt Yahoun, Brashit, and Tibnin. UNIFIL Press release PR12, 28 July 2006.

- On 29 July, UNIFIL reported that Hezbollah fired from the vicinity of six UN positions at Tibnin (2), At Tiri, Beit Yahoun, and Alma Ash Shab (2). UNIFIL Press release PR13, 29 July 2006.

- On 30 July, UNIFIL reported that Hezbollah fired rockets from the vicinity of three UN positions in the area of Tibnin, At Tiri, and Brashit. They also fired small arms fire from the vicinity of two UN positions in the area of Alma Ash Shab and Al Duhayyra. UNIFIL Press release PR14, 30 July 2006.

- On 31 July, UNIFIL reported that one aerial bomb impacted in the vicinity of a UN position in the area of Alma Ash Shab yesterday morning, causing damage to the parameter wall. It was reported that Hezbollah fired rockets from the vicinity of this UNIFIL position prior to the aerial bombardment. Hezbollah fired small arms fire from the vicinity of the same position. They also fired rockets from the vicinity of two UNIFIL positions in the area of Tibnin and At Tiri in the central sector. UNIFIL Press release PR15, 31 July 2006.

This same kind of reporting continued daily to the end of the war.

Photo courtesy of Lebanese Armed Forces

Remnants of a Syrian-made 220 mm rocket embedded in a Lebanese road. A significant portion of the civilian damage in south Lebanon was caused by Hezbollah weapons, including rockets that malfunctioned, Chinese-made submunitions that landed on Lebanese soil, mortars, rocket-propelled grenade launchers, and over 1,000 antitank missiles that were fired against Israel forces.

Hezbollah fired mortars, rocket-propelled grenades, and over 1,000 antitank missiles onto Lebanese soil, many at Israeli ground forces at civilian homes in frontline Lebanese villages. Scores of Hezbollah rockets malfunctioned and landed on Lebanese soil, as did a small number of Chinese-made submunitions.[64]

The number of civilian deaths and injuries can only be evaluated in the end in the context of what is to be expected when an enemy is intentionally embedded within civilian structures and civil society. Given Hezbollah's actions and Israel's level of response, civilian casualties also have to be compared to other

---

[64] This was observed by the author in Lebanon and communicated by UN officials on the ground. See also UN, Report of the Secretary-General on the implementation of *Resolution 1701*: "UNIFIL also strongly protested to the Lebanese authorities one incident of a Hezbollah-fired rocket impacting directly inside a UNIFIL position in the area of Ghanduriyah."

conflicts in terms of determining what is to be expected and what constitutes a suitable effort on the part of law-abiding, technologically advanced militaries to minimize civilian harm. Destruction and casualties can also only be assessed in light of alternative scenarios that might pursue the same objectives to achieve the same military results.

Chapter 6

Targeting for Effect

On 13 July, the Israeli government announced that it had attacked the following targets in Lebanon:

- headquarters, bases, training camps, installations, posts and arms "slicks" [depots];
- Al-Manar television in south Beirut, along with a transmission tower in Baalbek;
- runways at Beirut International Airport as well as two Lebanese Army military airfields—one in the north, and one in the Bekaa Valley;
- fuel storage at the Beirut airport and gas stations in southern Lebanon;
- bridges over the Litani, Zahrani, and Awali Rivers "connecting northern and southern Lebanon"; and
- the main road connecting Beirut and Damascus.[1]

With the exception of later attacks on Hezbollah-related financial institutions (and perhaps some factories associated with Hezbollah financiers), virtually every category of target that was bombed in the subsequent 34-day war was attacked in the first 24 hours. The Israeli military and government, in other words, had sufficient time to carefully plan and consider the legality, propriety, and importance of attacking each category of targets (e.g., bridges, roads, communications, gas stations, airfields, etc.) it selected in the 2006 war. Moreover, given Israel's previous experience in attacking terrorist forces and infrastructure in Lebanon, it also had more than sufficient experience with the controversies and effects associated with its contemplated attacks.

---

[1] Israeli MFA, "Summary of IDF operations against Hezbollah in Lebanon," 13 July 2006, http://www.mfa.gov.il/MFA/Terrorism+Obstacle+to+Peace/Terrorism+from+Lebanon+Hezbollah/IDF+operations+against+Hezbollah+in+Lebanon+13-Jul-2006.htm; and Israeli MFA, "Hezbollah attacks northern Israel and Israel's response."

Israel asserts that all the objects it attacked in Lebanon—including hundreds of residential high-rise apartment buildings in Beirut and thousands of homes and civilian "structures" throughout southern Lebanon and the Bekaa Valley—were attacked only as a result of a deliberate and careful determination of their Hezbollah connection and the military necessity associated with their destruction. It further avows that all attacks were based on positive identification by intelligence agencies and were done in strict compliance with the accepted obligations of the Geneva conventions, protocols, and international humanitarian law (the laws of war or the law of armed conflict).[2]

What was clear from the very beginning in Israel's political decision not to methodically attack Lebanon's electric power grid or water resources or the core assets of the Lebanese government—despite Israel's public stance that Beirut was equally responsible for Hezbollah's action and was ultimately the responsible party—was that the political and humanitarian "effects" of attacks were considered and were accepted to be just as important, if not more important, than the purely military calculations.[3] In other words, despite the internal demands of warfare and even Israel's stated objectives, Israel did not just attack what was "standard" to attack or what had previously been labeled a "legitimate" military objective. Even in the attacks into the center of highly urbanized south Beirut, Israel endeavored to safeguard civilians and civilian lives, even the lives of Hezbollah supporters, taking into consideration the direct and indirect results of what it otherwise justified as its necessary military course, given the nature of Hezbollah and the short time frame it anticipated for the conflict.

---

[2] Throughout the conflict and in its aftermath, the Israeli government has described high-rise buildings attacked in south Beirut and civilian structures in southern Lebanon and the Bekaa Valley as Hezbollah "structures," "headquarters," "weapons depots," and command and control targets.

[3] As an interesting aside, the Israeli press reported Israel had planned to attack the Lebanese government infrastructure but refrained from doing so after the United States asked Israel not to undermine the government of Fouad Siniora in its attacks on Hezbollah. See Aluf Benn, "Report: Interim findings of war won't deal with personal failures," *Haaretz*, 8 March 2007, http://www.haaretz.com/hasen/spages/834572.html.

Then why the almost universal international outcry claiming Israel's "disproportionate" actions and the accusations of excessiveness, indiscriminate attack, and even war crimes? Beyond the complex questions of Israel's position in the international community, the simple answer is quantity. The accumulation of destruction in Lebanon in just 34 days was unprecedented. Israel attacked with such seeming abandon that the comprehensiveness suggested a kind of callousness and cold-bloodedness that belied the country's stated adherence to either discrimination or humanitarian principles. Beyond the attacks on Hezbollah's direct military forces—rocketeers and units, even fixed infrastructure identified as command centers, barracks, and storage points—the repeated air and naval gunfire attacks on whole neighborhoods in south Beirut, the air and naval strikes and artillery and rocket attacks that resulted in such massive damage to southern Lebanese villages, the attacks on bridges, gas stations, ports, even on Lebanon's only international airport were unprecedented in a counterterror campaign. Without significant explanation and justification, the attacks appeared excessive to either mission of suppressing Hezbollah capabilities or impeding its future action. Israel clearly recognized that it had a limited amount of time to exact a certain level of damage, and it equated physical destruction with the objective of damaging Hezbollah's fighting ability and setting the organization back. The question is whether its targeting emphasis and all the destruction actually facilitated those goals.

Hezbollah Leadership and Infrastructure

The Israeli government has explicitly identified the home and offices of Hassan Nasrallah as targets that it attacked, and from the very beginning of Operation Change of Direction, it sought to kill Nasrallah and other Hezbollah leaders.[4] Hezbollah headquarters, bases, and main offices were attacked in-

---

[4] Specific high-rise buildings and complexes attacked, according to the IDF, included Hassan Nasrallah's house, Hezbollah bases, the "Fadlallah Center," a Hezbollah office building, a building complex "housing Hezbollah's headquarters," Hezbollah's "security center," and Al-Manar television. IDF, ITIC/CSS, Part Two, 66.

side the *dahiye* area of south Beirut, primarily in the Haret Hreik district and, to a lesser extent, in nearby Shi'a districts of Bir al-Abed and al Ruwais. Targets included, according to the IDF, "the main operations room, general staff functions (logistics, manpower, intelligence, and security), propaganda apparatuses (Al-Manar television), logistics sites, workshops, and apartments of the organization's leaders and operatives. Also situated in these districts are the offices of the Iranian Revolutionary Guards, which support Hezbollah."[5]

On 30 July, the IDF also said that these same types of leadership targets were being attacked in Sidon and Tyre, and included "organization headquarters and offices, the residences and hiding places.[6] There were also a number of commando operations in Lebanon that might have been related to leadership attack (either assassination attempts or attempts to capture Hezbollah leaders).[7]

Though Israel mostly focused its attacks on fixed infrastructure in south Beirut and the other Hezbollah strongholds, Hezbollah also "deployed" its military forces throughout the capital and other urban areas: Hezbollah stationed antiaircraft and antitank squads on the streets of the Shi'a districts and on the roofs of buildings in south Beirut.[8] It also stationed important military assets inside Beirut away from the southern suburbs, including its naval and antiship missile unit in the Ouzai port area near Beirut International Airport (a unit that successfully fired on an Israeli ship on 14 July),[9] as well as long-range

---

[5] IDF, ITIC/CSS, Part Two, 62–63. Earlier, the IDF had articulated that these were "targets belonging to the Hezbollah infrastructure which support the terrorist operative apparatus in the Shi'ite neighborhoods of south Beirut (e.g., *Dahiya*) [*sic*] and other locations in Lebanon: headquarters, offices, buildings serving Hezbollah's various branches, leaders' residences and the bunkers they are hiding in, as well as the organization's 'information' infrastructure (Al-Manar TV) and offices of the organization's social and financial infrastructure." IDF, ITIC/CSS, "The IDF-Hezbollah confrontation."

[6] IDF, ITIC/CSS, "News of the Israeli-Hezbollah confrontation (as of noon, Sunday, July 30)," 31 July 2006.

[7] These commando operations could have also been for the purpose of rescuing the Israeli soldiers.

[8] IDF, ITIC/CSS, Part Two, 63.

[9] According to the IDF, "the organization has a naval unit deployed along the shoreline, notably in the Shi'ite district of Ouzai, which is integrated into the organization's defensive and offensive plans." IDF, ITIC/CSS, Part Two, 64.

Zelzal (and other) rockets in the Kfar Shima and Wadi Shahrour southern neighborhoods.

There is no question that Hezbollah intentionally located itself and much of its military capability in predominantly civilian neighborhoods and in civilian buildings. The IDF says, and no one disputes, that Hezbollah offices and headquarters were "surrounded by civilian institutions and densely populated civilian residential buildings."[10] When Israel attacked Hezbollah in these areas, the international community did not necessarily call into question the attacks on leadership or objects that were otherwise civilian in character; it questioned the level of destruction Israel caused to civilians and civilian property overall.[11] Amnesty International said that "the extent of the damage suggests that Israeli strikes were aimed at any building that may have housed any activity associated with Hizbullah [*sic*], including non-military activities. As such they would have been direct attacks on civilian objects, and may also have been carried out as a form of collective punishment of Dhahiyeh's [*sic*] residents."[12]

A separate UN fact-finding group of Special Rapporteurs concluded that Israel failed to distinguish military from civilian objects in its attacks on Hezbollah infrastructure in south Beirut:

> While Hezbollah was in conflict with Israel, it does not follow that every member of Hezbollah could be justifiably targeted. Individuals do not become legitimate military objectives unless they are combatants or civilians directly participating in hostilities. Many members and supporters of Hezbollah do not meet either criterion. Similarly, not every building owned by or associated with Hezbollah constituted a legitimate military objective. Hezbollah is, in addition to being an organization using violence, a political movement and social services enterprise, particularly in the *Dahiye* [*sic*] and the areas of southern Lebanon with a Shiite majority population.[13]

---

[10] IDF, ITIC/CSS, Part Two, 62–63.

[11] Perhaps the one exception is the UN commission of inquiry, which states confusingly that, "the presence of Hezbollah offices, political headquarters and supporters would not justify the targeting of civilians and civilian property as military objectives." The statement suggests that the civilians and civilian property were the military objective. UN, "Implementation of General Assembly Resolution 60/251," 33.

[12] Amnesty International, Israel/Lebanon, "Out of all proportion."

[13] UN, "Implementation of General Assembly Resolution 60/251," 10–11.

The IDF nonetheless argues the fact that individual buildings remained standing next to others that were completely destroyed demonstrates that the targeting of Hezbollah leadership, even in civilian areas, was appropriately selective. The UN fact-finding group of Special Rapporteurs responds to this claim, saying that, "The mission's requests [of the Israeli government] for specific information as to the military objective pursued with the destruction of each building and the concrete and direct military advantage anticipated at the time of attack . . . remained unanswered on the grounds that such information must remain classified."[14]

If Israel could substantiate its intelligence with regard to the selection of each individual building attacked, the questions would still remain whether the destruction of so many civilian objects was proportional to the anticipated military benefit. It is true that Israel "warned" the Beirut population of its intention to attack, and clearly—given the extent of destruction and the relatively low level of civilian casualties in Beirut—its warnings were indeed highly effective. The warnings, nonetheless, point to an observation about the attacks that goes beyond the issue of legal justification and blame—they were largely ineffective. Israel did warn through leaflets, telephone calls, faxes, and broadcasts of potential attacks into the Hezbollah neighborhoods of Beirut. That warning no doubt also prompted Hezbollah commanders and fighters to relocate, reducing the attacks to being on largely "empty buildings," that is, to what many would describe as proscribed "civilian objects." Certainly some amount of militarily relevant Hezbollah equipment and assets—weapons, command and control equipment, even computers and files—was destroyed in attacks on buildings in south Beirut; but in its "precision" attacks on more than 150 buildings in the Shi'a neighborhoods, it is doubtful that Israel managed to destroy sufficient Hezbollah equipment or kill sufficient Hezbollah commanders or fighters to justify the overall civilian harm. What is more, if Israel is claiming that Hezbollah easily used civilian infrastructure to conduct it operations, then it is also saying that there is an endless supply left for the organization to use.

---

[14] Ibid.

Finally, there is the question of the secondary political "effects" associated with the attacks: Israel's campaign to weaken Hezbollah was shortened because of intense international pressure precipitated by the level of destruction in Beirut and the seeming harm to Lebanese civilians. And Hezbollah was immeasurably strengthened in its "martyrdom," raising the need for a conceptual alternative for attacking a terrorist organization like Hezbollah, one that avoids the reverberating effect of just strengthening its rolls in the future.

Al-Manar Television

From the first night of Operation Change of Direction, even before Israel attacked leadership targets in south Beirut, it attacked Hezbollah's Al-Manar television in Beirut. With up to 200 million viewers worldwide via satellite, the television station, the IDF says, is Hezbollah's "main tool for propaganda and incitement,"[15] a vehicle used to recruit new Hezbollah members and fighters, and the means "to relay messages to terrorists as well as incite acts of terrorism."[16] The US government agrees that Al-Manar is a propaganda organ and argues additionally that Al-Manar "regularly airs Hezbollah promotional videos featuring suicide bombers and rallies of Hezbollah fighters," thereby promoting and glorifying violence and terrorism.[17]

The IDF initially attacked Al-Manar's five-story headquarters and studio in south Beirut on the night of 12 July and followed up with attacks on other Al-Manar and Hezbollah-owned

---

[15] IDF, "Summary of events: July 13th, 2006," http://www.mfa.gov.il/MFA/Terrori sm+Obstacle+to+Peace/Terrorism+from+Lebanon+Hezbollah/IDF+operations+against +Hezbollah+in+Lebanon+13-Jul-2006.htm.

[16] Israeli MFA, "Responding to Hezbollah attacks from Lebanon: Issues of proportionality, Legal Background," 25 July 2006, http://www.mfa.gov.il/MFA/Government/ Law/Legal+Issues+and+Rulings/Responding+to+Hezbollah+attacks+from+Lebanon +Issues+of+proportionality+July+2006.htm.

[17] See Frank C. Urbancic, principal deputy coordinator for counterterrorism, Testimony before the House Committee on International Relations, Subcommittee on International Terrorism and Nonproliferation and Subcommittee on Middle East and Central Asia, 28 September 2006. The US Department of State *Report on Human Rights Practices 2005*, published in March 2006, initially remarked that "Hezbollah, through its media outlets, regularly directed strong rhetoric against Israel and its Jewish population and characterized events in the region as part of a 'Zionist conspiracy.'"

Al-Nour radio facilities, some in the same complex. Israel also jammed Al-Manar terrestrial signals and later conducted cyber warfare, managing to penetrate Al-Manar broadcasts and tamper with its signals to insert Israeli messages and programming.[18]

In addition to the initial strike on Al-Manar headquarters, Israel attacked relay and transmission stations on remote mountaintop locations overlooking Beirut and in other parts of Lebanon.[19] These attacks, though focused on Hezbollah media, damaged private and state-owned infrastructure belonging to the Lebanese Broadcasting Corporation (LBCI), National Broadcasting Network television, Future TV, New TV, and Télé Lumière as well as various radio enterprises and collocated cell phone service providers.[20] Yet despite Israel's claim that Hezbollah made extensive use of civilian facilities for actual military communications and intelligence collection, its attacks were clearly not meant to disable Lebanese civil communications. In fact, Israel did not attack the overall civil communications infrastructure in Lebanon.[21]

The question then, with regard to attacks on communications facilities, really relates solely to the issue of the legality of attacking Al-Manar. In December 2004, the US Department of State added Al-Manar television, Al-Nour radio, and other Hezbollah assets of the Lebanese Media Group to the Terrorism Exclusion List (TEL), designating them arms of Hezbollah

---

[18] "We struck their antennas, which prevented transmissions for a limited time," said Shuki Shacur, an IDF Reserves brigadier general who served as deputy commander for Northern Command during the war. "We also succeeded in penetrating their broadcasts and inserting our own programming. But . . . it's very difficult to block their satellite communication, since they're constantly changing their signals. After the war is over, we're likely to see more effort invested in denying Hezbollah its ability to use this means of communication." Barbara Opall-Rome, "Israel May Disrupt Commercial Broadcasts," *Defense News*, 28 August 2006, 28.

[19] According to research by the author and inspections on the ground, transmitters were attacked at Mt. Aitou, Deir al Baidar, Fatqa Heights, Hermel, Maroun a-Ras, Mt. Sannine, Terbol, and Toumat Niha.

[20] "Israel strikes TV, phone towers in Lebanon," 22 July 2006, http://www.lebanonwire.com; and UN, "Report of the Commission of Inquiry," 37.

[21] "Hezbollah made extensive use of the Lebanese civilian communications infrastructure, requiring the IDF to hit said infrastructure to disrupt Hezbollah's communications and intelligence." IDF, ITIC/CSS, Part Two, 98.

providing "fundraising and other material support." This act barred anyone in the United States from lawfully receiving Al-Manar's signal, a prohibition that was further strengthened in March 2006 when sanctions were imposed, assets were frozen, and dealings with Al-Manar were criminalized. These or similar prohibitions extend into much of Western Europe due to similar designations.[22]

Despite unambiguous Hezbollah ownership of these media assets, international news media and journalists protection organizations protested the attacks and disputed Israel's characterization of Al-Manar as a military entity. Reporters Without Borders stated that the station "cannot be viewed as [a] military" target.[23] The Committee to Protect Journalists stated: "While Al-Manar may serve a propaganda function for Hezbollah, it does not appear based on a monitoring of its broadcasts today to be serving any discernible military function.[24] The International Federation of Journalists (IFJ) condemned the attack on Al-Manar, warning that the attack "follows a pattern of media targeting that threatens the lives of media staff, violates international law and endorses the use of violence to stifle dissident media."[25]

The UN commission of inquiry chartered by the Human Rights Council also questioned whether Al-Manar's broadcasts of propaganda rendered it "a legitimate military objective." The

---

[22] Putting an organization on the TEL has immigration and deportation consequences for non-US citizens who have certain associations. Their addition to the TEL led to the removal of Al-Manar's programs from its main satellite television provider in the United States and made it more difficult for Al-Manar associates and affiliates to operate there. Al-Manar also lost access to its main satellite television service providers in Europe. On 23 March 2006, the US Department of Treasury further named the three Specially Designated Global Terrorist entities under Executive Order 13224. The 2006 terrorist designation of Lebanese Media Group (LMG), Al-Manar, and Al-Nour resulted in economic sanctions and their assets were frozen. Several European governments, including France and Germany, have also banned Al-Manar transmissions.

[23] Reporters Without Borders, "Reporters Without Borders in Beirut to express solidarity with Lebanese media," 27 July 2006, http://www.rsf.org/article.php3?id_article=18386.

[24] Aaron Glantz (OneWorld.net), "Lebanon: 7 Media Workers Injured in 48 Hours of Fighting," 15 July 2006, http://news.yahoo.com/s/oneworld/20060715/wl_one world/45361365131152986126.

[25] Quoted in UN, "Report of the Commission of Inquiry," 38.

commission argued in its report that a media outlet can only be a legitimate target if it calls upon its audience to commit war crimes, crimes against humanity, or genocide. The commission said it received no evidence that Al-Manar was indeed making such an "effective contribution to military action" or that its destruction offered "a definite military advantage."[26]

Israel disputes the strict legal characterization of immunity for media organs as articulated by the commission, arguing that "installations of broadcasting and television stations" have always been considered "accepted military objectives" by the International Committee for the Red Cross (ICRC). What is more, the Israeli Ministry of Foreign Affairs argues that the international committee established to review NATO bombings of Serbian radio and television in the 1999 Kosovo war noted, "If the media is used to incite crimes then it is a legitimate target. . . . Insofar as the attack [on Al-Manar] actually was aimed at disrupting the communications network it was legally acceptable."[27]

Legally acceptable, but also highly controversial in the overall information war for political support, leaving in the end the question of the military effectiveness of such attacks, first in their own right to stop Hezbollah propaganda and even incitement, and second when balanced against the negative political and other repercussions (the secondary and indirect effects). On the question of the effectiveness of the strikes themselves, Israel found, as the United States has found ever since it mounted attacks on Iraq's state-run media in the 1991 Gulf War and on Serbian media in 1999: modern broadcasting is far too dispersed and robust to disrupt. When Israel did attack Al-Manar in south Beirut, the signal reappeared within minutes; despite additional "nodal" targeting of transmitters and destruction of the fixed broadcasting studio in Beirut, Hezbollah was able to continue broadcasting throughout the conflict.

---

[26] UN, "Report of the Commission of Inquiry," 37–38. Regarding attacks on other transmission facilities, the commission additionally said that, "A clear distinction has to be made between the Hezbollah-backed Al-Manar television station and others. While the first is clearly a tool used by Hezbollah in order to broadcast propaganda, nothing similar can be said regarding the others."

[27] Israeli MFA, "Responding to Hezbollah attacks from Lebanon."

114

Robustness at Al-Manar and a Hezbollah "command and control" system that made use of civil assets—telephones, cell phones, and radio—largely proved impervious to physical destruction. The IAF failed to take Al-Manar off the air through "successful" physical attack; yet even if it had achieved the feat in the short term, it is certain that other Lebanese and Arab media outlets would have filled any gaps. As to Hezbollah command and control, the modest number of strikes against communications targets attests to the probability that Israel did not intend to destroy this target set. At the tactical level, Hezbollah made extensive use of low-power, short-range walkie-talkies and couriers, making attacks on fixed communications infrastructure likely a wasted effort in terms of producing a strictly military impact. Israel in the end seemed far more intent on exploiting Hezbollah's communications and the Lebanese communications infrastructure for intelligence value and to use that very infrastructure, even the cell phone system in southern Lebanon, to transmit its psychological operations messages, some of which were quite sophisticated. For the future then, not only does attack on "media" organizations still require an international consensus as to legality, but the military pursuit needs to be revisited, given the sheer difficulty of the task in the Internet-era.

A Bridge Too Many

If Israel chose not to methodically attack Lebanon's communications infrastructure because of its civilian character and because its inherent robustness made achievement of a coherent military objective an impossible endeavor, such logic did not extend to attacks on the transportation infrastructure, in particular, bridges. In its "emergency" response to the Hezbollah incursion and kidnapping on 12 July, the IDF implemented preplanned strikes against Lebanese bridges across the Litani River, following up daily with additional bridge strikes in southern Lebanon, eventually expanding attacks on bridges into the Beirut area, the Bekaa Valley, and northern Lebanon, accumulating the destruction of 109 bridges and overpasses[28] including 16 km of road sections in southern Lebanon[29] (see fig. 6.1). By the end of the war, 21 of the 29 bridges over the Litani River were reported damaged or destroyed (18 in the Tyre district and three in Marjeyoun).[30]

Israel says that it attacked bridges and transportation targets to prevent the movement and export of Israeli prisoners out of the country, to stem the flow of arms and military materiel to Hezbollah from Syria, and to interdict or prevent the movement of Hezbollah arms and forces, including rockets and launchers, internally within Lebanon.[31] Regarding attacks on bridges and roads, the Israeli government said, "The activity of terrorist groups in Lebanon is dependent on major transportation arteries, through which weaponry and ammunition, as well as missile launchers and terrorist reinforcements are transported. Damage to key routes is intended to prevent or obstruct the terrorists in planning and perpetrating their attacks."[32]

---

[28] The best specific accounting is 107 bridges and overpasses damaged and destroyed, 94 fully destroyed, nine partially destroyed, and four damaged. See UNDP, "Lebanon: Rapid Environmental Assessment," 2-3, 3-1. Other sources say 97–109 bridges. UN, "Report of the Commission of Inquiry," 37. The government of Lebanon says that as many as 97 bridges were damaged or destroyed, with additional damage to 630 km of roads. Government of Lebanon Fact Sheet, "Rebuilding Lebanon Together."

Six road sections in Beirut were destroyed or damaged, 240 in Bint Jbeil district, 251 in Marjeyoun district, and 251 in Tyre district. Road sections are defined as 15–50 meter sections of road. See JRC and EUSC, "Rapid preliminary damage assessment."

[29] UNDP, "Lebanon: Rapid Environmental Assessment," 3-1; JRC and EUSC, "Rapid preliminary damage assessment."

[30] Ibid. A later enumeration stated that 16 bridges over the Litani were destroyed and two damaged. Christopher Allbritton and Rania Abou Zeid, "Adding up the bill is itself a major challenge: Confusion still surrounds the extent of the damage in many parts of the country, *Daily Star* (Lebanon), 2 October 2006, http://www.dailystar.com .lb/article.asp?edition_id=1&categ_ id=1&article_id=75829.

[31] See, for instance, Israeli MFA, "Behind the Headlines: A measured response to Hezbollah missiles," 17 July 2006, http://www.mfa.gov.il/MFA/About+the+ Ministry/ Behind+the+Headlines/A+measured+response+to+Hezbollah+missiles+17-Jul-2006 .htm: "The bridges in northern and southern Lebanon serve as channels for transporting Hezbollah weapons and personnel. The same is true of the Beirut-Damascus Highway."

[32] Israeli MFA, "Responding to Hezbollah attacks from Lebanon."

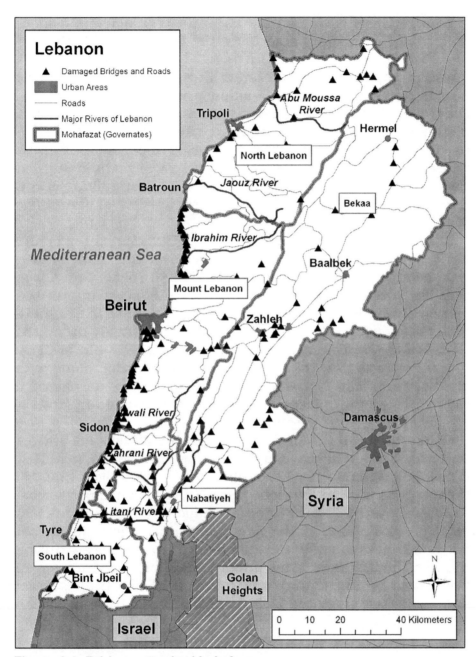

Figure 6.1: Bridges attacked in Lebanon

Though there is no dispute as to the legitimacy of bridges (and roads) as military objectives, the question is whether attacks on so many bridges furthered Israel's objectives. This question applies as well to Israel's attack on Lebanon's sole civilian airport, two Lebanese military airfields, and four ports. On the surface, such a question must seem absurd, for in a mountainous country like Lebanon with a dispersed and relatively sophisticated transportation grid, there are numerous redundant routes, a network that intrinsically would suggest the need for repeated and widespread attack for military effect. Such redundancy, nonetheless, ensures survival of alternative routes.

At least in southern Lebanon, the IDF's focus on roads and bridges—and not just on major bridges over the Litani River—was clearly directed at impeding Hezbollah rocket fire. Given that the rockets were widely dispersed and that improvised launch sites were only detected after launch, the IDF sought to limit movements in areas where rockets had already been fired by attacking nearby "access" points—both roads and bridges. The theory was that the isolation of launch areas, along with additional attacks focused on nearby structures as potential hiding and storage places, would ultimately constrain Hezbollah flexibility.

Given the nature of Hezbollah, were the attacks on bridges and access roads a reasonable strategy? Hezbollah says that it had no particular need to mobilize its forces, given that "all the weapons were in the right place."[33] American experts seem to agree, observing that: "Enough weapons and munitions had been pre-positioned in the south to reduce the requirement for dangerous resupply over distances."[34] Nonetheless, during the war, the IDF says "arms and ammunition were transferred from Syria by trucks and vans."[35] Some of this traffic, Israel says, was even disguised as humanitarian aid.[36] Initial strikes

---

[33] Shadid, "Inside Hezbollah, Big Miscalculations."

[34] Makovsky and White, "Lessons and Implications," 47.

[35] IDF, ITIC/CSS, Part One, 29. See also Fulghum, "Israel examines its military," 4.

[36] IDF, ITIC/CSS, "Hezbollah as a strategic arm of Iran."

Photo courtesy of Lebanese Armed Forces

A "bridge" in the Baabda section of Beirut, far from the Hezbollah area of *dahiye*, was inexplicably attacked. It lies far from the south and is not part of any major transit route. The attack could have been undertaken to signal a threat to the Lebanese government, as it is near the armed force headquarters. It could also have been part of the effort to find and destroy Hezbollah's Zelzal missiles, which reportedly were hidden in the hilly sections of greater Beirut. Or the damage could be collateral and simply the result of a weapon malfunction.

on Hezbollah shipments and traffic also seem to have had the effect of stopping or deterring further supply. On 25 July, the US State Department counterterrorism coordinator Henry Crumpton told reporters that US intelligence had not observed "anything in the last few days of missiles coming from Syria across the border into southern Lebanon." The flow, he said, "has been slowed if not completely stopped . . . of the large missile systems" because Israel was able to detect such missiles and most convoys were being attacked.[37]

---

[37] Ann Roosevelt, "Fighters Not Moving from Iraq to Lebanon, Official Says," *Defense Daily*, 28 July 2006.

By the most authoritative accounts then, Hezbollah attempted to resupply during the war, and Israel tried to prevent that supply through direct attacks on traffic.[38] Despite some successes, Hezbollah showed no shortage of rockets, is not known to have suffered any particular material shortages in the south, and the long-term effect of destruction of roads and bridges seemed negligible in preventing postwar resupply.[39] Attacks on road traffic did result in numerous civilian casualties and did precipitate much criticism, particularly with regard to supposed attacks on ambulances and humanitarian convoys.[40] One of the most controversial incidents occurred on 15 July, when a civilian convoy was attacked and more than 15 civilians were killed after Lebanese "civilians" heeded Israeli warnings in the border village of Marwaheen to evacuate.[41] Amnesty International observers on the ground described the incident:

---

[38] This is not to say that press or even expert reporting on the subject relating to the extent of that resupply or the impact of Israeli attacks is unanimous. Tony Cordesman says that experts "felt that they had prevented most Iranian and Syrian resupply of such rockets and other weapons, in spite of major Iranian and Syrian efforts during the war." Cordesman, "Preliminary 'Lessons,' " 4–5. Others are quoted in the Israeli news media as arguing that attacks on roads and bridges did not stop weapons from being moved from Syria. Yaakov Katz, "IDF: Hezbollah almost at full strength," *Jerusalem Post*, 21 December 2006, http://www.jpost.com/servlet/Satellite?cid=1164881 939862& pagename=JPost%2FJPArticle%2FShowFull. A UPI report quotes one source as saying that "during the war . . . Damascus did 'almost nothing' to help Hezbollah, although it did try to smuggle a few weapons systems to the organization." UPI (Brilliant), "Analysis."

[39] An advisor to the Lebanese Minister of Public Works and Transport even said that damage to roads was not a major problem. "Most of the damage is just holes that need to be filled, but the bridges are a big problem because they need careful study, they are very delicate." See Allbritton and Zeid, "Adding up the bill is itself a major challenge."

[40] See, for example, UN, "Mission to Lebanon and Israel," 12.

[41] UNIFIL press release PR01, 17 July 2006; AP (Beirut), "12 Lebanese killed in convoy attack," 15 July 2006, http://news.yahoo.com/s/ap/mideast_fighting_civilians _killed;_ylt=AkXPREPzihX.CrdFflsSI9oDW7oF;_ylu=X3oDMTBhcmljNmVhBHNlYwNtc m5ld3M; and Amos Harel and Yoav Stern, "Lebanon police: 15 die in IAF strike on van in south Lebanon," *Haaretz*, 15 July 2006, last update—15:05, http://www.haaretz .com/hasen/objects/pages/PrintArticleEn. jhtml?itemNo=738611.

Later, even when UNIFIL assisted in the evacuation of 283 civilian inhabitants of Marwaheen to Tyre, the UN convoy came under fire. UN, Report of the Secretary-General on the United Nations Interim Force in Lebanon (For the period from 21 January 2006 to 18 July 2006), S/2006/560, 21 July 2006.

See also Human Rights Watch, "Fatal Strikes: Israel's Indiscriminate Attacks against Civilians in Lebanon," August 2006, 15, 38; and Amnesty International, Israel/Lebanon, "Out of all proportion."

The convoy was traveling on the coastal road towards the town of Tyre but it came under Israeli artillery fire and had to turn back a couple of times and then continued. When it reached the vicinity of . . . al-Bayada the convoy again came under fire and the second and third vehicles, a pick-up truck and a car, were hit. The first shell was apparently fired by the Israeli navy, whose ships were besieging the Lebanese coast, followed by at least two missiles fired by Israeli helicopters. All the passengers of the pick-up truck and two passengers of the car behind it were killed and several others were injured.[42]

The UN Commission of Inquiry found that the Marwaheen convoy attack,

clearly was disproportionate, violated the principle of distinction, and cannot be justified on the basis of the convoy being a military objective. Moreover, the people of Marwaheen had been ordered by loudspeaker to leave town, although the routes for escaping were obstructed. . . . IDF command headquarters in the area must have known of the warning that had been issued and should then have ensured that orders were given throughout the chain of command to look out for evacuating civilians and ensure their safe passage.[43]

If one thing characterizes civilian action in the 2006 war, it was the huge number of Lebanese civilians who moved out of the south and the Hezbollah neighborhoods of Beirut once the bombing began. Tens and then hundreds of thousands of Lebanese civilians left their homes in search of sanctuary. Hundreds of thousands from the south made it north of the Litani—some 200,000 left Lebanon altogether for the safety of Syria.[44] A significant number, nonetheless—particularly the elderly and

---

[42] Amnesty International blogs, Lebanon mission: update 3, http://amnestyle banonisrael.blogspot.com/2006/08/lebanon-mission-update-3.html.

[43] UN, "Report of the Commission of Inquiry," 35.

[44] While some people in Beirut and other cities rushed to stock up on basics in anticipation of Israeli attacks on electric power and other targets, as had happened in 1996, there were initially few signs of panic in Lebanon, and no mass movements in the south. But by the third day of the war, after Israeli forces struck Nasrallah's offices and Hezbollah headquarters, the *dahiye* area of Beirut began to fully evacuate, and a huge population took to the roads in the south. By Friday, 14 July, with Israeli leaflets warning residents to leave Hezbollah areas, the main streets of Beirut's southern suburbs were virtually deserted, with residents either holed up in their homes or evacuated to safety outside identifiable Hezbollah neighborhoods. See Shadid, "Inside Hezbollah, Big Miscalculations"; Steven Erlanger, "Israel Vowing to Rout Hezbollah," *New York Times*, 15 July 2006, 1; and AP (Ghattas), "Israel bombs southern Lebanon."

infirm—could not make the trip, essentially because of the constant road attacks.[45] Israel at least acknowledges the connection between access to transportation and the livelihood of the civilian population, claiming a humanitarian purpose in its course of action: "In the current situation, notwithstanding the security justifications for targeting major roads, the IDF takes pains to ensure that sufficient routes remain open to enable civilians to leave combat zones, and to permit the access of humanitarian supplies. Efforts are also made to ensure that damage to civilian vehicles is minimized."[46]

That such a large number of civilians were able to leave their homes in southern Lebanon despite extensive attacks on bridges certainly raises questions about the military impact of bridge strikes (as opposed to road interdiction) on Hezbollah. Though attacks on key bridges and roads might have impeded the movement of the kidnapped IDF soldiers early on and even stopped (or complicated) the flow of Hezbollah rockets and supplies (and later, Hezbollah reinforcements), given the nature of the enemy—how it actually prepared and launched its rockets, how it moved its materiel in small numbers and on motorcycles, and how it prepared its defenses in the south (pre-positioning small amounts of weapons and materiel in a large number of locations)—it seems that the campaign of conventional attacks on bridges cannot be justified. Attacks on bridges in the north, moreover, seemed part of Israel's punishment strategy rather than part of a campaign of interdiction.

Attacks on bridges then are conceptually no different than attacks on civil communications, and one would think that Israel would apply the same criteria in deciding whether the effort required to halt militarily significant movements was worth the resources or the effects. It is an important calculation not only because bridges demand the use of a large number of precision-guided munitions—munitions that might otherwise be in short supply or be needed for other higher priority attacks—but also because attacks on civil transportation have a much greater potential for civilian casualties and negative humanitarian

---

[45] Amnesty International blogs, "Lebanon mission: update 3."

[46] Israeli MFA, "Responding to Hezbollah attacks from Lebanon."

effects (both direct and indirect) than communications strikes, particularly if the latter are directed at remote locations.

Israeli transportation-related attacks eventually expanded geographically and in scope well beyond key southern nodes. Eventually, the scope folded in all access points into Syria, both in southern and northern Lebanon, and all internal bridges of any consequence, with the seeming general justification that Hezbollah might use the disrupted routes for movement and resupply at some point in the future. However, as the attacks expanded beyond the Litani River and the south, they were naturally not as comprehensive, making the effect on transport more of a nuisance than militarily relevant and intrinsically increasing the effect on an otherwise intact civilian population.[47]

Fueling Anger

If Israel followed a mechanical approach to attacking transportation infrastructure, surely IDF attacks on Lebanese energy resources proved to be even more far-fetched in military justification, producing the potential for even greater civilian harm. The IDF attacked fuel resources throughout Lebanon, particularly in southern Lebanon, including two large fuel storage areas at Beirut International Airport and the Jiyyeh electric power plant, as well as more than 25 individual gas stations. The Beirut airport and Jiyyeh depots were attacked on 12 and 13 July, suggesting retaliations for Hezbollah urban attacks on Haifa and punitive damage to Lebanon as a signal to the Beirut government. The attacks on gas stations accumulated over time, though they also accelerated in the final days of the campaign, suggesting a desire to exact a long-term effect on Lebanon's ability to recover.[48]

---

[47] In the case of strikes in Beirut and northern Lebanon, many of the routes could be easily detoured and circumvented. See, for example, Allbritton and Zeid, "Adding up the bill is itself a major challenge."

[48] "There was also a fuel shortage caused by the blockade and the targeting by Israeli forces of fuel depots and petrol stations. Most of the petrol stations that had not run out of petrol or been destroyed were closed by their owners out of fear that they would be targeted. This meant that even those who had cars often could not find petrol." Amnesty International, Israel/Lebanon. "Out of all proportion."

Israel said that attacks on fuel were justified militarily and that fuel was needed for rocket launchers and for Hezbollah combatants to move around. According to the Israeli government, "Terrorist activity is dependent, *inter alia*, on a regular supply of fuel without which the terrorists cannot operate. For this reason a number of fuel depots which primarily serve the terrorist operations were targeted. From intelligence Israel has obtained, it appears that this step has had a significant effect on reducing the capability of the terrorist organizations."[49]

Taking into account the duration of the conflict, likely Hezbollah reserves, restricted movements, and the short distances involved (it was not as if fighters were traveling over huge areas even to get to and from southern Lebanon from Beirut or the Bekaa Valley), the anticipated military advantage associated with attacks on fuel resources seems quite minimal. In other words, only the civilian population was harmed by attacks on fuel and gas stations, and were it not indeed for the small distances involved in Lebanon and the duration of the conflict, the country might have indeed witnessed an energy "cluster bomb" in terms of shortages and deprivations.

As it was, a month into the war, Lebanese NGOs were reporting a "fuel crisis" with rationing and cars queuing for gasoline. Three hospitals in southern Lebanon were reported closed because of the lack of fuel, while others were running low on generator fuel.[50] By 12 August, the Lebanese Ministry of Public Health estimated that around 60 percent of the country's hospitals had ceased to function due to fuel shortages.[51] Hospitals in Bint Jbeil and Marjeyoun ceased functioning due to lack of fuel, electric power, water, and shortages of drugs.[52] On 12

[49] Israeli MFA, "Responding to Hezbollah attacks from Lebanon."

[50] Arab NGO Network for Development, "Update from a Lebanon under Unjustified Israeli War Rage, Wednesday August 2nd, 2006—22nd day of attack."

[51] Amnesty International, Israel/Lebanon, "Out of all proportion."

[52] WHO and Government of Lebanon Ministry of Public Health, Lebanon Crisis Service Availability Assessment, 29 August 2006, 32.

August, the Marjeyoun Hospital closed its emergency care altogether due to the absence of fuel.[53]

Despite Israel's decision not to attack the electric power grid, electric power was also cut off in large parts of Beirut after 14 July when fuel supplies at the nearby Jiyyeh power plant were bombed.[54] Though the IDF did not attack the generators at Jiyyeh or other plants, Israeli attacks on the three large fuel-oil storage tanks at the plant did lead to a marked reduction in the supply of electricity.[55] Centrally supplied electric power in the south also collapsed due to automatic and manual diversions in the national grid and damage to transmission lines.

Disruption of electric power, attacks on fuel and gas stations, Israel's blockade, attacks on bridges and roads, even attacks on civil communications, reverberated to create a magnified humanitarian effect.[56] According to Amnesty International:

> With the electricity cut off and food and other supplies not coming into the villages, the destruction of supermarkets and petrol stations played a crucial role in forcing local residents to leave. The lack of fuel also stopped residents from getting water, as water pumps require electricity or fuel-fed generators.[57]

After awhile, Amnesty said, "even those who could afford the journey often had no way of communicating with the cities to arrange for transport because by this time telephone and electricity networks had been put out of use by Israeli bombard-

---

[53] UNICEF Situation Report—Lebanon, 30–31 August 2006.

[54] Erlanger, "Israel Vowing to Rout Hezbollah."

[55] According to Lebanese authorities, the electrical shortages caused during July and August were caused when two of five generators at the Jiyyeh power plant were taken off-line after the IDF targeted two fuel-oil storage tanks at the plant on 13 and 15 July. The attacks also destroyed a third tank.

[56] The secondary and reverberating effects also had an economic impact. For example, an oil spill into the Mediterranean Sea of at least 15,000 tons of heavy fuel at Jiyyeh spread along 150 km of coast, impacting fishing and eventually the tourism sector. See UN, "Report of the Secretary-General on the implementation of resolution 1701."

[57] Amnesty International, "Israel/Lebanon: Deliberate destruction or 'collateral damage'?" 3.

ments and people could not use landlines or charge their mobile telephones as they had no power."[58]

Were the Lebanon conflict of longer duration, the humanitarian impact would have been greater as the effects of these deprivations accumulated. But the conflict was short, and Israel knew it would be short, thus not only softening the civilian impact but also demilitarizing the effect of the targeting emphasis. The destruction, moreover, did not just have a humanitarian impact. "IAF and artillery strikes that hit such facilities in populated areas created substantial problems in terms of perceived attacks on civilians and collateral damage," observed Anthony Cordesman. "Unless the IDF shows that the Hezbollah lost a major amount of weaponry in such attacks, the attacks may have done Israel as much harm in terms of future hostility as good in terms of immediate tactical benefits."[59]

Even if Israel could show Hezbollah losses of the type that might justify the damage caused in Lebanon, in the end the reality is that Hezbollah is not a conventional military force or a nation-state dependent on high technology or even military "equipment." Hezbollah was and is a terrorist organization that has evolved into a political force and a partisan movement fully woven into the fabric of Lebanese civil society and intrinsically embedded, indeed intentionally "shielded" behind civil society and the civilian population. Some might argue that Israel's attacks on civilian objects were the only alternative given this very nature of Hezbollah. Even inside Israel and among its defenders though, this argument has a diminishing number of adherents. Outside Israel, it is almost universally rejected. There has to be a more imaginative targeting scheme.

---

[58] Amnesty International, Israel/Lebanon, "Out of all proportion."

[59] Cordesman, "Preliminary 'Lessons.' " 5.

Chapter 7

Perfect Execution

Some refer to it as the "34-minute operation"; others, 39 minutes. It was a mythic attack that the Israeli Air Force had planned and rehearsed for many years to destroy Hezbollah's medium- and long-range Iranian-made Fajr and Zelzal rocket force.[1] On the night of 12 July, within hours of the Hezbollah cross-border attacks and the kidnapping, Israeli F-15 and F-16 fighters attacked and destroyed "most" of Hezbollah's long-range launchers, according to numerous postwar accounts,[2] hitting 54 Zelzal launchers one report says,[3] striking 59 launchers according to another,[4] destroying 18 out of 19–21 launchers according to yet another.[5] Two experienced American observers would later write: "In just 39 minutes on the night of 12 July, the Israeli air force destroyed most of Hezbollah's Iranian-made Zilzal [*sic*] long-range rockets, which were believed capable of hitting Tel Aviv."[6] An Israeli reporter wrote:

> The first 34 minutes of this war were dazzling. IAF fighter jets swept across Lebanon and wiped out in just over half-an-hour most of the guerrilla group's long-range missiles and launchers. In total, over 94 targets were hit, strikes made possible by precise intelligence and perfect execution by well-trained IAF pilots. Those first 34 minutes were characteristic of the IAF's overall contribution to the war in Lebanon.[7]

---

[1] Aluf Benn, "Report: IAF wiped out 59 Iranian missile launchers in 34 minutes," *Haaretz*, 24 October 2006, http://www.haaretz.com/hasen/spages/778485.html.

[2] Cordesman, "Preliminary 'Lessons,' " 17.

[3] Uzi Mahnaimi, "Humbling of the supertroops shatters Israeli army morale," *Sunday Times* (UK), 27 August 2006, http://www.timesonline.co.uk/article/0,,2089-2330624_1,00.html. See also "Halutz: 'Mr. PM, We Won the War'," *Ynetnews.com*, 27 August 2006, http://www.ynetnews.com/articles/0,7340,L-3296031,00.html.

[4] Makovsky and White, "Lessons and Implications," 18.

[5] Cordesman, "Preliminary 'Lessons,' " 4.

[6] Leslie Susser, "5766: A turbulent year," *Jewish Standard*, 21 September 2006, http://www.jstandard.com/articles/1619/1/5766-A-turbulent-year.

[7] Katz, "IDF report card."

127

With the 34-minute operation completed, according to press reports, IDF chief of staff Lt Gen Dan Halutz told Prime Minister Ehud Olmert that "all the long-range rockets have been destroyed." "We've won the war," he reportedly told Olmert.[8] Olmert in turn described the 34-minute operation as "an impressive, perhaps unprecedented, achievement." His aides compared the 12 July attack with the destruction of Arab air forces in the opening salvo of the Six-Day War.[9]

Some kind of preplanned "shock and awe" attack occurred on 12 July, and Halutz and Olmert evidently believed that some monumental and historic result had been achieved by Israeli airpower.[10] Yet the facts do not exist to substantiate whether 90 percent of Hezbollah's medium- and long-range launchers were indeed destroyed in half an hour on the first night of the war. There is, in fact, little evidence on the ground to indicate that the Israeli attacks undertaken on 12 July (or 13 July) were focused so intently on Hezbollah's rocket force, and there is no evidence that 94 such attacks were focused on the rocket force. An analysis on the ground and further review of the locations that were bombed in the first 48 hours in Lebanon indicates a far more dispersed and diffuse operation. In the case of the Zelzals, which were later reported to be located in southern and eastern Beirut, there were no attacks on 12 July and no major Israeli strike into the capital city on 13 July pursuing missiles, as some have otherwise reported. What is more, Hezbollah subsequently carried out extensive long-range rocket strikes, a fundamental reality that seems to call into question whether Israel had intelligence of such fidelity at the time to even validate the original bomb damage assessment.

On the other hand, that the IDF chief of staff could declare that Israel had won a war less than 24 hours into an operation,

---

[8] Mahnaimi, "Humbling of the supertroops." See also "Halutz: 'Mr. PM, We Won the War.' "

[9] Benn, "Report: IAF wiped out 59 Iranian missile launchers in 34 minutes."

[10] During the war, Halutz and Olmert said nothing publicly about the supposedly disabling strikes, perhaps taking a cue from the American playbook in 2003 to be more modest publicly. It may be that they were officially silent because of habitual secrecy and operational security. Israeli political leaders could also have additionally desired to dampen public expectations, given the monumental tasks ahead. Political leaders might even have intuited that the initial bomb damage assessments, if they existed as legend says, were overly optimistic or apocryphal, as first reports often are.

and that the prime minister could equally accept and believe such an absurdity indicates either an extraordinary level of naiveté or a grandiose and deeply flawed view of airpower. And then, the whole legend could be untrue. It is entirely possible, particularly given the postwar political battles that have raged in Israel over an extremely controversial war, that Halutz and Olmert (or at least Halutz) never actually said what is attributed to them or at least that they are being misquoted and taken out of context in terms of their attitudes about airpower and the war. The tale is repeated mostly by IAF and IDF defenders in Israel who think that they are countering an unfair indictment of airpower. The 34-minute tale is thus the perfect backdrop for analyzing the 2006 war; that is, if one can get beyond the parochial battles and ideological winds to understand what actually happened.

There are a million articulations of the adage that war is politics, and to understand the 34-minute operation and the 2006 war, one has to factor in international politics and attitudes about Israel, Israeli domestic politics during a time of transition and uncertainty, the state of civil-military relations under a new government, politics at the General Staff level, internal relations between different factions within the IDF, the role of the news media, and even the fog of war. There has been much speculation about the Israeli government's motivations in responding as decisively as it did to Hezbollah's 12 July incursion.[11] Some argue that a new Olmert government—elected barely three months earlier, with a prime minister lacking military background and with rookies in Foreign Affairs and Defense portfolios, all committed to a "civilian" agenda—either

---

[11] When asked in August about the proportionality of the Israeli response, Olmert stated that the "war started not only by killing eight Israeli soldiers and abducting two but by shooting Katyusha and other rockets on the northern cities of Israel on that same morning. Indiscriminately." He added, "No country in Europe would have responded in such a restrained manner as Israel did." Stephen Farrell, "The Times interview with Ehud Olmert," *The Times* (UK), 2 August 2006, http://www.timesonline.co.uk/article/0,,251-2296832,00.html.

Hassan Nasrallah himself claims that he was surprised with the Israeli government's rapid and decisive response to the kidnapping. Transcript, interview with Hassan Nasrallah on Al-Jazeera, 20 July 2006.

Nasrallah also later said that he would not have ordered the operation had he known beforehand what Israel would do. See also Shadid, "Inside Hezbollah, Big Miscalculations"; Claude Salhani, "Commentary: Nasrallah's mea culpa," *Middle East Times*,

overreacted to the kidnapping or deferred too much to the uniformed military leadership, specifically leadership dominated by air force officers.[12] In this narrative, naïve and inexperienced Olmert and his defense minister Peretz fell captive to the enticing assertion that the war could be won by airpower alone.[13]

---

30 August 2006, http://www.metimes.com/storyview.php?StoryID=20060830-070214-6184r; and Greg Myre and Helene Cooper, "Israel to Occupy Area of Lebanon as a Security Zone," *New York Times*, 26 July 2006. Nasrallah's statement seems at odds with other statements that Hezbollah felt that Israel was plotting a war to take place in October 2006 and that Hezbollah disrupted it in July. Nasrallah stated:

> Yes, the capture was exploited. And in our opinion, this was in our interest and the interest of Lebanon. It rushed a war that was definitely coming. Therefore, if I want to use expressions that cannot be taken out of context, I say that we did not err in the assessment. Our calculations were precise and correct. We are also not regretful, and I did not make any speech that I regretted, or a defeat, as some Israelis said. In fact, my speech was one of victory from the first day. On the first day, when the clouds were black, I was confident that victory was coming. And this is the consensus of every objective expert who assessed what happened. I believe, and I said this more than once, that what happened concerning the timing and decision of the operation what it led was heavenly success and kindness.

"Hezbollah's Nasrallah on Outcome of Hostilities, Role of Lebanese Army, UNIFIL," interview with Hezbollah secretary general Hasan Nasrallah by *As-Safir* chief editor Talal Salman in Beirut, n.d.; and "Comprehensive Political Dialogue with Hezbollah Secretary General on Repercussions of July War. Nasrallah to *As-Safir*: Resistance Has no Problem with National Army or UNIFIL," 6 September 2006.

[12] See, for example, Yehuda Ben Meir, "Israeli Government Policy and the War's Objectives," *Strategic Assessment* 9, no. 2 (August 2006) Jaffee Center for Strategic Studies; and Makovsky and White, "Lessons and Implications of," 49.

The decision itself to go to war was a major shift in Israeli policy. Since the IDF's withdrawal from Lebanon in 2000, Israel has largely restrained itself in the face of Hezbollah provocations. The kidnapping of three soldiers in 2000, as well as the attempted kidnapping in December 2005, all went unanswered by Israel, and Hezbollah guerrillas "were still allowed to maintain their outposts just a stone's throw from the northern border." This time however, the "Zimmer Policy," according to which Israel turned a blind eye to the Hezbollah buildup as long as the zimmers (rooms) and hotels in the North were full, was discarded and Israel went to war. "While there were many disagreements throughout the entire month of fighting, on a whole, the top IDF brass admitted that there has never been such a willing and supportive political echelon as the Ehud Olmert-Amir Peretz duo." See Katz, "IDF report card."

Nasrallah himself reportedly calculated that the government of Prime Minister Olmert, headed by "rookies" (his term) and committed to a "civilian agenda" (their term), would not react very strongly to a brief incursion across the border and the capture of a few Israeli soldiers. Yoav Peled, "Illusions of Unilateralism Dispelled in Israel," Middle East Report Online, 11 October 2006, http://www.merip.org/mero/mero101106.html.

[13] According to *Jane's*, " 'The CoS [chief of staff] did not prepare a clear operational plan for the campaign,' said Major General Udi Shani, who led a team investigating the General Staff performance. 'Halutz was unjustifiably locked on an idea of an aerial campaign, postponing time and again the launch of ground manoeuvres.' Once the ground operations began, 'forces were not given specific objectives and time frames to attain them.' As a result, said Gen Shani's report, 'the IDF failed to reduce rocket fire from Lebanon and shorten the operation' ": Alon Ben-David (Tel Aviv), "Debriefing teams brand IDF doctrine 'completely wrong,' " *Jane's Defence Weekly*, 3 January 2007.

The culprit here specifically is Lt Gen Dan Halutz, the IAF officer who was IDF chief of staff and the first and only airman to serve in that position. Halutz, a former fighter pilot who shot down five Arab planes in the 1973 Yom Kippur War, is described by critics as a narrow-minded airpower booster with an ideological dislike of ground forces.[14] "He emphasized again and again that to be a shepherd, you don't first need to be a sheep," one vocal Israeli ground forces general said, labeling the air force officer arrogant—both about what he knew about ground forces and what he could admit he did not know.[15]

According to his critics, Halutz not only had an irrational and parochial view of airpower, but in his prejudices, he undermined the IDF's ground war potential: in not preparing the required campaign plan, in not mobilizing the reserves in time, in hesitating to employ ground forces when it was clear that airpower "wasn't working," and by constantly changing orders and muscling in on what were tactical and command decisions even after ground forces were belatedly employed.[16]

Halutz for his part argues that many of the decisions and missteps critics point to were the responsibility of the politicians and not the General Staff. In his letter of resignation in January 2007, he asked the prime minister to keep the IDF "out of political struggles" in the future,[17] suggesting that the war and the military strategy were captive to behind-the-scenes political battles. By this account, it is Olmert and the civilian government who

---

[14] See, for example, "After the storm: Israel and the future of Olmert's government," *Jane's Intelligence Review*, January 2007; Makovsky and White, "Lessons and Implications," 14; and Cordesman, "Preliminary 'Lessons,' " 7. Even a "neutral" observer like Kenneth Katzman, a Middle East expert at the Congressional Research Service (CRS), said Israel initially "thought along the 'shock and awe' line," calculating that airpower "would be so overwhelming and so precise that Hezbollah would be scared into capitulating." When that did not happen, he said, Israel "settled into a pattern of making slow and steady degradation," incorporating ground forces. Quoted in Bloomberg (Tony Capaccio et al.), "Israel, Hezbollah Assess Arsenal, Consider Lessons as War Halts," 16 August 2006, http://www.bloomberg.com/apps/news?pid=20601070&sid=aJZ6iLvFjso0&refer=home.

[15] Amos Harel and Nir Hasson, "Pressure mounts on Halutz to 'take responsibility' for war," *Haaretz*, 13 November 2006, http://www.haaretz.com/hasen/spages/786933 .html.

[16] Amir Oren, "Unlearned Lessons," *Haaretz*, 2 November 2006; and Rabinovich, "Retired Israeli generals vent."

[17] IDF Spokesman's Office, Dan Halutz' letter of resignation as IDF chief of staff, 16 January 2007.

were unclear about Israeli objectives and goals, unable because of inexperience and a lack of military background to "ask the IDF hard questions" about proposed courses of actions beyond the preplanned response option, and confused or hesitant on the question of strategic objectives that might guide a subsequent military operation.[18] Halutz says that it was the Cabinet that had unrealistic expectations about airpower, and that it approved IAF strikes believing irrationally that Hezbollah's "spine" would be broken within "ten days, two weeks" even though Halutz and the IAF thought that at least eight to ten weeks would minimally be needed.[19]

Halutz himself is quoted as saying that "an air force cannot stick the flag on the hilltop,"[20] and IAF chief of staff Brig Gen Amir Eshel equally has spoken publicly, even during the war, questioning whether the airmen were claiming instant success or even an exclusive role. On 13 July, Eshel spoke to the press at length about the previous day's strikes and the air campaign. He said that the strikes had been "extremely complex" and that the campaign was Israel's largest ever "if you measure it in number of targets hit in one night." Eshel warned that "there is no instant solution or trick" to stop Hezbollah from attacking Israel and that to achieve the objectives would "take time" and a "very prolonged campaign." He stated specifically:

> I suggest that we begin thinking in terms of more than days. . . .
> This will neither end tomorrow nor the day after. Air power plays
> a very central and significant role in this operation thanks to the
> capabilities we have developed over the years, such as our ability
> to launch accurate strikes and coordinate with the ground forces.
> This means that the IAF will definitely have a key role in the activ-
> ity. Our aim at this stage of the campaign is to reduce their ability
> to strike at our territory. We cannot prevent them from doing this

---

[18] Makovsky and White, "Lessons and Implications," 7; and Cordesman, "Prelimi-nary 'Lessons,' " 9–10.

[19] Katz, "IDF report card"; and Nahum Barnea and Shimon Schiffer, "What Would Halutz Say," in *Yediot Aharonot* (Tel Aviv), 25 August 2006, quoted in Makovsky and White, "Lessons and Implications," 6.

[20] Arie Egozi, "Israeli air power falls as offensive in southern Lebanon fails to halt Hezbollah," *Flight International*, 1 August 2006.

but we are making a very intensive effort to reduce both the scope and accuracy of their strikes.[21]

Is there thus any validity to the claim and the conventional wisdom that Halutz or the General Staff exaggerated what air-power could do or ideologically snubbed a ground force option? Prime Minister Olmert addressed this question in September 2006, rejecting the notion that there was a failure at all in not employing ground forces from the beginning:

> If we had started a large-scale ground operation from day one and reached the Litani—forget about the price—the Katyushas would still have continued. There were launchers to the north of the Li-tani. Had we gone north of the Litani on the ground and reached the Awali, again regardless of the cost, there would still have been Katyushas. There were launchers beyond the Awali and beyond the Zaharani [sic]. The purpose was to act in a subtle, sophisticated and smart manner, to combine military power with political lever-age, to impose a new order. And that's precisely what we did.[22]

Maj Gen Benjamin Gantz, commander of the IDF army head-quarters confirms the Halutz and Olmert explanations: "There was absolutely no one in any military leadership position who claimed airpower alone could deliver the goods. I was sure it would not, and that we would have to go inside. By exploiting the air war, we could have gotten in simultaneously in full force and taken over the entire area, cleansing it from within. But that would have required . . . decisive ground-maneuver warfare, not the stage-by-stage operations that were ultimately executed."

Given the 2000 Israeli decision to withdraw ground forces from Lebanon and the "cost" that Olmert describes—the IDF reportedly made projections of 300 soldiers killed in a cam-paign to gain control of southern Lebanon south of the Litani River—it is not surprising that the prime minister felt that

---

[21] See BBC Worldwide Monitoring, "Israeli officials vow to remove Hezbollah from border"; and AP (Beirut, Sam F. Ghattas), "Israel blasts Beirut's airport as guerilla rockets hit Israel's third largest city in escalating battle," 13 July 2006, 1943 GMT.

[22] "Israel's Olmert Talks on Lebanon War, Iran, Prisoner Swap, Qadima Party Sur-vival," interview with Prime Minister Ehud Olmert in his Jerusalem Office by Herb Keinon and David Horovitz; n.d.; and "I Had No Illusions about This Job," *Jerusalem Post*, 29 September 2006.

public opinion would not support a full-scale ground war.[23] The conventional criticism from the army ignores these considerations, arguing that the politicians were guilty of "preventing" the ground forces from otherwise carrying out *their* preferred and *the* optimum plan. Maj Gen Yiftah Ron-Tal, the former commander of the Ground Forces Command, complained that politicians took a "hesitant course of action" and did not allow the army to operate in accordance with plans "for a wide-scale ground operation in southern Lebanon.[24] Gantz himself responds, expressing some frustration with lower-level critics: "It's the responsibility of the political leaders to adjust plans as they see fit." Gantz affirms what officers like Ron-Tal should know—that it is "the prerogative of political leaders to decide what is domestically and strategically desirable." Though his "professional opinion" might have been to act quicker on the ground to take advantage of tactical surprise and benefit from the initiative, Gantz says, "it was understandable, even crucial, for our leadership to want to fortify domestic legitimacy for the ground maneuver."[25]

Understandable. Crucial. And also necessary. Postwar reviews reveal that the political and IDF leadership also held a view of what was possible on 12 July because the ground forces were not ready anyhow to mount any kind of immediate and sustainable "wide-scale" invasion. In fact, even later when the ground forces were called upon to act decisively more than a week into the war, they were still unprepared, certainly suggesting that the Cabinet implemented the only feasible military option on 12 July. The lack of preparedness seems to have been the product of a combination of strategic missteps at the national level, prior decisions at the General Staff, as well as specific ground forces failures. At the strategic level, since the 2000 withdrawal from Lebanon, successive governments took

---

[23] Ben Caspit, "The Next War," *Maariv*, 13 August 2006, quoted in Makovsky and White, "Lessons and Implications," 14.

[24] Ryan R. Jones, "Israeli General: We Did Not Win Lebanon War," All Headline News, 4 October 2006, http://www.cynews.com/news/7005066917/.

[25] "Interview: Maj Gen Benjamin Gantz; commander, Israel Defense Forces' Army Headquarters," *Defense News*, August 2006, 38.

actions to avoid escalation, focusing the IDF away from the North and conventional ground war tasks and more on small-scale counterterrorism "head hunting" operations and targeted killings in Gaza and the West Bank.[26] The strategic decisions were responsible for significant organizational and resource decisions at the General Staff level, and were part of the reason behind the inability of the ground forces to make maximum use of the reserves or to concentrate Israeli fighting power even when called upon to do so.[27]

On top of these impediments, the ground forces, and specifically the Northern Command, also just were not ready. Forces were sent into battle with the wrong ammunition, without appropriate equipment such as body armor and night-vision devices, even lacking food and water.[28] The IDF chief infantry officer, on departing his command in 2006, admitted that he had not adequately prepared his troops for battle: "Despite heroic fighting by the soldiers and commanders, especially at the company and battalion level, we all feel a certain sense of failure and missed opportunity."[29] Once ground forces did cross into Lebanon, moreover, they failed to overtake Hezbollah strongholds, even those close to the border; ground units were initially sent into southern Lebanon and then withdrawn back into Israel; battles were dispersed rather than concentrated; ground units failed to fulfill the timetables levied upon them; and constant

---

[26] At the start of the fighting, for instance, Northern Command had no digitized brigades, since the IDF equipping focus prior to the 2006 war had been to provide networked command and control capabilities to forces fighting in Gaza and the West Bank. See "Interview: Maj Gen Benjamin Gantz."

[27] Ze'ev Schiff, "Ashkenazi to annul Halutz's organizational changes to IDF," *Haaretz*, 27 February 2007, http://www.haaretz.com/hasen/spages/830951.html. See also Makovsky and White, "Lessons and Implications," 32.

[28] There are a host of ground forces issues that have dominated the Israeli domestic debate that have to do with adequate support for the troops that are not the subject of this study. At the lowest echelons, no one in the regular units had even fought in Lebanon, further reducing preparedness and confidence (or realism) about the task. Kim Ellingwood and Laura King, "Warfare in the Middle East: Israel Wades into Bloodiest Day," *Los Angeles Times*, 27 July 2006.

[29] Amos Harel, "Outgoing Infantry Chief Says Military 'Guilty of Arrogance,' " *Haaretz*, 22 August 2006, http://www.haaretz.com/hasen/spages/752774.html. See also Amos Harel, "Army inquiries into Lebanon war will lead to personnel changes," *Haaretz*, 9 October 2006, http://www.haaretz.com/hasen/spages/772276.html.

"contact" was never kept with Hezbollah fighters. "The basic principles of war were neglected in this campaign," retired Gen Yoram Yair said after his review of the battles. "There was no initiative, persistence, onslaught, concentration of effort."[30]

And then there are the failures of Israeli intelligence, which did not properly forecast and analyze Hezbollah capabilities or disseminate what it did know to those who needed it. Apropos the ground war, Israeli intelligence did not understand or locate the Syrian rocket arsenal and did not have a clear picture of the short-range Katyusha force.[31] The IDF ended up being surprised by the number of antitank missiles in Hezbollah possession and the importance of the missiles to the organization's strategy.[32] The intelligence establishment did not appreciate the sophistication of Hezbollah's tunnel and bunker system or use of Lebanon's "nature reserves" in the south as cover. Intelligence also did not appreciate Hezbollah training and preparations at the village level, nor conceive of a targeting strategy that reflected its reliance on prestocked material rather than traditional lines of communication.

The IDF maybe could not ignore truck movements from Syria, or even movements within Lebanon away from the south, but it is a conventional picture supplied by intelligence and a fundamentally flawed view of Hezbollah as a conventional force with

---

[30] Alon Ben-David (Tel Aviv), "Debriefing teams brand IDF doctrine 'completely wrong,' " *Jane's Defence Weekly*, 3 January 2007.

[31] Former head of research for military intelligence Brig Gen Yossi Kuperwasser wrote that though the intelligence was aware of the number of rockets, "we also knew well what we did not know about Hezbollah, especially the exact location of the rockets." Senior air force officers said that had there been such intelligence about the Katyushas, they would also have been destroyed quickly and effectively. Amir Oren, "Intelligence is not only early warning," *Haaretz*, 10 November 2006.

Anthony Cordesman makes the assertion that "The IAF was able to destroy most of the Iranian Fajr 3 launchers the first night of the war, but the IDF did not know the Syrian rockets were present." According to Cordesman, "the size of Syrian deliveries of medium-range 220 mm and 302 mm rocket deliveries came as a major surprise, and it is unclear that there is an accurate count of launchers or that their count of rockets and missiles is as good." Cordesman, "Preliminary 'Lessons,' " 17.

[32] "What surprised the IDF was the amounts. They seemed at times to be endless." Katz, "IDF report card."

logistical constraints on its endurance that contributed to the excessive focus on bridges and roads as interdiction targets.

Some in the intelligence establishment of course dispute these claims, saying that they understood Hezbollah completely but that it was the operational and decision-making echelons that did not assimilate the information provided to them.[33] Evidently though, the Israeli intelligence establishment practiced the same kinds of compartmentalization and information hoarding so characteristic of American intelligence failures. Both Halutz and Brig Gen Gal Hirsch, commander of Division 91, said that crucial intelligence had not been transmitted to Northern Command or the actual fighting units. A former head of military intelligence even claims that the intelligence agencies were justified in not disseminating information about Hezbollah to the fighting units, saying it was too sensitive to share.[34]

Though intelligence shares some blame, it was not as if it or the IDF in general did not have sufficient information or experience to understand that Hezbollah had developed into a capable fighting force. Brig Gen Yossi Hyman, the chief infantry officer, says that "at times, we were guilty of the sin of arrogance" in describing Israel's view of both themselves as a fighting force and the Hezbollah threat.[35] Anthony Cordesman ascribes this sense of hubris to the nation as a whole, observing that Israel "seems to have felt it could deal with Hezbollah relatively simply, intimidate or persuade Lebanon with limited leverage, and assume that its defeat of the Hezbollah would counter Arab and Islamic anger and lead to only

---

[33] Makovsky and White, "Lessons and Implications," 35.

[34] Amos Harel and Avi Issacharoff, "Proceed with caution: For the first time since the war broke out, Peretz has managed to make it clear that he does not take orders from Halutz," *Haaretz*, 2 November 2006; and Amir Oren, "Unlearned Lessons." The investigation of the attack on the Israeli ship *Hanit* on 14 July found that military intelligence also did not pass vital information to the Navy. Josh Brannon, "Panel: '*Hanit*' attack was preventable," *Jerusalem Post*, 7 November 2006, http://www.jpost .com/servlet/Satellite?c=JPArticle&cid=1162378346651&pagename=JPost%2FJPArti cle%2FShowFull.

[35] Amos Harel, "Outgoing Infantry Chief Says Military 'Guilty of Arrogance,'" *Haaretz*, 22 August 2006, http://www.haaretz.com/hasen/spages/752774.html.

limited problems with outside states."[36] Finally, there was an attitude at the IAF and General Staff level that the Israeli Air Force was second only to the US Air Force, and in some ways even better, and that no other air force in the world was capable of executing such a complex and prolonged aerial campaign, adding to the mystique of the 34-minute legend and a false sense of accomplishment.[37]

As this telling suggests, there is ample responsibility to spread around. After much defending of his performance, Halutz resigned as IDF chief in January 2007, just five months after the war. Postwar public opinion polls show Olmert to be the least popular prime minister in Israeli history.[38] And these are not the only casualties. Maj Gen Udi Adam, the geographic combatant commander as head of Northern Command, also lost his command in September 2006. Brig Gen Gal Hirsch, commander of Division 91 (the Galilee division) and the field commander most responsible for southern Lebanon (and for the kidnapping), resigned after a scathing review of the division's performance.[39] Other senior officers at Northern Command and in the ground forces hierarchy have been relieved of command, left their service in disgrace, or have been denied promotion.[40]

Though we may never have a perfect picture of the internal deliberations of the Israeli government and military during Operation Change of Direction, despite all of this accountability,

---

[36] Cordesman, "Preliminary 'Lessons,' " 12.

[37] Noam Ophir, "Back to Ground Rules: Some Limitations of Airpower in the Lebanon War," *Strategic Assessment* 9, no. 2 (August 2006), Jaffee Center for Strategic Studies.

[38] A majority of Israelis also believe that Defense Minister Amir Peretz should resign from his job. Harvey Morris, "Israeli soldiers spend New Year holiday in Lebanon," *Financial Times* (UK), 24 September 2006, http://www.ft.com/cms/s/3fec977c-4bf1-11db -90d2-0000779e2340.html; and Yoel Marcus, "One leader with an agenda," *Haaretz*, 26 September 2006, http://www.haaretz.com/hasen/objects/pages/PrintArticleEn .jhtml?itemNo=766887.

[39] See, in particular, Oren, "Unlearned Lessons."

[40] For example, Maj Gen Eyal Ben-Reuven, Adam's deputy, stepped down after not being promoted. The Northern Command chief operations officer Col Boaz Cohen also announced his resignation in November. Maj Gen Yiftah Ron-Tal, former commander of the Ground Forces Command, who was on retirement leave and still drawing an army salary, was discharged in October.

and despite an unprecedented more than 50 internal probes examining all aspects of the fighting, Israel still has not reached a point of closure or understanding of the war. What we can say though is that a losing and frustrating war effort clearly brought out the worst in everyone, amplifying the tribal differences between political, military, and intelligence establishments, between the General Staff and the military services, and between air and ground arms. Senior commanders had tense and dysfunctional relationships,[41] and there have been suggestions that ground commanders even failed to follow orders.[42] Even when Halutz assigned his deputy, Maj Gen Moshe Kaplinsky, to manage the ground war and supplant the combatant commander, Maj Gen Udi Adam, midwar, the extraordinary step just came to symbolize the divide between air and ground.

---

[41] "The main failures that I identify and which I experienced during this war are ethical problems of loyalty, friendship and cordiality," Adam said at his retirement. "These cannot be fixed by a mechanism. These are rooted and fundamental problems of norms and values that require soul searching and they need to be fixed." Hanan Greenberg, "Adam: IDF needs moral rehab," *Ynetnews.com*, 23 October 2006, http://www.ynetnews.com/articles/0,7340,L-3318402,00.html.

[42] Yaakov Katz and JPost.com staff, "Report slams Halutz's management," *Jerusalem Post*, 6 December 2006, http://www.jpost.com/servlet/Satellite?cid=1164881834 350&pagename=JPost%2FJPArticle%2FShowFull; Yehuda Ben Meir, "Israeli Government Policy and the War's Objectives," *Strategic Assessment* 9, no. 2 (August 2006); and Rabinovich, "Retired Israeli generals vent."

Halutz in particular, has hinted at tensions between the General Staff and the forces in the field. He has spoken elliptically of instances where "officers did not carry out their assignments" and cases where officers "objected on moral grounds to their orders." This included the suspension of a senior officer, reportedly the commander of Brigade 300. AP (Jerusalem), "Israeli army chief admits failures in Lebanon war but won't resign," 2 January 2007.

On the question of the use of cluster bombs in Lebanon, Halutz also seemed to blame his subordinates for not following agreed upon rules, saying: "We need to check that we respected all the rules. The question was not if we could have used—but whether we respected agreed upon rules in all places in which we made use of cluster bombs. The use was not surprising but was disappointing." Hanan Greenberg, "Halutz: Criticism of IDF is out of proportion," *Ynetnews.com*, 20 November 2006, http://www.ynetnews.com/Ext/Comp/ArticleLayout/CdaArticlePrintPreview/1,2506,L-3330297,00.html. Conversely, one could not help but notice that many of the investigative cluster bomb stories in the Israeli press were also subtle, and not too subtle, attacks on Halutz, whom is described sarcastically as not being aware of what the Army was doing. Meron Rappaport, "Confusion clouds use of cluster bombs in Lebanon," *Haaretz*, 20 November 2006, http://www.haaretz.com/hasen/spages/789906.html.

To finally evaluate airpower in the 2006 war then, we need to first acknowledge that those who argue against what Israel did, or who favor a different approach, come to their view with their own ideologies, backgrounds, mind-sets, and motives. There is much to be desired in the standard narrative of the 2006 war, but many of these critics of Israeli performance and strategy are not interested in the facts of what happened; they rely instead upon a tired antiairpower case: that airpower can never be decisive in a war, that an airman cannot command an army, and that airmen live with a pernicious desire to win wars at the exclusion of ground forces.[43] Other critics are more explicitly intent upon reasserting the primacy of ground forces within the IDF and the Israeli system, a shift that they believe is necessary because an air force chief and an airpower-dominated strategy ultimately led Israel astray.[44] And then there are the critics who

---

[43] Philip H. Gordon, "Air Power Won't Do It," *Washington Post*, 25 July 2006; "An Enduring Illusion—Air Power," *The Economist*, 26 August 2006; Ralph Peters, "The myth of immaculate warfare," *USA Today*, 6 September 2006, http://news.yahoo.com/s/usatoday/20060906/cm_usatoday/themythofimmaculatewarfare; Maj Gen Robert H. Scales (USA, Ret.), "Enemy eyes," *Washington Times*, 1 August 2006; and Scales, "To win the long war," *Washington Times*, 10 October 2006. See also AP, "Military Analysts Question Israeli Bombing," 20 July 2006; Reuters (Dan Williams), "Air power assumptions shot down over Lebanon," 3 August 2006; Robert S. Dudney, "The Air War over Hezbollah," *Air Force Magazine*, September 2006; and Sarah E. Kreps, "The 2006 Lebanon War: Lessons Learned," *Parameters* 37, no. 1 (Spring 2007): 72–84.

"An air force man cannot command the army, certainly not oversee the operation of the ground forces," one reserve general asserted. Rabinovich, "Retired Israeli generals vent."

[44] One shrewd Israeli observer writes: "These former generals have time on their hands, as well as energy, memories and some scores to settle. They are often surprised to discover that their colleagues also have scores to settle with them. Their pretentious demand that future generations consult with them—and woe to him who fails to accept their recommendations, which are often contradictory—ignores human nature. Heirs do not want their predecessors, who are free of responsibility, to patronize them like an older chaperon accompanying a novice driver. And if the future is only meant to be a recycling of the past, there is no hope for progress, much less revolution. The armored corps officers who were second fiddle until they took the lead from the infantry corps in the Six-Day War, only to lose it again in the Yom Kippur War, went from being innovators to conservatives, reactionaries against the rule of the air force. Of course, if precedent were binding, the Wright brothers would never have left their bicycle workshop."

Amir Oren, "The wisdom of the 'has-beens,' " *Haaretz*, 28 September 2006, http://www.haaretz.com/hasen/spages/767578.html.

hold a different strategic conception of the Israeli national security challenge than that of the Olmert government. They believe
in the necessity for a stronger response against Hezbollah and
an even wider war against Syria and Iran because they believe
that those two countries (and their proxy force in Lebanon) represent a fundamental threat to Israel's existence.

None of this telling is to ultimately dismiss Olmert, Halutz,
or the General Staff for their actual sins or for their deeply
flawed view of what airpower (and military force) could achieve,
or for their erroneous conclusions regarding the connection between destruction and desired effects. Olmert for his part says
it was not his job to "baby-sit" the military,[45] a statement that
demonstrates a fundamental failure to understand not only his
civilian role as commander in chief but also his weakness in
not firing Halutz or other military leaders if indeed he felt that
things should have been going a different way. Airpower zealot
or not, Halutz seemed also unable to publicly explain what Israel
was doing, the role of airpower and its place, given the strategic
circumstances and the physical realities of ground force preparedness, and even the obvious integration of air and ground
capabilities when they were working together.

Despite postwar musings about naïve politicians and a
perfectly calibrated military understanding of the limitations
of airpower on the part of the General Staff, Halutz (and the
IDF leadership) did believe that airpower had "destroyed" more
than it did on 12 July and in the opening days and they did
confuse completion of a complex mission on 12–13 July with
the larger mission of weakening Hezbollah. Most important,
Halutz and the General Staff confused physical destruction of
a set of targets with actual destruction of capabilities, whether
in the form of empty buildings in Beirut equating to destruction of Hezbollah or the destruction of a set of rocket launchers

---

[45] Yoel Marcus, "One leader with an agenda," *Haaretz*, 26 September 2006, http://
www.haaretz.com/hasen/objects/pages/PrintArticleEn.jhtml?itemNo=766887.

equating to destruction of rockets (and thus the actual Hezbollah threat).[46]

Some airpower defenders, finally, might be content to argue that airpower achieved what the political authorities asked of it. Others might fall back upon lamenting yet another ideological crusade against airpower, particularly against so-called strategic attack, maintaining that airpower, despite its flaws, still did "more" and achieved more, with far less cost, than anything that ground forces could have achieved. Still others might lay blame on process and organization, arguing that the IDF did not have a "plan" for war beyond the 34-minute operation and thus somehow should not be judged for its subsequent improvisations. Yet none of these answers adequately captures the tragedy of the conflict nor helps with a clearer portrayal of the future task.

No matter what the IDF or IAF thinks it destroyed on 12 July, and no matter how the overall military achievements in destroying Hezbollah's rocket force (or its other infrastructure) are described and enumerated, we are left with a classic and unsatisfying articulation of warfare as physical destruction and "attrition," not of warfare as effects. Effects here is not meant to be some underhanded code for airpower, nor is the concept of "effects-based operations" meant as some calculation or reducible model that magically systematizes targeting or wipes away the inevitable fog of war. Israel went to war against Hezbollah in July 2006 and did so with the objective of at least weakening the enemy and improving its own security in the short and long term. While it may have achieved damage to Hezbollah as a fighting force, no one particularly would argue that the

---

[46] An explanation of irrational exuberance and/or bomb damage assessment that too easily translates physical achievement into actual mission accomplishment is seen in a similar legend from Operation Desert Storm in 1991. Many in the US military leadership were convinced that they had destroyed Iraq's chemical and biological weapons facilities and would later promote the achievement. DOD after-action reports then described the achievement as having been successful at destroying Iraq's "known" biological warfare facilities to take into consideration that targets had indeed been successfully attacked, but they just didn't turn out to actually be hosting the actual biological weapons. William M. Arkin, "Week Eight: Don't Know Much about Biology," The Gulf War: Secret History, *Stars and Stripes*, 2001, http://www.thememoryhole.org/war/gulf-secret.htm.

level of effort expended over 34 days—and the price paid—accrued a commensurate payoff for mid- or long-term security. The questionable outcome tends then to merely discharge airpower before a reasonable and forward-looking analysis can even be made as to whether the instrument was used appropriately or to its maximum potential. The primary task ahead then for military theorists and practitioners is to conceive of an integrated air-ground "effects-based" strategy that is suitable to the task of fighting terrorism and all of the inherent political realities associated with the modern use of force.

Chapter 8

Airpower against Terrorism

Every modern war has a complicated and controversial narrative. Desert Storm was the affirmation of modern technology and precision airpower. Yet to some, the first Gulf War proved that "strategic" bombing and coercion does not work and that ground forces were ultimately needed to exact Iraq's capitulation, to "occupy territory," and finish the job. The 1999 war over Kosovo was the first war "won" by airpower alone. But only, some argue, if one ignores that the threat of a ground war convinced Slobodan Milosevic to give in to NATO's demands. Operation Enduring Freedom (OEF) in Afghanistan defied predictions of a Soviet-style quagmire and affirmed a new era where a small force leveraging special operations and airpower defeated a much larger enemy. That is, as long as one limits OEF to the time frame of the 2001 "victory" and ignores the long war that followed. Finally, Gulf War Two—Operation Iraqi Freedom—is and was the repudiation of "shock and awe" and the one that got away because of a dubious expectation of instant and uncomplicated victory, because of too few resources employed a la Afghanistan, and because of deficient postwar planning.[1]

The 2006 Israel-Hezbollah conflict hardly disappoints in competing narratives. Hezbollah labels its endurance and survival in the face of Israeli attack a "Divine Victory," stating that it is rearming and more powerful than ever—militarily and politically in Lebanese internal politics and in the overall Arab world.[2] The Israeli government of Prime Minister Ehud Olmert equally asserts that the 2006 war was one of that country's

---

[1] The author has weighed in himself on these debates. See, for example, William M. Arkin, "Baghdad: The Urban Sanctuary in Desert Storm?" *Airpower Journal*, Spring 1997; "Desert Fox: The Difference Was in the Details," *Washington Post*, 17 January 1999, B1; Human Rights Watch, "Civilian Deaths in the NATO Air Campaign," February 2000 (written by the author); "Challenge to the '15,000-Foot Myth' Consumes Air Force Planners," *Defense Daily*, 2 March 2000; "Smart War, Dumb Targeting?" *Bulletin of the Atomic Scientists*, May–June 2000; and "Air heads: Misperceptions and rivalries obscure air power's potential," *Armed Forces Journal*, June 2006.

[2] See, for example, transcript, Hassan Nasrallah speech in south Beirut, aired on Al-Manar TV, 16 February 2007.

greatest military and political victories ever. Olmert argues that Israel set Hezbollah back in armaments and capabilities, pushed it from the northern border, achieved a cease-fire to suit Israel's political interests, and established a geopolitical reordering in Lebanon and the "moderate" Arab world.[3]

Airpower in the Israeli narrative is labeled "brilliant." Supporters claim that some huge percentage of Hezbollah's medium- and long-range capabilities was destroyed and point out that the IAF was able to exact a heavy toll, with almost zero losses. Even Maj Gen Benjamin Gantz, the IDF senior army officer, says airpower "set an historic precedent for its ability to identify launchers, pinpoint their exact location and very quickly close the sensor-to-shooter loop."[4] Others argue that airpower, through its rapid response, strategic reach, and punishing might, also strengthened Israel's deterrent, demonstrating the heavy price that Israel could impose on any attacker.[5]

---

[3] Prime Minister Olmert said in September 2006 interviews that the war "was an unvarnished success," insisting that *UNSCR 1701*, which brought about the cease-fire and called for the disarming of Hezbollah, was a codification of Israel's greatest military and political victory. Caroline Glick, "Column One: The world according to Olmert," *Jerusalem Post*, 28 September 2006, http://www.jpost.com/servlet/Satellite?cid=11 59193338867&pagename=JPost%2FJPArticle%2FShowFull. Olmert said in another September 2006 interview:

> This is the first time in a war between Israel and Arabs that . . . a war ends up not with a cease-fire imposed on us, against us, but with a cease-fire imposed by us to suit our political interest. This is what happened with [a vote of] 15–0 at the UN Security Council, without one word of criticism on Israel after fighting for 33 days against a Muslim society, when a large part of the world complained that Israel was destroying all of Lebanon, and that this was disproportionate and what not. . . . I think this was a very smart, subtle and sophisticated use—proportionally—of the military power together with the political power to achieve what we set forth to achieve . . . including a change in the entire political make-up in Lebanon, which is on the way, and a change in the posture of moderate Arab countries against the Shi'ites in Lebanon, which is an outcome of this war.

"Israel's Olmert Talks on Lebanon War"; and "I Had No Illusions about This Job."

[4] "Interview: Maj Gen Benjamin Gantz," 38.

[5] There are many different views on this question of deterrence. Some argue that attacks on Hezbollah and Lebanon weakened, not reinforced Israel's overall deterrence of the nonstate, Arab, and Iranian threat; weakened support for Israel in Europe and elsewhere; and stimulated a new wave of support for fighting Israel. Finally, there are those who argue that it will be difficult for Israel to prevent its "mismanagement" of the campaign against Hezbollah from damaging its deterrent profile. Feldman, "The Hezbollah-Israel War."

Photo by author

The Hezbollah flag still flies in the border village of Aiyt a-Shab less than a month after the cease-fire. Hezbollah initiated the 2006 war from Aiyt a-Shab, and the village was the location of intense fighting. But despite the cease-fire agreement, despite the presence of UN peacekeepers and the Lebanese Army, hundreds of Hezbollah flags were seen openly displayed in the village.

Arguing that Israel achieved what it set forth to achieve in the 2006 war, however, is a little like saying that the operation was successful but the patient died. The performance of airpower may have been superb, and the IDF may have indeed accomplished difficult internal transformational tasks under fire,[6] but in terms of Israel's objectives, the kidnapped Israeli soldiers were neither rescued nor released; Hezbollah rocket fire was never suppressed, not even its long-range fire; the extent of Israeli attacks evoked widespread condemnation; and

---

[6] Though not the subject of this study, the IDF did achieve a number of "firsts" in the campaign, such as digitizing its ground forces on-the-fly after the campaign began, refining its "sensor-to-shooter" capabilities as the war progressed, and applying many innovations incorporating unmanned vehicles. Some systems were used for the first time (e.g., MLRS) and others performed admirably (e.g., aircraft and PGMs), but talk about not being able to see the forest for the trees!

147

Israeli ground forces were badly shaken and bogged down by a well-equipped and capable foe. Even General Halutz labels the war results "mediocre"[7] and admits that the IDF did not achieve its internal objectives.[8] Great damage may have been done to Hezbollah by Israeli bombardment—air, sea, and land—but nothing Israel did was able to undermine its basic coherence or deplete its forces. Barely a month after the cease-fire, Nasrallah claimed that Hezbollah still had at least 20,000 rockets.[9] In March 2007 Israeli intelligence concluded that "south Lebanon has not become a demilitarized zone free of terrorist organizations and their weapons, Hezbollah as an organization was not disarmed, the process of rehabilitating its military strength continues, and an effective embargo on smuggling arms from Syria to Lebanon has not been imposed."[10] The US Defense Intelligence Agency agreed, opining less than six months after the cease-fire, "The Israel Defense Forces (IDF) damaged some of Hezbollah's arsenal and many of its buildings, but Hezbollah's leadership remains unscathed and probably has already replenished its weapons stockpiles with Iranian and Syrian

---

[7] JPost.com staff, "Halutz: 'War results mediocre, IDF far from that'," *Jerusalem Post,* 1 October 2006, http://www.jpost.com/servlet/Satellite?cid=1159193351994&pagename=JPost%2FJPArticle%2FShowFull.

[8] AP (Jerusalem), "Israeli army chief admits failures in Lebanon war but won't resign," 2 January 2007. Former IDF chief, retired Lt Gen Dan Shomron, a ground officer, also says "the prime minister instructed the army [the IDF] to halt the rocket fire on Israel, but the army failed to translate it into a military objective." Scott Wilson, "Israeli Head Of Military Quits After War Critique; Leadership in Conflict With Hezbollah Faulted," *Washington Post,* 17 January 2007, A10.

[9] "Today, the resistance has more—and I highlight the word 'more'—more than 20,000 missiles. Within a few days, even though it emerged from a fierce war, the resistance completely restored its military and organizational infrastructure, as well as its arsenal of weapons. Today, the resistance is stronger than on the eve of July 12." Transcript, Hezbollah Secretary-General Hassan Nasrallah, at a Victory Rally, 22 September 2006.

[10] IDF, ITIC at the Israel Intelligence Heritage and Commemoration Center (IICC), "The implementation of Security Council Resolution 1701 after six months; Interim report," 4 March 2007, http://www.terrorism-info.org.il/malam_multimedia/English/eng_n/html/res_1701e0307.htm. See also Yaakov Katz, "IDF: Hezbollah almost at full strength," *Jerusalem Post,* 21 December 2006, http://www.jpost.com/servlet/Satellite?cid= 1164881939862&pagename=JPost%2FJPArticle%2FShowFull; and Editorial, "Confronting the threats," *Jerusalem Post,* 4 December 2006.

assistance."[11] No wonder then that General Gantz reflects the view of many philosophical Israelis that despite achievements claimed and actual, the overall conflict with Hezbollah will not be solved "without another round of battle."[12]

Outside of the Israeli government and General Staff, and certainly outside Israel, Hezbollah's postwar survival and strength alongside Lebanon's seeming destruction drives observers to almost universal agreement that the 2006 war was illegally executed by Israel with meager if not counterproductive military justification and extreme humanitarian effects. In August, Amnesty International opined that Israel pursued a policy of "deliberate destruction of Lebanese civilian infrastructure," including commitment of "war crimes."[13] In September, Human Rights Watch said Israel made a "systematic failure to distinguish between combatants and civilians," questioning why so many civilian vehicles and homes had been targeted "despite the absence of military justification."[14] In November, the UN Commission of Inquiry cited "a significant pattern of excessive, indiscriminate and disproportionate use of force by IDF against Lebanese civilians and civilian objects,"[15] concluding that Israel's conduct demonstrated "an overall lack of respect for the cardinal principles regulating the conduct of armed conflict, most notably distinction, proportionality and precaution."[16]

---

[11] It went on to say that "Lebanon was compelled to deploy the Lebanese Armed Forces (LAF) to the south, though the LAF has not moved to disarm Hezbollah. Additionally, the Lebanese government has now been told it is accountable for what occurs on all Lebanese territory as a result of *UNSCR 1701*. Hezbollah leaders claimed victory and grew more assertive in their political demands as demonstrated by ongoing opposition demonstrations in Beirut. Hezbollah is currently focused on asserting political dominance in Lebanon. Iran and Syria remain committed to Hezbollah's survival. Israeli defense officials have publicly opined that due to the fluid situation the conflict could reignite during the summer of 2007." Lt Gen Michael D. Maples, director, Defense Intelligence Agency, "Current and Projected National Security Threats to the United States," Statement for the Record, Senate Select Committee on Intelligence Committee, 11 January 2007.

[12] "Interview: Maj Gen Benjamin Gantz," 38.

[13] Amnesty International, "Israel/Lebanon: Evidence indicates deliberate destruction of civilian infrastructure."

[14] Human Rights Watch, "Israel: Government Committee Should Probe Lebanon Laws of War Violations," Press Release, 26 September 2006.

[15] UN, "Report of the Commission of Inquiry," 3.

[16] Ibid, 27. "As with so many other cases investigated by the Commission, the IDF actions were indiscriminate and disproportionate. The destruction of so many civilian houses is not justifiable in terms of military necessity." Ibid., 32.

Given Israel's reliance on high technology and precision-guided munitions, given its decisions to spare Lebanon's direct life support infrastructure, given its specific targeting decisions and internal process of legal review, given Israel's view of itself as law abiding and morally based, given the nature of the enemy's explicit and intentional use of civil society as a shield and its own commission of war crimes in attacking Israeli civilians, no wonder this narrative of Israeli illegality is deeply frustrating to many. Some even argue that Israel's problem is one of perceptions: that the 2006 war was itself a war of competing narratives and Israel failed to "win" the public relations battle because of poor information warfare techniques or practices, because it had to "tell the truth" while Hezbollah told lies, or that Israel "lost" because of media biases.[17]

But perhaps part of the problem is in the nature and narrative of air warfare itself. Here are the facts regarding the 2006 war: 1,200 or more Lebanese civilian deaths, 4,000 civilians injured; destruction of as many as 130,000 homes and apartments in over 130 villages and towns; the destruction of hundreds of Beirut buildings and the leveling of entire city blocks; 100 bridges downed; two dozen gas stations destroyed; airports and ports attacked. Absent a decent explanation of what all these numbers really mean, or taken out of context or twisted to ignore Israel's care or where Hezbollah deployed its forces or how it fought, these isolated data points become any propagandist's tool. Whether it is the IDF's mechanically reciting how many "structures" it attacked daily and how many sorties it flew, or the news media's reporting civilian casualties and damage on the ground in the absence of Israel's compelling description of its dominant military effort (airpower), the context of Israel's choices, decision making, actions, and overall

---

[17] At the end of the year, Minister of Defense Amir Peretz argued at an event honoring soldiers who were injured in the war that, "The war against Hezbollah didn't receive appropriate recognition." Hanan Greenberg, "Peretz to war casualties: We achieved goals in Lebanon," *Ynetnews.com*, 28 December 2006, http://www.ynetnews.com/articles/0,7340,L-3345484,00.html.

Major General Gantz said, "in the long view, despite damage to our image, I think we achieved more from this war than the other side. Yes, we've had tremendous problems explaining this, because perceptions are created by negative snapshots rather than the more panoramic footage of all our achievements." "Interview: Maj. Gen. Benjamin Gantz," 38.

strategy was lost. Even Israeli commentary promoting the IDF's achievements built upon the same mind-numbing narrative of meaningless destruction. For example, here is how one Israeli journalist describes the war's outcome:

> Two-thirds of Lebanon lies in ruins. Major infrastructure was knocked out of commission. Bases, depots, headquarters, banks and financial institutions were destroyed. Most of Hezbollah's command centers were reduced to rubble. A million people were driven from their homes, and a quarter of a million scrambled to leave the country. With statistics like these, Nasrallah needs a healthy dose of chutzpah to get up in front of a crowd of hundreds of thousands and pass himself off as a hero and a savior.[18]

Two-thirds of Lebanon? No wonder that the UN Commission of Inquiry "saw" a country "destroyed" when it visited Lebanon, stating that "housing, water facilities, schools, medical facilities, numerous mosques and churches, TV and radio transmission stations, historical, archaeological and cultural sites . . . suffered *massive damage* . . . [and that] agriculture and tourism were particularly hit." (emphasis added)[19]

No wonder as well that the commission could write that Lebanon's economic infrastructure was intentionally targeted, suggesting not only an Israeli intent to ruin Lebanon but also that everything that was damaged, no matter how slight or peripheral, was actually destroyed and intentionally so.[20] No wonder because in spite of Israel's soothing reassurances of compliance with the Geneva protocols and legality in focusing on the difficult Hezbollah military target, Israeli leaders also issued threats suggesting a concealed agenda and intention to destroy Lebanon as a country. "Lebanon is responsible and Lebanon will bear the consequences" of Hezbollah's actions, Prime Minister Olmert declared on the first day of the campaign.[21] Halutz

---

[18] Yoel Marcus, "One leader with an agenda," *Haaretz*, 26 September 2006, http://www.haaretz.com/hasen/objects/pages/PrintArticleEn.jhtml?itemNo=766887.

[19] UN, "Report of the Commission of Inquiry," 4, 26.

[20] Ibid.

[21] Israeli MFA, "PM Olmert: Lebanon is responsible and will bear the consequences." Halutz also warned that the air strikes were aimed at sending a "message" to Lebanese officials to stop Hezbollah. Erlanger, "Israel Vowing to Rout Hezbollah"; and CNN, "Israel authorizes 'severe' response to abductions," 12 July 2006, 0227 GMT, http://www.cnn.com/2006/WORLD/meast/07/12/mideast/.

warned that the Israeli assault would "turn back the clock in Lebanon by 20 years."[22] A high-ranking IAF officer told reporters that Halutz had ordered the military to destroy 10 buildings in Beirut in retaliation for every rocket strike on Haifa.[23]

Israel signaled from the very beginning of Operation Change of Direction—through repeated attacks on bridges, in attacks on Lebanon's airport and ports, in attacking "buildings" in south Beirut for 23 of 34 days of the conflict—that it had a secondary agenda, as Prime Minister Olmert referred to it, of exerting political "leverage" over Lebanon.[24] Israel on the one hand was carefully calibrating its attacks and seeking to minimize civilian harm in limited war to achieve not just military results but long-term political benefits, while on the other hand it was simultaneously pursuing an intentionally punishing and destructive political campaign. Clearly Israel wanted to bring the war "home" to the Lebanese government and the people of Beirut. If Israel lost the war of narratives, it was not solely because Hezbollah hid among civilians, or even because Israel had a clumsy information campaign.

How then can we understand the Lebanon war beyond Israel's dual objectives, beyond its clumsiness, beyond Hezbollah's perfidy, and beyond an international community that was indeed predisposed toward being stacked up against Israel? "Nations fight in the real world, not in ones where they can set the rules for war or perceptual standards," Anthony Cordesman writes.[25]

---

[22] AP (Beirut), "Heavy clashes in southern Lebanon as Hezbollah announces capture of two Israeli soldiers." "The Lebanese government, which allowed Hezbollah to commit an act of war against Israel, will pay a heavy price," Justice Minister Haim Ramon also warned. AFP (Beirut), "Israel bombs Beirut airport, 27 killed in raids," 13 July 2006, 0614 GMT. A retired Israeli army colonel was quoted in the *Washington Post* as saying that the goal of Israel's military campaign was also to "create a rift between the Lebanese population and Hezbollah supporters." The message to Lebanon's elite, he said, "If you want your air conditioning to work and if you want to be able to fly to Paris for shopping, you must pull your head out of the sand and take action toward shutting down Hezbollah-land." Gordon, "Air Power Won't Do It."

[23] Yaakov Katz, "High-ranking officer: Halutz ordered retaliation policy," *Jerusalem Post*, 24 July 2006. IDF spokesmen vigorously denied any such objective, though there were authoritative reports and rumors that 10 buildings were hit in south Beirut on 13 July.

[24] Information based upon an attack and target database compiled by the author and Matthew McKinzie. The dates where no Hezbollah attacks occurred in the Beirut southern suburbs were 17, 21, 26–28, 30–31 July, 1–2, and 8 August. On 12 July, only the Beirut International Airport was bombed.

[25] Cordesman, "Preliminary 'Lessons'," 13.

In the real world, Israel fought against an opponent that not only defied the standards of conventional war making, but one that also proved to be sophisticated and prepared. Israel on some level understood Hezbollah's nature—something had to have sunk in with the selection of all of those civilian buildings and homes as Hezbollah assets—and yet Israel pursued a strategy to defeat Hezbollah in an old-fashioned and wrong-headed way.

Ultimately then, the characterization of the 2006 war as one of narratives or one big misunderstanding not only disobligates Israel of self-examination for its actual failures of conception and implementation, but also diverts Israel (and by extension, the United States) from the pressing task of getting beyond conventional military approaches to find a more effective way to "fight" terrorism.

An honest assessment of where Israel went wrong necessitates acknowledging from the beginning that the Israeli political leadership had many valid reasons to want to use the airpower tools associated with strategic attack and long-range strike. First, an "airpower"-centric approach best countered the enemy's strengths, particularly given how embedded Hezbollah was in Lebanese civil society and how much it had built up its basic capabilities north of the Litani River (and thus out of the reach of Israeli ground forces). Second, the existing conception of conventional ground combat, attrition, and occupation prevalent in the IDF was out of synch with either the nature of the enemy or the level of commitment Israeli leaders (and, in their view, the Israeli public) were willing to make. Third, the "airpower" decision was made easier if not de facto by the stark reality that the ground forces were not prepared to mount the very campaign they were promoting.

In his January 2007 letter of resignation to Prime Minister Olmert, Lt Gen Dan Halutz wrote: "One of the main things the [internal] investigations [of the 2006 war] taught us was that the military establishment is profoundly affected by long term processes. At times the effect is unnoticed and we are unaware of its full consequences. These processes affect the Israeli society in general and the capabilities of the military in particular."[26]

---

[26] IDF Spokesman's Office, "Dan Halutz' letter of resignation."

What were those long-term processes Halutz referred to and how had they influenced Israeli society, governmental decision making, and IDF strategy? Some were organizational and priorities-based, focusing more effort on Israel's hunt for high-value terrorist targets and the small-unit actions associated with the Palestinian challenges in the West Bank and Gaza, with the ground forces division, particularly in the north, receiving fewer resources.[27] Others were doctrinal and conceptual, particularly in the embrace of an "effects-based" operations mind-set and what IDF theorists call "cognitive" objectives rather than conventional approaches of attrition and "destroying" the enemy. Embrace of these long-term processes, some say, led to the "aerial arrogance" on the part of many senior IDF officers.[28]

To equate an effects-based approach with aerial arrogance is a mistake. But if one accepts that Israel had indeed adopted a new effects-based doctrine since 2000 to fight terrorism, the most important questions are how did the IDF implement it, and did it make the right choices? Like the United States in the global war on terror, Israeli leaders argue that they are fighting a "new" and different kind of enemy—a state within a state, a well-armed terrorist/guerrilla force shielded by the civilian population—and yet when the time for action came in 2006, the IDF designed the most conventional of wars built from the assumption that Hezbollah could be defeated, even eliminated, through some level of attrition and destruction. Somewhere in its recesses, Israel knew that Hezbollah was well armed and that it was a force with deep roots and enormous popular support in southern Lebanon, but it constantly intoned for domes-

---

[27] Organizational changes in the IDF from the 2000 withdrawal assigned greater responsibility (including command responsibilities) in both the General Staff and the Ground Forces Command. This was done at the expense of both Northern Command and the army Corps commands. Many of these organizational changes were done to restructure the IDF to "fight" in the Gaza and West Bank, where larger unit actions weren't perceived as needed.

[28] For instance, retired Maj Gen Amiram Levin, who wrote a report about the Northern Command's performance, pointed to the new doctrine, which he said "had a crucial contribution to the flaws exposed during the war against Hezbollah." He called effects-based operations "fundamentally wrong," saying it could not have succeeded and should not have been implemented. Alon Ben-David (Tel Aviv), "Debriefing teams brand IDF doctrine 'completely wrong'," *Jane's Defence Weekly*, 3 January 2007.

tic consumption and external propaganda that Hezbollah was weak, had no Lebanese support, and was losing and would lose. In short, Israel just could not seem to get away from seeing and then fighting Hezbollah in old ways.

In the last 24 hours of the campaign before the 14 August cease-fire, when the IAF attacked eight gas stations in southern Lebanon, pure punishment took over from an effects-based conception.[29] In the case of the gas stations and the blistering use of thousands of submunitions-dispensing weapons—"cluster bombs"—in the final 72 hours, some in Israel no doubt thought that Hezbollah's regeneration could be delayed and undermined; or if the cease-fire collapsed, that the cumulative effect of depletion of resources and obstacles to movement would accrue military advantages for the IDF. The same kind of thinking must have been applied to the accumulation of destroyed roads and bridges throughout northern Lebanon and the Bekaa Valley, that somehow movements and imports were being slowed or even stopped, and that the IDF was directly benefiting.

This is the most conventional of approaches, with each individual object justified for its legality and military importance, almost divorced from the overall campaign objective and desired strategic outcome. The assumption is that if the target is meticulously attacked, if the unit is defeated, if another combatant is killed, a connection will magically and naturally be made to the broader political objectives of the war. Now Israeli political leaders and military types hail their success in eliminating Hezbollah's long-range rocket threat, killing more than 600 Hezbollah fighters, setting back Hezbollah's military capabilities and infrastructure "two years," dislodging Hezbollah from southern Lebanon, demonstrating that Israel is no longer hesitant to respond to individual provocations, and creating a high "price tag" for anyone who attacks Israel.

[29] IDF, "Summary of IDF operations in southern Lebanon in the past 24 hours (prior to ceasefire [sic]), Monday 14/08/2006 14:40," [14 August 2006], http://www1.idf.il/DOVER/site/mainpage.asp?sl=EN&id=7&docid=56700&Pos=1&last=1&bScope=True.

Though Hezbollah never "defeated" Israel on the battlefield, because of Israel's bifurcated and destructive campaign waged against the people and the nation of Lebanon, Hezbollah was able to win the hearts and minds of many. Hezbollah's narrative was not only that Lebanese civilians were hit while only a few of its fighters were killed, but also that it survived the best that Israel could throw at it, and that it (and not Beirut and not Arab governments) uniquely stood up to Israel and achieved victory. Hezbollah's political strengthening in the face of massive Israeli attack—and the celebrations that rippled through the Arab world that Israel was thwarted (just as the United States has been in Iraq)—came from their "conventional" defeat.

When Israel made the decision to respond to Hezbollah on 12 July, beyond the immediate attacks on the border observation posts and nearby Hezbollah fighters and activity, beyond even attacks on the fixed rocket infrastructure and the 34-minute operation against Hezbollah's long-range force (whatever it was), did anyone in the IDF or Israeli leadership really believe their own articulation that attacks on a handful of Litani and Zahrani River bridges—even key choke points—would prevent Hezbollah from evacuating or hiding the kidnapped soldiers? When Israel bombed Beirut International Airport in the first 24 hours, with the public justification that it was further impeding the export of the soldiers or the import of military materiel, did anyone in the command structure really believe that? Did anyone in the IDF or the Israeli government think that the public or the international community would believe and accept these contrived explanations?

A fair, non-antiairpower assessment of the 2006 Israel-Hezbollah war is that Israel, in recognition of limited war and fully aware of its pessimistic prospects in the local and international struggle for hearts and minds, chose to just destroy as much as it could in as short a period of time as possible to at least set Hezbollah back and buy time for its security. Since security is the ultimate objective, at some point someone should have said "enough already" for what was being achieved. Someone should have said—and even recognized—that the accumulation of buildings and bridges and destroyed homes in villages in the south and in the Bekaa after awhile begins to tell a different story; and that story, if it is not the intent, is one to be avoided. That narrative is that "we" in the West, with all of our intelligence, drones, and technological and conventional military superiority, do everything with complete clarity and intention; that we are the ones who have no regard for civil society or civilians, particularly Muslims: we even destroy their gas stations. Given that "they" do not have F-16s to attack us with, they are reduced to using rockets, or suicide bombers, or airliners to strike back.

There is an argument to be made that probably no matter what Israel bombed, the Jewish state would have still provoked the hatred of Hezbollah sympathizers and much of the Lebanese and Arab world. But Israel could also have, and should have, pursued a different approach. Since Israel was not going to "win" the war against Hezbollah through statistical accumulation and was not going to fight Hezbollah to some total war victory, an equal objective had to be not only creating a stronger deterrent but also creating some degree of sympathy and support for Israel's right to defend itself, even if in doing so, Israel had to attack into another nation. Had Israel limited its attacks as much as possible to Hezbollah, had it concentrated its resources on military forces and capabilities in the south and the Bekaa, had it pursued a campaign more attuned to emerging humanitarian and international norms regarding the use of cluster bombs, had Israel shown greater transparency in describing what it was doing and the intelligence basis for its decisions, had Israel fought a war truer to its own political intuition about what was possible in the first place with an organization like Hezbollah, it might have—might have—bought more time and engendered greater sympathy and support, thus not only achieving more militarily, but also in the fundamental long-term objective of counterterrorism: not creating even more enemies tomorrow.

The "failure" of airpower in the 2006 Israel-Hezbollah war was not that it promised too much or that it did not deliver. It was instead a grand strategic failure in the application of force against terrorism. The war demonstrates and justifies a clear transition needed from conventional to wholly new modes of warfare required for counterterrorism in the future. Israel certainly failed to "tell" its airpower (and military) story effectively.

But to do so would have demanded that it understood the very flexibility of the instrument it was wielding, and that it had reconciled its competing impulses to seek "effects" while also exacting punishment that undermined the very agility. The failure then is that an instrument that has now been proven uniquely discriminating and reliable remains not only haunted by decades-old images of inhumanity, but also that it is held back and undermined by archaic and false conceptions of ground war preeminence and gentleness.

Appendix A

Israeli Order of
Battle and Dramatis Personae

Ehud Olmert, prime minister

Shimon Peres, vice premier/deputy prime minister

Tzipi Livni, deputy prime minister and minister of foreign affairs

Amir Peretz, deputy prime minister and minister of defense

Avraham Hirchson, minister of finance

Avi Dichter, minister of internal security/public security

Haim Ramon, minister of justice

Shaul Mofaz, minister of transportation

Israeli Security Cabinet (mid-2006)[1]

Ex-Officio	By Party Affiliation
Prime Minister	Vice Premier (Kadima)
Defense Minister	Minister of Transportation (Kadima)
Finance Minister	Minister of National Infrastructure (Labor:
Foreign Minister	Binyamin [Fouad] Ben-Eliezer)
Internal Security Minister	**By Invitation**
Justice Minister	Chief of IDF General Staff
	Israeli intelligence chiefs (Shin Bet and Mossad)

---

[1] The Security Cabinet is convened in emergencies to make decisions that cannot wait for regular meetings. Some of the 12 members convened by Prime Minister Olmert are ex-officio, and others are representatives of the parties in the ruling coalition. The chiefs of the IDF and the intelligence services also sit in the Security Cabinet.

Ministry of Defense

Maj Gen Gabi Ashkenazi, director-general, minister of defense (later chief of staff, replacing Halutz in January 2007)

Maj Gen Yitzhak Gershon, commander, Home Front Command

Israeli Defense Forces General Staff

Lt Gen Dan Halutz, chief of staff[2]

Maj Gen Moshe Kaplinsky, deputy chief of staff (assigned to manage the war and supplant Adam in Northern Command)

Maj Gen Gadi Eisenkot, head of Operations Directorate (later commander of Northern Command, replacing Adam)

Brig Gen Tal Russo, head of Special Operations (later head of Operations Directorate, replacing Eisenkot)

Maj Gen Yitzhak Harel, head of Planning Directorate

Maj Gen Ido Nehushtan, head of Planning Directorate

Brig Gen Yuval Halamish, chief IDF intelligence officer

Maj Gen Amos Yadlin, director, Directorate for Military Intelligence (DMI)

Brig Gen Yossi Baidatz, head of Research, DMI

IDF Commands and Services

Maj Gen Benjamin Gantz, commander of the IDF Army Headquarters

Maj Gen Eliezer Shkedy, commander of the IDF Air Force Headquarters

Maj Gen David Ben Ba'ashat, commander of the IDF Navy Headquarters

Brig Gen Amir Eshel, chief of staff, Israel Air Force (IAF)

Brig Gen Rami Shmueli, director of IAF Intelligence

---

[2] Appointed 1 June 2005 by Prime Minister Ariel Sharon, resigned on 16 January 2007.

Northern Command

Maj Gen Udi Adam, commander (headquarters in Safed (Zefat)[3]

Maj Gen Eyal Ben-Reuven, deputy commander (stepped down after not being promoted)

Brig Gen Shuki Shacur, deputy commander

Brig Gen Alon Friedman, chief of staff

Col Boaz Cohen, Operations chief (placed on leave from the military and announced his resignation in November 2006)

Maj Gen Yiftah Ron-Tal, former commander of the Ground Forces Command and a reserve officer on retirement leave and still drawing an army salary before being dismissed by Halutz[4]

Major Units

Division 91 (Galilee Division or Galil formation), HQ Biranit base, Israel. Brig Gen Gal Hirsch, division commander.[5]

- Armored Brigade 7 (7th Armored Brigade)—normally assigned to the 36th Division in the Golan; involved in the battle of Bint Jbeil, 24 July; controlled the Maroun al-Ras and Bint Jbeil areas at the cease-fire.

  Col Amnon Eshel, brigade commander (promotion suspended for two years after he publicly criticized superior officer Hirsch in September 2006).

- 35th Paratrooper (Parachute) Brigade—reportedly controlled the western sector at the cease-fire.

  Col Hagai Mordechai, brigade commander

  o Battalion 101—fought in Aiyt a-Shab, Lt Col Ariel Yohanon, battalion commander.

---

[3] Announced his retirement in mid-September 2006 and retired in October 2006.

[4] Ron-Tal said that the IDF "had plans for a wide-scale ground operation in southern Lebanon," but that the national leadership did not allow the army to "operate in accordance with those plans and took a hesitant course of action"; Ryan R. Jones, "Israeli General: We Did Not Win Lebanon War," *All Headline News*, 4 October 2006.

[5] Resigned in mid-November 2006 after report by Maj Gen Doron Almog concluded that he was responsible for the kidnapping of two IDF soldiers.

- Givati Infantry Brigade—organized into three main battalions: Shaked, Tzabar, and Rotem, in addition to associated reconnaissance, engineering, and other units. Col Yoel Streek, brigade commander.

- Golani Infantry Brigade (Brigade 1)—reported in Mais al Jabal on 4 August; reported deployed north of Bint Jbeil at the cease-fire. Col Tamir Yadai, brigade commander.[6]

  o Battalion 12, Barak battalion.

  o Battalion 13, Gideon battalion.

  o Battalion 51, "First Breachers" battalion, Merkava tanks—fought at Bint Jbeil and lost eight soldiers, Lt Col Yaniv Asor, battalion commander.

  o Egoz reconnaissance unit (company), Col Mordechai Kahane, commander.

- Brigade 300—served in the western sector. Col Chen Livni, commander. (Livni was the regional brigade commander at the time of the abduction in the North; Col Ofek Buhris, the former division coordinator for special operations in Lebanon, took over during the war).

- Brigade 769, Col Raviv Nir, brigade commander.

- Brigade 609, Alexandroni Brigade—operated in the western sector, crossed the border on the way to Ras al Bayyadah on the coast, through Shama; reported in Majdal Zoun on 4 August; Bayyadah on 6 August. Col Shlomi Cohen, brigade commander.

- Brigade 188 ("Barak") Armored Corps brigade—normally assigned to the 36th Division in the Golan; joined the fighting 2 August, operating under Brigade 609 in Rajmin; reported in the area south of the Nahal brigade at the cease-fire (included 74th Battalion).

---

[6] According to the IDF, the Golani Brigade is comprised of a number of battalions including Battalion 12, Battalion 13, Battalion 51, and the Gadsar reconnaissance battalion. It also includes the special Egoz counterterror battalion. See http://www1 .idf.il/DOVER/site/mainpage.asp?sl=EN&id=7&docid=54891.EN.

Division 162 ("Steel Formation" armored division), from Central Command—conducted assault on the Wadi Saluki and al-Ghandouriyeh; reportedly lost 12 soldiers overall. Brig Gen Guy Tzur, division commander.

- Armored Brigade 401—spent 36 hours in Lebanon over the weekend of 29–30 July in Kfar Kila, al-Adayseh, and al-Taybeh; located at Markaba on 4 August; reported at the Wadi Saluki on 12 August. Col Moti Kidor, brigade commander.

- Nahal Infantry (Mechanized) Brigade, HQ Beit Leed, Israel—transferred from Gaza; deployed to the high ground outside al-Ghandouriyeh and Froun to provide cover for armor; reported at the Wadi Saluki before the 401st Brigade; reportedly controlled the al-Taybeh area at the ceasefire. Col Roni Numa, brigade commander (included Battalion 931).

Armored reserve division—division fought on the eastern front of Lebanon, mainly during the last week of the war. Brig Gen Erez Zuckerman, division commander (included armored brigade).

Utzbat Haesh reserve infantry (paratrooper) division—from Central Command (fought only at the end of the war, crossing the border on August 8 towards Debel, where nine soldiers were killed by antitank missiles)[7] Brig Gen Eyal Eisenberg, division commander.

Northern Command artillery division—Lt Col Avi Mano, commander of the Keren artillery battalion, told the *Jerusalem Post* that his cannons fired 3,000 shells at Bint Jbeil in the 23–25 July time frame.[8]

---

[7] Josh Brannon, "What happened at the 'house of death'?" *Jerusalem Post*, 1 November 2006, http://www.jpost.com/servlet/Satellite?pagename=JPost%2FJPArticle%2FShowFull&cid=1161811247463.

[8] Yaakov Katz, "Army seals off Hezbollah stronghold of Bint Jbail," *Jerusalem Post*, 25 July 2006.

Special Operations Units

During the conflict, the IDF's special forces—Sayeret Matkal of AMAN, the IAF's Shaldag unit, and the Israel Navy's (IN) Shayetet 13 commandos—operated deep inside Lebanese territory.[9]

- Sayeret Matkal general headquarters reconnaissance unit, DMI/AMAN[10]

- Shayetet 13 Navy Commandos

- Shaldag IAF unit

- Yael special purpose engineering unit

---

[9] Alon Ben-David (Tel Aviv), "Israel Reflects—New Model Army?" *Jane's Defence Weekly*, 11 October 2006.

[10] Sayeret Maglan ("Ibis" in Hebrew) specializes in laser target designation for the IAF and employs long-range AntiTank Guided Missiles (ATGM).

Appendix B

Chronology

Day 1: Wednesday, 12 July

In the early morning, Hezbollah fires rockets and mortars into northern Israel simultaneous with an incursion near Zar'it that results in an ambush of a Division 91 border patrol. Three Israeli Defense Force (IDF) soldiers are killed and two are captured and taken back into southern Lebanon. Israeli forces implement "Hannibal" emergency procedures,[1] carrying out over 100 air attacks against Hezbollah positions in southern Lebanon and attacking 17 targets including Hezbollah "posts" and three bridges in two major waves of attacks at about 10:20 a.m. and 4:00 p.m.[2] Before noon, an Israeli armored unit enters Lebanon for the first time since 2000 to pursue the Hezbollah kidnappers. An Israeli tank is destroyed by an implanted explosive and four more IDF soldiers are killed. An eighth soldier is killed in subsequent clashes relating to the rescue.

In the afternoon, Hezbollah continues cross-border attacks, again reportedly firing rockets and mortars at Shlomi, at IDF outposts in the Shebaa Farms area, at Mount Meron, and engaging in sniper fire against Israeli positions at Rosh Hanikra on the coast. A total of 60 rockets are fired on 12 July.[3] A Hezbollah fighter is shot and killed trying to infiltrate into Israel at the Oranit outpost and another is killed trying to infiltrate the Biranit base.[4]

---

[1] IDF War Log, "First day of war, 12 July 2006," http://www.plint.us/idf/en.html.

[2] IDF, "Attacks on Israel from Lebanese Territory, Wednesday 12/07/2006 12:02," http://www1.idf.il/DOVER/site/mainpage.asp?sl=EN&id=7&docid=54183.EN.

[3] One source says Hezbollah conducted a total of six rocket attacks on 12 July. See Israel *Science and Technology* Homepage, "Chronology of Rocket Attacks on Israel, by Israel National News (INN)," 4 August 2006, http://www.science.co.il/arab-israeli-conflict/articles/INN-2006-08-04.asp.

[4] "Fighting on two fronts," *Jerusalem Post*, 13 July 2006, 1.

In the evening, the IDF issues a warning to United Nations Interim Forces in Lebanon (UNIFIL) that any person—including UN personnel—moving close to the Blue Line would be shot at.

Israeli Prime Minister (PM) Ehud Olmert describes Hezbollah's action on the border as "an act of war" by the state of Lebanon, saying that Israel would make the country pay a "heavy price."

"This was an act of war without any provocation on the sovereign territory—about which there is no dispute—of the State of Israel," Olmert says. "This morning's events were not a terrorist attack, but the action of a sovereign state that attacked Israel for no reason and without provocation. The Lebanese government, of which Hezbollah is a member, is trying to undermine regional stability. Lebanon is responsible and Lebanon will bear the consequences of its actions."[5]

Israeli Foreign Minister Livni adds: "Hezbollah is a terrorist organization, which is part of the Lebanese government. The international community, including the UN Security Council, has demanded, repeatedly, that the government of Lebanon dismantle Hezbollah. Lebanon has failed to act and today's aggression is the result."

Hezbollah says it will release the prisoners if Israel frees Lebanese prisoners held in Israeli jails. "Fulfilling its pledge to liberate the prisoners and detainees, the Islamic Resistance . . . captured two Israeli soldiers at the border with occupied Palestine," a Hezbollah statement says.

Hassan Nasrallah says: "You wanted open warfare, and we are going into open warfare. We are ready for it, a war on every level. To Haifa, and, believe me, to beyond Haifa, and to beyond Haifa. Not only will we be paying a price. Not only will our houses be destroyed. Not only will our children be killed. Not only will our people be displaced."

The Lebanese Council of Ministers issues a statement:

> The Lebanese government was not aware nor does it bear the responsibility and it disavows the events that have happened and are happening

---

[5] Prime Minister (PM) Olmert's remarks at his press conference with Japanese PM Junichiro Koizum. [12 July 2006].

along the international border. And it condemns strongly the Israeli aggression which has targeted and is targeting the vital facilities and the civilians. Hence the government calls for an urgent session of the UN Security Council to deal with those aggressions and it expresses its readiness to negotiate through the UN and third parties to deal with the events which took place and what resulted from them and the reasons behind them.

An Israeli Political-Security Cabinet meeting is held at 6 p.m. to discuss the Israeli response. The communiqué reads in part: "Israel views the sovereign Lebanese Government as responsible for the action that originated on its soil and for the return of the abducted soldiers to Israel. Israel demands that the Lebanese Government implement *UN Security Council Resolution 1559.*"

Lt Gen Dan Halutz, IDF chief of staff, is quoted in the media as saying: "If the soldiers are not returned, we will turn Lebanon's clock back 20 years."

"This affair is between Israel and the state of Lebanon," Maj Gen Udi Adam, commander of Israel's Northern Command says. "Where to attack? Once it is inside Lebanon, everything is legitimate—not just southern Lebanon, not just the line of Hezbollah posts."

US secretary of state Condoleezza Rice says Syria has a "special responsibility" for the Lebanese situation.

UN secretary-general (SG) Kofi Annan condemns the Hezbollah attack, calls for the return of the Israeli soldiers, and criticizes Israeli attack.

Lebanon reports five civilian casualties on 12 July and says that a bomb fell next to the Tajalli church in Rmeish town. A Lebanese TV staffer is also reported injured after an Israeli air raid on al-Aaishiyeh-Jarmaq.[6]

---

[6] "Day 1 of the Israeli war on Lebanon," 12 July 2006, http://www.lebanonlivenews .com/Day1.htm.

Amnesty International says: "Within the first 24 hours Israeli attacks killed at least 38 civilians in their homes, many of them children."[7]

Day 2: Thursday, 13 July

Israeli aircraft strike into Beirut for the first time, an escalation that prompts speculation of full-scale war. Israeli aircraft bomb the runways at Beirut's Rafiq Hariri International Airport, forcing flights to divert to Cyprus and other locations and closing the airport.

Air strikes in south Lebanon kill at least 44 civilians and wound 100 people, according to press reports.

Israel announces an air and sea blockade of Lebanon and says that Hezbollah will not be allowed to return to its former position along the border.

Hezbollah says it is retaliating for Israeli "massacres" and fires rockets at Nahariya in northern Israel, killing one.[8] Over the course of the day, Hezbollah fires 125 rockets into northern Israel, killing two civilians, one in Nahariya and one in Safed, and wounding about 100 overall.[9] As evening approaches, a Hezbollah-fired rocket hits Israel's third-largest city, Haifa.

Hezbollah issues an official statement: "As part of its continued retaliation to the Zionist aggression, the Islamic Resistance fired dozens of Grad rockets at 2:30 p.m. (1130 GMT) on the Israeli military command base in Safed."

The Lebanese Council of Ministers issues a second statement, condemning Israeli "aggression" and "salutes the souls of the martyrs and the resilience of the Lebanese and their determination to strengthen their solidarity and preserve their unity

---

[7] Amnesty International, Israel/Lebanon, "Out of all proportion—civilians bear the brunt of the war," MDE 02/033/2006, 21 November 2006.

[8] Reuters, "Chronology—Six months of rising Mideast tensions," 13 July 2006 9:44:18 a.m.

[9] Israel *Science and Technology* Homepage, "Chronology." IDF intelligence also said that 125 rockets were fired on 13 July.

which is an essential factor in facing aggression and protecting national concord."

Speaking in Germany, Pres. George W. Bush says Israel has the right to defend itself and says that Syria "needs to be held to account" for supporting Hezbollah.

The British Broadcasting Corporation (BBC) reports of "significant numbers of civilian casualties in Lebanese towns and villages close to Israeli targets, with at least 35 people reported killed.[10] *The Daily Star* (Lebanon) and Reuters report "at least 44 civilians" killed in air strikes across Lebanon, and 100 wounded.[11] Reuters later reports 52 civilians killed, "including more than 15 children" in Lebanon.[12]

Russia condemns the "disproportionate" use of force by Israel. "One cannot justify the continued destruction by Israel of the civilian infrastructure in Lebanon . . . with the disproportionate use of force in which the civilian population suffers," the foreign ministry says in a statement.

France and Italy also condemn Israel's "disproportionate" use of force.

The United Kingdom urges Israel to keep its military action in southern Lebanon "proportionate."

The Arab League announces that Arab foreign ministers would meet in Cairo on Saturday to discuss Israeli attacks on Lebanon and the Palestinian territories.

The UN Security Council convenes an emergency meeting at the request of the Lebanese government, which calls on the council to "adopt a complete and immediate position for a cease-fire." A draft resolution is introduced by Qatar on behalf of the Arab

---

[10] BBC News: "Day-by-day: Lebanon crisis—week one," http://news.bbc.co.uk/2/hi/middle_east/5179434.stm.

[11] Reuters, "Chronology"; and "July War 2006 Timeline," *Daily Star*, http://www.dailystar.com.lb/July_War06.asp.

[12] Reuters (Beirut), "Israel kills 52 civilians, including more than 15 children, in Lebanon," 13 July 2006, http://www.dawn.com/2006/07/13/welcome.htm.

Group that calls for the immediate and unconditional release of the two Israeli soldiers and calls for Israel to halt its "disproportionate use of force." Calling the draft "unbalanced and inflammatory," US ambassador to the UN, John Bolton, says the resolution "placed demands on one side of the Middle East conflict but not the other." The United States vetoes passage.

The UN announces that a three-person team of envoys would head to the region on behalf of the secretary-general to assess the situation.

The IDF says on 13 July that it has attacked about 80 targets, including 28 Hezbollah "organization headquarters, bases, posts, and outposts"; 17 access routes and bridges; and 28 "launching grounds, weapon warehouses, and Hezbollah centers."[13] The IDF releases drone and/or gun camera video showing a Hezbollah launcher firing 11 rockets in quick succession before it is destroyed.[14]

In the afternoon, the IDF drops leaflets on south Beirut urging residents to stay away from Hezbollah offices and buildings. The IDF attacks the building of Al-Manar TV in south Beirut and a transmission tower in Baalbek.[15] The Committee to Protect Journalists calls on Israel to explain its attacks on Al-Manar TV.[16]

The IDF attacks operational Hezbollah headquarters in southern Lebanon northwest of Ya'atar.[17]

In the afternoon, the IDF says it attacked two military airfields in Qulayaat and Riyaq.[18]

---

[13] IDF War Log; and IDF, "The IDF Operates Against Targets in Lebanon," n.d. (13 July 2006), http://www1.idf.il/DOVER/site/mainpage.asp?sl=EN&id=7&docid=54300.EN.

[14] IDF, "The IDF Operates."

[15] IDF, ITIC/CSS, "Hezbollah terrorist attack on Israeli's northern border: eight IDF soldiers killed and two abducted (Updated to July 13, afternoon)."

[16] Committee to Protect Journalists (New York), press release, "Lebanon: Israeli forces strike Al-Manar TV facilities," 13 July 2006.

[17] IDF, "The IDF Attacks Targets in Southern Lebanon," n.d. (13 July 2006), http://www1.idf.il/DOVER/site/mainpage.asp?sl=EN&id=7&docid=54274.EN; and IDF, "The IDF Operates."

[18] IDF, "Summary of IDF Attacks in Lebanon During the Past Day," n.d. (14 July 2006), http://www1.idf.il/DOVER/site/mainpage.asp?sl=EN&id=7&docid=54349.EN.

On the second day of the war, according to various postwar reports, Israel hits 59 of Hezbollah's permanent rocket launchers in a "34-minute" operation.

On the night of 13 July, the IAF attacks Hezbollah targets in the Shiite neighborhoods of southern Beirut.[19]

Day 3: Friday, 14 July

Hezbollah leader Hassan Nasrallah, in a dramatic telephone call to Al-Manar television, promises "open war" with Israel after the Hezbollah command compound and his offices are bombed in south Beirut. Celebratory gunfire erupts in the Lebanese capital and drivers honk their horns after Nasrallah's statement.

Hezbollah fires 103 rockets at Israel, killing two civilians in Meron. Shortly after 8:30 p.m., Hezbollah also fires an antiship cruise missile at the Israeli naval vessel *Hanit* off the coast of Beirut, killing four sailors. The missile is fired from the Ouzai port area of Beirut. Israel accuses the Lebanese army of assisting Hezbollah, specifically in the use of on-shore radar.

Defense Minister Amir Peretz vows to "break" Hezbollah after the first rockets land on Haifa the previous day. "Hezbollah has broken all the rules. So we plan to break the organization," he told reporters.[20]

IDF chief Lt Gen Dan Halutz vows to continue the offensive, saying that Israel wanted to deliver a clear message to "both greater Beirut and Lebanon that they've swallowed a cancer and have to vomit it up, because if they don't their country will pay a very high price."[21]

---

[19] IDF, ITIC/CSS, "Hezbollah terrorist attack on Israel's northern border."

[20] Yaakov Katz, "Israel vows to 'break' Hezbollah as rockets hit Haifa," *Jerusalem Post*, 14 July 2006, http://info.jpost.com/C002/Supplements/CasualtiesOfWar/2006_07_13.html.

[21] Steven Erlanger, "Israel Vows to Crush Militia; Group's Leader is Defiant," *New York Times*, 14 July 2006.

Israeli PM Olmert tells UN Secretary-General Annan that Israel will not accept a cease-fire until Hezbollah rocket attacks stop and Hezbollah is disarmed in accordance with *UNSCR 1559*.

Lebanese Health Minister Mohammad Khalifeh holds a press conference, saying that the death toll had reached at least 73.[22] The Lebanese government tells the UN that 190 have been injured.[23]

The UN Security Council meets and calls for an end to the fighting, saying it is causing the death of innocent civilians. Israel's ambassador to the UN says, "The Lebanese Government must seize the opportunity to wrest their country from the grips of terror."

President Bush telephones Lebanese PM Fouad Siniora and assures him he is pressing Israel to "contain the damage" to Lebanon and avoid civilian casualties. Asked whether President Bush had agreed to a request from the Lebanese PM that he rein in the Israelis, White House spokesman Tony Snow says: "The president is not going to make military decisions for Israel." Snow tells reporters that Bush believes that the Israelis have the right to defend themselves, but also that they should avoid civilian casualties and damage.

French president Jacques Chirac calls the Israeli air attacks "completely disproportionate."

UN High Commissioner for Human Rights Louise Arbour urges both sides to refrain from attacking civilian targets.

The Vatican strongly deplores Israel's attacks on Lebanon, saying they are "an attack" on a sovereign and free nation.

Saudi Arabia says that Hezbollah's actions were "not legitimate" and says that the "elements" inside Lebanon bear sole respon-

---

[22] Meris Lutz, "Death toll in onslaught mounts as 'barbaric' attacks continue; Army troops, Medics scramble to supply southern villages," *Daily Star* (Lebanon), 15 July 2006.

[23] UN, identical letters dated 14 July 2006 from the Charge d'affaires of the Permanent Mission of Lebanon to the United Nations addressed to the secretary-general and the president of the Security Council, A/60/940–S/2006/528, 17 July 2006.

sibility for the violence with Israel. Jordan and Egypt also criticize Hezbollah. President Bush had reportedly called on the Sunni governments to speak out.

Iranian president Mahmoud Ahmadinejad says an Israeli strike on Syria would be considered an attack on the whole Islamic world and would provoke a "fierce response."

Israeli Foreign Ministry spokesman Mark Regev says that Israel had information that Hezbollah guerrillas were trying to move the kidnapped soldiers to Iran.[24]

Maj Gen Gadi Eizenkot, head of the IDF Operations Directorate, says that "Lebanese civilians are not targets of IDF activities" and that Israeli forces are "bombarding known locations, only against terror targets and only with precise weapons."[25]

The IDF announces that it had struck 18 targets overnight,[26] and that it struck the south Beirut "security square" headquarters of Hezbollah, the permanent base of Hassan Nasrallah and Hezbollah senior leaders, as well as "bridges and access routes at the site."[27]

IDF air and naval forces attack three gasoline stations in southern Lebanon, the IDF says "as part of the effort to damage the Lebanese infrastructure that works to support terror activity."[28]

The Ministry of Foreign Affairs (MFA) says that the IDF attacked Hezbollah's "broadcasting compound" in Beirut after the IDF had attacked the Al-Manar TV station building on 13 July. "The compound has for many years served as the main tool for propaganda and incitement by Hezbollah, and has also helped the organization recruit people into its ranks," the MFA says.[29]

---

[24] Katz, "Israel vows to 'break' Hezbollah."

[25] IDF, Head of Operations Directorate: "IDF's Target is Terrorists," Sunday, 16 July 2006, 10:43, http://www1.idf.il/DOVER/site/mainpage.asp?sl=EN&id=7&docid=544 35.EN.

[26] IDF, Summary of IDF Attacks in Lebanon During the Past Day, n.d. (14 July 2006), http://www1.idf.il/DOVER/site/mainpage.asp?sl=EN&id=7&docid=54349.EN.

[27] Ibid.

[28] Ibid.

[29] MFA, "IDF targets Hezbollah's broadcasting compound" (communicated by the IDF spokesman), 14 July 2004, http://www.mfa.gov.il/MFA/Terrorism+Obstacle+to +Peace/Terrorism+from+Lebanon+Hezbollah/IDF+operations+against+Hezbollah+in+ Lebanon+14-Jul-2006.htm.

Press reports state that Israel is also bombing "power stations" after there is a sudden power cut in the Beirut area and Lebanon. Reuters reports that several mobile telephone relay stations were targeted in eastern Lebanon,[30] and cell phones reportedly stop working in the mountains and Bekaa Valley. The main highway connecting Beirut and Damascus is also reported as having been bombed.

The IDF begins a modern PSYOPS campaign, calling Lebanese political and local leaders on their cell phones with a recorded message, urging them to leave their villages immediately and to head north of the Litani River. The messages warn not to travel on motorcycles, vans, or trucks.

The US Department of Defense notifies Congress that it planned to sell up to $210 million in jet fuel to Israel.

Day 4: Saturday, 15 July

Speaking ahead of the G8 meeting in St. Petersburg, Russia, President Bush says it is up to Hezbollah "to lay down its arms and to stop attacking" Israel, urging Syria to put pressure on the organization. Russian president Vladimir Putin is more critical of Israeli bombing, saying that the "use of force should be balanced."

Lebanese Prime Minister Siniora says his country is a "disaster zone" and calls for international assistance to broker an immediate cease-fire to end Israel's offensive.

The news media report dozens killed in Lebanon after Israeli strikes on several convoys of civilians leaving the south of the country. Eighteen people, including nine children, are "burnt alive," the *Agence France-Presse* (*AFP*) says, after a helicopter gunship hits a convoy of families fleeing the south.[31] *Haaretz* reports that Israeli Air Force (IAF) strikes killed at least 27

---

[30] Reuters, "Developments in the Middle East on July 14," 14 July 2006.

[31] AFP (Beirut), "Eighteen civilians burnt alive in Israeli air blitz on Lebanon," 15 July 2006.

Lebanese civilians on Saturday.[32] Overall, some 100 deaths are reported, "according to an AFP tally compiled from medical and official sources," with 266 wounded. Three Hezbollah fighters have now been killed, the AFP says.[33]

Arab League secretary-general (SG) Amr Moussa says the Middle East peace process is dead after an emergency meeting of Arab foreign ministers. He calls on the UN Security Council to tackle the Lebanon crisis.

Hezbollah fires 100 rockets at Israel. After Hezbollah headquarters is destroyed in south Beirut on Friday, Hezbollah supposedly "responds" by firing two barrages of rockets on Tiberias (35 km from the Lebanese border) for the first time, the deepest rockets have landed in Israel since fighting began.[34]

According to UNIFIL, on the morning of 15 July, the IDF announced— via loudspeakers to the residents of Aiyt a-Shab and Marwaheen—that residents should vacate the villages. UNIFIL says it observed a large-scale exodus from the two villages as a result.

The IDF says it continues attacks against "Hezbollah main headquarters" in Beirut, including two buildings used by Hezbollah organization officials.[35] The IDF also reportedly destroys the Beirut office of senior Hamas official Mohammed Nazzal.

Attacks in Baalbek are reported as having destroyed Hezbollah headquarters in the al-'Asayreh neighborhood, the house of Nasrallah's executive deputy Hussayn al-Musawi in al-Ibrahim neighborhood, and the house of council member Sheikh Muhammad Yazbek.

---

[32] Amos Harel and Yoav Stern, "Lebanon police: 15 die in IAF strike on van in south Lebanon," *Haaretz*, 15 July 2006, Last update—15:05, http://www.haaretz.com/hasen/objects/pages/PrintArticleEn.jhtml?itemNo=738611.

[33] AFP (Beirut), "At least 39 killed in Israeli strikes on Lebanon," 15 July 2006.

[34] Yaakov Katz and Amir Mizroch, "Martial law in North as rockets hit Tiberias," *Jerusalem Post*, 16 July 2006, http://info.jpost.com/C002/Supplements/CasualtiesOf War/2006_07_14_1.html.

[35] IDF, "The IDF Attacks Hezbollah Headquarters," Saturday, 15 July 2006, 19:01, http://www1.idf.il/DOVER/site/mainpage.asp?sl=EN&id=7&docid=54383.EN.

The IDF attacks the Hezbollah broadcasting compound in south Beirut for the second time, focusing on Al-Nour radio, located about 300 yards from Al-Manar headquarters.[36]

After Hezbollah's attack on the naval ship *Hanit*, the IDF attacks coastal radar installations and Lebanese "ports." The MFA announces that Israel had attacked "all of the radar stations along the Lebanese coast" after it detected cooperation between the Lebanese military and Hezbollah in the 14 July attack.[37] Israel also accuses Iran of helping fire a missile that damaged an Israeli warship, a charge Iran denies.

A Lebanese army force fires at an Israeli aircraft flying near Lebanon's coast.[38]

Electricity du Liban (EDL) announces it had to halt energy production at the Jiyyeh facility to ensure the safety of its employees and equipment after fuel tanks were attacked on 13 and 15 July. It says that high-voltage lines in Tyre were targeted by Israel, damaging power plants in Zahrani, Zouk, and Deir Ammar and causing a complete blackout in the capital.[39]

Foreign governments make plans to evacuate their citizens from Lebanon.

Day 5: Sunday, 16 July

Hezbollah fires just 43 rockets at Israel. A train depot in Haifa's Shemen Beach area is hit by a Hezbollah rocket just after 9 a.m., killing eight Israeli civilians and wounding more than 20. It is the worst attack on Israel since the fighting started. Israeli PM Ehud Olmert says that the Haifa attack will have "far-reaching consequences."

---

[36] Harel and Stern, "Lebanon police."

[37] MFA, "IDF aerial attack of radar stations along the Lebanese coast," 15 July 2006, http://www.mfa.gov.il/MFA/Terrorism+Obstacle+to+Peace/Terrorism+from+Lebanon+Hezbollah/Summary+of+IDF+operations+against+Hezbollah+in+Lebanon+15-Jul-2006.htm.

[38] IDF War Log, "July 15th 2006."

[39] Nada Bakri, "Israel pounds key Lebanese infrastructure," *Daily Star*, 15 July 2006, http://www.dailystar.com.lb/article.asp?edition_id=1&categ_id=2&article_id=73990#.

Hassan Nasrallah says the battle against Israel is "just at the beginning." He says that Hezbollah is targeting the IDF and would avoid hitting "any Israeli colony or settlement in occupied northern Palestine." He says Hezbollah was justified to attack Haifa because of Israeli targeting of civilians. "Today we had no choice but to reject the pledge we had made to ourselves and proceeded to bomb the city of Haifa," Nasrallah says. "As long as the enemy undertakes its aggression without limits or red lines, we will also respond without limits or red lines."

In an emotional televised address, Lebanese PM Siniora calls for an immediate cease-fire and the end to the "collective punishment" of his country. UN envoys and European Union (EU) foreign policy chief Javier Solana arrive in Beirut to meet with Siniora and begin fact-finding tours.

At the G8 summit meeting in St. Petersburg, Russia, the nations issue a communiqué blaming Hezbollah for the outbreak of violence and calling on Israel to show restraint. The document states that "the immediate crisis results from efforts by extremist forces to destabilize the region and to frustrate the aspirations of the Palestinian, Israeli and Lebanese people for democracy and peace" but stops short of demanding an immediate cease-fire, and criticism of Israel's actions is removed after pressure from the United States and United Kingdom.

The *Jerusalem Post* reports a senior Israeli military official saying Lebanon could be "shut down for years, as long as necessary."[40]

In a Cabinet communiqué, the Israeli government states that "Israel is not fighting Lebanon but the terrorist element there, led by Nasrallah and his cohorts, who have made Lebanon a hostage and created Syrian- and Iranian-sponsored terrorist enclaves of murder."

Iran's supreme leader, Ayatollah Ali Khamenei, warns that Hezbollah will never disarm. Iran warns Israel that any attack on Syria will incur "unimaginable losses."

IAF headquarters command head Maj Gen Eliezer Shkedy says that Israel has conducted over 1,000 fighter and over 350 at-

---

[40] "Lebanon can be shut down for years," *Jerusalem Post*, 16 July 2006.

tack helicopter missions. "The country of Lebanon is a sovereign country and in our point of view all actions that emanate from its domain are the responsibility of those who stand at the head of the country," Shkedy says.[41]

The IAF says that it had destroyed about 60 percent of Hezbollah's long-range missile capabilities as of Saturday night, according to Brig Gen Rami Shmueli, head of IAF intelligence. He says that 100 rocket launching platforms had been hit, as well as 11 mobile rocket launchers.[42]

The IDF says that the IAF attacked more than 130 targets in Lebanon in the past 24 hours, including more than 50 overnight. In total, over 100 attacks are launched during the day.

Beirut's southern suburbs are attacked again early Sunday. The IDF says it conducted overnight air attacks on Al-Manar, the third attack on the station. "Al-Manar has been used for years as the central tool for propaganda, incitement, and recruitment for the Hezbollah terror organization, acting without interruption from Lebanese territory, [which] poses a grave terror threat against the citizens of Israel and against the soldiers of IDF, as proven by the continuing terror attacks," the IDF says.[43]

The houses of two senior Hezbollah officials in Baalbek, Sheikh Muhammad Yazbek and Hussein Musawi, have been destroyed, the Israeli press reports. According to a high-ranking IDF source, all of the Hezbollah leaders have gone into hiding.[44]

The IDF warns the residents of seven villages in southern Lebanon to evacuate: Bint Jbeil, at-Tiri, Yaroun, Kounin, Maroun a-Ras, Ya'atar, and al-Bazouriyeh.

The IDF says that a "large firefight" breaks out near al-Majidiyah in Hasbayya district for one and one-half hours after 9:30 p.m.

---

[41] IDF War Log, "July 16th 2006."

[42] Katz and Mizroch, "Martial law in North."

[43] IDF, "IDF Strikes Hezbollah Broadcast Station."

[44] Katz and Mizroch, "Martial law in North."

Senior IDF intelligence officials tell the *Jerusalem Post* that Iran had approximately 100 soldiers in Lebanon and that they were assisting Hezbollah in its attacks on Israel.[45]

The news media reports at least 16 civilians killed and 33 others wounded Sunday, bringing the total civilian deaths to 119 killed and 313 injured.[46] Nongovernmental organizations (NGO) report a "bloodbath" in Tyre when a high-rise apartment building housing Lebanese civil defense, "offices of politicians and religious officers," is hit.[47] Israel subsequently and convincingly identified the building as Hezbollah headquarters in Tyre.[48]

UNIFIL records 17 instances of IDF fire on UN observer posts, including two direct hits inside UNIFIL observer posts. An Indian peacekeeper is seriously wounded by IDF tank shell shrapnel.[49] UNIFIL later concedes that Hezbollah activities are repeatedly talking place close to UN posts.

The Lebanese press reports the use of "phosphoric" bombs in Kfar Shouba and the use of "internationally prohibited weapons" in southern Lebanon. Second generation bombs "without any noise" but with huge destructive power are also reported as having been used, and there are press reports of air attacks on a water purification plant. The BBC reports that a "major power station" is newly attacked in Beirut.[50]

Hezbollah claims to have repelled the first attempted Israeli ground forces incursion into southern Lebanon.

---

[45] Yaakov Katz, "Sailor killed, three missing as Hezbollah, helped by Iran, fires missile at Israeli ship," *Jerusalem Post*, 16 July 2006, http://info.jpost.com/C002/Supplements/CasualtiesOfWar/2006_07_14.html.

[46] AFP (Sidon), "16 killed in new Israeli air strikes on Lebanon," 16 July 2006.

[47] "Israel's War Against Lebanon A Third of the Victims are Children," Report compiled by Khiam Rehabilitation Center for Victims of Torture, Beirut, Lebanon; for the Second Session of the Human Rights Council in Geneva, 14 September 2006. See also Human Rights Watch, "Fatal Strikes: Israel's Indiscriminate Attacks Against Civilians in Lebanon," August 2006, 22–24; and Amnesty International, Israel/Lebanon, "Out of all proportion."

[48] IDF, ITIC/CSS, Part Two, 100.

[49] UNIFIL, press release PR01, 17 July 2006.

[50] BBC, "Deadly Hezbollah attack on Haifa," 16 July 2006, http://news.bbc.co.uk/1/hi/world/middle_east/5184428.stm.

Foreign governments continue plans for the evacuation of their nationals from Lebanon.

Day 6: Monday, 17 July

In a speech to the Knesset, Prime Minister Olmert says that the fighting in Lebanon would end only when the two Israeli soldiers were freed, Hezbollah rocket attacks stopped, and the Lebanese army deployed along the border. Olmert says: "We will search every compound, target every terrorist who assists in attacking the citizens of Israel, and destroy every terrorist infrastructure, everywhere. We will persist until Hezbollah and Hamas comply with those basic and decent things required of them by every civilized person. Israel will not agree to live in the shadow of missiles or rockets aimed at its residents."

Olmert says it is Israel's "national moment of truth. Will we consent to living under the threat of this Axis of Evil or will we mobilize our inner strength and show determination and equanimity?" He says that Hezbollah is nothing but a "sub-contractor . . . operating under the inspiration, permission, instigation and financing of the terror-sponsoring and peace-rejecting regimes, on the Axis of Evil which stretches from Tehran to Damascus." He says that "the majority of the international community supports our battle against the terror organizations and our efforts to remove this threat from the Middle East."

On the war, he says, "we will insist on compliance with the terms stipulated long ago by the international community, as unequivocally expressed only yesterday in the resolution by the 8 leading countries of the world:

- the return of the hostages, Ehud (Udi) Goldwasser and Eldad Regev,

- a complete cease-fire,

- deployment of the Lebanese army in all of Southern Lebanon, and

- expulsion of Hezbollah from the area, and fulfillment of United Nations Resolution 1559."

Olmert says that "when missiles are launched at our residents and cities, our answer will be war with all the strength, determination, valor, sacrifice and dedication which characterize this nation."

At the G8 summit meeting in St. Petersburg, Russia, an open microphone catches President Bush telling PM Tony Blair that Syria must "get Hezbollah to stop doing this [expletive deleted]."

After meeting with UN secretary-general Annan in St. Petersburg, PM Blair says that the only way there could be a cessation of hostilities is through the deployment of a multinational force in southern Lebanon. Annan appeals to Israel to abide by international law and spare civilian lives and infrastructure.

The UN envoys report "promising" steps after meetings in Beirut and head for Israel, where they are scheduled to hold talks with Israeli Foreign Minister (FM) Tzipi Livni.

Lebanon's president Emile Lahoud says he will never betray Hezbollah or its leader.

Meeting in Brussels, EU foreign ministers call on Israel not to resort to "disproportionate action" in Lebanon. French PM Dominique de Villepin calls Israel's action "violent and aberrant."

Hezbollah fires 92 rockets at Israel, one hitting an apartment in Haifa, injuring 11. Over 50 rockets are fired on Monday night. A Katyusha rocket hits the Rebecca Sieff Hospital in Safed, injuring five patients, two doctors, and two other hospital employees.

Hezbollah fighters reportedly attempt to fire rockets from the eastern town of al-Qlayeh. Hand-to-hand fighting reportedly breaks out between Hezbollah and local villagers, and Hezbollah is driven away.

An IDF officer is quoted in *The Jerusalem Post* stating that Israel would destroy Lebanese power plants if Hezbollah fires long-range missiles at strategic installations in northern Israel. "If their missiles hit petrochemical plants in Haifa we will consider bombing power plants in Lebanon," the senior officer warns.[51]

---

[51] "IAF continues attack on Lebanon," *Jerusalem Post*, 17 July 2006, http://www.jpost.com/servlet/Satellite?cid=1150886020269&pagename=JPost%2FJPArticle%2FShowFull.

The IDF says it has flown over 1,000 sorties since the start of Operation Change of Direction.[52] Overnight, it says the IDF struck upward of 60 targets, including targets in Baalbek, launch sites, and Lebanese army radar sites north of Beirut. The IDF says that the radars were used in the 14 July attack on Israeli ship *Hanit*.[53] Israeli aircraft attack the port of Beirut, and extend air strikes to northern Lebanon, including the Al Abda "port" north of Tripoli.

The IDF says it attacked Hezbollah headquarters in Tyre, as well as communications targets used by Hezbollah terrorists, among them the Al-Manar broadcasting station.[54] In Tyre, an Israeli weapon hits the middle of the town, 10 m away from what the media describe as a clearly marked Lebanese Red Cross ambulance and 30 m away from Tyre's main hospital.[55] Also bombed is the Liban Lait milk and derivatives factory near Baalbek.

According to the Israeli Ministry of Foreign Affairs, the IAF destroys "at least ten long-range Iranian-made missiles capable of hitting Tel Aviv, targeting a Hezbollah truck carrying the missiles before they could be launched."[56]

The Lebanese government provides the United Nations with the names of 63 "martyrs" and 166 civilians injured during the period 12–15 July.[57] The news media also report that the death toll has risen above 200–209 in Lebanon, 24 in Israel.[58]

---

[52] IDF, "IDF Strikes Hezbollah Headquarters," Monday, 17 July 2006 09:10, http://www1.idf.il/DOVER/site/mainpage.asp?sl=EN&id=7&docid=54479.EN.

[53] Ibid.

[54] Ibid.

[55] International Committee of the Red Cross (ICRC), Middle East; press briefing with Pierre Krähenbühl, ICRC director of operations, 19 July 2006.

[56] MFA, Israel-Hezbollah Conflict: Summary of Events, July-August 2006, http://www.mfa.gov.il/MFA/Terrorism+Obstacle+to+Peace/Terrorism+from+Lebanon+Hizbullah/Israel-Hizbullah+Conflict-+Summary+of+Events+July-Aug+2006.htm.

[57] UN, identical letters dated 17 July 2006.

[58] AP Jerusalem (Ravi Nessman), "Israel Softens Conditions for Cease-Fire," 17 July 2006; and AFP (Beirut), "At least 43 killed in Lebanon Monday, toll passes 200," 17 July 2006, http://www.dawn.com/2006/07/17/welcome.htm.

Following an attack on the village of Rumayleh, one of the treating doctors describes the symptoms of victims of the attack as having black skin with no signs of burns.[59]

An Israeli intelligence aerostat is reportedly shot down over the Bekaa.

Israeli ground forces briefly enter southern Lebanon to attack and destroy Hezbollah posts along the border.

The international community steps up its evacuation of foreigners from Beirut, as thousands of Lebanese flee their homes. Reuters reports that more than 100,000 civilians have escaped to Syria across four crossing points since 12 July. As many as 30,000 of the displaced are Persian Gulf and other foreign tourists, and 20,000 are Syrian citizens.

Day 7: Tuesday, 18 July

UNICEF labels the humanitarian situation in Lebanon "catastrophic" and says that 500,000 people have been displaced.

The Guardian (UK) reports that the United States is giving Israel a one-week "window" to attack and destroy Hezbollah.

Hezbollah fires 136 rockets at Israel, 100 of them within one hour and a half, with rockets landing in the Haifa area, Karmiel, Tiberias, Safed, Maalot, and Rosh Pina. One civilian is killed in Nahariya, and about 60 people are injured in Nahariya and Safed.

The Israeli Political-Security Cabinet again meets with IDF representatives.

The UN envoys meet with FM Livni. "While we continue to act to defend our citizens, we intend to cooperate with the international community, with a view to ensuring a successful and effective resolution of the crisis," she says afterwards in a statement.

---

[59] Nouveaux Droits de l'Homme (NDH Lebanon) and l'Association Libanaise pour l'Education et la Formation (ALEF), "International Humanitarian Law violations in the July-August 2006 conflict opposing Hezbollah (Lebanon) to the State of Israel," Third report, 4 September 2006.

PM Olmert meets with new Israeli ambassadors and says that "the timing of the [Hezbollah] action in the north was coordinated with Iran to divert international attention from the Iranian issue." In the House of Commons, PM Blair also accuses Iran of supplying weapons to Hezbollah.

The US Senate passes *Senate Resolution 534*, which calls for the release of Israeli soldiers who are being held captive by Hezbollah; condemns the governments of Iran and Syria for their continued support for Hezbollah; urges all sides to protect innocent civilian life and infrastructure; and strongly supports the use of all diplomatic means available to free the captured Israeli soldiers.

After a meeting with the Egyptian foreign minister in Washington, Secretary Rice says that a cease-fire will only be possible when the conditions are "conducive." Saudi Arabia says it will support the deployment of an international military force to stabilize Lebanon.

The IDF says that it has flown over 1,600 sorties since 12 July, attacking over 130 missile launch sites.[60]

The IDF says it flew over 250 sorties on Tuesday, attacking over 100 targets.[61] The Hezbollah center in south Beirut and targets in the coastal city of Tyre are attacked. During daylight hours, the IDF says it attacked 52 targets, including 12 "access routes connecting between Lebanon and Syria, in order to prevent the passage of weapons and terrorists."[62]

The IDF announces that overnight (Tuesday, 18 July) it attacked six targets associated with funding Hezbollah: in Beirut, in Beit Nebal, in Nabatiyeh, Baalbek, and Ba'al Azaia in the area of Tyre.[63]

---

[60] IDF, "Summary of IDF Airstrikes in Lebanon," Tuesday, 18 July 2006 10:21, http://www1.idf.il/DOVER/site/mainpage.asp?sl=EN&id=7&docid=54584.EN.

[61] IDF, "Over 100 Targets Attacked Yesterday in Lebanon," Wednesday, 19 July 2006 11:36, http://www1.idf.il/DOVER/site/mainpage.asp?sl=EN&id=7&docid=546 07.EN.

[62] IDF, "The Air Force Attacked 52 Targets Today," n.d. (18 July 2006), http://www1.idf.il/DOVER/site/mainpage.asp?sl=EN&id=7&docid=54599.EN.

[63] IDF, "IDF Attacked Hezbollah Organization Funding Targets," n.d. (18 July 2006), http://www1.idf.il/DOVER/site/mainpage.asp?sl=EN&id=7&docid=54643.EN.

The IDF drops warning leaflets over the villages of al-Abbasiyeh and al-Bazouriyeh advising residents to leave the sites of rocket launches. Warnings also advise that any vans or trucks moving south of the Litani River will be considered suspect.

Speaking on Sky News, Israeli Deputy PM Shimon Peres says that Israel will not "penetrate" Lebanon on the ground, and is instead "trying to control the roads . . . because all the 12,000 missiles and rockets that they have collected came from Iran and Syria."

Speaking of attacks on Hezbollah rockets, Maj Gen Udi Adam says that "The amounts are decreasing. . . . We damaged a large quantity of their weapons stores. They accumulated weapons for years and reached a huge arsenal of 13,000 or 15,000. Most of the weapons were provided by Iran, of course, and destroying all of these stocks takes time. . . . Let us put our best efforts into this and finish a situation that we have been suffering from for sixty years."[64]

The news media report that "at least" 233 civilians have been killed in Lebanon.[65] According to press reports, a medical convoy and ambulances of the United Arab Emirates are targeted near the Syrian-Lebanese border.[66]

Day 8: Wednesday, 19 July

France circulates proposals to the UN Security Council calling for an immediate cease-fire in Lebanon. UN Amb. John Bolton dismisses the proposals as "simplistic."

---

[64] Ibid.

[65] Reuters (Jerusalem), "One dead, 14 hurt in rocket attacks across N. Israel," 18 July 2006, http://www.dawn.com/2006/07/18/welcome.htm.

[66] Reuters (Beirut), "Israel pounds Lebanon, Hezbollah rockets hit Haifa," 18 July 2006, http://www.dawn.com/2006/07/18/welcome.htm; and UN, Identical letters dated 18 July 2006. See also Human Rights Watch, "Fatal Strikes: Israel's Indiscriminate Attacks Against Civilians in Lebanon," August 2006, 5.

Israel announces that the Political-Security Cabinet has defined the principles of a diplomatic solution to the Lebanese crisis:

- unconditional release of abducted soldiers,

- halt to the firing of rockets against Israel, and

- full implementation of *UNSCR 1559*.

After meeting Israeli FM Livni, the EU foreign policy chief Solana says the suffering of Lebanese civilians is "disproportionate" to the battle against Hezbollah. Livni says the Israeli military response is proportionate to the threat posed by Hezbollah to the entire region. "Israel is fighting to eliminate the threat posed by the axis of terror and hate: Hezbollah, Hamas, Syria and Iran," Livni says. "Specifically, Israel is fighting to end the control of the Hezbollah over the lives of both Lebanese and Israelis."

Solana also meets with PM Olmert and Vice-PM Peres.

The Daily Star reports at least 70 civilians killed in the deadliest day of Israel's Lebanon offensive.[67] The news media report that a total of 310 people, "mostly civilians," have been killed and hundreds injured since 12 July.[68] UN agencies express "serious concern" over civilian casualties in Lebanon and Israel.[69]

UN High Commissioner for Human Rights Louise Arbour says the killings in Lebanon could constitute war crimes: "The scale of the killings in the region, and their predictability, could engage the personal criminal responsibility of those involved, particularly those in a position of command and control," she says.

Hezbollah fires 116 rockets into Israel. Two children are killed and dozens are wounded in two Katyusha rocket attacks on the Israeli-Arab city of Nazareth.

---

[67] "July War 2006 Timeline," *Daily Star*, http://www.dailystar.com.lb/July_War06.asp.

[68] AFP (Tyre, Lebanon), "55 killed in deadliest day of Israeli raids on Lebanon," 19 July 2006, http://www.dawn.com/2006/07/19/welcome.htm.

[69] UN News Centre, 19 July 2006, http://www.un.org/apps/news/story.asp?NewsID=19243&Cr=Leban&Cr1.

The IDF says that since 12 July, it has flown over 2,000 sorties and struck over 1,000 targets, including about 180 missile- and rocket-launch sites.[70]

The IDF says it attacked over 200 targets in Lebanon,[71] including 75 sites from which Katyusha missiles were launched and the "routes leading to them."[72]

The Israeli military says its aircraft dropped 23 tons of explosives in an evening raid on a bunker in south Beirut where senior Hezbollah leaders, possibly including Hassan Nasrallah, were hiding. Hezbollah denies that any of its "leaders or personnel" was killed and says the Israeli raid hit a mosque under construction.

An Israeli F-16I fighter aircraft crashes while taking off from the Ramon base in the Negev in southern Israel. The pilot escapes unharmed.

Chief IDF intelligence officer Brig Gen Yuval Halamish says that despite the firing of 110 Katyusha rockets at Israel on Wednesday, the IDF had succeeded in delivering what he called a "significant blow" to Hezbollah. "We have struck some of their most strategic sites," Halamish says.[73]

Maj Gen Gadi Eizenkot, head of the IDF Operations Directorate and Brig Gen Amir Eshel, IAF chief of staff, brief journalists in Tel Aviv, saying that weapons are being smuggled from Syria to Lebanon, and that a number of trucks had been destroyed while engaged in that activity.[74]

Israeli ground forces carry out what the IDF calls "restricted pinpoint attacks" in southern Lebanon. Ground forces discover

---

[70] IDF, "Over 100 Targets Attacked."

[71] IDF War Log, "July 19th 2006," http://www.plint.us/idf/en.html.

[72] IDF, "Over 100 Targets Attacked."

[73] Yaakov Katz, "Two soldiers killed in clash with Hezbollah inside Lebanon," *Jerusalem Post*, 20 July 2006, http://info.jpost.com/C002/Supplements/CasualtiesOf War/2006_07_19.html.

[74] IDF, "The Head of the Operations Directorate, Major General Gadi Eizenkot, and the Head of IAF staff, Brigadier General Amir Eshel, held a journalist briefing at the Kirya base in Tel Aviv," n.d. (19 July 2006), http://www1.idf.il/DOVER/site/mainpage .asp?sl=EN&id=7&docid=54603.EN.

several underground Hezbollah tunnel and bunker complexes and engage in firefights with Hezbollah members. Two IDF soldiers are killed and seven more are wounded during exchanges of fire between the elite IDF paratrooper unit Maglan and Hezbollah in the Maroun a-Ras mountain ridge, about two kilometers from Moshav Avivim along the border.[75] Hezbollah then fires a mortar shell at a tank attempting to evacuate the wounded, wounding seven more Israel soldiers.[76] The MFA later says that the Israeli force had crossed the border to destroy the Hezbollah rocket-launching position at the former IDF outpost of Shaked.[77]

Day 9: Thursday, 20 July

After receiving the report of his fact-finding mission to Lebanon and Israel, Secretary-General Annan speaks before the UN Security Council and calls for an "immediate cessation of hostilities." He accuses Israel of "collective punishment" of the Lebanese people. Referring to Hezbollah, he says:

> Hezbollah's provocative attack on 12 July was the trigger of this crisis. It is clear that the Lebanese government had no advance knowledge of this attack. Whatever other agendas they may serve, Hezbollah's actions, which it portrays as defending Palestinian and Lebanese interests, in fact do neither. On the contrary, they hold an entire nation hostage [and] set back prospects for negotiation of a comprehensive Middle East peace. I have already condemned Hezbollah's attacks on Israel, and acknowledged Israel's right to defend itself under Article 51 of the UN charter. I do so again today. I also condemn Hezbollah's reckless disregard for the wishes of the elected Government of Lebanon, and for the interests of the Lebanese people and the wider region.

Annan and Secretary Rice are scheduled to meet on Thursday.

The UN warns that without an agreement allowing humanitarian aid agencies to begin the relief effort, there will be a "catastrophe."

The Russian Foreign Ministry says Israeli actions have gone "far beyond the boundaries of an anti-terrorist operation" and

---

[75] Katz, "Two soldiers killed in clash with Hezbollah inside Lebanon."

[76] IDF War Log, "July 19th 2006."

[77] MFA, Israel-Hezbollah Conflict: Summary of Events.

says that Lebanon is on the verge of a large-scale humanitarian catastrophe. Russia calls for "an immediate halt to firing and bloodshed."

The US House of Representatives passes *House Resolution 921*, which condemns Hezbollah's attack on Israel and urges the president to bring sanctions against the governments of Syria and Iran for their sponsorship of Hezbollah.

Hezbollah fires just 34 rockets at Israel, the lowest daily total of the war to date. Rockets kill two children in the Israeli Arab city of Nazareth. They are the first Arab Israelis to die in the rocket attacks. Nasrallah apologizes to the family for the deaths.

The IDF says it conducted 150 air strikes on Thursday during the day, attacking 1,500 targets (aim points), among them approximately 200 rocket launch sites. In addition, the IDF says, over 100 bridges and roads were attacked, as well as 21 vehicles transporting Hezbollah terrorists, among them one vehicle suspected of use as a Fajr 3 rocket launcher. Seven Hezbollah communications facilities were also attacked.[78]

The IDF says that it attacked about 80 targets overnight, including a bunker in Beirut used by Hezbollah officials, about 200 rocket "launching sites," 13 communications targets, 10 bridges, several roads, and an airport.[79]

An Israeli airman dies when two Apache attack helicopters collide near the northern Israeli border.

Senior IDF officers are quoted in the Israeli press as saying that air strikes had destroyed "about 50 percent" of Hezbollah's arsenal, but that more time was needed to complete the task. "It will take us time to destroy what is left," says Brig Gen Alon Friedman, chief of staff of the Northern Command.[80]

---

[78] IDF, "150 Airstrikes; 40 Armed Terrorists Targeted," Thursday, 20 July 2006 22:54, http://www1.idf.il/DOVER/site/mainpage.asp?clr=1&sl=EN&id=7&docid=54781; and IDF War Log, "July 20th 2006."

[79] IDF, "Summary of IDF Attacks During the Night in Lebanon and Gaza," n.d. [20 July 2006], http://www1.idf.il/DOVER/site/mainpage.asp?sl=EN&id=7&docid=54680.EN.

[80] Katz, "Two soldiers killed in clash with Hezbollah inside Lebanon."

Heavy fighting erupts between Israeli ground forces and Hezbollah inside Lebanon. Four IDF soldiers are killed and five more wounded during operations north of Avivim. One additional soldier was declared missing in action. In two separate incidents inside southern Lebanon, three IDF soldiers are wounded by gunfire and antitank missiles fired at them.[81] Two IDF tankers are wounded when an antitank missile strikes their vehicle.[82]

A company commander in the Egoz Battalion is killed in action on Thursday night in Maroun a-Ras.[83]

The IDF says that artillery is "continuously" firing at areas along the border where Hezbollah rockets are being launched.[84]

The IDF drops leaflets offering "attractive material rewards" to anyone providing information about Hezbollah. The leaflet directs people to a Web site and Internet address, All4Lebanon .org. Israel also generates cell phone calls to Lebanese civilians, some as early as 5:30 a.m., with recorded messages such as: "We don't want to harm you. We're bombing the infrastructure so Hezbollah will have no means of firing its rockets. We know you wanted to hit Israel, but you have confronted a house made of steel. This is the Israel Defense Forces." Later text messages are sent to cell phones, reading "Make your voice heard! Do you feel Hezbollah are to blame for the current violence?"

UNIFIL reports that Hezbollah had fired from the immediate vicinity of UN positions in Naqoura and Maroun a-Ras, prompting an IDF response.[85]

Day 10: Friday, 21 July

Italy announces it will host an international conference on Wednesday to discuss the Lebanon war, humanitarian assis-

---

[81] IDF War Log, "July 20th 2006."

[82] IDF, "150 Airstrikes; 40 Armed Terrorists Targeted."

[83] "IDF lays its fallen to rest," *Jerusalem Post*, 23 July 2006, http://info.jpost.com/C002/Supplements/CasualtiesOfWar/2006_07_20.html.

[84] IDF, "Summary of IDF Attacks."

[85] UNIFIL, press release PR02, 20 July 2006.

tance, a potential cease-fire, and deployment of an additional multinational peacekeeping force in southern Lebanon. Neither Israel, Iran, nor Syria will attend.

The UN Security Council discusses the situation in Lebanon but fails to reach a resolution.

Secretary Rice announces a visit to the Middle East and attendance at an upcoming international meeting in Rome. "At next week's meeting of the Lebanon Core Group, we will continue working to provide immediate humanitarian relief to the people of Lebanon," she says. "We urgently seek an end to the current violence. We also seek to address the root causes of that violence so that a real and endurable peace can be established. . . . A cease-fire would be a false promise if it simply returns us to the status quo."

Hezbollah also rejects a proposed cease-fire that calls for the release of two IDF soldiers. "The only thing accepted for us is an unconditional cease-fire followed by indirect negotiations on a prisoners' swap," a Hezbollah spokesman says.

Hezbollah fires 97 rockets at Israel. Hassan Nasrallah speaks to Al-Jazeera television, saying, "The victory we are talking about is when the resistance survives. When its will is not broken, then this is victory. . . . When we are not defeated militarily, then this is victory."

Visiting Beirut, French foreign minister Philippe Douste-Blazy says that his country is seeking a cease-fire to avoid the escalating conflict that could lead to a "catastrophe." He says that France denounces Hezbollah's action and "the disproportionate response of Israel." He denounces "attacks on the sovereignty" of Lebanon, particularly strikes on the Lebanese army.

Meeting in Moscow, Russian president Putin and German chancellor Angela Merkel call for concerted international efforts to end the Israel-Hezbollah conflict.

Speaking at the Security Council, Israel's ambassador to the UN says: "In spite of the very difficult situation on the ground, Israel is acutely aware of the humanitarian situation. I have received official confirmation from Israel that a two-way 'humanitarian corridor,' to meet the needs of those affected on the Lebanese side, has been established." The corridor used for the maritime evacuation of thousands of foreign residents and tourists from Lebanon to Cyprus will now also be used to bring in humanitarian aid.

The IDF begins an emergency reserve call-up in what the Israeli media see as a possible prelude to a larger ground offensive.[86]

The IDF says that it attacked 124 targets in Lebanon, and that during the previous night (20 July), it attacked more than 40 targets.

The Guardian (UK) reports that 55 bridges, three airports, three ports, Beirut's lighthouse, 21 fuel and gas stores, 12 gas stations, an electricity generator in Sibline, and various factories and warehouses have been destroyed in Lebanon during the 10-day campaign.[87]

Lt Gen Dan Halutz says that the IDF has killed nearly 100 Hezbollah fighters in the 10-day campaign so far.

Israel masses soldiers and tanks on the Lebanese border. Brig Gen Alon Friedman of Northern Command says that "It's possible that in the coming days our ground operations will increase."

The IDF drops leaflets warning residents south of the Litani River to flee north.

The news media say that Lebanese Health Ministry officials place the death toll at 344, one-third of them children, with over $4 billion in property losses. PM Siniora says 1,100 have been injured. Press reports also state that a hospital in Tyre has been so overwhelmed by the number of casualties it has begun burying the dead in a temporary mass grave.[88]

---

[86] IDF War Log, "July 21st 2006."

[87] Brian Whitaker, "Battered Lebanon counts the cost of Israeli onslaught," *Guardian* (UK), 21 July 2006, http://www.guardian.co.uk/syria/story/0,,1825669,00.html.

[88] Reuters, "Israel warns Lebanese to flee, calls up reserves," 21 July 2006, http://www.dawn.com/2006/07/21/welcome.htm.

Day 11: Saturday, 22 July

UN under secretary-general for Humanitarian Affairs and Emergency Relief Coordinator Jan Egeland says at least $100 million is urgently needed to help avert a humanitarian disaster in Lebanon over the coming months. He calls for the designation of secure routes for civilians to escape as thousands continue to attempt to flee. He estimates that "more than half a million people are directly affected" by the war.

British foreign secretary Margaret Beckett says that an Israeli ground invasion could have "dramatic effects." Minister of State at the Foreign and Commonwealth Office Kim Howells, after visiting Beirut, says that the Israeli government needs to think about "those children who are dying" and expressing bafflement at Israel's military tactics.

Hezbollah fires 129 rockets into Israel.

The news media report that 355 Lebanese, "mostly civilians," have died in the 12-day conflict, while Hezbollah attacks and rockets have killed 34 Israelis, including 19 soldiers.[89] The death toll, AFP says, "includes 25 Lebanese army soldiers and 12 Hezbollah fighters."[90] The Lebanese Ministry of Health later says over 362 Lebanese have been killed and 1,350 injured.

The IDF says it has struck roughly 2,000 targets and carried out more than 4,000 sorties since 12 July.[91]

The IDF says that it attacked some 150 targets across Lebanon in the past 24 hours and that the IAF had hit 90 targets in Lebanon throughout the day as of Saturday night. Among the targets that were hit were Hezbollah buildings, tunnels, Hezbollah communications systems, and Katyushas launchers.[92]

---

[89] Reuters, "Latest developments in the Middle East," 22 July 2006 11:54:30 p.m.

[90] AFP (Rashaya, Lebanon), "Israeli strikes kill four civilians in Lebanon," 22 July 2006, http://www.dawn.com/2006/07/22/welcome.htm.

[91] IDF War Log, "July 22nd 2006"; and IDF, Summary of IDF Airstrikes in Lebanon, Sunday 23/07/2006 11:23 [23 July 2006], http://www1.idf.il/DOVER/site/main page.asp?sl=EN&id=7&docid=54877.EN.

[92] IDF War Log, "July 22nd 2006."

The IDF says that it attacked over 150 targets in the past 24 hours, including 12 roads connecting Lebanon and Syria, sites used to launch rockets, as well as access roads and bridges leading to them.[93]

The Lebanese media report that mobile phone communication and local TV reception have been cut off between Beirut and north Lebanon after Israeli targeting of transmission stations.

Maj Gen Udi Adam says that the IDF objective is to "eradicate terror and to disarm the Hezbollah organization." He says that Katyusha fire has been declining in the past days and that most of what is hitting Israel is now mortars and not rockets.[94]

The Israeli army continues its ground operations in southern Lebanon, claiming to have gained control of the village of Maroun a-Ras after several days of fighting. "At most, we're talking about a few kilometers in," the IDF spokesman says of Israeli ground activity. "It will probably widen, but we are still looking at limited operations. We're not talking about massive forces going inside at this point."

During operations in Marwaheen, IDF forces uncover Hezbollah weapons in the basement of the village mosque.

The *New York Times* reports that the United States is expediting the delivery of precision-guided bombs that had been ordered by Israel in 2005.

Day 12: Sunday, 23 July

UN under secretary-general Egeland tours Beirut and calls the sight "horrific" and a "violation of humanitarian law."

The Norwegian government decides to provide an additional 200 million Norwegian krones (US $32 million) in humanitarian

---

[93] IDF, Summary of IDF aerial activity in Lebanon in the past 24 hours, Saturday 22 July 2006 13:57, http://www1.idf.il/DOVER/site/mainpage.asp?sl=EN&id=7&docid=54847.EN.

[94] IDF, GOC of Northern Command: "A big part of Hezbollah organization infrastructures has been hurt," Saturday 22 July 2006 16:37, http://www1.idf.il/dover/site/mainpage.asp?sl=EN&id=7&docid=54845.EN.

aid to Lebanon and the Gaza Strip. The Kuwaiti government announces that it would donate US $20 million.

Secretary Rice heads for the Middle East after White House talks between President Bush and Saudi officials.

Top diplomats from France, Germany, and the UK converge on Israel ahead of a visit by Secretary Rice.

After talks with the envoys, FM Livni says: "The situation that has been created in Lebanon over the years required us to establish objectives in order to remove the threat and to establish long-term stability—through both military and diplomatic means."

Israeli defense minister Amir Peretz indicates Israel would agree to the proposed NATO-led deployment of a multinational force in southern Lebanon.

Israeli PM Olmert accuses the international media of bias for not portraying the "murderous viciousness" of Hezbollah. "Hezbollah is operated by Iran and Syria. The Iranian issue is one that will preoccupy the world in the coming months and what is happening now is a preparation," he says. Olmert calls for an EU-based multinational peacekeeping force to be deployed to southern Lebanon.

The news media report 361 killed in Lebanon since 12 July, including 16 Hezbollah fighters.[95] Reports say that Israeli aircraft attacked "two clearly marked Red Cross ambulances" in the village of Qana.[96]

---

[95] AFP (Beirut), "11 more deaths push Lebanon's toll from Israeli attacks to 361," 23 July 2006, http://www.dawn.com/2006/07/23/welcome.htm; and Reuters, "Latest developments in the Middle East," 23 July 2006 10:34:00 p.m.

[96] IRIN (Tyre, Lebanon), "Number of civilian deaths likely to be higher—Red Cross," 26 July 2006, http://lebanonnewslive.com/IRIN-Tyre-2607.htm; Kerry Sander, "On a mission of mercy with Lebanon Red Cross; Horrors and heartaches as volunteers attempt to evacuate the wounded," MSNBC, 26 July 2006 (Updated: 2:20 p.m. ET 26 July 2006), http://www.msnbc.msn.com/id/14041670/; and AP (Kathy Gannon, Tyre, Lebanon), "Lebanese complain Israelis using banned weapons," 25 July 2006, http://www.hamiltonspectator.com/NASApp/cs/ContentServer?pagename=hamilton/Layout/Article_Type1&c=Article&cid=1153779011113&call_pageid=1020420665036&col=111210166267. See also Human Rights Watch, "Fatal Strikes: Israel's Indiscriminate Attacks Against Civilians in Lebanon," August 2006, 5, 41.

A UN military observer is also reported as seriously wounded near Maroun a-Ras from Hezbollah fire during an exchange with the IDF.[97]

Hezbollah leader Hassan Nasrallah acknowledges that Israeli troops can operate in south Lebanon at will. "I don't want to raise expectations. I never said that the Israelis cannot reach any place in southern Lebanon. Our dogma and strategy is: When the Israelis come (inside Lebanon) they must pay a high price. This is what we promise and this is what we will achieve, God willing."

Hezbollah fires 94 rockets into northern Israel, killing two civilians, one in Haifa and the other in Kiryat Ata, and wounding several others.[98] More than 2,200 Hezbollah rockets have hit Israel so far, Defense Minister Peretz says.

The IDF identifies a long-range 220 mm rocket launcher in the village of al-Halousiyeh (Hallousisyet al-Tahta), east of Bidyas. The launcher, hidden behind a residential dwelling, is attacked the same day.

Israeli Magen David Adom (MDA) says that it has been called to 505 rocket landing sites in which they have treated and evacuated 976 casualties (36 fatalities; 19 severely, 39 moderately, and 278 lightly injured; and 604 anxiety attacks).

Haaretz reports that Israeli officials estimate one-third to one-half of all residents of northern Israel have fled to escape Hezbollah rocket attacks.

The IDF says that it attacked 120 targets in the past 24 hours and 90 targets during the day, including 60 sites where Katyusha have been launched from and the access routes leading to them, vehicles, and communications arrays.[99]

---

[97] UNIFIL press release PR08, 24 July 2006; and AFP (Tyre, Lebanon), "UN observer injured in Lebanon fighting," 23 July 2006, http://www.dawn.com/2006/07/23/welcome.htm.

[98] IDF, "IDF Attacked Over 270 Targets in Lebanon," Monday 24 July 2006 19:33, http://www1.idf.il/DOVER/site/mainpage.asp?sl=EN&id=7&docid=54983.EN.

[99] IDF, "Summary of IDF Airstrikes in Lebanon, Sunday 23/07/2006."

The IDF attacks headquarters and structures in south Beirut and Sidon overnight, hitting inner Sidon city for the first time. (A Shi'a mosque known in Sidon as a Hezbollah mosque is hit.)

The IDF attacks about 88 rocket launch sites in Lebanon.[100] Overall the IDF carries out about 120 aerial attacks on terror-related targets during the day.[101]

The news media report that the signal of Hezbollah's al-Nour radio is electronically commandeered by Israel, which superimposes its own message. Leaflets also ask residents of a dozen named villages to leave their homes.

Large numbers of IDF ground forces cross the border Sunday night as the IDF expands its presence in southern Lebanon. Hezbollah admits that the IDF has taken over the village of Maroun a-Ras, where the two sides fought during the past 48 hours, but berates Israel's capabilities: "An army that fights with excellent forces and tanks with the assistance of an air force cannot go into a village directly on the border except after a battle that has continued for days with great losses against a number of opposition fighters is a failed and defeated army," the statement says.

The IDF says that it has fired upwards of 25,000 artillery shells since 12 July.[102]

Syria will enter the conflict if Israeli ground forces enter Lebanon and approach Syria, the Syrian information minister says.

Day 13: Monday, 24 July

UN secretary-general Annan says that the international ministerial talks to be held in Rome must not fail.

---

[100] IDF, "Twelve Days of War in the North," Sunday 23 July 2006 13:51, http://www1.idf.il/DOVER/site/mainpage.asp?sl=EN&id=7&docid=54889.EN.

[101] IDF, "Airstrike on Hezbollah Headquarters," Sunday 23 July 2006 11:09, http://www1.idf.il/DOVER/site/mainpage.asp?sl=EN&id=7&docid=54884.EN; and IDF War Log, "July 23rd 2006."

[102] IDF, "Summary of IDF Airstrikes in Lebanon, Sunday 23 July 2006."

Secretary Rice makes a surprise visit to Beirut on her way to Israel and Rome and puts forward new proposals for the Lebanese army to deploy in southern Lebanon alongside a UN-led multinational peacekeeping force. She also offers a significant US commitment in humanitarian aid and says she is "deeply concerned about the Lebanese people and what they are enduring."

Upon her arrival in Israel, FM Livni says: "This is a moment of truth for the government of Lebanon and for the international community. A cease-fire alone will create a vacuum that Hezbollah will fill with more terrorism."

After meeting with Iraqi PM Nouri al-Maliki, Prime Minister Blair calls the Lebanon war a "catastrophe" and says that he hopes to present an acceptable cease-fire plan in the next few days.

Al-Maliki expresses support for Hezbollah and says that Israeli attacks on civilian targets constitute a "violation of all the laws of war."

UN under secretary-general Egeland says Israel "has caused enormous damage to residential areas and key civilian infrastructure such as power plants, seaports, and fuel depots" and accuses Hezbollah of "cowardly blending" among Lebanese civilians. "Consistently, from the Hezbollah heartland, my message was that Hezbollah must stop this cowardly blending . . . among women and children. . . . I heard they were proud because they lost very few fighters and that it was the civilians bearing the brunt of this. I don't think anyone should be proud of having many more children and women dead than armed men."

UN refugee chief Antonio Guterres insists that Israel allow tens of thousands of people driven from their homes by Israeli bombing in southern Lebanon to move out of harm's way.

Hezbollah leader Hassan Nasrallah says in remarks published Monday that an Israeli ground invasion would not prevent Hezbollah from firing rockets into northern Israel. "Any Israeli incursion will have no political results if it does not achieve its declared goals, primarily an end to the rocketing of Zionist settlements in northern occupied Palestine," Nasrallah told the *As-Safir* newspaper. "I assure you that this goal will not be achieved, God willing, by an Israeli incursion."

On diplomatic efforts to end the fighting, Nasrallah said the priority was to end Israeli attacks on Lebanon, but added he was open to discussing initiatives. Nasrallah said it was "very noteworthy" that Israel first rejected and then accepted the idea of a NATO-led force. "This shift in Israel's position must be studied and considered well before taking a positive or negative stand on this idea," he said. Nasrallah said Israel's losses in the fighting for Maroun a-Ras showed the weakness of the Israeli army.

Hezbollah fires 83 rockets at northern Israeli communities, injuring over 30.

The death toll reaches at least 378 in Lebanon and 41 in Israel.[103] Four Ghanaian UNIFIL observers are lightly injured when an Israeli tank shell falls inside their UN post at Rmeish, one of six incidents of IDF fire on or close to UN positions recorded that day.

The IDF says that it attacked approximately 270 targets over the last 24 hours, including 50 buildings and structures used by Hezbollah, 21 launchers and launch sites, 35 suspect vehicles, and communications arrays.[104]

The UN says that the IDF hit the Rashidiyeh Palestine refugee camp in Tyre today for the first time, injuring six people. Two people are reported killed in a raid on a base of the Popular Front for the Liberation of Palestine in the Bekaa Valley.[105]

The IDF drops leaflets directed at Hezbollah fighters, which read:

> To Hezbollah militia activists: Do you really think that the battlefield looks like the propaganda clips on Al-Manar TV, and that you could sprint so fast and easily up the highest hills? Did you believe your leaders, who told you that those facing you are nothing but spider webs easily torn down by you? They lied to you all these years; they are lying to you now. You know very well that you were sent like sheep to be butchered, lacking military training and without proper combat gear. You know very well that the reassuring words of your leaders are not sufficient for a resilient stand against highly trained soldiers that fight

---

[103] Reuters, "Latest developments in the Middle East," 24 July 2006 11:24:10 p.m.

[104] IDF, "Summary of Yesterday's Airstrikes," Monday 24 July 2006 10:00, http://www1.idf.il/DOVER/site/mainpage.asp?sl=EN&id=7&docid=54953.EN; IDF "IDF Attacked Over 270 Targets in Lebanon;" and IDF War Log, "July 24th 2006."

[105] OCHA, "OCHA: Civilian death toll mounts in Lebanon Report," 24 July 2006, http://electronicintifada.net/v2/article5210.shtml.

to protect their homeland, their people and their home. You are nothing but mercenaries, and the Lebanese people do not support you. Run as far as you can, save your souls.

Ground forces of the Golani and Paratroopers brigades enter the area of Bint Jbeil town, about 4 km (2.5 mi) inside Lebanon, on Monday.[106] An IDF officer and soldier were killed, two severely wounded, five moderately wounded, and seven more lightly wounded during operations in the area of Bint Jbeil. An IDF soldier was severely wounded and five additional soldiers lightly wounded in a different incident.[107]

An IDF spokesman says nine Israeli soldiers were lightly wounded in heavy fighting around Maroun a-Ras village.

The IDF says that it killed Abu-Jafar, a Hezbollah commander in the Lebanese central sector on 24 July around Maroun a-Ras.[108]

An AH-64D Apache Longbow is lost when its main rotor separates during a fire suppression mission. There are reports that it may have been struck by friendly artillery fire. Hezbollah claims to have shot down the helicopter, a claim Israel denies.

Day 14: Tuesday, 25 July

Secretary Rice completes her visit to the Middle East, having visited Beirut and Israel, and holding separate talks with Palestinian president Mahmoud Abbas. After meeting Rice, PM Olmert says both agree that disarming Hezbollah and deploying multinational peacekeeping forces in southern Lebanon are keys to a cease-fire. "For over 12 days, more than 15% of the population of Israel has been forced to live in shelters because of the continuous rocket and missile attacks coming from Lebanon into the major cities of Israel," Olmert says.

---

[106] Yaakov Katz, "2 soldiers, 2 pilots killed," *Jerusalem Post*, 25 July 2006, http://info.jpost.com/C002/Supplements/CasualtiesOfWar/2006_07_24.html.

[107] IDF War Log, "July 24th 2006."

[108] IDF, "Summary of Warfare in Lebanon Yesterday," n.d. (25 July 2006), http://www1.idf.il/DOVER/site/mainpage.asp?sl=EN&id=7&docid=55101.EN.

Foreign ministers of the Association of Southeast Asian Nations (ASEAN) meeting in Kuala Lumpur express concern over "the deteriorating situation and the escalation of violence in the Middle East, particularly the disproportionate, indiscriminate and excessive use of force by Israel in the Occupied Palestinian Territory and in Lebanon."

Iranian president Ahmadinejad comments on the war in Lebanon while in Dushanbe, saying that the conflict between Israel and Hezbollah could trigger a "storm" in the region with destructive consequences.

Hassan Nasrallah suggests the beginning of a "second phase of our struggle" in which rockets would "go beyond Haifa." He says Hezbollah will not accept any "humiliating" conditions for a ceasefire. Hezbollah fires 101 rockets at Israel, killing a 15-year-old girl in the Galilee village of Mrar (Maghar), home to Israeli Druze and Moslems.

Mahmoud Komati, the deputy chief of the Hezbollah politburo, says he did not expect Israel to react so strongly to the group's capture of two Israeli soldiers.

Defense Minister Peretz says Israel is now carving out a "security zone" in south Lebanon until a multinational force can take over security responsibilities.

The IDF attacks over 115 targets in Lebanon,[109] and resumes air strikes on Beirut's southern suburbs after a 24-hour lull that coincided with Rice's visit to the Middle East.[110]

The Guardian (UK) reports an Israeli strike on "two clearly marked Red Cross ambulances," a story repeated in the international press.

Israeli ground forces enter the town of Bint Jbeil for the first time; Israel says it kills up to 30 Hezbollah fighters. In a Hezbollah ambush on the outskirts of Bint Jbeil, eight IDF soldiers

---

[109] IDF War Log, "July 25th 2006."

[110] Reuters (Beirut), "Israeli planes continue to blast Beirut; 12 civilians killed," 25 July 2006, http://www.dawn.com/2006/07/25/welcome.htm.

from Battalion 51 of the Golani Brigade are killed, and 24 are injured.[111]

An IDF officer is killed and three IDF soldiers are injured when attacked with an antitank missile on the outskirt of Maroun a-Ras.[112]

Human Rights Watch accuses Israel of using artillery-fired cluster bombs. The death toll is reported as 418 in Lebanon and 42 in Israel.[113]

An Israeli weapon hits a UN Observer Group Lebanon (OGL) post near al-Khiyam at about 7:30 p.m., demolishing a three-story building and killing four unarmed observers from Austria, Canada, Finland, and China. UN SG Kofi Annan describes the attack as "apparently deliberate." Israel is accused of ignoring repeated warnings that it was shelling close to UN observers. Observer posts have been subjected to numerous hits and near misses by Israeli and Hezbollah weapons.

The White House calls the deaths "horrible." In London, British PM Blair's office says the incident was "deeply regrettable." French president Jacques Chirac issued a condemnation.

Day 15: Wednesday, 26 July

Hezbollah fires 169 rockets at Israel, the highest daily total since 12 July.

Prime Minister Olmert phones UN secretary-general Annan and expresses his deep regret over the death of the four UN observers the previous day. He promises to conduct a thorough investigation, stating that "It's inconceivable for the UN to define an error as an apparently deliberate action."

Israel's killing of the four observers piles pressure on an international conference opening in Rome to end the 15-day-old

---

[111] Yaakov Katz, *Jerusalem Post* staff, and AP, "Names of nine soldiers killed in Lebanon released," *Jerusalem Post*, 25 July 2006, http://info.jpost.com/C002/Supplements/CasualtiesOfWar/2006_07_26.html.

[112] Ibid.

[113] Reuters, "Latest developments in the Middle East," 25 July 2006 11:26:52 p.m.

conflict. China condemns Israel for killing the four observers, including a Chinese national, and calls for a full investigation.

The international conference convenes in Rome with delegates from Europe, Canada, the United States, Israel, Lebanon, and select Middle East nations (not including Iran or Syria). They vow to "reach with the utmost urgency a cease-fire that puts an end to the current violence and hostilities" and urge Israel to show "utmost restraint" in its offensive. Calls for an immediate cease-fire without preconditions are blocked by the United States and UK.

In his address to the Rome conference, PM Siniora praises Hezbollah as having been key to ending Israel's occupation of southern Lebanon and as a legitimate part of the Lebanese government. He says Lebanon will sue Israel for the "barbaric destruction" suffered. "Is the value of human rights in Lebanon less than that of citizens elsewhere? Are we children of a lesser God? Is an Israel teardrop worth more than a drop of Lebanese blood?" he asks, calling for "an immediate and comprehensive cease-fire."

"We have to have a plan that will actually create conditions in which we can have a cease-fire that will be sustainable," Rice says at the closing news conference.

Israel's response to the statement: "Israel joins the international community in its demand to bring about the full and immediate implementation of *UN Resolution 1559* and the G-8 statement."

Hezbollah demands an immediate cease-fire and indirect talks to secure a prisoner exchange. Mohamad Raad, the leader of Hezbollah's 14-member parliamentary bloc, says "anything other than that is not acceptable."

The news media report a death toll of 418 people in Lebanon and 42 in Israel.[114] As of 26 July, the World Health Organization (WHO) reports that 365 Lebanese have died and more than 1,267 people have been injured.[115] The Lebanese Red Cross in

---

[114] Reuters, "Latest developments in the Middle East," 26 July 2006, 6:06:40 a.m.

[115] USAID, Lebanon—Complex Emergency Information Bulletin #6, Fiscal Year (FY) 2006, 26 July 2006.

southern Lebanon say dozens more civilians could have died than accounted for so far.[116]

The UN Food and Agriculture Organization (FAO) says that Lebanon is heading for a "major food crisis."

A Jordanian military plane transporting UN humanitarian aid lands at Beirut International Airport, the first flight to land after a two-week closure.

The IDF says that it carried out close to 180 air attacks in the past 24 hours, and that it attacked approximately 60 targets during the day (Wednesday), striking 45 buildings and headquarters, rocket launch sites and access routes leading to them, and vehicles.[117]

The IDF says it attacked a headquarters of Amal in the vicinity of Anatzrya (al-Ansariyeh).[118]

The news media report an Israeli strike on a refugee convoy waving white flags that had been fleeing southern Lebanon under Israeli orders.

According to news media reports, Israel "hacks into" the Al-Manar TV satellite signal, replacing it for 90 seconds with a transmission that shows Hezbollah command sites and rocket launching pads that have been destroyed.

Four officers and five IDF soldiers are killed and two officers and 23 additional soldiers are injured during IDF operations in Bint Jbeil and Maroun A-Ras.[119]

The IDF says that since Operation Change of Direction began, it has fired 45,000 artillery shells.[120]

---

[116] Integrated Regional Information Networks (IRIN) (Tyre, Lebanon), "Number of civilian deaths likely to be higher."

[117] IDF, "60 Targets Attacked Today in Lebanon," Wednesday 26 July 2006 22:34, http://www1.idf.il/DOVER/site/mainpage.asp?clr=1&sl=EN&id=7&docid=55125.

[118] Ibid.

[119] IDF War Log, "July 26th 2006."

[120] IDF, "60 Targets Attacked Today in Lebanon."

Day 16: Thursday, 27 July

The UN Security Council adopts a statement expressing shock and distress at Israel's bombing of the outpost on 25 July that killed four unarmed UN observers.

Italy's foreign minister, host of the international conference in Rome, says that the call for restraint from Israel has fallen on deaf ears.

President Bush says he wants an end to the conflict as soon as possible but that he does not want a "fake peace."

Syria's ambassador to the United States Imad Moustapha tells the Associated Press that there has been "not a single contact" by the US government with Syria since the fighting began.

In a taped message, al-Qaeda leader Ayman al-Zawahiri calls on Muslims to join the war against "crusaders" and "Zionists" in Lebanon. He says al-Qaeda will respond with force to attacks in Lebanon and Gaza.

Hezbollah fires 109 rockets into northern Israel. The launching of the "Khaibar-1" is announced against Afula. The IDF says that the Khaibar-1 is a modified Iranian Fajr rocket.

The Israeli Security-Political Cabinet agrees to continue air strikes while maintaining a limited ground offensive and approves the call up of 15,000 more military reservists.

Israeli justice minister Haim Ramon says Israel has been implicitly "authorized" to continue its attacks in Lebanon by the failure of Wednesday's international conference in Rome to call for an immediate and unconditional cease-fire. "Maximum firepower has to be used," he said. "We have to exploit the advantages that we have over Hezbollah with the air force and artillery and be cautious when we use ground troops. Everyone who is still in south Lebanon is linked to Hezbollah, we have called on all who are there to leave. Bint Jbeil is not a civilian location, we have to treat it like a military zone."[121]

---

[121] "You're all targets, Israel tells Lebanese in South," *Daily Telegraph* (UK), 28 July 2006, www.telegraph.co.uk/news/main.jhtml?xml=/news/2006/07/28/wmid28.xml.

Hezbollah official Nur Shalhov is killed in an IDF attack. The IDF says that Shalhov was responsible for Hezbollah's weapon smuggling activities, including the acquisition of long-range rockets.[122]

The IDF says it attacked over 90 targets during the night, including a Lebanese army radar north of Beirut.[123]

The Israel Air Force attacked about 67 targets in Lebanon during the day.[124]

Nine Israeli soldiers are killed and more than two dozen injured in the worst 24 hours for casualties in a 16-day-old conflict.

After the death of Israeli soldiers in Bint Jbeil, Lt Gen Dan Halutz says that many Hezbollah terrorists were killed and that Israel is continuing towards the achievement of its goals. "I'm certain that with this blow we have struck Hezbollah at the strategic level," Halutz says. "Never have so many countries united against this terror organization." He says that hundreds of Hezbollah terrorists have been killed and that "parts of the Hezbollah rocket system have been severely hit."[125]

News media reports say that at least 445 people, "most" of them civilians, have been confirmed killed in Lebanon, with 51 Israelis, including 18 civilians, killed.[126] The Lebanese minister of health says up to 600 people may have died in the 16-day war. He says hospitals had so far received 401 bodies of victims of the Israeli campaign. "On top of those victims, there are 150 to 200 bodies still under the rubble. We have not been able to pull them out because the areas they died in are still under fire," he said.[127]

---

[122] IDF War Log, "July 27th 2006."

[123] IDF, Summary of IDF Attacks in Lebanon During the Night, n.d. (27 July 2006), http://www1.idf.il/DOVER/site/mainpage.asp?sl=EN&id=7&docid=55151.EN; and IDF War Log, "July 27th 2006."

[124] IDF War Log, "July 27th 2006."

[125] MFA, "Chief of Staff Halutz: 'We have no intention of hurting Syria or the citizens of Lebanon'," 27 July 2006, http://www.mfa.gov.il/MFA/Terrorism+Obstacle+to+Peace/Terrorism+from+Lebanon+Hezbollah/Chief+of+Staff+Halutz+No+intention+of+hurting+Syria+or+citizens+of+Lebanon+27-Jul-2006.htm.

[126] Reuters, "Latest developments in the Middle East," 27 July 2006 11:22:42 p.m.

[127] Reuters (Beirut), "Lebanon says up to 600 killed in Israeli campaign," 27 July 2006.

Day 17: Friday, 28 July

At a joint press conference in Washington, President Bush and PM Blair announce that Secretary Rice will return to the Middle East Saturday to discuss a final UN resolution to secure a cease-fire. The two throw their support behind a UN-backed multinational peacekeeping force and warn Iran and Syria to curtail their support for Hezbollah.

The US State Department announces that the administration is requesting an additional $10 million in military aid to help prepare the Lebanese army, in conjunction with international forces, to deploy to the Israeli-Lebanese border in the future.

UN under secretary-general Egeland asks Israel and Hezbollah to stop fighting for 72 hours to enable relief workers to evacuate the elderly and disabled from southern Lebanon and get in emergency aid supplies.

Hezbollah fires 111 rockets into Israel, using long-range Khaibar-1 (Syrian 302 mm) rockets for the first time in five strikes on Afula, more than 50 km (30 mi) south of the Lebanese border. Al-Manar broadcasts pictures of the 302 mm rockets being fired at Afula. The rockets, according to the IDF, were launched from north of the Litani River from the Al-Zrariye area.

Nabih Berri, speaker of Lebanon's parliament and a leading Shi'a politician, says his Shi'a Amal movement and Hezbollah would join forces against Israel's offensive in Lebanon.

Minister of Defense Peretz states that "we have no intention of an offensive toward Syria" but warns that "[w]e hope Hezbollah does not drag Damascus into the conflict."

The IDF says that it attacked over 130 targets in Lebanon, with air attacks on over 60 targets on Friday.[128]

The Lebanese Higher Relief Commission states: "An Israeli missile also destroyed a four-story building belonging to speaker Nabih Berri in the southern port city of Tyre."[129]

---

[128] IDF, "IDF Attacks Over 60 Targets"; and IDF War Log, "July 28th 2006."

[129] Higher Relief Commission (HRC), Daily situation report (SITREP) no. 004, 28 July 2006.

The Independent (UK) claims that Israel is using depleted uranium in southern Lebanon.

Israeli forces pull back from Bint Jbeil late Friday and returned to Maroun a-Ras, which the IDF entered on 23 July.

The government of Lebanon reports 600 dead and 3,225 injured in Lebanon, including its estimate of bodies still uncovered.[130] Other reports say the death toll is 426, including 355 civilians.[131]

Day 18: Saturday, 29 July

Israel rejects the UN call for a 72-hour pause in fighting to evacuate people from south Lebanon and send in emergency aid, saying it has already opened a humanitarian corridor.

Prime Minister Siniora says that if Israel wants secure borders it must withdraw from the disputed Shebaa Farms area that it has occupied since 1967.

Hassan Nasrallah suggests that Hezbollah would accept a cease-fire and said he believed Israel wanted a cease-fire but was being pressured by Washington to continue the conflict. He said Secretary Rice, who arrived in Israel on Saturday, had come to "impose conditions that serve Israel."

Hassan Nasrallah says in a televised speech: "It is clear that Israeli enemy cannot achieve any military success. The whole world knows that." He threatens more rocket attacks on Israeli cities if Israel does not quickly end its air and artillery strikes.

Secretary Rice arrives in Israel to seek agreement for the specific mandate and arrangements for a multinational force in southern Lebanon.

British Cabinet ministers Jack Straw and Hilary Benn speak out against the Lebanon war. Straw says that the war has killed 10 times more innocent Lebanese than Israelis.

Hezbollah fires 86 rockets at Israel.

---

[130] Ibid.

[131] AFP (Beirut), "Six civilians killed in new wave of Israeli air raids on Lebanon," 28 July 2006, http://www.dawn.com/2006/07/28/welcome.htm.

The IDF announces that it attacked over 60 terror-related targets in Lebanon on 29 July.[132] Aircraft strike the main highway linking Beirut and Damascus. The Israeli military says it hit the road, closing the border crossing between Lebanon and Syria, "to prevent smuggling of weapons."

The IDF says that ground forces disengaged from the village of Bint Jbeil in southern Lebanon after completing their operations in the area.[133]

The government of Lebanon says that 615 Lebanese civilians have died and 3,020 have been injured.[134] The news media say 439 Lebanese have been killed, including 368 civilians.[135] Reuters says at least 475 people, "mostly civilians," have been killed in Lebanon in the conflict, and 51 Israelis have died.[136]

Day 19: Sunday, 30 July

Initial reports say that more than 60 civilians were killed in an Israeli attack in the southern village of Qana, the same site of an Israeli bombing of a UN base on 18 April 1996 that killed 105 civilians who had taken refuge there during Israel's Grapes of Wrath offensive.

UN secretary-general Annan's representative in Lebanon Geir Pedersen says he was "deeply shocked and saddened by the killing of tens of Lebanese civilians, including many children in Qana, south Lebanon, and calls for an immediate cease-fire and investigation," a statement said.

Lebanese PM Siniora denounces Israel's "war crime" in Qana, saying that there would be no talks on a cease-fire until the bombing ceased. He thanks Hezbollah leader Hassan Nasrallah and "all those who sacrifice their lives for the independence

---

[132] IDF War Log, "July 29th 2006."

[133] Ibid.

[134] HRC, SITREP No. 005, 29 July 2006.

[135] AFP (Tyre, Lebanon), "Death toll in Lebanon hits 439," 29 July 2006, http://www.dawn.com/2006/07/29/welcome.htm.

[136] Reuters, "Latest developments in the Middle East," 29 July 2006, 10:27:12 p.m.

and sovereignty of Lebanon." Lebanese officials also say that Secretary Rice is unwelcome in Beirut for talks.

World leaders quickly condemn the Qana attack, and France, Jordan, Egypt, the EU, and others call for immediate cease-fire. Thousands of demonstrators flocked to downtown Beirut to join the protestors, breaking into the UN headquarters. Gunmen also storm the UN compound in Gaza City.

At Lebanon's request, the UN Security Council convenes an emergency meeting Sunday in the wake of the Qana attack. France circulates a draft resolution calling for an immediate cease-fire. A permanent cease-fire, the resolution says, would involve "the release of the abducted Israeli soldiers and the settlement of the issue of the Lebanese prisoners detained in Israel."

In his first public comment since the Lebanon conflict began, Syrian president Bashar al-Asad describes the Israeli strikes on Qana as "state terrorism," saying that "the Syrian people are ready to offer anything that might support, help and bolster Lebanon."

Israel later says that over 130 Hezbollah rockets were launched towards the city of Nahariya and the communities in the western Galilee from the vicinity of the village of Qana, and that residents were warned to leave the village. More than 50 rockets were launched from within the village itself, and launchers were routinely situated in close proximity to residential buildings.[137]

An Israeli Cabinet communiqué says, "The State of Israel deeply and sincerely regrets the killing of civilians during operations to halt firing intended to murder Israelis." Israel agrees to suspend air attacks in south Lebanon for 48 hours. Israel is also to coordinate with the UN to allow a 24-hour window for residents of southern Lebanon to safely leave the area if they wish.

Secretary Rice meets with Israeli Foreign Minister Livni and Defense Minister Peretz.

Hezbollah fires at least 156 rockets into northern Israel.

---

[137] MFA (communicated by the IDF spokesman), "Incident in Kafr Qana," 30 July 2006, http://www.mfa.gov.il/MFA/Government/Communiques/2006/Incident+in+Qana+IDF+Spokesman+30-Jul-2006.htm.

The IDF says that it carried out over 80 "aerial attacks" in the past 24 hours (midnight July 30–midnight July 31). IDF aircraft attacked rocket launch sites southeast of Tyre, sites from which Hezbollah had launched missile attacks against Nahariya and the area of western Galilee.[138]

Lebanon's main international border crossing was closed on Sunday, 30 July, a day after Israeli attack struck the road leading to Syria. Bombs had gouged out large craters on the road leading to the Masnaa border crossing. The closure left only one route through northern Lebanon to Syria as the only relatively safe passage out of the country.[139]

The village of Kafra southeast of Tyre was hit by 13 Israeli raids overnight, with the Israeli navy firing 80 shells in the area and artillery blasting 50 shells over the border.[140]

Reuters says that Israeli tanks were massing near the border village of Metula, and Israeli forces are reported making another new incursion into Lebanon on Sunday to the outskirts of the village of al-Taybeh.

An IDF soldier is moderately wounded during IDF operations in the village of al-Adayseh during which large stockpiles of weaponry were uncovered.[141]

The government of Lebanon reports 670 Lebanese been killed and 3,125 people injured to date.[142] The Lebanese health minister says that the death toll is closer to 750, including bodies buried in rubble.[143] The news media report at least 483 Lebanese, "mostly civilians," and 51 Israelis have been killed.[144]

---

[138] IDF War Log, "July 30th 2006."

[139] AFP (Qana, Lebanon), "51 killed in Israeli blitz on Lebanon village," 30 July 2006, http://www.dawn.com/2006/07/30/welcome.htm.

[140] AFP (Tyre, Lebanon), "21 casualties in Israeli raid on Lebanon house," 30 July 2006, http://www.dawn.com/2006/07/30/welcome.htm.

[141] IDF War Log, "July 30th 2006."

[142] HRC, SITREP no. 006, 30 July 2006.

[143] Reuters, "Latest developments in the Middle East," 30 July 2006 11:07:27 p.m.

[144] "List of collective massacres perpetrated by Israeli Army in its attack against Lebanon in summer 2006," in annex 6, Report of the Commission of Inquiry on Lebanon pursuant to *Human Rights Council Resolution S-2/1*, Advanced Unedited Version, 10 November 2006.

Day 20: Monday, 31 July

Prime Minister Olmert again apologizes to the Lebanese people "for the pain caused" in Qana and in the war, and says that Israel's fight is against Hezbollah, not Lebanon.

Israel reportedly suspends air attacks on southern Lebanon for 48 hours. The suspension is to allow investigation into civilian deaths in Qana, although air cover is still provided for ground forces in the border area.

Hezbollah evidently follows its own suspension of rocket attacks on Israel, shooting just six rockets (or possibly mortars) on 31 July.

As of 31 July, the government of Lebanon's Higher Relief Council (HRC) reports that 784 people have been killed and 3,240 people have been injured,[145] an increase of 124 deaths in one day. The Lebanese minister of health puts the death toll at 750 dead.[146]

Prime Minister Olmert tells Prime Minister Blair in a telephone call that Israel will accept an effective multinational force to deploy along the Blue Line and at the border crossings between Syria and Lebanon.

President Bush says any peace between Israel and Lebanon has to be "long-lasting and sustainable," again resisting calls for an immediate cease-fire. Secretary Rice says she believes a sustainable cease-fire to end the fighting between Israel and Hezbollah could be forged this week.

British foreign secretary Margaret Beckett calls Qana "appalling" and argues that an agreement for a cease-fire had to be reached "this week."

EU foreign ministers hold an extraordinary meeting in Brussels and agree on the key principles for a political settlement in Lebanon. They call for an immediate cessation of hostilities to be followed by a sustainable cease-fire, stating that they

---

[145] USAID, Lebanon Humanitarian Emergency USG Humanitarian Situation Report #5, Fiscal Year (FY) 2006, 31 July 2006.

[146] HRC, SITREP No. 007, 31 July 2006.

strongly support UN efforts to define the political framework for a lasting solution.

Shi'a leader Ayatollah Ali al-Sistani issues a statement threatening unspecified "dire consequences" if an immediate ceasefire to stop "this Israeli aggression" is not imposed.

The Israeli ambassador to the UN tells the Security Council: "Is it not time that Lebanon took its fate into its own hands, rather than keep crying out to the Security Council and to the international community? Is it not time that the Lebanese army, which is there, acted in order to rid itself of the very beast which is bringing this horror and this destruction upon its people?"

In an address to Israeli mayors, Olmert says: "Since the war in Lebanon began, we have reached substantial and important achievements. Hezbollah suffered a major blow. We succeeded in damaging the organization's long-range missile system. Hezbollah and its leader are isolated in both the Lebanese and Arab arenas. This is almost a one time opportunity to change the rules of the game in Lebanon."

He says that Hezbollah would take a long time "if ever," to recuperate: "Hezbollah does not look today as it did 20 days ago —threatening, arrogant and dangerous." Of the war, he says:

> We succeeded in damaging the organization's long-range missile system deep inside Lebanon, and we will continue to do so. We have destroyed Hezbollah's command and control systems, as well as its headquarters, and damaged its infrastructures. Hezbollah's military bases and compounds in Beirut, Ba'al-Beq and other places no longer look the same. The system of Katyushas spread in south Lebanon was severely damaged. We have succeeded in locating and striking the smuggling of ammunition from Syria to the Hezbollah, which continues at this very moment, and we will continue to do this. . . . The organization's leadership is hiding, it operates in the dark, in fear for its life, and we will continue to pursue it, everywhere, any time. It is a leadership under pressure, engaged in a web of lies and manipulations designed to conceal the true reality.[147]

Defense Minister Peretz says Israel will step up its offensive despite the 48-hour suspension of air strikes.

On Monday, a Royal Jordanian Air force plane landed in Beirut, carrying a shipment of UNICEF emergency supplies to Lebanon.

---

[147] Transcript, address by PM Conference of Heads of Local Authorities, 31 July 2006.

Israel reportedly uses an armed UAV in a daylight air strike in Lebanon for the first time.

The IDF announces: "In accordance with the decision made by the political echelon regarding the partial suspension of aerial activity, the IDF carried out a number of aerial attacks overnight."

Three IDF soldiers are lightly wounded on Monday in the Kfar Kila area when an antitank missile hits their armored personnel carrier. A tank that follows to rescue the injured troops is also hit by a missile and three soldiers are injured.

Writing in the *Guardian* (UK), Human Rights Watch Emergencies Director Peter Bouckaert says: "The pattern of Israeli behavior in southern Lebanon suggests a deliberate policy. . . . Israel blames Hezbollah for the massive civilian toll in Lebanon, claiming that they are . . . fighting from within the civilian population. This is a convenient excuse."

The UN Security Council extends the mandate of the UNIFIL for one month.

Day 21: Tuesday, 1 August

Israel's Political-Security Cabinet gives a green light to widen the ground offensive inside southern Lebanon.

Prime Minister Olmert signals that a cease-fire may also be on the horizon. In televised remarks, Olmert says: "I believe one can say today. . . that there is no way to measure this war according to the number or range of the rockets being fired at us. From the very first day, neither I, nor the defense minister, nor the Israeli government, nor the military leadership—and this is to its credit—ever promised for even one moment that when the fighting ended, there would be absolutely no rockets within firing range of the State of Israel. No one can make such a promise."

Haaretz reports that while the IAF investigation into the 30 July Qana incident was ongoing, "questions have been raised over military accounts of the incident." The IDF had changed its original story, the newspaper said, "it now appears that the military had no information on rockets launched from the site of the building, or the presence of Hezbollah men at the time."[148]

The European Union failed to reach consensus on calling for an immediate cease-fire in Lebanon, calling instead for an "immediate cessation of hostilities."

Senior Iranian cleric Ayatollah Ahmad Jannati calls on Muslim countries to send weapons to Hezbollah to fight Israel.

Speaking at the World Affairs Council in Los Angeles, PM Blair says that there is a lack of "any understanding of the Israeli predicament." Blair supports Israel in not pursuing "diplomacy" to fight Hezbollah, saying that Israel did what any nation would do: defend its sovereignty and fight terrorists who glorify hatred and bigotry.

Hezbollah fires only nine "rockets" into Israel.

Israel's justice minister says about 300 of an estimated 2,000 Hezbollah fighters have been killed so far, while the tourism minister puts the number at 400. Hezbollah denies both claims.

Israeli press reports say that the IDF, under the assumption that only a few days are left for operations against Hezbollah, gear up for a massive ground incursion on three different fronts, utilizing reservists for the first time in Lebanon.[149]

Press reports from southern Lebanon indicate IDF ground forces engaged in four separate incursions; in the region of al-Taybeh, al-Adayseh, and Kfar Kila; in Aiyt a-Shab (where IDF forces reportedly entered on the afternoon of August 1); around Houla in the southeast; and in the Maroun a-Ras and Bint Jbeil areas.

An IDF officer and two soldiers of Battalion 101 of the Paratrooper Brigade are killed, and 25 additional soldiers are injured while operating "to destroy Hezbollah organization infrastructure" in the village of Aiyt A-Shab.[150]

---

[148] Yoav Stern, Yuval Yoaz, and Amos Harel, "Livni: Qana Attack Led to Turning Point in Support for Israel," *Haaretz*, 1 August 2006, http://www.haaretz.com/hasen/pages/ShArtVty.jhtml?sw=livni+qana&itemNo=745185.

[149] Yaakov Katz, "3 soldiers killed in Hezbollah ambush; 5 brigades battle village by village in S. Lebanon," *Jerusalem Post*, 2 August 2006, http://info.jpost.com/C002/Supplements/CasualtiesOfWar/2006_08_02.html.

[150] Ibid.; and IDF War Log, "August 1st 2006."

A commando operation is conducted by IDF special forces in the area of Baalbek. The commandos attack a suspected Hezbollah headquarters located inside the Iranian-funded Hikmeh Hospital and confiscate much Hezbollah equipment, according to the IDF. During the operation, Israeli forces kill about 10 terrorists and capture five others.[151] Reuters reports that the Baalbek special operation killed 19 civilians, including four children.

IDF reservists enter Lebanon for the first time during the current campaign in western Lebanon along the coast.[152]

The government of Lebanon now puts the death toll at 828; civil defense and Red Cross personnel are reported as having retrieved many bodies during the lull in bombing.[153]

Gas shortages are reported in Lebanon.[154]

Electricity du Liban (EDL) says that electrical power in Lebanon will return to normal today.

Day 22: Wednesday, 2 August

Israel resumes full air operations, and Hezbollah fires its highest single-day total of rockets since the war began. Some land as far as 70 km inside Israel.

Lebanese PM Siniora unveils a "seven step" plan to achieve an immediate and comprehensive cease-fire:

- An undertaking to release Lebanese and Israeli prisoners and detainees.

- Withdrawal of the Israeli army behind the Blue Line.

---

[151] IDF War Log, "August 1st 2006."

[152] Yaakov Katz, "IDF soldier killed in battle with Hezbollah in Aita a-Sha'ab [Aiyt a-Shab]," *Jerusalem Post*, 2 August 2006, http://info.jpost.com/C002/Supplements/CasualtiesOfWar/2006_08_03.html.

[153] HRC, SITREP no. 008, 1 August 2006.

[154] Under the heat of August, thousand of Lebanese citizens lined up at gas stations to fill their cars. "I have been waiting for two hours and I don't know how much longer I am going to wait to fill 20 liters," George said. "Petroleum products are available in sufficient quantities and threatened to punish gas stations that refuse to sell gasoline or try to increase its prices," Energy and Water ministry said. See HRC SITREP no. 008.

- Placement of Shebaa Farms and the Kfar Shouba hills under UN jurisdiction until Lebanese sovereignty is "fully settled."

- Lebanese army authority in the south and "no weapons or authority" other than the Lebanese state.

- Enhancement of the UN force operating in South Lebanon to guarantee stability and security.

- Return to the 1949 Armistice Agreement between Lebanon and Israel.

- International commitment to support Lebanon, especially in the areas of relief, reconstruction, and rebuilding of the national economy.

The UN Security Council embarks on intensive talks to craft a final resolution setting out the terms of an enduring cease-fire.

Prime Minister Olmert says that fighting will continue until a multinational force deploys to southern Lebanon and Hezbollah is disarmed. Israel's offensive had already "entirely destroyed" Hezbollah's infrastructure, Olmert says. "All the population which is the power base of the Hezbollah in Lebanon was displaced," he continues. "They lost their properties, they lost their possessions, they are bitter, they are angry at Hezbollah and the power structure of Lebanon itself has been divided and Hezbollah is now entirely isolated in Lebanon"

Deputy PM Peres says that 70 percent of Hezbollah's long- and medium-range missiles and 20 percent of short-range missiles have been destroyed. He says that the IDF has destroyed about 1,000 structures used by Hezbollah and killed more than 250 Hezbollah fighters, including regional commanders.[155]

Hezbollah fires 212 rockets at Israel, the most since 12 July. One modified Fajr hits near Beit She'an, about 65 km inside Israel, the deepest rocket strike into Israel so far, while another hits the West Bank for the first time.[156] Hezbollah rockets reportedly hit

---

[155] "Peres: 70 percent of Hezbollah's long- and medium-range missiles destroyed," 2 August 2006, *YnetNews.com*, http://www.ynetnews.com/articles/0,7340,L-3285044,00.html.

[156] Katz, "IDF soldier killed in battle with Hezbollah."

the Zarít military base, Israeli military headquarters for northern Israel, as well as the Ami'ad military base. One Israeli civilian is killed in Saar, the first civilian casualty since July 25.

Mahmoud Qomati, deputy of Hezbollah's political bureau, says Hezbollah has enough rockets to last months: "Our missile capacity is still untouched. It is sufficient at two levels, in quantity for the missiles they know of, and in quality for those they still don't know about—the type or the range." He added, "We have enough missiles for months."

Starting in the morning hours, the IDF says it attacks over 120 targets across southern Lebanon.[157]

The IDF drops leaflets over Nabatiyeh calling on Hezbollah guerrillas to surrender and warning them that "we will get you wherever you flee."

IDF deputy chief of staff Maj Gen Moshe Kaplinsky is quoted in the *Jerusalem Post* saying that the military was working on a plan for ground forces to push to the Litani River, some 20 km from the border with Israel.

The *Jerusalem Post* reports that nearly 9,000 IDF soldiers were operating on the ground in Lebanon.[158] The IDF officially states that reserve forces called to active duty took part in operations inside Lebanon for the first time.

An IDF soldier from the Golani Brigade is severely wounded and two more are lightly injured during the morning in the village of Muhaybib.[159]

In battles during the day, the IDF says that it killed about 35 armed Hezbollah terrorists and wounded many more.[160]

The government of Lebanon reports 835 killed and 3,210 injured.[161]

---

[157] IDF War Log, "August 2nd 2006."

[158] Katz, "IDF soldier killed in battle with Hezbollah."

[159] IDF War Log, "August 2nd 2006"; and Katz, "IDF soldier killed in battle with Hezbollah."

[160] IDF War Log, "August 2nd 2006."

[161] HRC, SITREP no. 009, 2 August 2006.

Day 23: Thursday, 3 August

Hassan Nasrallah appears in a taped broadcast on Al-Manar TV and offers to stop rocket attacks on northern Israel in return for an end to air strikes, the first such offer since 12 July. "Anytime you decide to stop your campaign against our cities, villages, civilians and infrastructure, we will not fire rockets on any Israeli settlement or city," Nasrallah says. He also vows to attack Tel Aviv if Beirut continues to be attacked. "If you bomb our capital Beirut, we will bomb the capital of your usurping entity. . . . We will bomb Tel Aviv," he says. Nasrallah goes on to say:

> I want to say to our Lebanese people, the peoples of our nation, and the world. . . . What has happened since the first day of this war, and is still happening, even today—the killing, massacres, destruction, brutality, and barbarism—the ones responsible for all this are, first and foremost, Bush and his administration. In our opinion, Olmert and his government are no more than tools in this war. I'd like to stress this by saying that the blood of the women and children in Qana and the blood of all the elderly and the innocent civilians that has been spilled in Lebanon stains the faces of Bush, Condoleezza Rice, Rumsfeld, and Cheney.[162]

Diplomats from the UK, France, and the United States are reported close to agreeing on a UN Security Council resolution implementing an immediate cease-fire.

In a live address beamed to the Organization of the Islamic Conference (OIC) in Malaysia, PM Siniora calls on the OIC to back his seven-point plan to end the Lebanon war and provide humanitarian aid to the country. The OIC calls for an immediate cease-fire, and accuses Israel of "blatant and flagrant" human rights violations in carrying out its "indiscriminate and massive" air strikes.

After speaking with Syrian president Bashar al-Assad, Spanish foreign minister Miguel Angel Moratinos says that Syria is ready to help put an end to the Israel-Hezbollah war and is eager to take part in talks on a "comprehensive and lasting peace" for the region.

---

[162] Transcript, Hezbollah Secretary-General Hassan Nasrallah, Al-Manar TV, 3 August 2006.

Jordan's King Abdullah says that the Israeli offensive against Hezbollah has turned its fighters into heroes among ordinary Arabs. "They want to destroy Hezbollah by tanks and air force. Peace comes by returning occupied territory and setting up a Palestinian state," he says. "Okay, if you [Israel] destroy Hezbollah and, let's say, after a year or two there is no solution to the Palestinian cause or Lebanon or Syria . . . then a new Hezbollah would emerge, maybe in Jordan, Syria or Egypt. . . . Israel should know this," he adds.

Hezbollah fires 241 rockets, the highest daily total of the war, bringing up to 2,300 the total number of Hezbollah rocket attacks since the war began.[163] Eight Israeli civilians die in Acre and Tarshiha after a massive rocket barrage involving more than 130 Katyushas within a 90-minute period.[164] Hezbollah fires the Iranian-made Fajr-5 (Khaibar-1) for the second time in an attack on the West Bank town of Jenin. A Katyusha volley is fired against Acre.

IAF aircraft resume attacks on Beirut, after a reported lull of several days. Israel Army radio reports that the IDF has expanded ground operations in southern Lebanon, with elements of seven brigades and up to 10,000 troops fighting Hezbollah.

The IDF drops leaflets over the southern suburbs of Beirut, warning residents to immediately leave areas where Hezbollah activity is being carried out.

The Israeli offensive against Hezbollah has no predetermined limit, PM Olmert tells *Le Monde*. Asked if the Israeli objective was to reach the Litani River, Olmert told the French newspaper that "there is no limit. . . . We are not going to fight all the

---

[163] IDF War Log, "August 3rd 2006." Israel MDA says that from dawn until 21:03, over 200 Katyushas fell on Israel, most of them within one-half hour in the afternoon. MDA News, MDA Daily Activities—4 August 2006, http://www.ukmda.org/news/?content_id=151.

[164] Yaakov Katz, "8 civilians, 4 soldiers killed in bloodiest day of war," *Jerusalem Post*, 4 August 2006, http://info.jpost.com/C002/Supplements/CasualtiesOfWar/2006_08_06.upd.html.

way to Beirut. But as for the rest, I don't think I have to announce my plans."

The *Jerusalem Post* reports that elements of seven IDF brigades have taken up positions in more than 20 villages in southern Lebanon as the army begins to carve out "a security zone" that would be clear of Hezbollah. Ground Forces commander Maj Gen Benny Gantz says that the IDF plans to make the security zone larger than the previously planned depth of 6–8 km.[165]

Three IDF soldiers are killed and one is severely injured by an antitank missile fired at their vehicle in the village of Rajmin.[166]

IDF forces expose two weapon caches in civilian structures in the Lebanese villages of Markaba and al-Taybeh.[167]

The government of Lebanon says that 860 have died and 3,265 have been injured.[168]

HRW issues a report branding some Israeli attacks as "war crimes." "Our research shows that Israel's claim that Hezbollah fighters are hiding among civilians does not explain, let alone justify, Israel's indiscriminate warfare," a statement said accompanying the 50-page report. "In many cases, Israeli forces struck an area with no apparent military target. In some instances, Israeli forces appear to have deliberately targeted civilians."

A chronic fuel crisis is reported in Lebanon, with only two to three days of supplies left, owing to Israel's blockade of the country and attack on gas stations. "We have negotiated for two tankers, now off Cyprus, to go into Beirut and Tripoli ports," a World Food Program spokeswoman says.[169]

The WHO says that the main hospital in Baalbek has been severely damaged and that the Ghandour hospital in Nabatiyeh has also been extensively damaged from attacks. Serious shortages of drugs, fuel, electricity, and water supplies are affecting the health care system, the WHO says.[170]

---

[165] Katz, "8 civilians, 4 soldiers killed in bloodiest day of war."

[166] IDF War Log, "August 3rd 2006."

[167] Ibid.

[168] HRC, SITREP no. 010, 3 August 2006.

[169] Ibid.

[170] Ibid.

Day 24: Friday, 4 August

Hezbollah fires 195 rockets at Israel, killing three civilians, one in Mrar and two in Majdal Krum. At least two rockets land in or near the Israeli city of Hadera, about 80 km inside Israel, the deepest rocket attack so far.

Israeli aircraft are reported bombing into northern Lebanon "for the first time," attacking five bridges in Christian areas between Beirut and the north, attempting to cut off the last significant road link with Syria.[171]

The European Commission issues a statement expressing its concern about the worsening access situation for humanitarian aid following Israeli attacks on Lebanon's main transportation routes.

The United States and France are reported to be inching closer to a deal on a UN resolution calling for an end to fighting.

Arab foreign ministers say they will hold an emergency meeting in Beirut on Monday to press for a cease-fire.

The IDF says it attacked nine Hezbollah targets in south Beirut during the night, including a house of a senior Hezbollah official, a bunker underneath a soccer stadium used for weapons storage "used by the Hezbollah terror organization to direct terror activity," and a security office. A Hamas office is also attacked.[172]

The IDF attacks the "Hadi Nasrallah" harbor in Ouzai, near the Beirut airport, heavily damaging "terror infrastructure at the harbor and maritime craft in the area."[173]

The AFP reports that Israel bombs a major power station serving the Bekaa Valley.[174]

---

[171] HRC, SITREP no. 011, 4 August 2006; and HRC, SITREP no. 012, 5 August 2006.

[172] IDF War Log, "August 4th 2006"; and IDF, "Airstrikes on Beirut Hezbollah Targets," Friday, 4 August 2006, 16:04, http://www1.idf.il/DOVER/site/mainpage.asp?sl=EN&id=7&docid=55693.EN.

[173] Ibid.

[174] AFP (Beirut), "Israelis bomb major power station in Lebanon," 4 August 2006.

Ground fighting intensifies around areas of the latest incursions near Markaba and the coastal town of Naqoura. Israel says 10 Hezbollah fighters were killed.

Three IDF soldiers from an armored battalion belonging to the 188th Armored Brigade and the reserve's Alexandroni Brigade are killed in Rajmin when their tank is hit by an antitank missile.[175]

An IDF officer and two soldiers from the Golani Brigade are killed by antitank missile fire in the village of Markaba.[176]

Two IDF soldiers are injured by another antitank missile fired at their tank in the village of al-Taybeh.[177]

The government of Lebanon says that 863 have died and 3,280 have been injured.[178]

The Lebanese minister of health says that the fuel crisis in Lebanon has taken a dramatic turn for the worse and that hospitals might be forced to close within the next seven to 10 days.[179]

Day 25: Saturday, 5 August

The United States and France reach agreement on a joint draft Security Council resolution aimed at securing a cease-fire in Lebanon. President Chirac's office announces that "an accord has been found between the French and Americans on the draft resolution prepared by France to call for a complete cessation of hostilities and work towards permanent cease-fire and long-term solution."

The UN Security Council meets to discuss the resolution.

Thousands of people demonstrate in Britain and France to demand an end to the war.

An Israeli minister says time is running out for Israel's military campaign in Lebanon, following the completion of the draft UN resolution.

---

[175] Katz, "8 civilians, 4 soldiers killed in bloodiest day of war."

[176] IDF War Log, "August 4th 2006."

[177] Ibid.

[178] HRC, SITREP no. 011, 4 August 2006.

[179] Ibid.

Hezbollah fires 170 rockets into Israel. Three civilians die in the Bedouin village of Arab al-Aramshe near the border, and an elderly woman dies of a heart attack in Kiryat Ata while taking cover in a bomb shelter during the rocket strikes on the Haifa suburbs. Five are injured, police and medics say.

Maj Gen Udi Adam says on Israeli Army radio that he expects to see a decrease in the extent and range of the Hezbollah rocket attacks on Israel, as the organization is pushed further and further northward. Adam said the IDF goals were to reach and neutralize rocket-launch sites and to strike Hezbollah infrastructure and terrorists. The Northern Command commander said that the IDF was meeting the goals that it had set.[180]

Israel launches what is reported in the news media as its heaviest bombardment of southern Lebanon since 12 July, carrying out 250 air attacks and firing some 4,000 shells, according to Lebanese press reports. The area around Aitaroun alone is reportedly hit with 2,000 shells. During the day, IDF aircraft attacked over 70 targets in Lebanon.[181] The IDF, however, states that overnight (from 4 August), the IAF attacked over 80 Hezbollah targets.

Israel warns residents of Sidon to evacuate south Lebanon's biggest city.

The Israeli Navy's "Shayetet 13" commando squad raids the city of Tyre to strike at rocket launchers and Hezbollah cells responsible for the launches of long-range missiles against Israel that earlier had struck Hadera. During the operation, an IDF officer and soldier are severely wounded and six additional soldiers are lightly injured. "The purpose of the commando raid was to reach Hezbollah officials and to raid several targets that have useful [intelligence] materials and information," Maj Gen Adam says.[182] Hezbollah says it repelled the commandos.

---

[180] Yaakov Katz, "Two reserve soldiers were killed," *Jerusalem Post*, 5 August 2006, http://info.jpost.com/C002/Supplements/CasualtiesOfWar/2006_08_06.upd.html.

[181] IDF War Log, "August 5th 2006."

[182] Ibid.

An IDF reservist from Brigade 2 is killed Saturday and 21 soldiers are injured when an antitank missile hits a building in Aiyt a-Shab.[183]

An IDF soldier from the engineering corps unit is killed and another is slightly injured in Nabi al-Awadi near al-Taybeh late Friday night (1 a.m. Saturday morning) when a mortar hits his vehicle.[184]

An IDF soldier is severely wounded in the afternoon when a Hezbollah mortar shell strikes an IDF base on the Israeli-Lebanese border.[185]

Press reports say that Nahr al-Barid dam, which provides electric power to northern Lebanon, is attacked.

The government of Lebanon says that 907 have died and 3,293 have been injured.[186] According to an AFP count, at least 993 people, "mostly civilians," have been killed. Hezbollah says 48 of its fighters have died; Amal says it has lost seven fighters. The war has also forced 915,672 people from their homes, including 220,000 who left Lebanon, according to the HRC. The figure includes 100,000 foreigners and dual nationals who were evacuated.[187]

Amnesty International criticizes the Israeli investigation of the Qana "massacre" as a "whitewash."

Day 26: Sunday, 6 August

The UN Security Council meets to discuss the draft French resolution, but Russian ambassador Vitaly Churkin says the council is not close to an agreement that could allow a resolution to be passed. The Lebanese government rejects the initial draft, saying it would not end hostilities and asking for the text

---

[183] Ibid.; and Katz, "Two reserve soldiers killed."

[184] "Sgt. Or Shahar, 20, killed in Lebanon," *Jerusalem Post*, 5 August 2006, http://info.jpost.com/C002/Supplements/CasualtiesOfWar/2006_08_06.upd.html.

[185] IDF War Log, "August 5th 2006."

[186] HRC, SITREP No. 012, 5 August 2006.

[187] AFP (Beirut), "Israeli offensive kills at least 993 in Lebanon: latest toll," 5 August 2006, http://www.dawn.com/2006/08/05/welcome.htm.

to be amended. The Beirut government insists on the Siniora seven-point plan that calls for an immediate cease-fire and an exchange of prisoners. Prime Minister Siniora tells CNN that the draft is "not adequate" and "does not really achieve the objective that they have set for themselves."

The Syrian foreign minister also condemns the draft resolution, saying it is a "recipe for the continuation of the (current) war" and also "civil war" in Lebanon.

Israel says it will continue its offensive until an international force arrives to take over in southern Lebanon. Aircraft continue to attack roads and bridges in north Lebanon.

Secretary Rice says that there will be violence in the Middle East "for some time to come" even after the adoption of a UN resolution aimed at ending the Lebanon conflict.

Thousands march through Brussels for the second consecutive Sunday to call for peace in Lebanon.

Prime Minister Olmert, in an interview with a German newspaper, tells European leaders to stop preaching to him about civilian casualties.

Hezbollah fires 163 rockets of varying types on Sunday, killing three civilians and 12 soldiers. Israeli MDA says it treated 148 casualties during 69 Katyusha incidents: 13 dead (including soldiers), seven severely wounded, six moderately wounded, and 64 anxiety patients.[188] It is Hezbollah's deadliest wave of rocket attacks on Israel since fighting began on 12 July. A Syrian-made rocket, filled with ball bearings, kills 12 IDF reservists near Kibbutz Kfar Giladi while they are preparing to enter Lebanon.[189] Later on the same day Hezbollah launches rockets at seven residential locations in Haifa, killing three and injuring over 100.

---

[188] MDA News, "MDA Daily Activities August 6th–7th, 2006," 8 August 2006, http://www.ukmda.org/news/?content_id=153.

[189] MFA, Israel-Hezbollah Conflict: Summary of Events; and IDF War Log, "August 6th 2006."

The government of Lebanon says that 933 have died and 3,322 have been injured since 12 July.[190]

The IDF says that during the night, aircraft attacked over 80 targets in Lebanon, and that in the past 24 hours, it carried out 170 "aerial attacks across Lebanon."[191] The IDF says that it has attacked more the 4,600 targets since 12 July, including:

- seven Hezbollah terror training camps,
- more than 60 Hezbollah bunkers and tunnel openings,
- over 260 Hezbollah headquarters and other buildings,
- upwards of 70 weapons-storage sites,
- 90 missile launchers and truck-mounted missile launchers,
- over 100 suspect vehicles,
- varied Hezbollah infrastructure, and
- more than 50 bridges and access roads.[192]

An IDF soldier is severely wounded and another soldier is lightly injured during exchanges of fire in the village of al-Bayyadah, in the western sector of southern Lebanon. During the battles, Hezbollah fired antitank missiles at IDF forces, which returned fire and confirmed hitting the attackers.[193]

Later, an IDF soldier was severely wounded and four more were lightly wounded in the village of Muhaybib in southern Lebanon.[194]

A UNIFIL request to erect a temporary bridge over the Litani River is rejected by Israeli authorities.[195]

---

[190] HRC, SITREP no. 013, 6 August 2006.

[191] IDF War Log, "August 6th 2006."

[192] IDF, "Day 26: 4,600 Airstrikes So Far," 06/08/2006, 14:18, http://www1.idf.il/DOVER/site/mainpage.asp?sl=EN&id=7&docid=55849.EN.

[193] IDF War Log, "August 6th 2006."

[194] Ibid.

[195] Amnesty International, "Israel/Lebanon: Deliberate destruction or 'collateral damage'? Israeli attacks on civilian infrastructure," MDE 18/007/2006, August 2006, 3.

Day 27: Monday, 7 August

A UN Security Council vote on the draft French resolution is delayed. Lebanon proposes amendments on both the cease-fire and on the Shebaa Farms territorial dispute.

Speaking to Arab foreign ministers, Lebanese PM Siniora demands a "quick and decisive cease-fire" and calls for immediate withdrawal of Israeli troops from south Lebanon and assistance to reconstruct the Lebanese economy. He says that the Arab ministers support Lebanon's seven-point plan and Lebanon will send 15,000 troops to the south when Israeli troops begin to withdraw from the area.

Saudi FM Saud al-Faisal calls for an end to Israeli attacks on Lebanon, saying that Saudi Arabia's patience was wearing thin. "If Israel wants to live in this region it has to learn to stay in peace with the people of the region," he says, adding, "They are destroying the whole country because two soldiers were captured. It is a tragedy."

President Bush and Secretary Rice meet to discuss the UN resolution. The statement issued says:

> The first resolution, which the Security Council is now considering, calls for a stop of all hostilities. In addition, the resolution calls for an embargo on the shipment of any arms into Lebanon, except as authorized by the Lebanese government. A second resolution will help establish a sustainable and enduring cease-fire and provide a mandate for a robust international force that will help the legitimate government of Lebanon extend its authority over all of Lebanon's territory.

Press reports in Israel suggest that the civilian political leadership was restraining the IDF, a suggestion that receives a vigorous and direct denial from PM Olmert.

Hezbollah fires 185 rockets into Israel. At 15:30 the IDF identifies a rocket launcher on the back of a pickup truck in the center of the village of Haneen near a bombed building that serves as local Hezbollah headquarters.

The IDF says that since 12 July, it has flown more than 9,300 sorties and attacked over 5,000 targets.[196]

The IDF announces that it carried out attacks on 82 targets overnight, including 42 "structures," upwards of 30 access roads, and six launchers.[197]

The IDF says it attacked over 150 targets over the past 24 hours, including about 50 Hezbollah structures, 10 tunnels and caves, 60 launching sites and access routes, and launchers and vehicles.[198]

IDF carries out aerial attacks on over 150 targets across southern Lebanon during the day.[199] The Chiyeh area of Beirut is attacked for the first time.

The last crossing over the Litani River is reported destroyed, cutting all supply routes to Tyre and south Lebanon.[200]

A Médecins sans Frontières (MSF) convoy transporting emergency supplies is attacked north of the Litani. The humanitarian workers pass their aid by hand over the river, using a tree trunk as a makeshift bridge.[201]

The ICRC complains that the IDF has denied permission for aid groups to move food and medicine to besieged villages in southern Lebanon for two days.

The news media report that more than 1,000 Lebanese civilians have died since the war began, with one-third being children under the age of 13. They say that the Israeli raid has

---

[196] MFA, "Summary of IDF operations against Hezbollah in Lebanon," 7 August 2006 (communicated by the IDF spokesman), http://www.mfa.gov.il/MFA/Terrorism+Obstacle+to+Peace/Terrorism+from+Lebanon+Hezbollah/Summary+of+IDF+operations+against+Hezbollah+in+Lebanon+7-Aug-2006.htm.

[197] Ibid.

[198] IDF,"IDF Attacks over 150 Targets in Lebanon in the past 24 Hours," 7 August 2006, 08:23, http://www1.idf.il/DOVER/site/mainpage.asp?sl=EN&id=7&docid=55970.EN.

[199] IDF War Log, "August 7th 2006."

[200] NDH and ALEF, "International Humanitarian Law violations in the current conflict opposing Hezbollah (Lebanon) to the State of Israel," second report, 14 August 2006.

[201] Amnesty International, "Israel/Lebanon," 3.

killed 69 people, one of the highest death tolls in a single day.[202] The government of Lebanon says that 958 have died and 3,369 have been injured.[203]

At the Arab foreign ministers' meeting, PM Siniora breaks down in tears as he says that 40 people have died in a "horrific massacre" and "deliberate bombing" in the southern village of Houla. An hour later, the PM backtracks and says only one person died.[204]

Day 28: Tuesday, 8 August

France said a new draft resolution was being prepared while an Arab League delegation warned the Security Council there would be civil war in Lebanon if Israel's troops did not leave Lebanon, and Russia called for an interim resolution calling for "humanitarian cessation of fire" in Lebanon.

The Israeli ambassador to the UN says: "The critical test this Council faces is not whether it can adopt a resolution. The question is whether this Council and the international community can adopt a course of action, a blueprint for change, which will end the threat that Hezbollah and its sponsors pose to the people of Israel and Lebanon, and to the region as a whole. Both the forces of terror and the forces of moderation in the Middle East are looking to the Council to see if it is up to that challenge."

Lt Gen Dan Halutz appoints his deputy chief of Staff, Maj Gen Moshe Kaplinsky as his personal representative in the north and the coordinator of IDF ground, sea, and air efforts in the Leba-

---

[202] Reuters (Beirut), "Lebanon says 1,000 dead or missing in war with Israel," 7 August 2006; UNRWA Lebanon Field Office, Situation Report: 24 hours up to 14:00, 8 August 2006; and HRC, SITREP no. 015, 8 August 2006.

[203] HRC, SITREP no. 014, 7 August 2006.

[204] AP (Beirut), "Lebanese prime minister now says one dead, not 40 in Houla attack," 7 August 2006, http://www.dawn.com/2006/08/07/welcome.htm; CNN, "Lebanon proposes plan to end violence; Two Israeli strikes kill 17 people; Hezbollah fires 140 rockets," 7 August 2006, 0228 GMT, http://www.cnn.com/2006/WORLD/meast/08/07/mideast.main/index.html; and HRC, SITREP no. 015.

nese sector. The press says that the appointment effectively side-lines Maj Gen Adam, the Northern Command commander.[205]

Hezbollah fires 159 rockets on Israel Tuesday, injuring two.[206]

During the night IDF attacked a total of about 100 targets in Lebanon.[207] The IDF says it attacked 82 targets overnight, including 42 structures, upwards of 30 access roads and six launchers.[208]

The IDF announces that it has imposed a "prohibition on all travel" south of the Litani River as of 2200, 7 August. It says that travel for humanitarian purposes is permitted "solely and exclusively if coordinated with the IDF."[209]

Israeli military officials say that the Israeli army is now holding land up to 8 km inside Lebanon.

Three IDF soldiers are killed when antitank missiles hit vehicles and an infantry force operating in the village of Debel. Other IDF soldiers are lightly wounded and are evacuated for medical treatment at a hospital in Israel.[210]

Two IDF soldiers from the Paratroopers Brigade are killed in an operation in Bint Jbeil on Tuesday night.[211]

An IDF soldier is seriously wounded during exchanges of fire in the early morning hours in the area of Bint Jbeil, in the western sector of southern Lebanon.[212]

---

[205] IDF War Log, "August 8th 2006"; and Yaakov Katz, "Three soldiers killed in southern Lebanon," *Jerusalem Post*, 9 August 2006, http://info.jpost.com/C002/Supplements/CasualtiesOfWar/2006_08_08.html.

[206] Katz, "Three soldiers killed in southern Lebanon."

[207] IDF War Log, "August 8th 2006."

[208] IDF, "82 Targets Hit in Lebanon Overnight," Tuesday, 8 August 2006, 12:32, http://www1.idf.il/DOVER/site/mainpage.asp?clr=1&sl=EN&id=7&docid=56105.

[209] Ibid.

[210] IDF War Log, "August 8th 2006"; and Yaakov Katz and AP, "3 IDF soldiers killed, five wounded in heavy fighting near Bint Jbeil," *Jerusalem Post*, 8 August 2006, http://info.jpost.com/C002/Supplements/CasualtiesOfWar/2006_08_07_3.html.

[211] JPost.com staff, "Two Paratroopers killed in gun battle in Bint Jbeil," *Jerusalem Post*, 9 August 2006, http://info.jpost.com/C002/Supplements/CasualtiesOfWar/2006_08_09.html.

[212] IDF War Log, "August 8th 2006."

Two IDF reserve soldiers are killed during exchanges of fire in the area of Labouneh, in the western sector of southern Lebanon. Two reserve soldiers are wounded in the same incident and are evacuated for medical treatment at a hospital in Israel.[213]

The government of Lebanon says 987 have been killed and 3,408 injured.[214]

Day 29: Wednesday, 9 August

The Israeli Political-Security Cabinet orders an expanded ground offensive in Lebanon and announces that Israel will continue with the efforts to achieve a political agreement to accomplish the following goals:

- immediate, unconditional return of the kidnapped soldiers,
- immediate cessation of all hostilities,
- full implementation of *UNSCR 1559*,
- deployment of an effective international force, together with the Lebanese army, along the Blue Line, and
- a program to prevent Hezbollah from rehabilitating its military capabilities, mainly by preventing transfer of weapons and ammunition from Syria and Iran.

Israeli deputy PM Eli Yishai says that Israel's offensive could drag on for another month or more, commenting on the Cabinet decision to expand operations. "It is believed that it will last another 30 days," Yishai told public radio after the six-hour cabinet meeting, adding, "I fear it could last much longer."

Hezbollah fires 168 rockets into northern Israel. Hassan Nasrallah says that Israeli attacks had not weakened its rocket capabilities, and its fighters would turn south Lebanon into a "graveyard" for invading Israeli troops. Nasrallah calls upon Arab residents of Haifa to leave the city:

---

[213] Ibid.

[214] HRC, SITREP no. 015.

> To the Arabs of Haifa, I have a special message. We have grieved and we are grieving for your martyrs and wounded people. I beg you and turn to you asking you to leave this city. I hope you will do so. Over the past period, your presence and your misfortune made us hesitant in targeting this city, despite the fact that the southern suburbs and the rest of the heart of Lebanon were being shelled, whether Haifa was being shelled or not. Please relieve us of this hesitation and spare your blood, which is also our blood. Please leave this city.

Nasrallah says Hezbollah accepts the deployment of the Lebanese army to the south but that Washington was trying to impose Israeli demands on Lebanon through the current draft UN resolution. Nasrallah said that the seven-point plan presented by the Lebanese government was the least the country should accept as part of a draft resolution to end the fighting.

After meeting with US envoy, assistant Secretary of State David Welch, PM Siniora says that there has been no progress towards a new draft UN Security Council resolution. "There is no progress so far. We are still at the same place," he tells reporters.

After meeting with the German foreign minister, FM Livni says: "It is very important that the Lebanese army also be accompanied by international forces that will enable it to reach the south in an organized fashion and guard the area once the Hezbollah are gone."

During the night, IDF aircraft attack over 120 terror-related targets across Lebanon.[215]

Israel is estimated to have about 10,000 ground troops in southern Lebanon, while Israeli television announces the start of a new ground attack in Lebanon.

Intense shelling of Al-Khiyam and the area around Marjeyoun precedes a late-night advance towards the towns.

A letter from Tunisia to the UN Human Rights Council, backed by Russia and China, calls for the body to take action "on the gross human rights violations by Israel in Lebanon," including "country-wide targeting of innocent civilians."

The government of Lebanon says 1,020 have been killed and 3,508 injured.[216]

---

[215] IDF War Log, "August 9th 2006."

[216] HRC, SITREP no. 016, 9 August 2006.

Day 30: Thursday, 10 August

France newly proposes a staggered Israeli withdrawal, reportedly in a bid to break a deadlock with the United States over a Security Council cease-fire resolution. The new proposal calls for Lebanese troops to start deploying in south Lebanon in coordination with UNIFIL as the Israeli forces start withdrawing.

Prime Minister Blair speaks with several world leaders and tells them that he believes an agreement on a UN resolution to end the conflict in Lebanon could be reached within the next 24 hours.

The IDF reportedly delays its expanded ground offensive after Defense Minister Peretz freezes a planned thrust up to the Litani River on Thursday night. Peretz says Israel would first exhaust the diplomatic front before launching the operation. IDF chief Lt Gen Halutz hints that the military is disappointed with the political decision. "The State of Israel is defending its home," he said. "We don't go backwards. Only forward."[217]

Hezbollah fires 166 rockets at northern Israel, many from the very hills in the south where Israeli forces are operating. An Arab-Israeli mother and her young daughter are killed in Deir el-Assad.[218]

The IDF says that it conducted attacks on over 150 targets in the past 24 hours, including attacks on 70 "structures," six launchers, two bridges, and three gas stations.[219] Lebanese press reports an Israeli attack on a historic lighthouse in western Beirut—the first strike on Beirut proper since Hezbollah warned that rockets would be fired at Tel Aviv if the capital itself were hit.

---

[217] Yaakov Katz, "Reservist slain as fierce fighting rages on in Lebanon," *Jerusalem Post*, 11 August 2006, http://info.jpost.com/C002/Supplements/CasualtiesOfWar/2006 _08 _11_1.html.

[218] Ibid.

[219] IDF, "Air Force Attacks Over 150 Targets in Southern Lebanon," 10 August 2006, 11:38, http://www1.idf.il/DOVER/site/mainpage.asp?sl=EN&id=7&docid=56363.EN.

The IDF again drops leaflets on Beirut, warning residents of adjacent suburbs to *dahiye* to leave immediately. Israel also drops leaflets for the first time on northern Lebanon, warning that all trucks must be off the roads by 8:00 p.m.

The IDF says it has accelerated ground operations in southern Lebanon and destroyed rocket launchers in Bint Jbeil, al-Hamra, and Ras al-Bayyadah. Ground forces artillery also fired artillery at over 55 targets.[220]

Israeli ground units push 7 km (4 mi) into Lebanese territory in the direction of al-Khiyam and Marjeyoun, a Christian enclave to the northwest of Khiyam.

An IDF soldier is killed and two are wounded, one seriously and the other lightly, when antitank missiles hit IDF tanks in the vicinity of al-Qlayeh, west of Khiyam.[221]

IDF artillery shelled 25 Hezbollah buildings, an ammunition storage facility, and 30 other targets to disrupt the launching of missiles from southern Lebanon.[222]

UN under secretary-general Egeland criticises both sides for not stopping the fighting long enough to allow aid to reach 120,000 civilians who need help in southern Lebanon, calling the lack of access a "disgrace." Lebanese hospitals are again reported as running out of fuel and other supplies.

Day 31: Friday, 11 August

The UN Security Council adopts the amended US-French draft resolution (*UNSCR 1701*) that would end the Lebanon fighting and lead to the formation of a new multinational peacekeeping force in the south. The resolution, unanimously approved, calls for "full cessation of hostilities," tells Hezbollah to stop all attacks immediately, and tells Israel to end "all offensive operations." Secretary Rice, in an address to the Security Council, calls on Iran and Syria to respect the terms of the UN resolution.

---

[220] IDF, "Air Force Attacks Over 150 Targets."

[221] IDF War Log, "August 10th 2006."

[222] Ibid.

UN secretary-general Annan condemned the Security Council's failure to act more quickly, saying that the delay had "badly shaken" the world's faith in the United Nations. "I would be remiss if I did not tell you how profoundly disappointed I am that the council did not reach this point much, much earlier," he says.

The IDF announces an expansion of its ground offensive in accordance with the new Cabinet decision on the evening of 11 August, "in the direction of the Litani River and in areas from which rockets are launched at Israel."[223]

Hezbollah fires 123 rockets, hitting Haifa and wounding at least two. Hezbollah also claims to have sunk an Israeli Super Dvora fast patrol boat off the coast of southern Lebanon.

The IDF announces that the IAF carried out over 120 air strikes in Lebanon, striking among other targets 60 Hezbollah headquarters.[224] At dawn, Israel reportedly conducts heavy bombing of Beirut's southern suburbs, attacking leadership targets.

The IDF drops leaflets on Sidon and Beirut accusing Hassan Nasrallah of hiding facts about the "great losses" among the Hezbollah fighters. The leaflet contains a list of 100 Hezbollah members killed in the fighting.

An IDF reservist is reported killed when an antitank missile hits his tank in al-Qlayeh, west of Khiyam.[225]

A UN contingent is dispatched to provide a convoy to remove approximately 350 Lebanese soldiers held in their barracks by Israeli soldiers in Marjeyoun.

According to *An Nahar* newspaper, a Red Cross ambulance carrying bread and medical equipment to Tibnine is directly targeted by Israeli aircraft.

The government of Lebanon puts the current civilian toll at 1,044 deaths and 3,600 injuries.[226]

---

[223] IDF, "Summary of IDF Operations in Lebanon in the past 24 Hours," 12 August 2006, 14:04, http://www1.idf.il/DOVER/site/mainpage.asp?sl=EN&id=7&docid=56532.EN.

[224] IDF War Log, "August 11th 2006."

[225] Katz, "Reservist slain as fierce fighting rages on in Lebanon."

[226] HRC, SITREP no. 018, 11 August 2006.

The UN Human Rights Council votes to set up a commission of inquiry into "systematic" Israeli attacks on civilians in Lebanon. "There is a clear and urgent need to bring clarity to a situation in which facts and allegations are now given the same credit but without the benefit of systematic, independent, thorough and independent scrutiny," UN human rights chief Louise Arbour tells a special session of the 47-member UN Council.[227]

Day 32: Saturday, 12 August

Hassan Nasrallah says Hezbollah would abide by the UN cease-fire resolution but would continue fighting as long as Israeli troops remained in southern Lebanon. He calls continued resistance to the Israel offensive "our natural right." Hezbollah fires 64 rockets into northern Israel on Saturday, killing one Israeli civilian in Yaara.

Israel announces that *UNSCR 1701* "reflects the interests of the State of Israel" and says it plans to halt offensive operations on 14 August, making its deepest push into southern Lebanon since 12 July, with some ground troops reportedly reaching close to the Litani River, some 30 km north of the border.

Lebanese PM Siniora accepts the UN resolution calling for an end to the hostilities, saying it was in Lebanon's interest. "If this resolution proves anything, it shows that the entire world stood by Lebanon," he said, vowing that "just like Lebanon waged a diplomatic battle during the war, it will continue it in the same rhythm after the war."

President Bush praises the UN resolution: "I welcome the resolution adopted yesterday by the United Nations Security Council, which is designed to bring an immediate end to the fighting." He tells PM Siniora that it is critical to "dismantle" Hezbollah and end "unwanted" Iranian and Syrian influence in Lebanon.

President Bush reportedly speaks to PM Olmert for the first time since the opening days of the war.

---

[227] AFP (Geneva), "UN rights chief calls for probe of civilian attacks in Lebanon, Israel," 11 August 2007.

Lebanese representative of UN secretary-general Annan says he expects an immediate cessation of hostilities: "After the Lebanese government meets today and after the Israeli cabinet has met tomorrow, we do expect to see an immediate cessation of hostilities," Geir Pedersen says after meeting with Lebanese foreign minister Fawzi Sallukh.

Pursuant to a decision by the Cabinet, the IDF begins widening its ground operations in southern Lebanon, and IDF forces begin advancing to and across the Litani River, according to the IDF. In fighting during the day, 24 IDF soldiers are killed.[228]

The IDF says that ground forces operating in the area of Ghanduriyah secured positions near the Wadi Saluki. Forces destroyed a missile launcher near Debel.[229]

Hundreds of Israeli troops are airlifted into south Lebanon on more than 50 transport helicopters. An Israeli CH-53 transport helicopter is reported destroyed by an antitank missile, killing the five-man crew. The helicopters had just delivered ground forces as part of the expanded offensive.

Israel said its troops killed more than 40 Hezbollah fighters in the last 24 hours; Hezbollah announced four deaths Friday and none on Saturday.

Israel Army radio says that 54 IDF soldiers were wounded in fighting in southern Lebanon. Israeli Radio later reports that nearly 100 Israeli soldiers were wounded on Saturday, the highest one-day injury toll of the war.

The IDF says it carried out attacks on more than 80 targets in the past 24 hours, including 32 "structures," a Hezbollah command center south of Tyre, nine bridges and access routes, and 10 launch sites in the area of Nabatiyeh.[230]

---

[228] IDF War Log, "August 12th 2006."

[229] IDF, "Summary of IDF Operations in Lebanon in the past 24 Hours," 12 August 2006, 14:04.

[230] Ibid; and IDF, "80 Targets Struck Yesterday in Lebanon," n.d. (13 August 2006), http://www1.idf.il/DOVER/site/mainpage.asp?clr=1&sl=EN&id=7&docid=55375.

Aircraft strike an apartment building in the heart of Baalbek that the media report as housing a Hezbollah charity organization.

Israel again "hacks" into Hezbollah radio and television broadcasts with recordings of the names of Hezbollah fighters it says it has killed. Video of Israeli air attacks and gun-camera video is aired.

The government of Lebanon puts the number of casualties at 1,071 deaths and 3,628 injuries.[231]

The AP reports that electricity is out in Tyre and Sidon, after Israeli aircraft attacked transformers at power plants in both coastal cities.

Day 33: Sunday, 13 August

UN secretary-general Annan announces that the governments of Israel and Lebanon have agreed to halt fighting in the month-long war at 0500 GMT (8 a.m. local) on Monday.

Maj Gen Udi Adam, commander of Northern Command, says he hoped the estimated 30,000 ground troops involved in the expanded Israeli offensive launched will have secured control of most of south Lebanon by Monday.

Hezbollah fires 220 rockets into Israel, the second highest single-day total since the war began. The IDF detects Hezbollah firing 220 mm Syrian-made rockets from the outskirts of Tyre at Haifa.

The IDF says it has flown over 6,800 sorties and attacked over 3,300 targets since 12 July.[232]

Intense Israeli strikes are reported in south Beirut, with at least 20 "huge explosions" reported in a two-minute period on Sunday afternoon. The IDF says that the IAF continued operations on Sunday, 13 August, carrying out 178 overnight attacks through the cease-fire. Targets included 122 Hezbollah "structures" and houses belonging to fighters in Nabatiyeh and

---

[231] HRC, SITREP no. 019, 12 August 2006.

[232] IDF, "80 Targets Struck Yesterday in Lebanon."

Marjeyoun, 11 rocket launchers, a bridge on the Zahrani River, four tunnels, an "aluminum factory" near Nabatiyeh, and eight gas stations.[233]

The Ain al-Helweh Palestinian refugee camp is reported attacked near Sidon. Air strikes are reported on factories in al-Naemeh and Shwayfat, and two bridges in northern Lebanon are attacked.

The IDF says that ground forces yesterday operated in the vicinity of al-Taybeh, al-Adayseh, and Kila, west of Metula. Nine IDF soldiers are killed Sunday.

Two IDF reservists are killed, four are seriously injured, and six slightly wounded when Hezbollah fires antitank rocket and mortar shells at troops near al-Qantara.[234]

Four IDF soldiers are killed and 14 are hurt, two of them seriously, when an antitank rocket hit reserve infantry troops near Abu Tawil, north of Aiyt a-Shab.[235]

A large cache of weapons is found in al-Adayseh. Soldiers are injured by antitank missile fired near al-Adayseh when a missile hits their tank.[236]

An officer is killed when Hezbollah mortar fire strikes a tank in the village of Tal al-Nahhas.[237]

IDF forces in the village of Aiyt a-Shab discover a Hezbollah bunker containing weaponry, infrastructure, and a radio transmitter and destroy 20 structures in the village that had been used to hide weapons including dozens of antitank missiles.[238]

The government of Lebanon says that 1,071 have died and 3,628 have been injured.[239]

---

[233] IDF, "Events in Southern Lebanon during the Night," 14 August 2006, 10:20, http://www1.idf.il/DOVER/site/mainpage.asp?sl=EN&id=7&docid=56690.EN.

[234] IDF War Log, "August 13th 2006."

[235] Ibid.

[236] IDF, "80 Targets Struck Yesterday in Lebanon."

[237] IDF War Log, "August 13th 2006."

[238] Ibid.

[239] HRC, SITREP no. 020, 13 August 2006.

Day 34: Monday, 14 August

The cessation of hostilities goes into effect at 0500 hours GMT (0800 local time), the date and time mutually agreed to by the prime ministers of Israel and Lebanon. Some of the fiercest fighting of the month-long conflict takes place in the final hours up to the UN cease-fire coming into effect.

The IDF says that the IAF continued to attack Hezbollah targets overnight, carrying out 178 attacks.

Israel says it will retain its blockade of Lebanon "until a mechanism is put in place to control smuggling of arms" to Hezbollah.

Israeli MDA says that from 12 July until 14 August, MDA personnel, employees, and volunteers had been called to 1,477 incidents in which they have treated and evacuated 2,586 casualties (135 fatalities; 70 severely, 115 moderately, and 807 lightly injured; and 1,465 anxiety attacks).[240]

Prime Minister Olmert speaks to the Knesset regarding the war, saying that the UN resolution is a political accomplishment with the support of the Security Council. "There is no longer a state within a state," Olmert says. "There is no longer sponsorship for a terror organization by a state. And no longer is a terror organization allowed to operate within Lebanon, as the long arm of the axis of evil which reaches out from Teheran to Damascus, uses Lebanon's weakness and transforms it, its citizens and its infrastructure into a tool for its war." He describes the military accomplishments:

> IDF soldiers dealt a severe blow, the dimensions of which are not yet publicly known, to this murderous organization, its military and organizational infrastructure, its long-term ability, the huge weapons arsenal it has built and accumulated for many years, and also to the self-confidence of its people and leaders. In every battle, in every encounter with Hezbollah terrorists, the fighters of the IDF had the upper hand—of this there is no doubt.
>
> The leaders of this terrorist organization went underground, and from there they are busy spreading lies and hiding the truth of the cost to them and their people. . . . We also suffered painfull [sic] blows, both on

---

[240] MDA News, "MDA Weekend Activities August 11th–14th, 2006," 14 August 2006. http://www.ukmda.org/news/?content_id=155.

the home front and on the front line. We did not mislead ourselves when we embarked, because of the inevitability of the circumstances, on this war. We did not mislead anyone. We said rockets would fall, missiles would fall, and that we would pay a heavy price—the most precious—in human lives.

Hassan Nasrallah appears on Al-Manar TV: "We are facing a strategic and historic victory," he says. "This is no exaggeration. This is a victory for Lebanon—all of Lebanon—for the resistance, and for the entire Islamic nation."[241]

The Daily Star reports that Hezbollah is distributing posters throughout Beirut claiming a "Divine Victory."

---

[241] Hezbollah secretary-general Nasrallah, on Al-Manar TV, 14 August 2006.

Appendix C

Lebanon Gazetteer and Target List

The list of locations in this appendix is based upon information provided by the Lebanese and Israeli governments, by contemporaneous press reporting of attacks in Lebanon, and by the author's research. Location names have been harmonized (alternative spellings are included), and the named places themselves have had to be located, not a simple task, given great variations in spelling from Arabic to the English language and the specificity of the villages and neighborhoods, some of which are quite small.

For each location, the common entry endeavors to include some geographic setting, district (*kaza*); alternate spellings as reported in the news media, in official gazetteers, or as reported by the IDF; and specific objects (e.g., bridges) that were reported as attacked. Those locations in bold are locations where IDF ground forces were reported as operating.

Common Arabic words used in place names:

ain	fountain, spring
bayt	house (of)
burj	fort
deir	courtyard, church
hamam	hot baths
jabal	mountain
kaza	district
kfar	village
majdal	tower
qala	fort
qasr	palace
ras	summit

Lebanon is a coastal Mediterranean country bordered by Syria to the north and east and by Israel (and the Golan Heights) to the south. With a total area of 4,000 sq. mi. (10,400 sq. km.), it is significantly smaller than the state of Connecticut and one of the smallest countries in the Middle East region. The population of Lebanon—the July 2006 population estimate, according to the US Central Intelligence Agency, is 3.87 million[1]—is predominantly urban. The capital, Beirut, is the largest city, housing about one-third of the total. Other principal cities are Tripoli, Tyre, and, Jounieh (see Gazetteer).[2]

Lebanon also has an extremely diverse population. Though 95 percent of the population is Arab, only about 60 percent is Muslim, with most of the remaining being Christians. The principal Muslim sects are Shi'a, Sunni, and Druze, with over one million Shi'a constituting Lebanon's largest single community. Most Christians are Maronite Roman Catholics.

Lebanon's current government structure is derived from the 1989 Charter of National Reconciliation (the "Taif Agreement"), the document that helped end the long civil war.[3] The agreement made revisions to the 1943 constitution in order to adapt government to the demographic makeup of the nation, and it provided for the disbanding of independent militias. Politically, it reduced the authority of the president (a Maronite Christian) by transferring executive power to the prime minister (a Sunni), a council of ministers (with portfolios equally divided between Christians and Muslims), and a president of the National As-

---

[1] Lebanon also hosts some 405,000 Palestinians, most in refugee camps, and a significant immigrant-worker population, estimated to be more than 1 million, predominantly from Syria, East Asia, and Africa.

[2] The 2006 population distribution per Mohafazah (governorate) is estimated to be:

Mohafazah	Population	Percent
Beirut	403,337	10
Beirut suburbs	899,792	22
Mount Lebanon	607,767	15
North Lebanon	807,204	20
South Lebanon	472,105	12
Nabatiyeh	275,372	7
Bekaa	539,448	14
Total	4,005,025	100

Adapted from FAO Technical Cooperation Programme Lebanon, "Damage and Early Recovery Needs Assessment of Agriculture, Fisheries and Forestry," November 2006, vii.

[3] At the end of September 1989, the Lebanese National Assembly met in Taif, Saudi Arabia, to discuss a charter of national reconciliation. The session was attended by 62 members of Parliament (31 Christian and 31 Muslim). On 22 October, they endorsed the Charter of National Reconciliation.

sembly (a Shi'a).[4] The National Assembly was also reconfigured to 128 seats with an equal number of Christian and Muslim members instead of a previous six-to-five ratio.

The Lebanese armed forces under the Ministry of Defense number some 55,000, almost all ground forces, with another 13,000 in the Internal Security Forces (ISF) under the Ministry of the Interior. Since 1978, the United Nations Interim Force in Lebanon (UNIFIL) has conducted a peacekeeping operation in the country, assisted by a small observer group.[5] UNIFIL is mandated to monitor the Blue Line, the border demarcation created by the UN. As of the outbreak of war in July 2006, the UN Security Council authorized 1,990 troops to UNIFIL.

Though Lebanon is a middle-class, modern country, the economy is highly dependent on remittances from Lebanese abroad. Lebanon has experienced a significant exodus, with some 1.3 million leaving since 1975 to seek a better life and escape the long civil war. Tourism and investments, as well as summer visits by expatriate Lebanese, are the major factors in the economy of the country. Lebanon has not reclaimed its pre–civil war position as a Middle Eastern banking hub. The country has no significant major industry and is predominantly a service economy. Though Lebanon remains the most urbane and Westernized of Arab countries, its diverse population and formal sectarian structure, enshrining Christian, Sunni and Shi'a power and recognizing almost two dozen separate religious communities, also promotes near-feudal groupings and loyalties.

Lebanon's geography is predominantly mountainous, with four north-south lowland-highland sectors between the Mediterranean Sea and Syria: the coastal plane; the Lebanon mountains (or Mount Lebanon) nearest the coast (branching off to form the Shuf mountains near the southern end); the Bekaa

---

[4] The president is responsible for the promulgation and execution of laws enacted by the National Assembly, but all presidential decisions (with the exception of those to appoint a prime minister or to accept the resignation of a government) require the cosignature of the prime minister, who is head of the government, implementing its policies and speaking in its name. The president must receive the approval of the Cabinet before dismissing a minister or ratifying an international treaty. The ministers and the prime minister are chosen by the president of the republic in consultation with the members and president of the National Assembly.

[5] *UN Security Council Resolution (UNSCR) 425, 19 March 1978.*

central highland (or valley) east of the Lebanon mountains; and the anti-Lebanon mountain range east of the Bekaa, which includes Mount Hermon. The Litani River flows south from the Bekaa Valley and then west, where it is formally called the Qasimiyeh River. The Litani River, 13 miles from the Israeli border, has generally served as a dividing line for "southern Lebanon."

Southern Lebanon, encompassing about 200 villages south of the Litani River, is normally home to some 625,000 people, about 75 percent of whom are Shi'a.[6] The area south of the Litani can broadly be divided into three zones (not counting the urban area of Tyre): a coastal strip of approximately five kilometers where citrus fruit and banana agriculture flourishes; a central hilly and verdant zone, where tobacco and olives are the main agricultural crops; and an ever-hillier eastern area of significantly lower population where agriculture gives way to shepherding. Tyre (Sour), Nabatiyeh, Bint Jbeil, and Marjeyoun are the main towns, but villages are dotted throughout the countryside, along the main roads, and perched on top of steep hills.

Israel and Hezbollah battled in four zones in Lebanon: in the extreme south, where Hezbollah had established full control since May 2000 and operated without interference from either the Lebanese government or UN peacekeepers and observers; in a "midzone" area of southern Lebanon and the Bekka Valley, where Hezbollah operated extensively; in south Beirut, where Hezbollah had its headquarters and high command and operated many of its longest-range rockets; and in northern and central Lebanon and the rest of the country, where Israeli designated targets of "strategic" importance but Hezbollah was not a major direct factor. Israel treated each of these battle zones—if not explicitly at least in practice—separately, selecting targets, escalating, and conducting operations to achieve its objectives.

Lebanon is divided into six administrative regions or governorates called *mohafazahs* (*mohafazat*, singular), which are further subdivided into 25 districts, called *cazas*.[7] Each *caza* is made up of several municipalities and cadastral (tax) zones. In total, there are 1,492 cadastral zones.

---

[6] This population grows as much as fivefold in some areas during the summer months when expatriate Lebanese return from North America, Latin America, and West Africa.

[7] The six are Bekaa, Beirut, Mount Lebanon, Nabatiyeh, North Lebanon, and South Lebanon. Some sources refer to eight governorates, adding Akkar and Baalbek-Hermel.

Caza (District)	Mohafazah (Governate)
Akkar	North
Alay/Aaley	Mount Lebanon
Baalbek	Bekaa
Baabda	Mount Lebanon
Batroun	North
Bcharre	North
Beirut	Beirut
Bint Jbeil	Nabatiyeh
Hasbayya	Nabatiyeh
Hermel	Bekaa
Jbeil	Mount Lebanon
Jezzine	South
Kesrouane/Kesrouan	Mount Lebanon
Koura	North
Marjeyoun	Nabatiyeh
Metn	Mount Lebanon
Minieh-Dinnieh	North
Nabatiyeh	Nabatiyeh
Rachaiya	Bekaa
Shuf (Chouf)	Mount Lebanon
Sidon (Saida)	South
Tripoli	North
Tyre (Sour)	South
West Bekaa	Bekaa
Zahleh	Bekaa
Zgharta	North

Gazetteer

Aadshit, southeast of Nabatiyeh, Nabatiyeh district (Aidsheet, 'Adshit, At-Sjeet, Aadchit ech Chqif) long-range rocket launch point

Aadshit al Qsair, Marjeyoun district (Atsheit, Habsheet)

al-Aamiliyeh, Tyre district

Aandqit, Akkar district (Andakit, Andqit)

    Aandqit road at al-Sha'ar intersection

    Aandqit-Akroum main road, assessed as destroyed[8]

---

[8] UNDP. "Lebanon: Rapid Environmental Assesment," 3-12.

Aaqtanit, Zahrani

al-Aaishiyeh, north of Marjeyoun town, Jezzine district ('Ayshi-yah, Aaichiye, Aishiye)

    al-Aaishiyeh-Jarmaq (Jormuk)

    al-Aaishiyeh-al-Rihan road

    al-Aaishiyeh heights

'Aba, southwest of Nabatiyeh, Nabatiyeh district (A'aba, Aaba, Abba)

    'Aba-al-Zrariyeh road

    'Aba-Jibsheet road

Ablah, Zahleh district

Ablah-Riak bridge over Litani River (Ablah-Baalbek-Tel Aamara bridge, Ablah Riyak bridge) ID 77, assessed as destroyed[9]

Abu El Aswad, north of Tyre on the coast, Tyre district (Abou El Aswad, Abuol Aswad)

    Abu El Aswad national road bridge/Abu El Aswad over-pass/underpass) ID 137, assessed as destroyed[10]

    Palestinian refugee camp

Abu Jajeh bridge, assessed as destroyed)[11]

Abu Tawil

Abu Zeble, Hasbayya district (Abou Zeble, Aboo Zebli, Abu Zableh)

    Abu Zeble bridge, ID 4, assessed as destroyed[12]

al-Abbasiyeh, northeast of Tyre near Bidyas near the Litani, Tyre district (Abbasiyyeh, Al Abbassiya, Abbasiyeh, al-Abasiyyeh, al-Aabbasiyeh, Al Abasseyia)

    Mabneen in al-Ruz complex "at entrance of al-Abbasiyeh"

Abel a-Saki (see Ibl al-Saqi)

---

[9] Ibid.

[10] Ibid.

[11] Ibid.

[12] Ibid.

Al Abda, north of Tripoli on the coast, Akkar district (Aabde, Abdeh)

Lebanese navy base/"port," attacked 17 July

Al Aboudiyeh main road, Akkar district (Abboudiyyeh), limited damage[13]

Abraj al-Nada in Bayt Lahia

al-'Abadah, near Wadi Jilo, Tyre district

al-Adayseh, south of Kfar Kila on the border, Marjeyoun district (Adeisseh, Adaisseh, Aadayse, Aadayseh, al-Adaiyseh, Al-Adisa, Al Adeisa, Udaysah)

Addousiyeh bridge/overpass, Zahrani district, assessed as destroyed[14]

Adloun on the coastal road (Aadloun)

Adloun bridge/Al-Mashru (Project) bridge, assessed as destroyed[15]

Adweh bridge/culvert, Akkar district, ID 142, (Adwi) assessed as destroyed[16]

al-Ain, Hermel district

Ain Arab, Hasbayya district/western Bekaa? (Ayn 'Arab, Ain Aarab)

Ain Arab new bridge near Al Khiyam

Ain Ba'al, south of Tyre on the road to Qana, Tyre district (Ain Baal)

Ain Bourday, south of Baalbek, Baalbek district (Ain Bourdai, Budai village, Bouday, Boudai, Ain Borday, Ein Bourdai)

(Hassaniya Bouday?)

Awadhad gas company

Hassan gas station

Hayy al-Wadi Colonel Al-Taqih fuel station

Ain Bouswar, Iqlim al-Toufah, Nabatiyeh district (Ain Boswar)

---

[13] Ibid.

[14] Ibid.

[15] Ibid.

[16] Ibid.

Ain Ebel, near the border, south of Bint Jbeil, Bint Jbeil district (Ain Ibel, Ain Ibl)

Ain Helweh, Sidon (Ain Al Hilweh, Ein-el-Helweh)

Ain Helweh, small bridge, assessed as destroyed[17]

Palestinian refugee camp

Ain al-Mizrab road

Ain Qana, north of Habboush, Nabatiyeh district

Ain al Sawda ("Black Eye") bridge, assessed as destroyed[18] (Ain elsawda, Ein Al-Sawda)

Ain al-Tineh, western Bekaa

Ainata, village near the border just north of Bint Jbeil, Bint Jbeil district (Aainata, 'Inata, Ainatha)[19]

Ainata al-Arz road

al-Freiz hill

Aita al-Fukhar, Rashaya district (Aita El Fukhar, Ayta al Fokhar)

Aita al Zot, north of Bint Jbeil on the Tyre main road, Bint Jbeil district (Aaita ez Zott)

Aitman, Shuf district (Atyman)

Aitman overpass, south of Aitman gas station

Aitanit, western Bekaa (Aitaneet)

Aitaroun, on the border, Bint Jbeil district (Aytroun, Aytaroun, Itrun)

Aitou (Mount Aitou), Ehden (Qarn Ito)

transmission station, Lebanese radio and television

Aitit, north of Qana, Tyre district (Aiteet, Aaitit, Aytit)

Hezbollah territorial subdivision headquarters

---

[17] Ibid.

[18] Ibid.

[19] There is also an Ain Aata in Rachaya district near Mount Herman.

Aiyt a-Shab, on the border, Bint Jbeil district[20] (Aita al-Shaab, Aita al-Chaab; Ayta a-Shab, Ayata-Shav, Aiyt a-Shaab, Aita El Shaeb)

Ajar (see al-Ghajar)

Akibeh square bridge, assessed as destroyed[21]

Akkar, north Lebanon, Akkar district (Aakkar; see also Aarqa)

Akroum, Akkar district

    Akroum road/retaining wall, ID 94

Alaak bridge, assessed as destroyed[22]

Ali al-Nahri, central Bekaa Valley (Ali Annahr)

    Ali Annahri bridge, assessed as destroyed[23]

    Hezbollah regional headquarters[24]

'Ali al-Tahir, Nabatiyeh district

Alma a-Shab, on the border, Tyre district[25] (Aalma ech Chaab, Alma ash-Shaab, Alma al-Chaab, Alma Shaib, 'Alma al-Sha'b, Alma Chaab)

Alman, north of Sidon, Chuf district (Almane)

    Alman steel bridge (Almane bridge), assessed as destroyed[26]

---

[20] "About 30 squads of Hezbollah fighters operated in the Aiyt a-Shab village region. IDF forces identified three anti-tank squads, ten flat-trajectory fire squads, and three reconnaissance squads. A front command post was situated in the village. It coordinated the activities of Hezbollah fighters and operated through the territorial subdivision headquarters near the village of Aitit (southeast of Tyre). According to a testimony given by one of the Hezbollah detainees, about 25 regular anti-tank operatives resided in the village." IDF, Intelligence and Terrorism Information Center at the Center for Special Studies (ITIC/CSS), Hezbollah's use of Lebanese civilians as human shields: the extensive military infrastructure positioned and hidden in populated areas; Part Two: Documentation; Hezbollah's Military Infrastructure and Operational Activities Carried Out from Within the Civilian Population, November 2006, 85–86.

[21] UNDP, Lebanon: Rapid Environmental Assessment," 3-12.

[22] Ibid.

[23] Ibid.

[24] ITIC/CSS, Part Two, 129.

[25] "Local youngsters from the villages of Rmaish (central sector) and Alma al-Shaab (western sector) thwarted several attempts to fire rockets from those villages' houses (in practice, rockets were fired from the southern outskirts of the village of Alma al-Shaab)." IDF, ITIC/CSS, Part One, 35.

[26] UNDP, "Lebanon: Rapid Environmental Assessment," 3-12.

Alman Bqosta bridge, assessed as destroyed[27]

Alman underpass/Rmeileh/Alman interchange, ID 67, 20 percent damage[28]

'Alman, southwestern Marjeyoun district (Aalmane)

'Alman-Shumariya road, Marjeyoun

'Alman-Taybeh road, Marjeyoun

Amchaki-Baalbek road?

Amees gas station

'Amishki Hill, east of the city of Baalbek, Baalbek district

Al-Manar television and Al-Nour radio stations, attacked 13 July

Amshit, 40 km north of Beirut, Jbeil district (Amchit, Amsheet)

Amshit port radar, attacked 15 July

transmission station, near the Lebanese army barracks, Radio Liban, attacked 28 July, 10 August

Anduriya/Wadi al-Slouqi, western sector, southern Lebanon (A-Naduriya, Randuriya, Randuyia)

Anqoun/Sarba road, Iqlim al-Toufah, Nabatiyeh district

Ansar, western Nabatiyeh district (Insar)

Ansar/'Aba area

Ansar/al-Zrariyeh area

al-Ansariyeh, Zahrani district (al-Ansariya, Ansarieh, Ansari-yah, Anatzrya)

al-Ansariya/al-Babliyeh bridge

al-Ansariyeh main road/Ansariyeh overpass/underpass, south of Zahrani, ID 146

Ansariyeh Deir Takla overpass/underpass, south of Zahrani, ID 135

al-Arab bridge near Zahrani

Arab al-Jal/Sarba triangle in Iqlim al-Toufah, Nabatiyeh district

---

[27] Ibid.

[28] Ibid.

Arab al-Loueizeh, on the border south of al-Khiyam, Marje-youn district (al-Loueizeh, al-Louaizeh)

al-Loueizeh/Mleikh?

Arabsalim, north east of Nabatiyeh, Nabatiyeh district (Arab Salim, Arabsaleem, Arab Aalim, Aarab Aalim)

Arabsalim/al-Khiyam road

al-Areeda bridge, northern Lebanon

Arid Dbien?

Arqa, Zouk Haddara municipality, Akkar district (Aarqa, Ar-qah, Araqa, Arki)

Arqa bridge/Old Arqa-Halba main road bridge, ID 127, at-tacked 4 August, assessed as destroyed[29]

Arqa coastal bridge/marine bridge, ID 81, damaged[30]

al-Arqoub (al-Aarqoub)

Arnoun, north of Yohmur, Nabatiyeh district

Arsaal in Bekaa (Ersal, Arsal, Aarsal)

Arzai, near the Litani River

Arzoun, west of Srifa, Tyre district (Arzun)

al-A'asayreh, Baalbek district

Ashrafieh (see Beirut)

Asham bridge

Al-Assi, Hermel district (Alassi, al-Aassi, al-Assi, Al-Asi, Al Assy)

Al Assi bridge/Al-Heesah bridge, outskirts of al-Qaa and north of Hermel, ID 80, assessed as destroyed[31]

Al-Assi dam/Al-Sayyid Ali reservoir (at al-Dourah?)

al-Awali, north of Sidon city, Sidon district (Ouwali, Owali)

al-Awali bridge (old) (a.k.a. Alma/Al-Awali bridge/Alman Awali bridge), attacked 12 July,[32] ID 107, assessed as de-stroyed[33]

---

[29] Ibid.

[30] Ibid.

[31] Ibid.

[32] "Fighter jets also struck a minor bridge that helps form the main entrance to southern Lebanon, on the Awali River north of the provincial capital of Sidon, witnesses said. The main bridge and highway remained intact, however." AP (Sam F. Ghattas, Beirut), "Israel bombs southern Lebanon after Hezbollah fighters snatch 2 Israeli soldiers," 12 July 2006 1948 GMT.

[33] UNDP, "Lebanon: Rapid Environmental Assessment," 3-12.

al-Awali bridge (new), ramp to Sidon East Boulevard, assessed as destroyed[34]

Awjh al-Hajar radar

Ay'aat, west of Baalbek, Baalbek district

Ayara Bayde (see al Bayyadah)

Ayara Al-Mantuzi (see al-Mansouri)

Ayun al-Samak, Akkar district (Uyun A-Siman?)

Al-Mazar neighborhood transmission station and building belonging to the Lebanese Institution for Transmission power station (power station at the Nahr al-Barid dam?),[35] reportedly attacked 16 July, 15 August

al-Aziyeh (al-Aziya, al-Eziyeh)

Baabda, southeastern Beirut, Baabda district[36]

Baabda roundabout/road

Baabda bridge (Baabda Al Hadath bridge), ID 88, assessed as destroyed[37]

Baalbek (Ba'albak, Baalbeck)

Baalbek-Homs road

Baalbek-Riyaq road

Al-Dabas gas station

Ghosn gas station

Hezbollah headquarters (al-'Asayreh neighborhood), attacked 15 July

Hikmeh Hospital (Dar al-Hikmah, Dar-el-Hekma), site of commando operation on 1 August

Ibn Sina Hospital

---

[34] Ibid.

[35] http://www.assafir.com/iso/today/front/1888.html.

[36] "The road leading to the Baabda Municipality has been cut by a missile. This road can be easily contoured. Baabda has no strategic targets, controls no key roads, and its population of 60,000 is almost entirely Christian." Christopher Allbritton and Rania Abou Zeid, "Adding up the bill is itself a major challenge: Confusion still surrounds the extent of the damage in many parts of the country," *Daily Star* (Lebanon), 2 October 2006, http://www.dailystar.com.lb/article.asp?edition_id=1&categ_id=1&article_id=75829.

[37] UNDP, "Lebanon: Rapid Environmental Assessment," 3-12.

Imam Alys' mosque

"Justice Palace," reportedly attacked 18 July

Liban Lait (see Talba)

Moussaoui establishment on Baalbek-Riyaq road

Musawi Building Supplies (near Baalbek)

"Plastics factory," reportedly attacked 18 July

Ras al-Ein neighborhood gas station

Sheikh Abdallah camp[38]

Tabeekh gas station

Zayan Hospital

al Babliyeh, Nabatiyeh district (al-Babiliyeh)

Babliyeh bridge/interchange/overpass, ID 138, assessed as destroyed[39]

Baflay, east of Tyre, Tyre district (Bafliyah, Baflieh, Biflay, Bafliye)

Balzac? (Baalbek)

Baka

Baka/Kfar Kouk road

Baka/Yanta road

Balat (Balad), Marjeyoun district

Bani Haya?

Al-Barbarah Al-Daghlah bridge

Barda reservoir bridge, Ras al-Naba' neighborhood

Bareish, east of Tyre, west of Srifa, Tyre district (Bareesh, Barish, Barich, Bariesh)

Barine

Barouk (Mount Barouk)

transmission station, attacked 7 August

Barr Elias, Bekaa Valley (Bar Elias) Palestinian refugee camp

Bastarah farms, Hasbayya district (Basta Farms)

al-Batiri (see At-Tiri)

---

[38] Hezbollah training camp, formerly used by the Lebanese army and the Iranian Revolutionary Guards, situated on the outskirts of Baalbek.

[39] UNDP, "Lebanon: Rapid Environmental Assessment," 3-12.

Batouliyeh, north of Deir Qanun, Tyre district (Battouliyeh, Batoulay)

Batroun, Jbeil district

Lebanese army post/radar, possibly at Hamat, attacked 15 July

al-Madfoun/al Madhoun bridge in al-Batroun, linking north Lebanon with Mount Lebanon (El Madfoun bridge) ID 36, attacked 4 August, assessed as destroyed (a.k.a. Madfoun ["buried"] bridge and Madfoun ["anointed"] river bridge)[40]

Bawadi, 15 km west of Baalbek, Baalbek district

Bayt Ayyoub, Akkar district (Beit Ayyoub)

Al Jerd main road near Saqaqa area, cratered

Mechmech Bayt Ayyoub bridge, assessed as destroyed[41]

Bayt Hanoun (Bait Hanoun)

Bayt Jaafar, Akkar district

Akkar-Hermel bridge, assessed as destroyed[42]

Bayt Lif, near the border, western Bint Jbeil district[43] (Beit Lif, Bait Lif, Beit Leif, Bayt Ayf, Beit Ayf)

Bayt Wlaih, east of Sidon, Sidon district (Bait Wlaih)

Bayt Yahoun, north of Bint Jbeil, Bint Jbeil district (see also Yahoun) (Bait Yahoun, Bayt Yahoun, Beit Yahun, Bayt Yahun)

Bayyad, east of Qana, Tyre district (Bayad, Biyad)

al-Bayyadah, on the coast, Tyre district (see also Ras al-Bayyadah) (Bayada, al-Bayada, Biyyadeh, El Biyada, Ayara Bayde, Al-Beideh)

al-Bayyadah al-Ads road (Bayader)

Bayzoun bridge, assessed as destroyed[44] (Batroun bridge?)

Bazaliyeh, north of Baalbek, Bekaa (Bazalieh)

---

[40] Ibid.

[41] Ibid.

[42] Ibid.

[43] "On 23 August, UN assessment teams visited the villages of Beit Lif, Yater and Sidiqqin, where they reported massive destruction; Beit Lif is in particular need for drinking water and hygiene kits." Lebanon response, OCHA SITREP no. 33, 25 August 2006.

[44] UNDP, "Lebanon: Rapid Environmental Assessment," 3-12.

al-Bazouriyeh, on the main road from Tyre to Bint Jbeil, Tyre district[45] (Bazzouriyyeh, Bazourieh, Bazzouriyeh, al-Baysariyeh, Al Bazoureyi, Baysariyyeh)

    Bazouriyeh main line highway bridge, assessed as destroyed[46]

    Safieddin plant, manufactures medical supplies

    Sharnay road east of al-Bazouriyeh

Bchmoun (see Proctor and Gamble warehouse in Shwayfat)

Bednayel in Baalbek, Baalbek district (Bidnayel)

    al-Shehaynieh bridge/Bednayel bridge, ID 131 (Badnail/ Shahimiyah road bridge) Beirut[47]

    Abbas Al Mousawi Street

    Abdelnour Street gas station, attacked 25 July

    Ashrafieh (Achrafieh)[48]

    Bahman Hospital (*dahiye*)

Beirut port (see Ouzai)

    Beirut viaduct over highway (Bir al-Abed) ID 115

    Bir al-Abed (Bir al-Abd, Bir El Abed) (adjacent quarter to Haret Hreik)[49]

    Bir El-Abd/Rouis bridge, assessed as destroyed[50]

    Al-Moallem gas station

    Bir Hassan area

    Burj al-Barajneh municipality (Bourj El Barajina)[51]

        al-Manshiyeh mosque

        Palestinian refugee camp

---

[45] The birthplace of Hassan Nasrallah.

[46] UNDP, "Lebanon: Rapid Environmental Assessment," 3-12.

[47] Dahiyah (Dahyeh, Dahyieh) is literally the Arabic section of Beirut, commonly used to refer to the southern Shi'a suburbs of the city centered on the Haret Hreik neighborhood.

[48] "In Beirut, in the Christian neighbourhood of Achrafieh, on 19 July, IDF bombed two engineering vehicles used to drill water." UN General Assembly, Human Rights Council, Report of the Commission of Inquiry on Lebanon pursuant to *Human Rights Council Resolution S-2/1*, A/HRC/3/2, 23 November 2006, 37.

[49] After the district of Haret Hreik, the nearby Shi'ite districts of Bir al-Abed and Al-Ruwais were the main Hezbollah targets in south Beirut. IDF, ITIC/CSS, Part Two, 62.

[50] UNDP, "Lebanon: Rapid Environmental Assessment," 3-12.

[51] IDF, ITIC/CSS, Part Two, 62.

Chiyeh municipality (Shiyah, Chiyah)

Dar al-Hawra health facility (*dahiye*)

Galerie Semaan crossing, southeast Beirut (Gallery Semaan)

Hadi Nasrallah street/bridge in southern suburb, "close to the heavily guarded Iranian Embassy compound"[52] (Beirut Ashiyah highway over Hadi Nasrallah highway), ID 116, attacked 15 July

Hamas offices, attacked 15 July

Haret Hreik municipality[53] (Harit Hriek, Haret Horaik, Harat Hreik, Harat Hurayk)

Al-Manar TV and Hezbollah broadcasting compound (including Al Nour radio), attacked 12, 13, 14, 23 July, and 9 August

Hashem petrol station in al-Jamous, attacked 25 July

Hayy al-Abiad near Sayed al-Shuhada complex

Hayy al-Sulum (Hay al-Sulum)[54]

Hayy Madi

Hazmiyeh airport road/viaduct 1/viaduct 2 (a.k.a. Ghobeiry airport bridge) (Hazmieh, Hazmeyeh) attacked on the evening of 13 July, ID 117[55]

al-Imamain al-Hassanain mosque

Jamhour (Jmhour, Jumhour)

Lebanese army barracks (public works/engineer regiment)

Khaldeh, Alayh district just south of Beirut airport on the coast (see also Ouzai)

---

[52] Nada Bakri, "Israel pounds key Lebanese infrastructure," *Daily Star*, 15 July 2006, http://www.dailystar.com.lb/article.asp?edition_id=1&categ_id=2&article_id=73990#.

[53] Haret Hreik housed the main Hezbollah headquarters, administrative offices, and military and civilian "infrastructures" and was the main focus of Israeli attack inside south Beirut. For a satellite graphic portraying before and after damage, see *New York Times*, 4 August 2006, http://graphics.nytimes.com/packages/html/world/20060804_MIDEAST_GRAPHIC/index.html.

[54] IDF, ITIC/CSS, Part Two, 62.

[55] The bridge connects the southern outskirts of Beirut with the airport. "The Hazmieh-Airport bridge going through the Shiite southern suburbs was targeted at the beginning of the conflict. It is unfinished on both sides. It does not lead to Hazmieh or to the Airport. The middle section has been targeted. It can be easily contoured." Allbritton and Zeid, "Adding up the bill."

Khaldeh bridge

Kfar Shima, southeast Beirut (Kfarshima)

Lebanese army base, attacked 17 July

Zelzal rocket base

Qreitem "Old Lighthouse" (Qraitem), near American University, facing the Qarijan mosque

Lebanese Broadcasting Corporation (LBCI) antenna, attacked 10 August

Rafiq Hariri Beirut International Airport, attacked 13 July[56]

Rammal COOP

al-Ruwais (al-Rowais, al-Ruwis, Al-Rawis), adjacent quarter to Haret Hreik)[57]

Sayyed al-Shuhadaa complex, attacked 25 July

Sfeir (Sufayr)[58]

Sfeir bridge, Haret Hreik

Al-Shiyakh (IDF says it did not bomb the location)[59] Sultan Ibrahim-Marriott bridge, "close to the heavily guarded Iranian Embassy compound,"[60] attacked 14 July, damaged[61]

Bekaa Valley (Biqa Valley, Beqaa)

Bqosta-Karkha bridge (Baqsatah, Bkasta, Sidon district, attacked 13 July,[62] assessed as destroyed[63] (see also Alman)

---

[56] Airport authorities estimated that 25 bombs struck the airport's three runways and taxiways, crippling operations. The terminal buildings were undamaged. The airport was back in limited commercial operations on 18 August, four days after the cease-fire. See "Bombed Beirut airport on road to restoration," *Flight International*, 29 August 2006.

[57] After the district of Haret Hreik, the nearby Shi'ite districts of Bir al-Abed and Al-Ruwais were the main Hezbollah targets in south Beirut. IDF, ITIC/CSS, Part Two, 62.

[58] Ibid.

[59] Ibid.

[60] Nada Bakri, "Israel pounds key Lebanese infrastructure."

[61] UNDP, "Lebanon: Rapid Environmental Assessment," 3-12.

[62] "Air raids targeted the metal bridge of Baqsatah at the edge of town that connects it with 'Alman al-Shufiyah. The bridge was assessed as destroyed and fell into the Awwali River. The bridge was built by the Lebanese army in the aftermath of Grapes of Wrath in 1996 and is mainly used by the army and the inhabitants of the two towns." *As-Safir*, http://www.assafir.com (20060714).

[63] UNDP, "Lebanon: Rapid Environmental Assessment," 3-12.

Bidyas, near al-Abbasiyeh south of the Litani River, north Tyre district (Beddias, Badias?/Badyas?, Bedyas, Badias Abassieh)

Bidyas/Burj Rahhal road

Bint Jbeil, Bint Jbeil district (Bnt Jbeil)

Al-Hourani/Bint Jbeil gas station (Saff al-Hawa)

Bir al-Abed (see Beirut)

Bir Amnit?

Birket Jabbour, western Bekaa

al-Bisariyeh valley near al-Zahrani (Bissariyeh)

Blida, on the border, Marjeyoun district (Bleida, Blaida, Al-Beideh)

Bouday (see Ain Bourday)

Bra'shit, east of Tibnine, Bint Jbeil district (Barachiya, Bara-ashit, Barachit, Baraasheet, Brachit, Bri'shit, Baraachite; see also Barich)

122 mm rocket launch point

Brayqi', north of Qusaybeh, south Nabatiyeh district (al-Breiqe' a.k.a. al-Brayqaa, on the Zahrani River?)

Brital, near the Syrian border north of Nabbi Sheet, Baalbek district, Bekaa (Britel, Breetal)

Brital road

Brital Husseiniyeh

Budai (see Ain Bourday)

al-Burghuliyah, north of Tyre on the coast, Tyre district (Bourghliye)

Palestinian refugee camp

Burj al-Barajneh (see Beirut)

Burj al-Moulouk/Tal al-Nahhas, north of Khirbe, Marjeyoun district (Burj al-Mulouk, Bouj Al Malouke)

Burj Chamali, on the main road from Tyre to Bint Jbeil, Tyre district (Borj Shamali, Burj al-Shemali, Al-Borj al-Shemali, al-Burj al-Shamali)

Ghabris detergent factory, sustained major damage from direct attack[64]

---

[64] Ibid., 5-1.

Palestinian refugee camp

Saffieddine Plasti-med (Plastics Factory, a.k.a. Sada al-Din Plastics factory/Pastech medical factory[65]/Plati Med factory [medical supplies]) in Tyre,[66] attacked 18 July, sustained major damage[67]

Burj Qalawi, south of Ghandouriyah, Bint Jbeil district (Borj Qalaouiye, Burj Qalawiyeh, Burj Qulwiyeh, Borj Kalaway) (see also Qalawi)

Burj Qaloubeh

Burj Rahhal, off the Sidon-Tyre coastal highway north of Tyre near Abbasiyeh, Tyre district (Rahal)

Skayki Orchard

Bustan, on the border, Tyre district (Boustane) (also Boustane, eastern suburb of Tyre)

al-Bustan in west Bekaa (al-Boustane)

al-Butm mountains (see Jabal al-Butm)

Byblos (see Jbeil)

Casino bridge (see Jounieh)

Chanouh (see Shanuh)

Charoun bridge, assessed as destroyed[68]

Chehabiyeh

Chehemiyeh-Turkman bridge (Cheheimieh)

Choueifat (see Shwayfat)

Chtoura, on the Beirut-Damascus highway in mid Bekaa, Zahleh district (Chtaura, Shtura)

al-Dabsheh hill, Nabatiyeh district

al-Dadweer

---

[65] Ministry of Industry, Report of Damaged Factories, n.d., 2007.

[66] Ibid.; and UN, Report of the Commission of Inquiry, 38.

[67] UNDP, "Lebanon: Rapid Environmental Assessment," 5-1.

[68] Ibid., 3-12.

Dahal gas station

al-Dalafeh, west Bekaa district (al-Dalafa, Dlafy, Delafa) Delafa bridge/Dallafa Esper bridge, west Bekaa, assessed as destroyed[69]

al-Dalhamiyah (see Al Sa'adiyat) (Dahimiya, Dalhamiyah)

Dalhmieh village, Iqlim al-Kharroub, Shuf district (same as Dalhamiyah?)

Damour, Shuf district (Aldamoor, Damur, Djamour)

    Damour old bridge/Jisr Haret el Rouss, ID 51, attacked 12 July,[70] assessed as destroyed[71]

    Damour bridge/Damour Oceana Beach bridge, ID 61, attacked 13 July, assessed as destroyed[72]

    Damour interchange—Oceana, ID 58, assessed as destroyed[73]

    Damour interchange—N1, ID 59

    Damour interchange—S1, ID 68

    Damour–Beit Eddine interchange/Shuf interchange, ID 60

    Lebanese army barracks

Davin (see Dibeen)

Dbaiyeh, Metn coast, Shuf district (Debbiyyeh, Debiyeh, Debieh)

    Dbaiyeh overpass/underpass, ID 62, assessed as destroyed[74]

Debaal, north of the Tyre/Bint Jbeil main road near Jouwaya, Tyre district (see also Debel)

Debel, west of Bint Jbeil near the border, Bint Jbeil district (Debel et Emmeya, Dibil, Dbil) (see also Debaal)

---

[69] Ibid.

[70] "In the evening, warplanes made their closest strike to Beirut, destroying a seldom-used coastal bridge near a hilltop Palestinian guerrilla base 16 km (10 mi.) to the south. Palestinian guerrillas said the base was not hit as previously reported." AP (Ghattas), "Israel bombs southern Lebanon."

[71] UNDP, "Lebanon: Rapid Environmental Assessment," 3-12.

[72] Ibid.

[73] Ibid.

[74] Ibid.

Deir Ahmar bridge/Shlifa-Deir Al Ahmar bridge, assessed as destroyed,[75] "near Lebanese army checkpoint" (Der El Ahmar, Dier Al Ahmar)

Deir Aamis, northeast of Sidiqine, Tyre district (Deir Amess, Dayr 'Aamis, Deir Amess)

Deir Antar, off the main Tyre/Bint Jbeil road, Bint Jbeil (Dayr Antar, Deir Ntar, Deir Intar)

Deir Antar-Mazrait Meshref bridge/Mafraq Deir Antar bridge, ID 98

Deir Ashayer

Deir al Baidar (Baidar summit), Bekaa (see also al-Namliyeh) (Dahr al Baidar, Daher Al Baydar, Dahr al-Baydar Dahr-el-Baidar)

MTC mobile phone company transmission antenna,[76] attacked 14 July

Dahr al Baidar road

Dahr al Baidar-Mdeirej road

Deir Dibba, east of Tyre

Deir Jennine, Akkar district (Deir Jannein)

Deir Jennine-Fseyqeen main road, 10 m deep crater

Deir Kifa, eastern Tyre district north of the Tyre/Bint Jbeil main road, Tyre district (Deir Keefa, Dayr Kifa)

Deir Mimas, north of Kfar Kila, Marjeyoun district

Deir Qanun Ras al Ain, west of Qana, south of Tyre, Tyre district (Deir Kanoun, Deir Qanoun, Deir Qanoon, Deir Kanoun Ras, Dayr Qanun Ras al-'Ayn, Deir Qanon town near Tyre)

Deir Qanun gas station

Deir Qanun en Nahr, north of Tyre just south of the Litani River, Tyre district (Deir Qanun al-Nahr, Dir Al-Nahr, Qanoun al-Nahr, Deir Kanoun El-Nahr)

Deir Siryan, just north of Taybeh, Marjeyoun district (Dir Sirhan, Deir Siriane, Deir Seriane, Dir Sirin, a.k.a. Dir Yassin?)

---

[75] Ibid.

[76] "Israel strikes TV, phone towers in Lebanon," 22 July 2006, http://www.lebanonwire.com.

Deir az Zahrani, north Nabatiyeh district

> Deir az Zahrani/Rumin bridge, on the Zahrani River, (Dayr Zahrani), assessed as destroyed[77]

> Deir az Zahrani water treatment/sewage treatment plant, widely reported as having been attacked

Deir Znoun/al-Faour in Bekaa Valley (Deir Jennine, Deir Zanoun, Dayr Znun)

> "cement warehouse," reported attacked 16 July

> Deir Znoun road

Derb El-Sim bridge "west of Said," assessed as destroyed[78] (Darab Al-Sim, Darb el Seem, Darb Essim)

Derdghiya, east of Ma'aroub, west of Srifa, Tyre district (Derdghaiya, Dardeghya)

> Derdghiya/Ma'aroub road

> Derdghiya/Arzoun road near Tyre

> Derdghiya/al-Houmaira road

Dhaira, on the border near Bustan, Tyre district (al-Dhera, Duheira, Duhayrah, al-Dahira, Al Duhayyra)

Dhour al-Choueir

> Dhour al-Choueir road

> Dhour al-Choueir/Zahleh road (Dhour Shoueir-Zahleh)

> Dhour al-Choueir/Tarshish road

Dibeen, suburb north of Marjeyoun town, Marjeyoun district (Debbine, Dibbine, Dibbin, Dabine, Davin)

> Dibeen hills, Hezbollah base, attacked 12 July

Dibil (see Debel)

Dibsheh, Nabatiyeh district

Dimashkieh bridge, assessed as destroyed[79]

al-Diniyeh road, northern Lebanon

Douris near Baalbek, Baalbek district (Drous)

> Douris/Brital bridge

---

[77] UNDP, "Lebanon: Rapid Environmental Assessment, 3-12.

[78] Ibid.

[79] Ibid.

ad-Duwayr, west of Nabatiyeh, Nabatiyeh district (Douir, Duwair, al-Dowair, Dweir)

Ebil al-Saqi (see Ibl al-Saqi)

Ersal (see Arsaal)

Fakiha Hill

Fana

al-Faour, central Bekaa

Faour Litani River bridge, assessed as destroyed[80]

Faraya/Aayoun al-Simane road

al-Fardis, north of Rashaya, Hasbayya district (al-Freidis, Kfardiss)

Fardis bridge, ID 122

Fatqa heights, in the Kesrouan (Kesrwan) mountains, 10 mi. (16 km) northeast of Beirut, east of Jounieh (Fatqa-Kesrwan, Satqa, Fagra?)

television and cellular phone[81] transmission station (Ojiro company/Lebanese Instition of Transmission, Lebanese Broadcasting Corporation (LBCI), Future TV), attacked 22 July

al-Fayda (see Zahleh)

Fidar, south of Jbeil (Byblos), Bint Jbeil district (Fedar)

Fidar bridge (Halat-Fidar bridge) connecting the villages of Halat and Madfoun, ID 37,[82] attacked 4 August, assessed as destroyed[83]

Fih, Al Koura, north Lebanon, television station

Ferzol, Bekaa Valley, Zahleh district (Forzoi? Firzil, Fourzol)

Jarmicheh railroad bridge (Ferzol Jarmashiyyeh Bridge), assessed as destroyed[84]

---

[80] Ibid.

[81] "Israel strikes TV, phone towers in Lebanon."

[82] The Fidar bridge was the second tallest bridge in Lebanon and a key link between Beirut and Tripoli. The bridge spans over 300 m in length, standing 24 m above a deep chasm.

[83] UNDP, "Lebanon: Rapid Environmental Assessment," 3-12.

[84] Ibid.

Ferzol-Turbol bridge, Litani River, ID 113, assessed as destroyed[85]

Ferzol culvert

Froun, about 2 km north of Ghandouriyeh, Bint Jbeil district (Fru, Faroun/Faroun al Madjidiya, Froune)

al-Ghajar, on the border, south of al-Khiyam, Marjeyoun district (Aljar, Al Gajar, Rajar)

al-Ghandouriyeh, east of Srifa, northern Bint Jbeil district (Ghanduriyah, Ghandourieh, Ghandouriye, Ghandouriyé)

Gharbiyah (see Zawtar al-Gharbiyah)

Ghariefa bridge, ID 79

al-Ghassaniyeh, Sidon district

Ghazir, Jounieh? Kesrouane district

Ghazir bridge (Haret Sakher-Ghazir bridge) ID 130, attacked 4 August, damaged[86]

al-Ghaziyeh, south of Sidon, Sidon district (Ghazieh, Ghazeyi)

Ghaziyeh overpass, ID 70, assessed as destroyed[87]

al-Riji bridge/al Zahrani bridge (in Ghazeyi) attacked 17 July

"plastics factory," reportedly attacked 20 July

Ghazzah, Bekaa Valley (Ghazeh, Ghazeyh)

al-Ghurfa al-Faransiya (French Room) in Dahr al-Qadeeb "in Cedars region"

al-Habariyyeh, near Shebaa Farms, Hasbayya district (Habarieh, al-Habariyeh, Hibbariyah)

Habboush, north of Nabatiyeh, Nabatiyeh district (Hbush, Habouch, Haboush, Habbouch)

302 mm rocket launch point

Habboush bridge in the Nabatiyeh area, ID 92

Habboush River

Habboush-Arabsalim bridge, ID 13, assessed as destroyed[88]

Habboush interchange/overpass interchange, ID 91, damaged[89]

---

[85] Ibid.
[86] Ibid.
[87] Ibid.
[88] Ibid.
[89] Ibid.

Hadatha, north of Bint Jbeil, Bint Jbeil district (Hadath, Hadatha, Hadetha, Haddata, Haddatha, Hadta)

Chamoun Street in Hadath

Hadeth Baalbek

Hadid bridges (two separate bridges)

Al-Hadid (iron) bridge, connecting Qasta with Alman, Shuf
mountains

al-Hajjah, on the Zahrani River, Sidon district (Hajje, Hajjeh,
al-Hejjeh, al-Hijjeh, Alhaja, Hadja)

al-Hajjah town bridge between al-Msayleh and Nabatiyeh,
ID 39, assessed as destroyed[90]

al-Hajjah Maamariya bridge/ferry in Maamarieh, ID 40

al-Hajjah valley

al-Hajjah-al Mi'mariyah road

Halab town bridge, "near the center of the Lebanese Army intelligence"

Halat, Bint Jbeil district (see Fidar)

Halba, Akkar district

Halba bridge/Aawik Halba bridge, bridge on Al-Awik River,
ID 35, attacked 13 August

al-Halousiyeh, east of Bidyas, Tyre district (a.k.a. al-Halousiyeh
at Tahta, al-Halousiyeh Maaroub, al-Haloussiyeh, Halloussi-
yeh, Halouseh, al-Halousieh, Halusiyah, Hallusiyat at Tahta,
also Hallousiyet el Fao)

220 mm rocket launch point

Halta near Shebaa Farms on the border, Hasbayya district
(Halbta?)

Halta Farm

al-Hamra, on the border east of Metulla, Marjeyoun district
(Hamre, Aamra, Hemera)

Hamana heights (in the Maten), north of Batroun (al-Hamamis
hill, Hammana)

Hamana radar (a.k.a. Hamat airport radar)

---

[90] Ibid.

Hanawiyeh, northwest of Qana, Tyre district (Hanaouay, Han-
nouiye, Hanawayy, Hannaouiye)

Haneen, near the border, western Bint Jbeil district (Hanine,
Hanin)

Harbta, northern Bekaa

Hareess, northwest of Bint Jbeil, Bint Jbeil district (Haris, Ha-
riss, Harees)

Haret al-Marj in Kfar Ruman

Haret Hreik (see Beirut)

Haret Sakher-Ghazir bridge (see Ghazir)

Haret Sidon, Mar Ilyas hill, overlooking Sidon, Sidon district
(Mar Elias)

    Lebanese army antenna/radar, attacked 16 July[91]

    Palestinian refugee camp

Harouf, west of Nabatiyeh, Nabatiyeh district (Haruf)

    Harouf triangle, Nabatiyeh

Hasbani, Hasbayya district (Hasbany)

    Hasbani water station (Jisr Abu Wadi)

    Hasbani bridge/Hasbani roads, assessed as destroyed[92]

Hasbayya, Hasbayya district (Hasbaya, Hasbayia)

    Hasbayya-Marj al-Zuhur road

    Hasbayya-Marjeyoun road

Al-Hasbeh

    Shawqi Antar gas station

Hassiniya Boudai? (Husseiniyeh? see Ain Bourday)

Hassiniya Wadi al-Hadjir

Hatzor

al-Hawza al-Diniya, Tyre district

Hayy al-Aasireh

Hayy al-Bayad, Nabatiyeh district (Hayy al-Bayyadah)

Hayy al-Sharawneh in Baalbek, Baalbek district

---

[91] Lebanese media reports stated that a water tower/tank was attacked.

[92] UNDP, "Lebanon: Rapid Environmental Assessment," 3-12.

Hayy Rahbat in Nabatiyeh, Nabatiyeh district

al-Helaniyeh, Bekaa

Hamyri, north of Arzoun, Tyre district (Haumeiri) (see also Hamra)

Hermel, north Lebanon (El-Hermel) (see also Al-Assi)
Hermel transmission station

Heshmesh Valley, Bekaa
Popular Front for the Liberation of Palestine-General Command (PFLP-GC) camp

al-Hijjeh (see al Hajjeh)

al-Hineyeh, near Izziyah on the coast, Tyre district (al-Hiniyeh, al-Henniyeh, Hiniye, Hynya, Hanniye)

al-Hissah, Akkar district (Hasieh, Haissa, Al-Heisa; see also Al-Assi)
al-Hissah bridge over the Oustwan River, about 3 kms from the Dabboussiyeh, Syria, border crossing (same as Aboudiyeh bridge?), ID 47, assessed as destroyed[93]
Hissah Ballaneh culvert, ID 85

Hokbane hill?

Homa Arnoun

Homeen al-Fawqa

Houmine (see Sarba Houmine)

al-Hosh, suburb of Tyre, Tyre district (al-Housh, Hawsh, Al-houch)
al-Hosh road near Lebanese army barracks
al-Hosh Safee al-Din gas station

Hosh Barada

Hosh Basmeh, Tyre district

Hosh al Rafka bridge, Baalbek district, assessed as destroyed[94] (Houch el Rafqa, Hawsh el Rafka, Hawch al Rafiqua)
Hosh-Ar Rafka-Hosh Misraya culvert, ID 84

---

[93] Ibid.

[94] Ibid.

Houla, on the border, Marjeyoun district (Hula, Howla, Hawla)[95]

Al-Zahra gas station

al-Hujair

Husseiniyeh? ("Upper Husseiniyeh"; see also Ain Bourday)

Ibl al-Saqi, eastern Marjeyoun district (Ibles Saqi, Ibl al-Saqqi, Ebil al-Saqi, Abel a-Saki, al-Saqi)

Hezbollah base (east of), attacked 12 July

Al-Ichiya?

Iqlim al-Kharroub, area east of Jiyyeh, Shuf district (Ikleem Alkharroub)

Palestinian refugee camp

Iqlim al-Toufah ("Apple District") north of Nabatiyeh, Nabatiyeh district (Iqlim al Tuffah, Eklim al Toufah)

Iqlim al-Toufah heights

Ain Bouswar/Jebaa/Sarba/Houmine roads

Itrun (see Aitaroun)

Iskandaroun, north of Naqoura on the coastal road, Ras al-Bayyadah, Tyre district (Iskandarouna, Eskandaroun)

Izza, Zahrani River, Nabatiyeh district (Izzah)

al-Izziyah (Izya) Valley, Tyre district (al-'Izziyeh, Izzié)

Izray, north of the Litani River near Qasimiyeh, Sidon district

Jabal Abu-Rashid, Bekaa

---

[95] "Some Hezbollah positions remained in close proximity to United Nations positions, especially in the Hula area, posing a significant security risk to United Nations personnel and equipment, as demonstrated during the heavy exchanges of fire on 28 May. In letters to the Foreign Minister, dated 23 March, 27 June and 5 July 2006, the Force Commander, General Pellegrini, expressed grave concern about the Hezbollah construction works in close proximity to United Nations positions and requested that the Government of Lebanon take necessary actions to rectify the situation. However, the situation remained unchanged despite repeated objections addressed by UNIFIL to the Lebanese authorities. UNIFIL observed the reconstruction of Hezbollah positions that were damaged or assessed as destroyed during the 28 May exchange of fire." UN, Report of the Secretary-General on the United Nations Interim Force in Lebanon (For the period from 21 January 2006 to 18 July 2006), S/2006/560, 21 July 2006.

Jabal al-Ahmar

Jabal al-Bat

Jabal al-Butm, north of Zibqine, Tyre district (Jbal al-Botm, Jbal al-Butom, Jibal al-Butm, Jibal LBotom, Batm Mountain in Sidiqine, Jbeil al-Baten)

    Jabal al-Butm bridge, ID 118

Jabal al-Malah heights, east of Baalbek, Baalbek district

Jabal al-Rafi' (Jabal al-Rafee')

Jabal al-Safi (Mount Safi), Iqlim al-Toufah (Jebel Safi)

    Jabal al-Safi radar

Jabal Sannin (Mount Sannine, 2,695 m)

    television and radio transmission station (LBCI and Radio Free Lebanon), attacked 22 July

Jabal Siddaneh, near Shebaa Farms

Jabal Terbel (see Terbol)

Jabanet Macchouk near Tyre

al-Jabbour pond, Bekaa

al-Jadid (New) bridge, Al-Mdeirej international road

Jadra interchange/Jadra-Wadi Zaineh bridge, ID 65, assessed as destroyed[96]

Jal al-Shomar

Jlala Bridge, central Bekaa, assessed as destroyed[97] (Jalala)

al-Jamaliyeh, north of Baalbek, Baalbek district (near Hikmeh Hospital in Baalbek)

Jamil Gemajel port (Jamil Gemayel), reported as attacked

Jamhour (see Beirut Jamhour)

Janata, south of Deir Qanoun en Nahr, Tyre district (Jnata, Janta)

---

[96] UNDP, "Lebanon: Rapid Environmental Assessment," 3-12.

[97] Ibid.

Jarjou', Iqlim al-Toufah (Jarju north of Arabsalim in Nabatiyeh district) (Jarjoua)

Jarjou'/Arab al-Loueizeh road

Jarmaq, northwest of Marjeyoun, Jezzine district (Jarmak, Jurmuq, al-Jarmaq, Jurmaq, Jarmouk)

Jarmaq bridge, attacked 12–13 July, assessed as destroyed[98]

al-Jarmishah

Al-Jarmishah bridge connecting Al-Farzad plans to the town of Al-Jarmishah

Al-Jarmishah iron bridge

Jba'a in Iqlim al-Toufah region, north of Nabatiyeh, Nabatiyeh district (Jbaa, Jbea?)

Jbeil (Byblos), Jbeil district (Jbail)

al-Jbien, on the border north of Yarin, Tyre district (al Jibbayn, Jibbin, al-Jebbayn, al-Jbein, Jebbain)

Jdeidet Yabous, Masnaa area, Syrian border (Jdayded)

Jibsheet, southwest of Nabatiyeh, Nabatiyeh district (Jibshit, Jabshit, Jabsheet, Jebchit, Jebshit)

Jibsheet bridge

Jisr Beach bridge, Shuf district

Jiyyeh, coastal south of Beirut, Shuf district (El Jiye, Jiyeh, Jieh, Al-Jiya)

Jiyyeh electric power plant fuel storage, attacked 13 and 15 July[99]

Jiyyeh interchange north of Jammoul bakery/Jiyyeh overpass/Jiyyeh bridge, ID 64, assessed as destroyed[100]

---

[98] Ibid.

[99] "The power station's Director, 'Abd al-Razaq al-Eitani, told Amnesty International that the first tank, containing 10,000 tons of fuel, was hit in an air strike on 13 July. Two days later the 15,000-ton fuel tank was hit and caused a 25,000-ton fuel tank to catch fire. He said one person was slightly injured in the attacks, and that several people, including himself, had suffered from smoke inhalation." Amnesty International, Israel/Lebanon, "Out of all proportion—civilians bear the brunt of the war," MDE 02/033/2006, 21 November 2006.

[100] UNDP, "Lebanon: Rapid Environmental Assessment," 3-12.

Jmayjmeh, eastern Bint Jbeil east of Tibnine, Bint Jbeil district (Jmaijmeh, Jumayjimah, Jmaijime)

al-Josh road, Tyre

Joun (same as al-Jurn east of Tibnine?)

    tire factory, reported attacked on 13 August

Jounieh, Maamaltein area, Kesrouane district, northern Lebanon, coastal resort (Juniyah, Junieh, Jernaya)

    Casino bridge, Ghazir municipality (a.k.a. "Maamaltein bridge, North Lebanon road"), ID 33, attacked 4 August, damaged[101]

    Jounieh culvert? assessed as destroyed[102]

    Jounieh port radar (located on Lebanese navy base), attacked 15 July

    (see also Ghazir bridge)

Jouwaya, on the main road from Tyre to Bint Jbeil, Tyre district (Jouaya, Juwayya, Jwayya, Jounaya)

    Jounaya to Tyre bridge, ID 99

Kaakieh bridge (see al-Qa'qa'iyah)

Kabeet, Akkar district

    Al Jerd main road near Habsheet intersection, assessed as destroyed[103]

Kafra, western Bint Jbeil district

    Kafra-Ain Zhalta road in Shuf Cedars Reserve?

Kafrouwa (see al-Kfour)

Al-Kaliya (see al-Qlayeh)

Kaliyet (see Qulayaat)

Kamed al-Louz road, western Bekaa

Kantara (see al Qantara)

Karak near Zahlah, Zahlah district (al-Karak, AlKark)

    Karak bridge connecting Karak to Turbol

Kasmieh (see Qasimiyeh)

---

[101] Ibid.

[102] Ibid.

[103] Ibid.," 5-1.

273

Kawkaba in Rashaya, off the main Marjeyoun-Bekaa road, Hasbayya district (Kaoukaba)

Kayfoun hills in Mount Lebanon

Kbayet Akkar bridge, Akkar district, ID 93

Kefraya, western Bekaa

Kfar Bater, southern Lebanon

Kfar Dounine, Bint Jbeil district (Kfardounine)

Kfar Hamam, north of Kfar Shouba, Hasbayya district (Kfarhamam, Kfarmam, Kafarhmam)

Kfar Harra bridge, Akkar district (Swaysseh), ID 87

Kfar Hatta, Sidon district (Kfarhety)

Kfar Houna

Kfar Jarrah, east of Sidon on the Sidon-Jizzin road, Sidon district

fine tissue factory/Hassan al-Za'tari cardboard factory, attacked 16–17 July, assessed as completely destroyed[104]

Kfar Jouz (Kfarjouz), Nabatiyeh district

Kfar Kila, on the border, Marjeyoun district (Kfarkellah, Killah, Kufrkala, Kurfkala)

Kfar Kila/Deir Mimas/al-Khiyam road

Fawaz gas station

Sheet gas station

Kfar Mashki in western Bekaa, Hasbayya district (Kfar Mashki, Kfarmeshkeh)

Kfar Mashki-Hasbayya culvert 1/2/Lebanese army checkpoint

Kfar Rumman, Nabatiyeh district (Kfar Ruman, Kfar Roumaine)
Kfar Rumman/Arabsalim bridge (Green Valley bridge; a.k.a. Arabsalim Al-Wadi Al-Akhdhar bridge, Wadi elakhdar/Arabsalim/Kfar Remman bridge), ID 134, attacked 13–14 July, assessed as destroyed[105] (see also Habboush)

Kfar Shima (see Beirut Kfar Shima)

---

[104] Ibid.

[105] Ibid., 3-12.

Kfar Shouba hills, on the border, Hasbayya district (Kfarshuba, Kfarshiuba, Kfarshouba)

Kfar Selwan? (Kafarselwan)

Kfar Sir (Kfarsir), north of the Litani River, south Nabatiyeh district (Kfar Seer)

Kfar Tibnit, north of Arnoun, Nabatiyeh district (Kfar Tibneet, Kafartebnit; see also Khardali)

    Kfar Tibnit hill

    Jarmaq Farm

Kfar Zabad, south of Rayak, Zahleh district, Bekaa (Kafarzbd, Kafarzied? Kfar Zibd)

    Maalqa-Kfar Zabad bridge

    PFLP-GC camp

    transmission station (New TV), attacked 14 July

al-Kfour, Iqlim al-Toufah, Nabatiyeh district (Kafrouwa)

    Kfour crossing in Nabatiyeh

    Kfour Valley near Nabatiyeh

Khaldeh (see Beirut)

al-Khardali-Kfar Tibnit highway bridge, Litani River, Marjeyoun district, ID 17 (El Khardaly, Khandali), assessed as destroyed[106]

Kharis (see Hareess)

Khayzaran Viaduct, Zahrani district, ID 103(?), (Hahn Khaizarane; see also Sarafand)

Al-Kheyr plain

    Khaled Hamoud gas station

al-Khidr highway bridge, Sidon district, ID 104

Khirbe, Marjeyoun district (a.k.a. Khirbet Kasif, Hirbat Kasif, Hirbet Kseif)

Khirbet Silim, off the main Tyre/Bint Jbeil road, Bint Jbeil district (Khirbet Sulum, Kherbet Selm, Khirbet Sahlem)

al-Khrayeb, Zahrani region, Sidon district (al-Kharayeb)

al-Khraybeh, west of al-Khiyam, Marjeyoun district (Khirbe)

---

[106] Ibid.

al-Khiyam, Marjeyoun district (al-Khiam, al-Khyam)
    Al-Khiyam prison
    al-Khiyam/Marjeyoun road

Kilya (see Qalya)

Kleyate (see Qulayaat)

al-Knaisseh, western slopes of Mount Lebanon (Knayseh)

Kouseia hills, Bekaa (Koseia, Qousaya, Qussaya)
    PFLP-GC camp

al-Koueikhat/al-Qubayat, Akkar district (Kuowiakhat, Koway-khat, Kowikhat, Kuwaikhat)
    Koueikhat bridge/Akkar international road, Halba-Koueikhat main road over Outswan River (Kowayhkat 1/Kowaykhat 2), ID 34, assessed as destroyed[107]

al-Kousaybeh (see Qusaybah)

Kouza (see Qawzah)

Kssara near Zahleh

Kawthariyet al-Ruz

Kroum

Kunin, north of Bint Jbeil, Bint Jbeil district (Kounine, Ko-neen)

Labouneh, on the border, Tyre district (Lebona, Labouna)

al-Laqis in Baalbek, Baalbek district

al-Loueizeh (see Arab al-Loueizah)

Loussia, west Bekaa district ("Lucy in the Bekaa," "Lucy Farms")

Maamaltein (see Jounieh)

Maalaqa bridge, near Salhab house, Zahleh district

al-Ma'aliyeh, near Qlayleh, Tyre district (al-Ma'liyeh, Ma'aliya, Maaliye)

Maamariya? (Maamariya Haadja)

Ma'araka (see Ma'rakeh)

Ma'aroub, east of Tyre, central Tyre district (Maroub)

---

[107] Ibid.

Mabarat al-Imam Ali in Ma'aroub

Maaraboun village, near the Syrian border, south Bekaa

    Maaraboun bridge

Madfoun (see Batroun) (Madhoun)

Mafraq Deir Antar bridge (see Deir Antar)

Mahloussiyeh

al-Mahmoudiyeh, Jezzine district (Mahmoudieh)

    al-Mahmoudiyeh/Dimashqiyeh bridge ("Liberation Bridge")
Dimashkieh/Tahrir bridge "between Mahmudiyah Farm
and Marji'yun on the Litani River," attacked 12 July, ID
125, assessed as destroyed[108] (see also Tayr Filsay)

Mahrounah, south of Jouwaya off the Tyre to Bint Jbeil road,
Tyre district (Mahrouneh, Mahrouna, Mahroumeh)

Mahrouhine (see Marwaheen)

Mais al-Jabal, on the border, Marjeyoun district (Mayss al-Jabal,
Mays al-Jabal, Mis al-Jabel, Mis Al Jbeil, Miss El-Djabal, Meis
al-Jabal, Meiss El-Jabel)

    Hezbollah headquarters

    Mais al-Jabal Hospital

Majadel, east of Jouwaya, Tyre district (al-Majadil, Mjadel, Ma-
jaydal)

    Majaydal bridge

Majdal Silm, near the border, southern Marjeyoun district
(Majdel Selm)

    Hezbollah construction unit

Majdal Zoun, near the border, Tyre district (Majdel Zoun, Majdal Zun Majdel Zun)

Majdaloun (Majdloun) (same as Majdal Zoun?)

    Saideh-Majdaloun bridge, assessed as destroyed[109]

al-Majidiyah, on the border, Hasbayya district (al-Majidiyeh,
al-Majida)

al-Malikiyeh, north of Qlayleh, Tyre district (Malkiya)

---

[108] Ibid.

[109] Ibid.

al Mamoura, Tyre district (Ma'murah) (located between al Her-ish and al-Bazouriyeh)

al-Manara, on the border, Bekaa (Al Khyaray-Al Manara)

Al Arz textile factory, attacked 23 July, sustained major damage[110]

al-Mansouri, south of Tyre off the coastal road, on the way to Majdal Zoun, Tyre district (Mansouri, Mansuri, El-Man-souri, al-Mansoura, Mansoureh, a.k.a. Ayara Al-Mantzuri)

Lebanese army post

al-Maqaleh

Maqna in Baalbek, Baalbek district (Mekeni)

Maqna/Younin road

Maqsaba interchange, ID 63

Ma'rakeh, near Tayr Diba east of Tyre, Tyre district (Maaraka, Ma'arakeh, Maarake, Maarakeh)

Maaraka crossroad

Mar Ilyas hill (see Haret Sidon; see also Barr Elias)

al-Mari, east of al Khiyam on the border, Hasbayya district (al-Mary, El-Meri)

El Mari bridge, ID 121

Marj al Zohoor bridge, assessed as destroyed[111]

Marj Debeen in Yohmor al-Shqaif area

Marjeyoun, Majeyoun district (Marjiayoun)

Marjeyoun electrical power station fuel storage, reported as attacked

Markaba, on the border, Marjeyoun district (Markabeh, Markhava)

Markaba-Hayy al-Husseini

---

[110] Ibid., 5-1.

[111] Ibid., 3-12.

Maroun a-Ras, highest point in Jabal A'amel, on the border, Bint Jbeil district (Maroun el Rass, Maroun al-Ras, Maroon Al Rass)

Al-Manar television transmitter, attacked 12 July

Marwaheen, on the border near Bustan, Tyre district (Marwahin, Marwahine, Mervachin, Marouahine)

122 mm rocket launch point

Mashghara, southern section of western Bekaa, west Bekaa district (Mashgharah)

Mashghara/Aitanit road

Iranian Revolutionary Guard camp

al-Masnaa, on the Syrian border, northern Lebanon

Masnaa customs crossing, ID 109

al-Masnaa road near Syrian border

Masnaa Road Litani bridge, ID 75, assessed as destroyed[112]

Masnaa border point

Maydoun, western Bekaa

Mayfadoun, south of Nabatiyeh town, Nabatiyeh district (Maifadoun, Mifdun)

Mazra'at Balde bridge, Halba-Deir Jennine main road, Akkar district, ID 48 (Mazraat Baldeh)

Mazra'at al-Khreibeh

Mazra'at Meshref (see Deir Antar) (Mazrait Meshref)

Mdeirej, Aley district (Mdayrej, Mdairege, Al Mdayrij, Mdeirej-Hammana bridge)

"Radar Hill"

---

[112] Ibid.

Mdeirej bridge/viaduct (old Mdeirej bridge) on the Beirut-Damascus international road,[113] ID 74, attacked 12 and 21 July,[114] assessed as destroyed[115]

M'doukha

Mechref bridge, assessed as destroyed[116]

al Mi'mariyah, Zahrani, Sidon district (Maamarieh, al-Ma'amariyeh, Maamariya)

(Maamariya bridge)

Minyara bridge, northern Lebanon

al-Minyeh, al-Rawdah

al-Minyeh iron bridge, connecting al-Dinniyah and al-Minyeh, attacked 15 July

Miskaf Aam

Mleekh

Mleita (Mleeta, Mletha)

Msayleh?

---

[113] "One example is the Mdeirej Bridge, the only bridge in Lebanon adopted by USAID. A spectacular modern construction more than 70 meters high, it was struck early in the war by Israeli bombs. One of its spans is marked by a huge crater that took out an entire section, about one-third of the bridge's length. The other span is too unstable to allow traffic. The crucial artery between Beirut and Chtoura, and on to Syria, is closed, along with the trade and travel that are vital to Lebanon's recovery. The USAID official said the bridge would be rebuilt with $20 million and the help of the original Italian company that designed and constructed it." Allbritton and Zeid, "Adding up the bill."

Fadl Shalak said that replacing the bridge connecting Mount Lebanon to the Bekaa Valley above the Sulfi River on the road to Damascus would cost an estimated US $65 million. "A beautiful bridge, its columns 70 meters, it's one of a kind in the whole Middle East. Why would they destroy such a bridge?" he asked. "They could have bombed the beginning and the end and stopped the traffic. But they made a point to bomb this bridge several times." Another observer said, "This bridge is not used by Hezbollah since it lies in a mountain resort area of Mount Lebanon, far away from the south of Lebanon. Hence it has no strategic value for the Israeli fight against Hezbollah. But it was a beautiful bridge and was the symbol of the reconstruction of Lebanon after the civil war." Quoted in Amnesty International, "Israel/Lebanon: Deliberate destruction or 'collateral damage'? Israeli attacks on civilian infrastructure," MDE 18 July 2006, August 2006, 6.

[114] "Israel destroys the highest bridge in Lebanon," *YaLibnan.com*, 22 July 2006, http://yalibnan.com/site/archives/2006/07/israel_destroys.php.

[115] UNDP, "Lebanon: Rapid Environmental Assessment," 3-12.

[116] Ibid.

al-Mtariyyeh "in al-Zahrani," east of Zahrani, Sidon district (Al-matareya, al-Matriya?, al-Matariyeh, al Mutayriyah)

Mtoula

Al-Mu'aqin ("handicapped") bridge

Muhaybib, on the border north of Blida, Marjeyoun district (Mhaybib, Mahbib, Mehibev, Mhaibib)

al-Muraifaa

al-Naemeh, north of Jiyyeh, north of Damour, Shuf district (al-Naimeh, Naameh, Alnaamey, Na'emeh, Na'imah, Al-Ni'ma)

   paper factory, reported attacked on 13 August

   al-Naemeh heights, south of Beirut

   al-Naemeh entry bridge, ID 55, assessed as destroyed[117]

   al-Naemeh interchange—Hara, ID 54, assessed as destroyed[118]

   al-Naemeh interchange—N3, ID 57, assessed as destroyed[119]

   al-Naemeh interchange—N4, ID 56

   al-Naemeh old tunnel

   al-Naemeh autostrad bridge

   PFLP-GC camp

Nabatiyeh (Nabatieh, Nebatya, Nabateyieh)

   Al-Manar TV station, al-Bayyad neighborhood, attacked 17 July

   Ghandour hospital, damage reported 24 July

   Habboush-Nabatiyeh bridge

   Jarmaq bridge in Nabatiyeh

   Nabatiyeh–Iqlim al-Tufah bridge

   Nabatiyeh culvert, assessed as destroyed[120]

   Salim Dhaher gas station (see also al-Shqif)

Nabbi Sheet, near the Syrian border, Baalbek district, south Bekaa (Nabi Shit, Nabi Chit)

---

[117] Ibid.

[118] Ibid.

[119] Ibid.

[120] Ibid.

Nabi al-Awadi, south of Kfar Kila, west of Metulla, Marjeyoun district (Nabi El Awadi)

Nabi Ayla bridge, assessed as destroyed[121]

Nabi Omran

Al-Nabi ("Prophet") Shubat bridge, connecting Rital with the towns of Homs and Al-Kharabi

Nafkhah, near Srifa, Tyre district (Nafkha, Naffakhiye)

Nahleh

Nahr al-'Asi Valley, east of Hermel

Nahr al-Bared dam, north of Tripoli

Palestinian refugee camp

al-Najjariyeh petrol station, attacked 16 July

al-Namliyeh, Bekaa (Namlieh, Namliya-on-Baydar)

al-Namliyah bridge at Deir al Baidar ("al-Baydar summit"), attacked 14 July, assessed as destroyed[122]

al-Naqoura, on the south coast, Tyre district (Nakoura, Naqurah)

Naqoura-to-Tyre bridge, ID 96

al-Naseriyeh, Bekaa

al-Nassar area, between Hannawiyah and Deir Qanun Ras al-Ain

al-Numairiyeh, Nabatiyeh district (Nmeiriyeh, Noumeyriyyeh, Almayriyeh)

al-Numairiyeh/al-Sharqiyeh area, Nabatiyeh

Oudein

Ouwali (see al-Awali)

Ouzai, near Beirut International Airport, Baabda district (Ouzaai, Owzaai, Al Uza'i)

"Costa Brava beach," Khaldeh, attacked 14 July

Costa Brava bridge (A-Cost Brafa)

---

[121] Ibid.

[122] Ibid.

Beirut port, attacked 15–16 July,[123] 17 July,[124] 4 August
Hezbollah navy unit[125]

Lebanese army post

Palestinian refugee camp (Al-Jnah-Ouzai)

al-Oweida village, near Marjeyoun (al-Ouwaida)
    al-Owaida hills

al-Qaa, Lebanese-Syrian border, Baalbek district
    Qaa culvert (government hospital), ID 126

Qaaqaaiyet al-Snoubar

al-Qa'qa'iyah al-Jisr, north of the Litani, Nabatiyeh district
    (Qaaqaiya, Kaakaa-iyyit Al Jisir, Kaakieh, Qaaqaait Jisr)
    al-Qa'qa'iyah bridge, Litani River/Zahrani River? (al
    Qa'qa'iyah/al Froun Bridge, a.k.a. Kaakieh bridge), ID 42,
    attacked 12 July, assessed as destroyed[126]
    Qaaqaeit aljisr bridge, ID 119

Qabreeha

Qabrikha, west of Markaba, Marjeyoun district (Qabrika)

Qadmus (see Tyre)

Qalya, western Bekaa (Kilya)
    "fish raising tanks," reported destroyed

Qala'et Meis between al-Zrariyeh and Aaba

Qalawi, south of Burj Qalawi, Bint Jbeil distrct (Qalawiyeh,
    Qalawiya, al-Qulaiyaa, Qalya)

Qana, Tyre district (Kana, Kfar Qana)
    Hezbollah regional headquarters

---

[123] Attacks on the Beirut port on 15–16 July are reported as having assessed as destroyed the "Greater Beirut Power Station," the Beirut "lighthouse" (housing radar, observation posts, and communications), and "grain silos."

[124] "On 17 July, the Israeli Air Force launched a pre-dawn attack on the port of Beirut, striking a fuel tank, which exploded, killing two workers. The port of Beirut, which had been badly damaged in previous conflicts, had recently undergone an extensive reconstruction programme." See Amnesty International, "Israel/Lebanon."

[125] According to the IDF, "the organization has a naval unit deployed along the shoreline, notably in the Shi'ite district of Ouzai, which is integrated into the organization's defensive and offensive plans." IDF, ITIC/CSS, Part Two, 64.

[126] UNDP, "Lebanon: Rapid Environmental Assessment," 3-12.

Qana/Ain Ba'al road
122 mm and 220 mm rocket launch point

Qanoun al-Nahr (see Deir Qanoun en Nahr)

al-Qantara, on the main road, Marjeyoun district (Qantarah, Kantara, Al Kantara)

al-Qaraoun Dam, near Aitaneet, Bekaa
Lebanese army checkpoint, attacked 18 July
Qaraoun Dam, reportedly attacked 30 July

al-Qasimiyeh, on the Litani River, Tyre district (al-Qassmiyeh, Qassimieh, Kassimiyeh, Kasmieh, Kasmeyeh)

al-Qasimiyeh main (new) bridge (Muhammad Sa'd and Khalil Jaradi Bridge) on the "international road," Litani River; a.k.a. al-Qasimiyeh bridge between Sidon and Tyre and Qasimiyeh bridge west, ID 23, attacked 12 July, assessed as destroyed[127]

al-Qasimiyeh old bridge/local road bridge, Litani River (Qasimiyeh bridge east), ID 29, attacked 12 July, assessed as destroyed[128]

Qasimiyeh river ferry

Lebanese army barracks (Kasmieh Lebanese army camp), reportedly attacked 31 July

Palestinian refugee camp

al-Qawzah, near the border, western Bint Jbeil district (al-Qouwzah, Qouzah, al-Qaouzah, Kouza)

Christian Maronite church[129]

Kouza dam?

---

[127] Ibid.

[128] Ibid.

[129] "Of particular note was the damage caused to the Christian Maronite church, which was damaged by bombing in the early days of the conflict and was later occupied by Israeli forces and used as its base. The roof had been badly damaged and there was a large shell hole in the front right corner of the wall. The damage to the church's roof and wall of the church appeared to have been caused by a tank round. Furthermore, during their 16-day occupation IDF vandalized the church, breaking religious statues, leaving behind garbage and other waste. The Commission saw a statue of the Virgin Mary that had been smashed and left in the church grounds. When the villagers returned, they found the church had been wrecked, the church benches and confessional box smashed. Silver items remained but had been deliberately broken. There were sandbagged defensive positions within the church grounds. There was no evidence to suggest fighting in and around the church to capture it. It therefore appears that IDF simply took it over. The damage was either caused on their occupation of the village or on their departure." UN, Report of the Commission of Inquiry, 47.

al-Qaysiyeh

Qinarit/Zeita valley in Zahrani, Sidon district (Qanareet)

Qinarit overpass

al-Qlayleh, west of Qana, Tyre district (Klayleh, al-Qleileh, al-Qulaiyaa, al-Qlayleh, al-Qalaileh, al-Qalila, al-Qliyeh al-Maaliyeh, El-Kleile)

al-Qlayleh Choubrikha (Qalila)

al-Qlayeh, west of al-Khiyam, Marjeyoun district[130] (Al-Kaliya, al-Qlei'a, al-Qleia'a, al-Qalaya, al-Koulaya'a)

al-Qubayat, Akkar district (Kobayat)

Qubayat-Aandqit main road, two large craters

Qulayaat military airfield, near Tripoli (a.k.a. Rene Mouawad airfield), attacked 13 July (Kaliyat, Qoleiat, Qulayate, Kleyaat, Qaliate, al-Qali'at)

Qulayaat road

al-Qura, north Lebanon

TV transmission station (state-run Tele-Liban), attacked 22 July

al-Qusaybeh, Nabatiyeh district (Qusaibeh, Al-Qsaibe, al-Qusaiybeh, al-Kousaybeh)

302 mm rocket launch point

al-Qusaybeh road

al-Qusaybeh/A'adsheet road

Rab al-Thalathine, on the border, Marjeyoun district (Rab a-Tiltin, Rub Thalatheen)

Rachiya (see Rashaya)

al-Radar hills, Iqlim al-Toufah, Nabatiyeh district

Al-Rafi'ah town bridge

Al-Rafiqah Reservoir town bridge

Rahaiya Al Wadi bridge

al-Rahrah

Rajar (see al-Ghajar)

---

[130] "On July 17, Hezbollah operatives attempted to fire rockets from the eastern town of Qlaiaa. Hand-to-hand fighting broke out between the Hezbollah operatives and local villagers, and the operatives were driven away." IDF, ITIC/CSS, Part One, 35.

Rajmin (Rajamin, Ramjamin, see Ramiya)

al-Raki, Zahrani

Al-Ram bridge

Ramiya, on the border just east of Aiyt a-Shab, western Bint Jbeil district (Ramiye, Ramya, Ramyah, Al Rmya)

Ramjil (see Ramiya)

Ras al-Ain, on the coast south of Tyre, Tyre district (see also Baalbek)

    Ras al-Ain beach

Ras Baalbek

    Ras Baalbek bridge—Essahel, ID 86, assessed as destroyed[131]

Ras al-Bayyadah, on the coast, Tyre district (Ras Al Beidah, Ras al-Bayyadah)

Ras al-Mal area, Hermel district

Ras al-Naqoura, Tyre district (see also Naquoura)

Rashaf, near the border, Bint Jbeil district (Rshayf, Rachaf)[132]

Rashaya, Rashaya district (Rachiya, Rachaiya)

Rashaya Alwadi, Bekaa Valley

    Alarez Lilnasij/Cedars Textile SARL factory[133]

Rashaya al Fukhar, near the border, Hasbayya district (Rashia Fukhar, Rashayia, Rashaya Fukhar, Rashaya al-Fakhar, Rashaya al-Foukhar, Rachaya Al Foukhar)

al-Rashidiyeh, north of Ras al-Ain on the coast, south of Tyre, Tyre district (Al Rashideyia, Rachidiye)

    Palestinian refugee camp

Regie overpass, ID 71, assessed as destroyed[134]

Reshknanay, far eastern Tyre district near Sidiqine, Tyre district (Rishknaniyah)

---

[131] UNDP, "Lebanon: Rapid Environmental Assessment," 3-12.

[132] "In the village of Rashaf (in the central sector), mosques served as primary firing positions and command and control headquarters from which the fighting was directed." IDF, ITIC/CSS, Part One, 50.

[133] Ministry of Industry, Report of Damaged Factories.

[134] UNDP, "Lebanon: Rapid Environmental Assessment," 3-12.

al-Rihan, Tyre (al-Rihani)

Rihaniyeh/Al Qaiteh bridge over Bared River, linking Akkar with Dinnyeh region, Akkar district

Al-Riji (see al-Ghaziyah)

al-Rimadiyeh (see Rmadiyeh)

Riyaq, Bekaa Valley, Zahleh district (Riak, Rayaq)

> Riyaq Hospital
>
> Riyaq military airfield (Riyaq Al-Askari, Al-Biqa al-Sharqi), attacked 13 July
>
> Riyaq road
>
> Riyaq railroad bridge over Nahr al Litani, ID 114

al-Rmadiyeh, north of al-Sha'aytiyeh south of Qana, Tyre district (Rmadiye, al-Rimadiyeh, Ramadiyeh, Ramadiyyeh)

Rmeish, south of Aiyt a-Shab on the border, Bint Jbeil district (Christian village)[135] (Rmaish, Rmaich, Remich, Rumaysh, Al-Ramich)

> Tajalli church, reported damaged

Rumayleh, on the coastal road, north of Sidon, Shuf district (Rmeyleh, Rumaileh, Rmayleh, Rmeili, Rmayel, Ramlieh, Rmeileh, Ramileh)

> Rumayleh petrol station/Dagher gas station, attacked 15 July
>
> Rumayleh-Deir Rumayleh interchange, ID 73, assessed as destroyed[136]
>
> Rumayleh overpass
>
> Rumayleh-Wardaniyeh bridge, north of Sidon, ID 72, assessed as destroyed[137]

Rumin, north Nabatiyeh district (Roumine, Romeen, Roumayne)

> Roumine-Deir az-Zahrani bridge, ID 140 (Roumayne bridge?)

---

[135] According to one report, "local youngsters from the villages of Rmaish (central sector) and Alma al-Shaab (western sector) thwarted several attempts to fire rockets from those villages' houses (in practice, rockets were fired from the southern outskirts of the village of Alma al-Shaab)." IDF, ITIC/CSS, Part One, 35.

[136] UNDP, "Lebanon: Rapid Environmental Assessment," 3-12.

[137] Ibid.

al-Ruwais (see Beirut)

al-Sa'adiyeh, Baalbek district (Saaydeh, Saadiyat, Sa'adiyat, al-Sa'idah)

> Sa'adiyeh-Majdaloun bridge/culvert (a.k.a. Al-Dabiayah bridge), ID 129, assessed as destroyed[138]
>
> Dalhamieh bridge (Al-Sa'adiyat), assessed as destroyed[139]
>
> Dalhamieh Zahleh bridge, assessed as destroyed[140]

Saath, north of Baalbek (Shaath)

Sabah ("morning") hill, Al-Nabi Misha' neighborhood

> telephone antennas (reported completely destroyed)

Sabine (Saghbin)

Sadd al-Barid road, northern Lebanon

Safad al-Battikh, east of Tibnine, Bint Jbeil district (Safad al-Batteekh, Safad Al Batikh)

Safir bridge (see Sofar)

Sainiq, Sidon district (Sayniq)

> Sainiq bridge/Sainiq steel bridge (two separate bridges) (Sanig Maghdoucha bridge?), assessed as destroyed[141]

al-Saksakiyeh, south of Sidon, Tyre district (Saksakiyah, Saksakiya)

> al-Saksakiyeh heights
>
> al-Saksakiyeh bridge/overpass near Bablieh, ID 50, assessed as destroyed[142]

Salaa, south of Bafly, north of Jouwiya near Deir Kifa, eastern Tyre district (Sel'a, Selaa, Salaa, Silaa)

Salaata

Salhab bridge (Zahleh-Kfar Zabad), Zahleh district, ID 124

al-Sama'iyeh, Tyre district (al-Samaeiyeh, al Samayieh)

Sarafand, Zahrani district (Sarfand)

---

[138] Ibid.

[139] Ibid.

[140] Ibid.

[141] Ibid.

[142] Ibid.

Sarafand bridge/overpass, ID 49

Sarafand highway bridge, "over Hahn Khayzaran," ID 103, assessed as destroyed[143]

Sarba, Iqlim al-Toufah, north Nabatiyeh district (Sarba Houmine)

Lebanese army 2nd Brigade headquarters, reportedly attacked 30 July, 2 August

Sarba-Kfar Hatta bridge

(see also Anqoun/Sarba road)

Sarbine (same as Sabine?)

Sardeh, near the border south of al-Khiyam, Marjeyoun district (Sarda)

Sarri

Satqa (see Fatqa)

Sawwanah, near Khirbat Silim, Marjeyoun district (As-Souana)

Saydoun, western Bekaa

Seble plant electric transformer station?

Sejoud in Iqlim al-Toufah

Sere'en, Bekaa Valley (Seryin, Sereine)

Sere'en road

Sere'en plateau

al-Sha'aytiyeh, south of Qana, Tyre district (al-Shaittiyeh, al-Sheaaytiyeh, al-Shietiyeh, al-Sha'atiyeh, Sh'aytiyah, Chaatiyyeh)

Al-Shaf'a bridge?

al-Shahabiyeh, east of Jouwaya, Tyre district (al-Shahabiyah, Shehabiyeh, Shehabiyyeh, Chahabiya, Chehabiye)

Shahour, north of Arzoun, just south of the Litani River, Tyre district (Shahrour, Shahur, Shour near Tyre, Sh'hour, Sh-hour, Chohour, Chahour)

Shahrour/Arzoun triangle

Shahrour (see Wadi Shahrour)

---

[143] Ibid.

Shama, near Majdal Zoun, Tyre district (Chamaa, Shema?)

Abu Shamra, near Syrian border (Sham', Shema?, Abu Shamra)

    Abu Shamra bridge

    Abu Shamra petrol station

Shanuh Farm (Chanouh)

Shaq'ah bridge, Hasbayya district (Chakaa), assessed as destroyed[144]

Shaqra, east of Tibnine, Bint Jbeil district (Chakra, Chaqra)

Sharbiha, just north of Tyre city, Tyre district (Chabriha)

Sharnayh, (Sharnai, Charnaiye), east of Burj Chamali between Tayr Diba and Ma'rakah

al-Shariqiyeh, west of Nabatiyeh, Nabatiyeh district

Sharqiyeh (see Zawtar ash Sharqiyah)

Shatila Kafaat bridge (Chatila), assessed as destroyed[145]

Shawakir, area of Burj al-Chamali, Tyre district

Shebaa Farms, on the border, Hasbayya district, Mount Dov slopes (Shib'a, Sheeba, Shabaa)

Shiheen, near Tayr Harfa on the border, Tyre district (Shihin, Chihine, Shhin)

    122 mm rocket launch point

Shiyah (al-Shiyah) (see Beirut Chieh)

Shlifa falls, west of Baalbek, Baalbek district (Shalifa, Chlifa)

    Shalifa crossing Rajul al-Hifr neighborhood fuel storage

Shmaa, near Majdal Zoun, Tyre district (Shama)

Shmeiss (Shheem/Mount Lebanon)

Shmestar, west of Brital, Baalbek district, Bekaa (Chmistar)

    Husseiniyeh in Shmestar

al-Shnaiyeh

---

[144] Ibid.

[145] Ibid.

Shoukine, south of Nabatiyeh, Nabatiyeh district (Shoukein, Shokein, Shokeen, Shukin)

al-Shqif/Qalat ash Shqif, south Nabatiyeh district (al-Shqeef, Shaqif)

> al-Shqif fortress

Shrafiyat in al-Abasiyeh, Tyre (Shreifat)

Shuf district

> Shuf bridge north of Shuf interchange

> Shuf bridge south pedestrian overpass

Shuf Cedars (Arz al-Shouf)

> Cedars/Ain Zhalta road

Shumariyah (Choumariya)

Shwayfat, south of Beirut, Aaliyah district, Mount Lebanon[146]

(Shoefat? Choueifat, Chouwifatt, Showeifat)

> Lebanese Company for Catron Mince and Industry, collateral damage[147]

> Transmed Sal food and paper goods storage warehouse,[148] industrial zone (a.k.a. Proctor and Gamble detergent and foodstuffs warehouse), sustained major damage, supposedly hit with "bunker buster" bombs[149]

---

[146] Other industrial facilities in Shwayfat also are reported as having been attacked. The Sinno factory (Snow lumbermill?), Serum products factory, Transtec, the Wood trading company, and metal workshop all sustained "low" damage. A Pepsi factory, the Ghandour factory, and ITA Plast sustained no damage. See UNDP, "Lebanon: Rapid Environmental Assessment," 5-1. Damage was also reported to the Tabara pharmaceutical plant. The Ghandour factory was widely reported as having been attacked on 13 August.

[147] UNDP, "Lebanon: Rapid Environmental Assessment," 5-1.

[148] William Wallis, "Industrialists count cost of bombing," *Financial Times* (UK), 5 August 2006, http://www.ft.com/cms/s/4e2d7094-241f-11db-ae89-0000779e2340.html; and Caritas Internationalis, "Caritas Lebanon's Overwhelming Task of Caring for Civilians," 20 July 2006, http://www.caritas.org/jumpNews.asp?idChannel=3&idLang=ENG&idUser=0&idNews=4264.

[149] UNDP, "Lebanon: Rapid Environmental Assessment," 5-1.

Sibline electricity generator? reportedly attacked 21 July[150]

Sidiqine, southeast of Qana, Tyre district (Sidiqeen, Siddiqeen, Siddiquine, Saddiqin)[151]

    Jaafar petrol station, reported attacked 13 August

    122 mm and 220 mm rocket launch point

Sidon (Saida)

    Al-Hilaliyah electric transformer station

    Al-Kilani gas station

    Mar Elias hill

    Sidon Eastern Boulevard overpass, ID 69, assessed as destroyed[152]

    Sidon el Sim East bridge (Darb-el-Sin)

    fine tissue paper factory (see Kfar Jarrah)

    al-Awali bridge (see al-Awali)

    Sidon highway bridge NE over road/Sidon bridge (north), ID 108, assessed as destroyed[153]

    Sinniq bridge (Sidon), ID 106

    al-Zahraa complex, Sidon

Slouqi (see Wadi al-Slouqi)

Sofar, Aley district (Saofar, Sawfar, Safir)

    Sofar-Charon bridge/al-Safir bridge, ID 141

    old Sofar road

    Sofar-Chtaura international road

    Sofar viaduct

Sohmor near Litani River, west Bekaa district (Suhmur)

al-Soueida, near Tayr Diba (Swayda')

---

[150] Brian Whitaker, "Battered Lebanon counts the cost of Israeli onslaught," *Guardian Unlimited* (UK), 21 July 2006, http://www.guardian.co.uk/syria/story/0,,1825669,00.html.

[151] "In Sidiqqin, the main urgency is the clearance of tobacco fields from cluster bombs and UXOs, since cultivation of tobacco is the main source of income." Lebanon response OCHA SITREP no. 33, 25 August 2006.

[152] UNDP, "Lebanon: Rapid Environmental Assessment," 3-12.

[153] Ibid.

Souk al-Khan, south of Hasbaya

Sour district (see Tyre)

al-Sreireh, western Bekaa

Srifa, east of Tyre, Tyre district (Sraifa, Sreifa, Tzrifa, Sreefa, Sarifa)

> Srifa hill in Deir al-Jouz (Shriefa)

Srobbine, western Bint Jbeil district (Sirbeen, Sribbin)

Sultan Yacoub, Bekaa (Sultan Yaacoub)

> Florence General Trade furniture factory[154]

as-Sultaniyeh, on the main Tyre/Bint Jbeil road north of Tibnine, Bint Jbeil district (A-Sultania, al-Soltaniyeh)

> Hezbollah base (north of), attacked 12 July
>
> electric transformer station (near Hezbollah storehouse)
>
> al-Sultaniyeh/Qalya main road
>
> Sultaniyeh cell phone relay station

al-Suwayra, east of Hasbayya, Hasbayya district (Shwayya)

> al-Suwayra–Rashaya road

Taanayel, Bekaa Valley, Zahleh district[155] (Ta'nayel, Taanayeh, Ta'neil)

> Dalal Steel Industries factory (prefabricated house manufacture), attacked 23 July[156]
>
> Lamartine Food industry, sustained major damage from direct hit[157]

---

[154] Ministry of Industry, Report of Damaged Factories.

[155] Factories reported attacked in Taanyael include Akar Establishment (granite and marble), the Amwaj Leban stone industry, Lamartine Food industry, L'Origine Cos Sal, Massaya & Co Sal brewery, the Muller industry (ice cream), and the Turner SARL glass raw material factory. Ibid.

[156] Ibid.; Amnesty International, Israel/Lebanon, "Out of all proportion"; and IRIN (Bekaa Valley), "Lebanon: Factories come under fire," 4 August 2006.

[157] UNDP, "Lebanon: Rapid Environmental Assessment," 5-1.

Maliban Sal Glass works, attacked 18–19 July,[158] sustained major damage[159]

Taanayel Bardawni River bridge (at al Marj on the Beirut-Damascus highway)

Taanayel Taalbaya bridge, ID 133

(Taanayel-Barr Elias bridge near Alba)

Tabreekh, Bint Jbeil district

Tafahta culvert, assessed as destroyed[160]

al-Taher/Tahrir (see Tayr Filsay; see al-Mahmoudiyeh)

Tal Abbas bridge, Akkar district

Tal Abu al-Taweel near Aiyt a-Shab, Bint Jbeil district

Tal al-Abiad near Baalbek, Baalbek district (Tal al-Abyad)

Tal al-Nahhas (see Burj al-Moulouk) (Tel-Nahs, Tel-Nahess)

Tal Masoud, Bint Jbeil district (Tallat Mas'ud)

Talabayyeh, Bekaa (Taalabayyeh, Talbaya?)

Palestinian refugee camp

Talat El-Rahib (see Tallet al-Rahib)

Talba Baalbek, Bekaa Valley

---

[158] Ministry of Industry, Report of Damaged Factories. "Maliban, the second largest glassworks in the Middle East, was an exception, with production reaching some 200 tonnes a day for sale around the region. It was one of five Bekaa factories assessed as destroyed. A journalist who visited the ruined factory floor said, "It's impossible to discern what this space was used for. All that's visible is churned up soil with twisted metal, powdered glass and wrecked machinery. It is possible to discern the cause of the disruption, though: four distinct craters have been gouged out of the factory floor." One of the plant managers said, "The planes came around 12:45 so most people were at lunch, fortunately. Two people were killed, both Indians, and two injured. If they had come an hour earlier or later it would have been a massacre . . . they even assessed as destroyed the workers' residence." Quoted in Amnesty International, "Israel/Lebanon," 17.

[159] UNDP, "Lebanon: Rapid Environmental Assessment," 5-1. The attack also caused damage to a chicken farm, killing hundreds of chickens, the Shamsin bakery opposite the farm, and an adjacent gas station.

[160] UNDP, "Lebanon: Rapid Environmental Assessment," 3-12.

Liban Lait Dairy Plant, the country's largest dairy farm, attacked 17 July,[161] sustained three direct hits[162]

Tallet al-Rahib (Talat El-Rahib)

Tallet al-Rumtani at foot of Barouk mountains, above Kefraya

Tallet al-Khazzan

Tallet Hamamess in Bint Jbeil, near Marjeyoun (Tallet al-Hamamess, Tallat al-Hamamis)

Tallet Mar Elias, Sidon district (Talit Mar Elias)

Talouseh, near the border, southern Marjeyoun district (Talloussa, Tallousa, Talousa, Tallousseh)

Tanieh, Tyre district

Tariya, Baalbek district (Taraya)

> Taraya/Afqa road, connecting Bekaa with Mount Lebanon
>
> Taraya/Afqa/Aayoun al-Siman road in Mount Lebanon

Tarshish-Zahleh road

al-Tasseh River, southern Lebanon

al-Taybeh, on the border west of Kfar Kila, Marjeyoun district[163] (al-Teebeh, al-Tibo, Tiba, A-Teibeh, Taybe, Al-Taibe, Tibbiya)

Tayr Diba, east of Tyre, Tyre district (Tair Dibba, Tayr Dibba, Tier Diba, Tair Debba)

Tayr Filsay, on the Litani River, Nabatiyeh district (Tayr Filsiyeh, Tair Falsay, Teir Felseih)

---

[161] "Amnesty International visited the Liban Lait milk and derivatives factory, which was assessed as destroyed in an air strike at about 3 am on 17 July. The control room, processing plant and canning and cheese-making sections were all left in ruins. Liban Lait had produced over 90 percent of Lebanon's long-life pasteurized milk, as well as fresh milk, yoghurt, cheese and lebneh. Its chief engineer, Hisham Oraybi, told Amnesty International at the end of August that the company had employed 160 workers at the factory, of whom only 18 now had work. The destruction of Liban Lait disrupted the provision of fresh milk to schoolchildren that was coordinated by non-governmental and intergovernmental organizations. Hisham Oraybi said the attack had cost the company an estimated US $20 million in damage alone and that 'while we paid the staff for the first half of the war we don't know when we'll next be able to do so.'" Amnesty International, Israel/Lebanon, "Out of all proportion."

[162] UNDP, "Lebanon: Rapid Environmental Assessment," 5-1.

[163] "In Taibe, the Commission gathered information on the occupation of part of the town by IDF, which set up sniper positions in the castle from which they could dominate the surrounding area; 136 houses and 2 schools were assessed as destroyed in Taibe." UN, Report of the Commission of Inquiry, 31.

February 6 (Tahrir) Bridge over the Litani River[164]/Tayr Fil-say-al-Zrariyeh bridge, ID 43, attacked 12 July, assessed as destroyed[165]

Tayr Harfa, on the border, Tyre district (Tair-Haif)

Terbol, near Tripoli, Zgharta area, Zahleh district (Tirbil, a.k.a. Jabal Tarbal)

television and cellular phone transmission station[166] (Al-Manar, state-run Tele-Liban, LBCI, New TV, Avenir TV, and Future TV), attacked 22 July

Terbol main road, larger crater

Kark Terbol bridge, assessed as destroyed[167]

Terfa

Tibnine, on the main Tyre/Bint Jbeil road, Bint Jbeil district (Tebnine, Tibneen)

122 mm rocket launch point

Tibnine hospital[168]

At-Tiri, Bint Jbeil district (Tayri, Al Tire, Batiri)

Fawzi Safir natural gas station

Jamal Saleh gas station

Toul (Tul)

Toulin, southern Marjeyoun district (Toleen, Touline)

Toumat Niha (Tumat Neiha), central Bekaa (Toumat Neha, a.k.a. Jebal Toumat Niha)

Jezzine district transmission station (Al-Manar TV, NBN), attacked 15 July

---

[164] Reuters (Marjayoun), "Israel bombs Lebanese bridge—security sources," 12 July 2006, 1052 GMT: "Israeli warplanes bombed a key bridge in south Lebanon on Wednesday shortly after Hezbollah guerrillas seized two Israeli soldiers in a cross-border attack. . . . They said the February 6 Bridge linking the south's major cities of Tyre and Nabatiyeh was assessed as destroyed. There were no reports of casualties."

[165] UNDP, "Lebanon: Rapid Environmental Assessment," 3-12.

[166] "Israel strikes TV, phone towers in Lebanon."

[167] UNDP, "Lebanon: Rapid Environmental Assessment," 3-12.

[168] "In Tibnin[e], the governmental hospital showed signs of being hit by direct fire weapons, possibly a tank shell or a missile strike from a helicopter. The Commission saw at least five direct hits on the hospital's infrastructure." UN, Report of the Commission of Inquiry, 42.

Toura, near Deir Qanoun en Nahr, Tyre district (Tura)

Tripoli (Al-Abdeh)

   Beddawi refugee camp

   Tripoli port

   Tripoli port naval radar/Tripoli harbor antenna

   Tripoli port antenna "belonging to the maritime operations room"

Tufahta

Tyre, Tyre district (Tyr, Sour)

   Amal offices, Salaa neighborhood, attacked 27 July

   Benoit Barakat army barracks

   Qadmus area/Qadmus hill (Kadmous, Cadmous, Cadmouns)

   Najim (Najem) hospital

   Tyre-al Hosh road

   "Center of operations for Hezbollah's unit in charge of Fajr and 220 mm rockets"[169]

Umm at-Tout, near Marwaheen, Tyre district

Wadi al Akhdar (Alwadi al Akhdar, Wadi El-Akhdar; see Kfar Rumman)

Wadi al-Aaziyeh

Wadi Chahrour (see Wadi Shahrour)

Wadi El-Hadjir (Hassaniya Wadi El-Hadjir)

Wadi al-Hujair, near Bra'shit (Wadi al-Hjayr)

   Wadi al-Hujair–Shumariyah road

Wadi Jilo, east of Tyre on the main Bint Jbeil road, Tyre district (Wadi Jilu, Ouadi Jilou)

   electric power station, reported attacked on 12 July[170]

   pumping station

Wadi al-Jeer

Wadi Kfur

   "fireworks factory," reported attacked 16 July

Wadi Khansa, Hasbayya district

---

[169] IDF, ITIC/CSS, Part Two, 101.

[170] Bahrain News Agency (Al-Arabiya TV, Dubai, in Arabic), "Two civilians killed in South Lebanon," 12 July 2006, 1351 GMT.

Wadi al-Qaysiyeh, near Bra'shit (Wadi Qayssiyya, Wadi al Qaysiyah)

Wadi Shahrour, southeast Beirut, east of Kfar Shima, Beirut district (Ouadi Chahrour, Wadi Shahrur)

    Bleibel/Wadi Shahrour road

    suspected long-range (Zelzal) rocket base

    Wadi Shahrour bridge/Toshai-Wadi Shahrour bridge, assessed as destroyed[171]

Wadi al-Sluqi [Saluki River], south of the Litani River, near Bra'shit (Wadi Slouqi, Wadi Saluki)

Wadi al-Wanah, near Bra'shit

Wadi Yanta on Lebanese-Syrian border

Wadi al-Zaynah, north of Sidon on the coastal highway at Jadra, Shuf district

    (Wadi Al-Zineh, Wadi al-Zayneh, Wadi Zina)

    Wadi al-Zaynah bridge/viaduct/Wadi al-Zaynah-Chhime overpass, ID 66, reported attacked 12–13 July, damaged)[172]

Wadi Zibqine (see Zibqine)

Wardaniyeh, Shuf district (see also Rumayleh)

    Wardaniyeh interchange/overpass

al-Wardiyeh

al-Wazzani, on the broder south of al-Khiyam, Hasbayya district

    Wazzani bridge, ID 120

Ya'atar, western Bint Jbeil district (Yatar, Yater, Yatir)[173]

    Hezbollah headquarters northwest of (Nasr unit's Second Territorial Subdivision)

    122 mm rocket launch point

Yahoun (see Bayt Yahoun)

al-Yammouneh

---

[171] UNDP, "Lebanon: Rapid Environmental Assessment," 3-12.

[172] Ibid.

[173] "In Yater (almost half of which has been assessed as destroyed) assets such as blankets, mats and kitchen sets are needed which will be provided by UNHCR." Lebanon response OCHA SITREP no. 33, 25 August 2006.

Yanouh, north of the Tyre/Bint Jbeil main road, Tyre district (Ynouh)

Yanta, near the Syrian border, Rachiya district (see also Wadi Yanta)

Yarin, on the border, Tyre district

Yaroun, on the border, south of Bint Jbeil, Bint Jbeil district (Yurin)

    water processing plant

Yohmor, north of the Litani River, Nabatiyeh district (Yuhmor)

Yohmor-al-Shqif region

Youneen fields, "in depth of eastern chain of Mount Lebanon" (Youneed)

    Youneed bridge

Zaarourieh-Allek culvert, Baalbek district, ID 128

Zaghla bridge, Hasbayya district, ID 123

Zahlah, southern Bekaa Valley, Zahlah district (Zahle, Zahleh)

    al-Fayda/Zahlah road

    Iranian Revolutionary Guards camp

Zahrani, south of Sidon, Zahrani district

    Zahrani highway bridge over the Zahrani River, ID 139, attacked 12 July,[174] assessed as destroyed[175]

    Zahrani interchange to Nabatiyeh, ID 90

    Zahrani old bridge—Tall al Buraqi highway/old Zahrani road bridge, ID 95, assessed as destroyed[176]

    Zahrani overpass main highway, ID 89

    Zahrani power plant, reported attacked on 15 July

    al-Qa'qa'iyah bridge, Zahrani River

Zamraya crossing near Hasbayya

---

[174] The AP reports that an Israeli attack hit a major road junction at Zahrani where the main north-south coastal highway meets the road connecting the coast with the interior of southern Lebanon. AP (Beirut), "Hezbollah captures two Israeli soldiers, sparking Israeli bombardment in south Lebanon," 12 July 2006, 1546 GMT; and AP (Ghattas), "Israel bombs southern Lebanon."

[175] UNDP, "Lebanon: Rapid Environmental Assessment," 3-12.

[176] Ibid.

Zawtar al-Gharbiyah (West Zawtar), south of Nabatiyeh, Nabatiyeh district

Zawtar ash Sharqiyah (East Zawtar), south of Nabatiyeh, Nabatiyeh district (Zaoutar, Zouter, Zoter, Zotor, Zawtar)

Zawtar/Mayfadoun road

Zboud (near Hermel)

Zefta, south of the Zahrani River, Sidon district (Zifta, Zafta)

Amal offices, attacked 26 July

Zefta road bridge over the Beirut-to-Tyre highway, ID 105

Zibdine, south of Nabatiyeh, Nabatiyeh district (Zebdine, Zib-
din)

Zibqine, Tyre district (Zibqeen, Zebqine, Zabqine, Zebkin, Ze-
bkine)

122 mm and 220 mm rocket launch point

Zighreen—Marjaheen in Hermel

al-Zrariyeh, north of the Litani River, south Sidon district (see
also Tayr Filsay) (al-Zararieh, al-Zrariyyeh, Al Zrareyi, Al-
zrareyia)

220 mm and 302 mm rocket launch point

Abbreviations

AFP	*Agence France-Presse* (French press agency)
AP	Associated Press
BLU	bomb live unit
CSS	Center for Special Studies (IDF)
DPA	*Deutsche Presse-Agentur* (German press agency)
FM	Foreign Minister
GMT	Greenwich Mean Time
HRC	Human Rights Council (UN); Higher Relief Commission (Lebanon)
IAF	Israeli Air Force
ICRC	International Committee of the Red Cross
IDF	Israel Defense Force(s)
IRIN	Integrated Regional Information Network (UN news network)
ITIC/CSS	Intelligence and Terrorism Information Center at the Center for Special Studies
MDA	*Magen David Adom* (Israeli "Red Cross")
MFA	Ministry of Foreign Affairs
MLRS	multiple-launch rocket system
OCHA	Office for the Coordination of Humanitarian Affairs
OGL	Observer Group Lebanon
OHCHR	Office of the High Commissioner for Human Rights
PM	Prime Minister
SLA	South Lebanon Army
UAV	unmanned aerial vehicle
UNDP	UN Development Programme
UNHCR	UN High Commissioner for Refugees
UNICEF	UN Children's Fund
UNIFIL	UN Interim Forces in Lebanon
UNMACC	UN Mine Action Coordination Centre
UNOSAT	UN Institute for Training and Research (UNITAR) Operational Satellite Applications Programme

UNSC	UN Security Council
UNSCR	UN Security Council Resolution
UPI	United Press International
UXO	unexploded ordnance
WHO	World Health Organization

Bibliography

"A war-torn Lebanese city in ruin." *Houston Chronicle*, 23 September 2006. http://www.chron.com/disp/story.mpl/headline/world/4209972.html.

"After the storm: Israel and the future of Olmert's government." *Jane's Intelligence Review*, January 2007.

Agence France-Presse (AFP) Beirut. "28 killed as Israel pounds Lebanon in soldier crisis." 13 July 2006, 0851 GMT.

———. "Dozens killed as Israel bombs Lebanon." 13 July 2006, 2258 GMT.

———. "Gruesome scenes after Israeli air raids on south Lebanon." 13 July 2006, 1158 GMT.

———. "The heavy human and economic cost of Lebanon war." 14 August 2006.

———. "Israel bombed Beirut airport to halt Hezbollah arms: army." 13 July 2006, 0510 GMT.

———. "Israel bombs Beirut airport, 27 killed in raids." 13 July 2006, 0614 GMT.

———. "Israel strikes Lebanon over seized soldiers, dozens killed." 13 July 2006, 1133 GMT.

———. "Israeli aircraft bomb Beirut international airport." 13 July 2006, 0418 GMT.

"Air heads: Misperceptions and rivalries obscure air power's potential." *Armed Forces Journal*, June 2006.

Allbritton, Christopher, and Rania Abou Zeid. "Adding up the bill is itself a major challenge: Confusion still surrounds the extent of the damage in many parts of the country." *Daily Star* (Lebanon), 2 October 2006. http://www.dailystar.com.lb/article.asp?edition_id=1&categ_id=1&article_id=75829.

"Ambulances fired on by Israel, says Red Cross." *Sunday Morning Herald*, 25 July 2006. http://www.smh.com.au.

Amnesty International. "Israel/Lebanon: Deliberate destruction or 'collateral damage'? Israeli attacks on civilian infrastructure." MDE 18/007/2006, August 2006.

———. "Israel/Lebanon: End immediately attacks against civilians." Press release. 13 July 2006.

303

———. "Israel/Lebanon: Evidence indicates deliberate destruction of civilian infrastructure." n.d.

———. "Israel/Lebanon: Hezbollah's deliberate attacks on Israeli civilians." MDE 02/026/2006, 14 September 2006. http://web.amnesty.org/library/Index/ENGMDE0202620 06?open&of=ENG-2D2.

———. "Israel/Lebanon; Out of all proportion—civilians bear the brunt of the war." MDE 02/033/2006, 21 November 2006.

———. "Lebanon mission: update 3." Blogs. n.d. http://amne stylebanonisrael.blogspot.com/2006/08/lebanon-mission -update-3.html.

"An Enduring Illusion—Air Power." *Economist*, 26 August 2006.

"Analysis: Iran, Syria use Lebanese militia." UPI, Beirut, 12 July 2006, 1646 GMT.

"Annan condemns Israel attack in Lebanon." *Ynetnews.com.* 12 July 2006, 18:03. http://www.ynetnews.com/Ext/Comp/ ArticleLayout/CdaArticlePrintPreview/1,2506,L-3274607,00 .html.

Arkin, William M. "Week Eight: Don't Know Much about Biology." The Gulf War: Secret History, *Stars and Stripes*, 2001. http://www.thememoryhole.org/war/gulf-secret.htm.

Ashkenazi, Eli, Ran Reznick, Jonathan Lis, and Jack Khoury. "The Day After/The War Numbers—4,000 Katyushas, 42 civilians killed." *Haaretz*, 15 August 2006.

Asmolov, Grigory. "We Are Ready for the Next War." *Kommersant* (Russia), 9 November 2006. http://www.kommersant .com/p719977/r_527/Israel_ Lebanon_Syria_Hizballah.

Associated Press (AP), Beirut. "12 Lebanese killed in convoy attack," 15 July 2006. http://news.yahoo.com/s/ ap/mideast_fighting_civilians_killed;_ylt=AkXPREPzihX .CrdFflsSI9oDW7oF;_ylu=X3oDMTBhcmljNmVhBHNlYw Ntcm5ld3M.

———. "Heavy clashes in southern Lebanon as Hezbollah TV announces capture of two Israeli soldiers," 12 July 2006, 0813 GMT.

————. "Heavy clashes in southern Lebanon as Hezbollah TV announces capture of two Israeli soldiers," 12 July 2006, 1435 GMT.

————. "Hezbollah and Israeli forces clash across the border in southern Lebanon," 12 July 2006, 0735 GMT.

————. "Hezbollah captures two Israeli soldiers, sparking Israeli bombardment in south Lebanon," 12 July 2006, 1546 GMT.

————. "Hezbollah denies firing rockets on Israel's Haifa," 13 July 2006, 1752 GMT.

————. "Japan's Koizumi urges Israel to show restraint, not seek 'eye for eye,'" 12 July 2006, 1146 GMT.

————. "Military Analysts Question Israeli Bombing," 20 July 2006.

————. Nahariya, Israel. "Rockets hit northern city of Haifa, causing no injuries," 13 July 2006, 1740 GMT.

————. "Nine Palestinians killed in Israeli airstrike, Hezbollah claims to kidnap two Israeli soldiers." (Gaza City), 12 July 2006, 0920 GMT.

Association Libanaise pour l'Education et la Formation (ALEF) and Nouveaux Droits de l'Homme (NDH). "International Humanitarian Law violations." Second report, 14 August 2006.

Bahrain News Agency. "Two civilians killed in South Lebanon." (Al-Arabiya TV, Dubai), in Arabic, 12 July 2006, 1351 GMT.

Barnea, Nahum, and Shimon Schiffer. "What Would Halutz Say?" *Yediot Aharonot* (Tel Aviv), 25 August 2006.

Bazzi, Mohamad. "Hezbollah cracked Israeli radio code during war." *Yaliban*, 21 September 2006. http://yaliban.com/site/archives/2006/09/Hezbollah_crack.php.

Ben-David, Alon. "Debriefing teams brand IDF doctrine 'completely wrong.' " *Jane's Defence Weekly* (Tel Aviv), 3 January 2007.

————. "Israel probes use of cluster munitions in Lebanon." *Jane's Defence Weekly* (Tel Aviv), 6 December 2006.

Ben Meir, Yehuda. "Israeli Government Policy and the War's Objectives." *Strategic Assessment,* Jaffee Center for Strategic Studies (JCSS), Tel Aviv University-affiliated, Israel 9, no. 2 (August 2006).

Benn, Aluf. "Report: IAF wiped out 59 Iranian missile launchers in 34 minutes." *Haaretz*, 24 October 2006. http://www.haaretz.com/hasen/spages/778485.html.

———. "Report: Interim findings of war won't deal with personal failures." *Haaretz*, 8 March 2007. http://www.haaretz.com/hasen/spages/834572.html.

Blanford, Nicholas. "Deconstructing Hizbullah's [*sic*] surprise military prowess." *Jane's Intelligence Review*, November 2006.

———. "Hizbullah [*sic*] and the IDF: Accepting New Realities along the Blue Line." *MIT Electronic Journal of Middle East Studies*, Summer 2006. Massachusetts Institute of Technology: Cambridge, MA.

Blanford, Nicholas, Ian MacKinnon, and Stephen Farrell. "How Israel was pulled back into the peril of Lebanon." *Times* (London), 13 July 2006, 4.

Brannon, Josh. "Panel: '*Hanit*' attack was preventable." *Jerusalem Post*, 7 November 2006. http://www.jpost.com/servlet/Satellite?c=JPArticle&cid=1162378346651&pagename=JPost%2FJPArticle%2FShowFull.

Brannon, Josh, and jpost.com staff. "Halutz slammed for promoting generals." *Jerusalem Post*, 30 October 2006. http://www.jpost.com/servlet/Satellite?cid=1161811237367&pagename=JPost%2FJPArticle%2FShowFull.

Brilliant, Joshua. "Analysis: Hezbollah's Recovery Timetable." UPI, 6 September 2006. http://www.upi.com/InternationalIntelligence/view.php?StoryID=20060906-045027-8532r.

British Broadcasting Corporation (BBC) News. "(Correction) Israel bombs Beirut airport; twenty-six Lebanese killed—Al-Jazeera." 13 July 2006, 0420 GMT.

———. "Day-by-day: Lebanon crisis—week one." http://news.bbc.co.uk/2/hi/middle_east/5179434.stm.

———. "Hezbollah warns Israel over raids." 12 July 2006. http://news.bbc.co.uk/1/hi/world/middle_east/5173078.stm.

———. "Israel Air Force bombs Beirut airport, isolates South Lebanon [Studio talk between correspondent Miki Gurdus and Ya'aqov Ahime'ir—live]." 13 July 2006. Excerpt from report by Israel radio, 13 July, 0405 GMT.

———. "Israel bombs Lebanese villages, Hezbollah shells targets—TV." Al-Arabiya TV, in Arabic, 12 July 2006, 0718 GMT.

———. "Israeli general says 'this is war'; pledges 'forceful' response to Lebanon," live news conference with Maj Gen Udi Adam, commander of the Israeli Defense Force (IDF), Northern Command: site unknown, Israeli Channel 2 TV, 12 July 2006, 1512 GMT.

———. "Israeli officials vow to remove Hezbollah from border." *Voice of Israel*, Jerusalem, in Hebrew, 13 July 2006, 0905 GMT.

Brookes, Andrew. "Air War over Lebanon." International Institute for Strategic Studies, London, 8 August 2006.

Capaccio, Tony, Timothy R. Homan, and Jonathan Ferziger. "Israel, Hezbollah Assess Arsenal, Consider Lessons as War Halts." *Bloomberg News*, 16 August 2006. http://www.bloomberg.com/apps/news?pid=20601070&sid=aJZ6iLvFjso0&refer=home.

Caspit, Ben. "The Next War." *Maariv*, 13 August 2006. Quoted in Makovsky and White, "Lessons and Implications."

CBS News, "Israel Bombs Foreign Ministry in Gaza," 12 July 2006.

Central Intelligence Agency. *World Factbook 2007.* "Lebanon" entry (Age Structure). https://www.cia.gov/cia/publications/factbook/geos/le.html#People.

"Comprehensive Political Dialogue with Hezbollah Secretary General on Repercussions of July War. Nasrallah to *As-Safir*: Resistance Has no Problem with National Army or UNIFIL." *As-Safir*, 6 September 2006.

"Confronting the threats." Editorial. *Jerusalem Post*, 4 December 2006.

Cordesman, Anthony H. "Preliminary 'Lessons' of the Israeli-Hezbollah War." Washington, DC: Center for Strategic and

International Studies (CSIS). Working draft, 17 August 2006.

Daily Star (Lebanon). July War 2006 Timeline. http://www .dailystar.com.lb/July_War06.asp.

Deutsche Presse-Agentur (DPA). "2ND ROUNDUP: Israel strikes Beirut airport, suburbs; over 40 killed." 13 July 2006, 1438 GMT.

———. "4TH ROUNDUP: Israel strikes Beirut airport, rockets land in Haifa." 13 July 2006, 2110 GMT.

———. "5TH LEAD: Israeli airstrikes hit Beirut airport, suburbs; 27 killed," 13 July 2006, 0542 GMT.

———. "7TH LEAD: Israel strikes Beirut airport, suburbs; at least 31 killed." 13 July 2006, 1004 GMT.

———. "Israel retaliates with Lebanon attacks; Gaza targeted." 13 July 2006, 12:54 a.m. EST.

———. "Israeli troops enter Lebanon in hunt after soldiers." 12 July 2006, 1050 GMT.

———. "Two projectiles fired from Lebanon land in northern Israel." 12 July 2006, 0712 GMT.

Dudney, Robert S. "The Air War over Hezbollah." *Air Force Magazine*, September 2006.

Egozi, Arie. "Israeli air power falls as offensive in southern Lebanon fails to halt Hezbollah." *Flight International*, 1 August 2006.

Ellingwood, Kim, and Laura King. "Warfare in the Middle East: Israel Wades into Bloodiest Day." *Los Angeles Times*, 27 July 2006.

Erlanger, Steven. "Israel Vowing to Rout Hezbollah." *New York Times*, 15 July 2006.

Erlich, Dr. Reuven. "Attacks on Israel from Lebanese Territory." 12 July 2006, 1202 GMT. http://www1.idf.il/DOVER/site/ mainpage.asp?sl=EN&id=7&docid=54183.EN. Parts I–III. IDF, ITIC/CSS. Report is now declassified. November 2006.

European Commission Joint Research Centre (JRC) and European Satellite Centre (EUSC). "Rapid preliminary damage assessment—Beirut and S Lebanon: Joint JRC and EUSC assessment of damage caused by the recent conflict in view of the Stockholm Donor conference (31st August) and re-construction efforts." Version 3, 30 August 2006.

Farrell, Stephen. "Our aim is to win—nothing is safe, Israeli chiefs declare." *Times* (UK), 14 July 2006, 1.

———. "The Times interview with Ehud Olmert." *Times* (UK), 2 August 2006. http://www.timesonline.co.uk/article/0,,251-2296832,00.html.

Federal News Service. "Interview with Silvan Shalom, Former Israeli Finance Minister and Member of The Knesset's Sub-committee for Intelligence And Secret Services, Discussing the Need to Act Decisively in Damascus and Beirut Following Hezbollah's Attack on Northern Israel (Iba Reshet Bet Radio, 12:44 (GMT+3)." 13 July 2006, 0944 GMT.

Feldman, Shai. "The Hezbollah-Israel War: A Preliminary Assessment." Middle East Brief. Waltham, MA: Brandeis University, Crown Center for Middle East Studies, September 2006.

"Fighting on two fronts." *Jerusalem Post*, 13 July 2006, 1.

Fulghum, David A. "Israel examines its military during Lebanon fighting lull." *Aerospace Daily and Defense Report*, 21 August 2006, 4.

———. "Israel's military changes to fight after a nuclear attack." *Aerospace Daily and Defense Report*, 12 September 2006.

Fulghum, David A., and Douglas Barrie. "The Iranian Connection; New operations, advanced weapons, Iranian advisers are influencing the course of Lebanon/Israel conflict." *Aviation Week & Space Technology*, 14 August 2006, 20.

Fulghum, David A., and Robert Wall. "Lebanon Intermission; Israel starts examining the military's roles, missions and technology during lull in Lebanon fighting." *Aviation Week & Space Technology*, 21 August 2006.

Gantz, Maj Gen Benjamin, commander of the IDF army head-quarters. Quoted in "Mideast Crisis to Guide Future Needs," *Defense News*, August 2006, 38.

Ghattas, Sam F. "Israel attacks Beirut international airport runways, airport closed; Civilians killed in south Lebanon." AP (Beirut), 13 July 2006, 0522 GMT.

———. "Israel blasts Beirut's airport as guerilla rockets hit Israel's third largest city in escalating battle." AP (Beirut), 13 July 2006, 1943 GMT.

———. "Israel bombs southern Lebanon after Hezbollah fighters snatch 2 Israeli soldiers." AP (Beirut), 12 July 2006, 1948 GMT.

Glantz, Aaron. "Lebanon: 7 Media Workers Injured in 48 Hours of Fighting." *OneWorld.net*, 15 July 2006. http://news.yahoo.com/s/oneworld/20060715/wl_oneworld/45361365131152986126.

Gleis, Joshua L. "A Disproportionate Response? The Case of Israel and Hezbollah." Jerusalem Center for Public Affairs, December 2006. http://www.jcpa.org/JCPA/Templates/ShowPage.asp?DBID=1&LNGID=1&TMID=111&FID=442&PID=0&IID=1456.

Glick, Caroline. "Column One: The world according to Olmert." *Jerusalem Post*, 28 September 2006. http://www.jpost.com/servlet/Satellite? cid=1159193338867& pagename=JPost%2FJPArticle%2FShowFull.

Goldenberg, Suzanne. "Red Cross ambulances destroyed in Israeli air strike on rescue mission." *Guardian* (UK), 25 July 2006.

Goose, Steve, director of Human Rights Watch (HRW) Arms Division. "Convention on Conventional Weapons (CCW): First Look at Israel's Use of Cluster Munitions in Lebanon in July–August 2006." Briefing. Geneva, Switzerland: 15th Meeting of the Group of Governmental Experts, 30 August 2006.

Gordon, Philip H. "Air Power Won't Do It." *Washington Post*, 25 July 2006.

Government of Lebanon. "Damage to Infrastructure." (last updated on 15 August 2006). http://www.lebanonundersiege.gov.lb/english/F/Info/Page.asp?PageID=130.

———. "Rebuilding Lebanon Together." Fact Sheet, n.d.

———. "Setting the stage for long term reconstruction: The national early recovery process." Stockholm Conference for Lebanon's Early Recovery, 31 August 2006.

Grant, Greg. "Hezbollah Missile Swarms Pounded Armor, Infantry." *Defense News*, August 2006, 8.

Greenberg, Hanan. "Adam: IDF needs moral rehab." *Ynetnews. com*, 23 October 2006. http://www.ynetnews.com/articles/ 0,7340,L-3318402,00.html.

———. "Almog: Kidnappings could have been avoided." *Ynetnews.com*, 12 November 2006. http://www.ynetnews.com/ articles/0,7340,L-3327332,00.html.

———. "Halutz: Criticism of IDF is out of proportion." *Ynetnews.com*, 20 November 2006. http://www.ynetnews.com/ Ext/Comp/ArticleLayout/CdaArticlePrintPreview/1,2506,L -3330297,00.html.

———. "Halutz: I don't need a lawyer." *Ynetnews.com*, 20 September 2006. http://www.ynetnews.com/Ext/Comp/ArticleLay out/CdaArticlePrintPreview/1,2506,L-3306396,00.html.

———. "Halutz: 'Mr. PM, We Won the War.' " *Ynetnews.com*, 27 August 2006. http://www.ynetnews.com/articles/0,7340,L -3296031,00.html.

———. "Most Long, Medium-Range Rockets Destroyed." *Ynet-News.com*, 31 July 2006. http://www.ynetnews.com/ articles/0,7340,L-3284302,00.html.

———. "Peretz to war casualties: We achieved goals in Lebanon." *Ynetnews.com*, 28 December 2006. http://www.ynetnews .com/articles/0,7340,L-3345484,00.html.

"Halutz: 'War results mediocre, IDF far from that.' " *Jerusalem Post*, 1 October 2006. http://www.jpost.com/servlet/Sate llite?cid=1159193351994&pagename=JPost%2FJPArticle% 2FShowFull.

Harel, Amos. "Army inquiries into Lebanon war will lead to personnel changes." *Haaretz*, 9 October 2006.

———. "Outgoing Infantry Chief Says Military 'Guilty of Arrogance.' " *Haaretz*, 22 August 2006. http://www.haaretz .com/hasen/spages/752774.html.

Harel, Amos, and Avi Issacharoff. "Proceed with caution: For the first time since the war broke out, Peretz has managed to make it clear that he does not take orders from Halutz." *Haaretz*, 2 November 2006.

Harel, Amos, and Gideon Alon. "Defense sources: Winograd war probe to last at least a year." *Haaretz*, 23 October 2006.

Harel, Amos, and Nir Hasson, "Pressure mounts on Halutz to 'take responsibility' for war." *Haaretz*, 13 November 2006. http://www.haaretz.com/hasen/spages/786933.html.

Harel, Amos, and Yoav Stern, "Lebanon police: 15 die in IAF strike on van in south Lebanon." *Haaretz*, 15 July 2006, last update—15:05. http://www.haaretz.com/hasen/objects/pages/PrintArticleEn.jhtml?itemNo=738611.

Hasson, Nir. "Gal Hirsch: MI warning would have prevented soldiers' abduction." *Haaretz*, 15 November 2006.

Hasson, Nir, and Meron Rappaport. "IDF admits targeting civilian areas in Lebanon with cluster bombs." *Haaretz*, 6 December 2006. http://www.haaretz.com/hasen/spages/789876.html.

"Hezbollah leader promises enemy 'more surprises.' " *Daily Star* (Lebanon), 17 July 2006. http://www.freerepublic.com/focus/f-news/1666790/posts.

"Hezbollah made extensive use of the Lebanese civilian communications infrastructure, requiring the IDF to hit said infrastructure to disrupt Hezbollah's communications and intelligence," n.d.

Human Rights Watch (HRW). "Fatal Strikes, Israel's Indiscriminate Attacks against Civilians in Lebanon." August 2006. http://hrw.org/reports/2006/lebanon0806/lebanon0806web.pdf.

———. "Hezbollah Must End Attacks on Civilians." 5 August 2006.

———. "Israel: Government Committee Should Probe Lebanon Laws of War Violations." Press Release, 26 September 2006.

"IAF continues attack on Lebanon." *Jerusalem Post*, 17 July 2006.

"IDF Spokesman: Hezbollah attack on northern border and IDF response." 12 July 2006. http://www.mfa.gov.il/MFA/Terrorism+Obstacle+to+Peace/Terrorism+from+Lebanon+Hizbullah/Hizbullah+attack+on+northern+border+and+IDF+response+12-Jul-2006.htm.

IDF Spokesman's Office. Dan Halutz' letter of resignation as IDF chief of staff, 16 January 2007.

"I Had No Illusions about This Job." *Jerusalem Post*, 29 September 2006.

"In the cockpit, by MAJOR 'Y.' " *Jerusalem Post*, 18 July 2006, 1524 (updated 19 July 2006, 0819). http://www.jpost .com/servlet/Satellite?cid=1150886035223&pagename=JP ost/JPArticle/ShowFull.

International Committee of the Red Cross. "Lebanon/Israel— ICRC Bulletin No. 11/2006." 11 August 2006.

"International Humanitarian Law violations in the July–August 2006 conflict opposing Hezbollah (Lebanon) to the State of Israel." Third report, 4 September 2006.

International Labor Organization (ILO). "An ILO Post Conflict Decent Work Programme for Lebanon." Report of the September 2006 Multidisciplinary Mission to Lebanon.

"Interview: Maj Gen Benjamin Gantz, commander, Israel Defense Forces' Army Headquarters." *Defense News*, August 2006.

"Iranian-made Hezbollah UAV shot down by Israeli fighter." *Flight International*, 15 August 2006.

"Israel authorizes 'severe' response to abductions." *Cable News Network* (*CNN*), 12 July 2006, 0227 GMT. http://www.cnn .com/2006/WORLD/meast/07/12/mideast/.

"Israel encounters top-line Russian weaponry in Lebanon." *Aerospace Daily and Defense Report*, 5 September 2006, 1.

"Israel praises UAV abilities." *Flight International*, 29 August 2006.

"Israel strikes TV, phone towers in Lebanon." *Lebanonwire.com*, 22 July 2006. http://www.lebanonwire.com.

"Israel used Delilah missile in Lebanon." UPI (Tel Aviv), 21 November 2006. http://www.upi.com/SecurityTerrorism/ view.php?StoryID=20061120-120755-2918r.

"Israeli army chief admits failures in Lebanon war but won't resign." AP (Jerusalem), 2 January 2007.

Israeli Defense Force (IDF). "Hezbollah attacks northern Israel and Israel's response." MFA/Terrorism+Obstacle+to+Peac e/Terrorism+from+Lebanon+Hizbullah/Hizbullah+attack +in+northern+Israel+and+Israels+response+12-Jul-2006 .htm.

———. "Hezbollah as a strategic arm of Iran." Intelligence and Terrorism Information Center (ITIC), Center for Special

Studies (CSS), 8 September 2006. http://www.intelligence .org.il/eng/eng_n/html/iran_Hezbollah_e1b.htm.

———. "The IDF-Hezbollah confrontation (Updated on the morning of Thursday, July 20)." 20 July 2006.

———. "The implementation of *Security Council Resolution 1701* after six months; Interim report." 4 March 2007. http://www .terrorism-info.org.il/malam_multimedia/English/eng_n/ html/res_1701e0307.htm.

———. "News of the Israeli-Hezbollah confrontation (as of noon, Sunday, July 30)." 31 July 2006.

———. "Responding to Hezbollah attacks from Lebanon: Issues of proportionality, Legal Background." 25 July 2006. http://www.mfa.gov.il/MFA/Government/Law/ Legal+Issues+and+Rulings/Responding+to+Hezbollah+attack s+from+Lebanon+Issues+of+proportionality+July+2006.htm.

———. "Summary of events: July 13th, 2006." http://www .mfa.gov.il/MFA/Terrorism+Obstacle+to+Peace/Terrorism +from+Lebanon+Hezbollah/IDF+operations+against+Hezb ollah+in+Lebanon+13-Jul-2006.htm.

———. "Summary of IDF operations against Hezbollah in Lebanon." 13 July 2006. http://www.mfa.gov.il/MFA/Te rrorism+Obstacle+to+Peace/Terrorism+from+Lebanon+H ezbollah/IDF+operations+against+Hezbollah+in+Lebanon +13-Jul-2006.htm.

———. "Summary of IDF operations in southern Lebanon in the past 24 hours (prior to cease-fire), Monday 14/08/2006 14:40." 14 August 2006. http://www1.idf.il/DOVER/site/ mainpage.asp?sl=EN&id=7&docid=56700&Pos=1&last=1 &bScope=True.

"Israel's War with Hezbollah: Facts and Figures." Embassy of Israel Backgrounder, 15 August 2006.

Japan Economic Newswire. "Israeli bombs Beirut airport, imposes sea, air blockade." 13 July 2006, 1116 GMT.

Jones, Clive. "Israeli offensive may not meet long-term objectives." *Jane's Intelligence Review*, 9 September 2006.

Jones, Ryan R. "Israeli General: We Did Not Win Lebanon War." *All Headline News*, 4 October 2006. http://www.cynews .com/news/7005066917/.

Katz, Gregory. "Bint Jbeil bears the scars of weeks of fighting with Israeli forces, but many regard Hezbollah's charge to battle as a point of pride." *Houston Chronicle*, 23 September 2006.

Katz, Yaakov. "Eyeballing different Lebanese at the kidnapping site," *Jerusalem Post*, 10 December 2006. http://www.jpost.com/servlet/Satellite?cid=1164881865641&pagename=JPost%2FJPArticle%2FShowFull.

———. "High-ranking officer: Halutz ordered retaliation policy." *Jerusalem Post*, 24 July 2006.

———. "IDF: Hezbollah almost at full strength." *Jerusalem Post*, 21 December 2006. http://www.jpost.com/servlet/Satellite?cid=1164881939862&pagename=JPost%2FJPArticle%2FShowFull.

———. "IDF report card." *Jerusalem Post*, 24 August 2006. http://www.jpost.com/servlet/Satellite?cid=1154525936817&pagename=JPost/JPArticle/ShowFull.

———. "IDF set for massive assault on Lebanon. Eight soldiers killed, two kidnapped in Hizbullah attack on northern border." *Jerusalem Post*, 13 July 2006, 1. http://www.jpost.com/servlet/Satellite?cid=1150885985413& pagename=JPost%2FJPArticle%2FPrinter.

Katz, Yaakov, and JPost.com staff. "Report slams Halutz's management." *Jerusalem Post*, 6 December 2006. http://www.jpost.com/servlet/Satellite?cid=1164881834350&pagename=JPost%2FJPArticle%2FShow Full.

Keinon, Herb, and David Horovitz. "Israel's Olmert Talks on Lebanon War, Iran, Prisoner Swap, Qadima Party Survival." Interview with Prime Minister Ehud Olmert, Jerusalem, n.d.

Kreps, Sarah E. "The 2006 Lebanon War: Lessons Learned." *Parameters* 37, no.1 (Spring 2007): 72–84.

Lebanon Higher Relief Commission. Fact sheet. http://www.lebanonundersiege.gov.lb/english/F/Info/Page.asp?PageID=130.

———. Fact sheet. 31 August 2006. http://www.lebanonundersiege.gov.lb/english/F/Main/index.asp?

———. FAQ, Presidency of the Council of Ministers Communication Unit. n.d. http://www.rebuildlebanon.gov.lb/english/f/Page.asp?PageID=46.

Lavrov, Foreign Minister Sergei, and Italian Foreign Minister Massimo D'Alema. Interview by Interfax, Russian news agency. n.d.

Macintyre, Donald "Israel launches ferocious assault on Lebanon after capture of troops." *Independent* (UK), 13 July 2006, 4.

Mahnaimi, Uzi. "Humbling of the supertroops shatters Israeli army morale." *Sunday Times* (UK), 27 August 2006. http://www.timesonline.co.uk/article/0,,2089-2330624_1,00.html.

Makovsky, David, and Jeffrey White. "Lessons and Implications of the Israel-Hezbollah War: A Preliminary Assessment." Washington Institute for Near East Policy, October 2006.

Maples, Lt Gen Michael D., director, Defense Intelligence Agency. "Current and Projected National Security Threats to the United States." Statement for the Record. Senate Select Committee on Intelligence Committee, 11 January 2007.

Marcus, Yoel. "One leader with an agenda." *Haaretz*, 26 September 2006. http://www.haaretz.com/hasen/objects/pages/PrintArticleEn.jhtml?itemNo=766887.

McGreal, Chris. "Capture of soldiers was 'act of war' says Israel." *Guardian* (UK), 13 July 2006. http://www.guardian.co.uk/israel/Story/01819123,00.html.

"MDA Daily Report—Emergency Urgency." http://www.ukmda.org.

Ministry of Foreign Affairs (MFA). "Behind the Headlines: A measured response to Hezbollah missiles." 17 July 2006. http://www.mfa.gov.il/MFA/About+the+Ministry/Behind+the+Headlines/A+measured+response+to+Hezbollah+missiles+17-Jul-2006.htm.

Ministry of Health and World Health Organization (WHO). "Lebanon Crisis: Service Availability Assessment," 29 August 2006.

Ministry of Industry. Report of Damaged Factories, n.d.

Morris, Harvey. "Israeli soldiers spend New Year holiday in Lebanon." *Financial Times* (UK), 24 September 2006. http://www

.ft.com/cms/s/3fec977c-4bf1-11db-90d2-0000779e2340
.html.

Myre, Greg, and Helene Cooper. "Israel to Occupy Area of Lebanon as a Security Zone." *New York Times*, 26 July 2006.

Nasrallah, Hassan. Interview on Al-Manar television, 27 May 2006.

————. Transcript. Interview with Hassan Nasrallah on Al-Jazeera, 20 July 2006.

————. Transcript. Interview with Hassan Nasrallah on Lebanese NTV, 27 August 2006.

————. Transcript. Speech in south Beirut, aired on Al-Manar TV, 16 February 2007.

————. Transcript. Victory Rally, 22 September 2006.

Nessman, Ravi. "Israeli Cabinet approves strikes in Lebanon after Hezbollah captures two soldiers in raid." AP (Jerusalem), 13 July 2006, 0354 GMT.

————. "Israeli troops raid Lebanon after Islamic militants capture two soldiers in cross-border raid." AP (Jerusalem), 12 July 2006, 2227 GMT.

Office for the Coordination of Humanitarian Affairs (OCHA), UN. Situation Report (SITREP), no. 35, 31 August 2006. http://iys.cidi.org/humanitarian/hsr/ixl79.html.

Office of the Prime Minister. Transcript. "PM Olmert's remarks at his press conference with Japanese PM Junichiro Koizum," 12 July 2006.

Opall-Rome, Barbara. "Did Hezbollah Fire U.S. Missiles at Israeli Tanks?" *Defense News*, September 2006, 1.

————. "IMI Shows Signs of Recovery; Israeli Firm Reshapes Portfolio to Heed Lebanon War Lessons." *Defense News*, 4 December 2006.

————. "Israel May Disrupt Commercial Broadcasts." *Defense News*, 28 August 2006.

Ophir, Noam. "Back to Ground Rules: Some Limitations of Airpower in the Lebanon War." *Strategic Assessment* 9, no. 2 (August 2006). JCSS, Tel Aviv University-affiliated, Israel.

Oren, Amir. "Analysis: In Lebanon, government hamstrung troubled division." *Haaretz*, 15 October 2006. http://www .haaretz.com/hasen/spages/774974.html.

———. "IDF preparing for another conflict by next summer." *Haaretz*, 6 November 2006. http://www .haaretz.com/hasen/objects/pages/PrintArticleEn .jhtml?itemNo=784074.

———. "Intelligence is not only early warning." *Haaretz*, 10 November 2006.

———. "Unlearned Lessons." *Haaretz*, 2 November 2006.

———. "The wisdom of the 'has-beens.' " *Haaretz*, 28 September 2006. http://www.haaretz.com/hasen/spages/767578 .html.

Peled, Yoav. "Illusions of Unilateralism Dispelled in Israel." Middle East Report Online, 11 October 2006. http://www .merip.org/mero/mero101106.html.

Peters, Ralph. "The myth of immaculate warfare." *USA Today*, 6 September 2006. http://news.yahoo.com/s/usato day/20060906/cm_usatoday/themythofimmaculatewarfare.

"Preparing to rebuild the north." *Ynetnews.com*, 14 August 2006.

Rabinovich, Abraham. "Retired Israeli generals vent." *Washington Times*, 27 September 2006. http://washingtontimes .com/world/20060926-105117-2517r.htm.

Rappaport, Meron. "Confusion clouds use of cluster bombs in Lebanon." *Haaretz*, 20 November 2006. http://www .haaretz.com/hasen/spages/789906.html.

———. "Israeli Defense Forces commander: We fired more than a million cluster bombs in Lebanon." *Haaretz*, 12 September 2006.

———. "When rockets and phosphorous cluster." *Haaretz*, 30 September 2006. http://www.haaretz.com/hasen/spages/ 761910.html.

Reporters Without Borders. "Reporters Without Borders in Beirut to express solidarity with Lebanese media." 27 July 2006. http://www.rsf.org/article.php3?id_article=18386.

Reuters. "Chronology—Six months of rising Mideast tensions." 13 July 2006, 09:44:18.

———. "Israel kills 52 civilians, including more than 15 children, in Lebanon." (Beirut), 13 July 2006. http://www .dawn.com/2006/07/13/welcome.htm.

———. "UPDATE 3—Hezbollah says seizes Israeli soldiers in border raid (Recasts with Hezbollah saying captured Israeli soldier)." 12 July 2006, 6:32:39 a.m.

Roosevelt, Ann. "Fighters Not Moving From Iraq to Lebanon, Official Says." *Defense Daily*, 28 July 2006.

Rubin, Uzi, Institute for Contemporary Affairs. "Hezbollah's Rocket Campaign against Northern Israel: A Preliminary Report." *Jerusalem Issue Brief* 6, no. 10 (31 August 2006).

Salhani, Claude. "Commentary: Nasrallah's mea culpa." *Middle East Times*, 30 August 2006. http://www.metimes.com/ storyview.php?StoryID=20060830-070214-6184r.

Salman, Talal. "Hezbollah's Nasrallah on Outcome of Hostilities, Role of Lebanese Army, UNIFIL." *As-Safir* chief editor's interview with Hezbollah secretary-general Hasan Nasrallah (Beirut), n.d.

Save the Children. "Rapid Livelihoods Assessment in Southern Lebanon: Tyre Caza (South Lebanon) and Bint Jbeil Caza (Nabatiyeh)." Final Report, 29 August 2006.

Scales, Maj Gen Robert H., USA, ret. "Enemy eyes." *Washington Times*, 1 August 2006.

———. "To win the long war." *Washington Times*, 10 October 2006.

Schiff, Ze'ev. "Ashkenazi to annul Halutz's organizational changes to IDF." *Haaretz*, 27 February 2007. http://www .haaretz.com/hasen/spages/830951.html.

———. "The War's Surprises." *Haaretz*, 19 August 2006. http:// www.haaretz.com/hasen/pages/ShArt .jhtml?itemNo=751958.

Shadid, Anthony. "Inside Hezbollah, Big Miscalculations; Militia Leaders Caught off Guard by Scope of Israel's Response in War." *Washington Post*, 8 October 2006, A1.

Shapir, Yiftah. "Artillery Rockets: Should Means of Interception be Developed?" *Strategic Assessment* 9, no. 2 (August 2006). (JCSS, Tel Aviv University-affiliated, Israel).

Shavit, Ari. "Six months of failures." *Haaretz*, 17 November 2006.

Siniora, Fouad, Lebanese Prime Minister. Address to the Lebanese People, 15 July 2006, n.p.

"Smart War, Dumb Targeting?" *Bulletin of the Atomic Scientists*, May–June 2000.

Susser, Leslie. "5766 A turbulent year." *Jewish Standard*, 21 September 2006, http://www.jstandard.com/articles/1619/1/5766 -A-turbulent-year.

United Nations (UN). "Implementation of General Assembly *Resolution 60/251* of 15 March 2006, Entitled 'Human Rights Council.' "

———. "Lebanon: Rapid Environmental Assessment for Greening, Recovery, Reconstruction and Reform 2006." UN Development Programme (UNDP), March 2007.

———. "Mission to Lebanon and Israel (7–14 September 2006)." A/HRC/2/7, 2 October 2006.

———. Presentation of Israel before the UN Security Council's 5508th meeting. S/PV.5508, 8 August 2006.

———. Report of the Secretary-General on the United Nations Interim Force in Lebanon (UNIFIL) for the period from 21 January 2006 to 18 July 2006. S/2006/560, 21 July 2006.

———. Report of the Secretary-General on the implementation of Resolution 1701.

———. Report of the Commission of Inquiry on Lebanon pursuant to Human Rights Council Resolution. S-2/1, A/HRC/3/2, 23 November 2006.

———. *Security Council Resolution 1559*. 2 September 2004.

UN Children Fund (UNICEF). "Hezbollah, Israel trade bombing threats." (Jerusalem), 13 July 2006, 1036 GMT.

———. SITREP (Lebanon), 30–31 August 2006.

———. SITREP (Lebanon), 1–8 September 2006.

UNIFIL Press Release. PR01, 17 July 2006.

———. PR02, 18 July 2006.

———. PR03, 19 July 2006.

———. PR04, 20 July 2006.

———. PR11, 27 July 2006.

———. PR12, 28 July 2006.

————. PR13, 29 July 2006.

————. PR14, 30 July 2006.

————. PR15, 31 July 2006.

Urbancic, Frank C., principal deputy coordinator for counterterrorism. Testimony before the House Committee on International Relations, Subcommittee on International Terrorism and Nonproliferation and Subcommittee on Middle East and Central Asia, 28 September 2006.

US Department of State. *Report on Human Rights Practices 2005*, March 2006.

Wall, Robert, David A. Fulghum, and Douglas Barrie. "Israel Tries to Identify Latest Hezbollah Rocket Threat." *Aviation Week & Space Technology*, 7 August 2006, 28.

————. "Israel Tries To Identify Latest Hezbollah Rocket Threat: Harsh Trajectories." *Aviation Week & Space Technology*, 6 August 2006, 28.

Williams, Dan. "Air power assumptions shot down over Lebanon." *Reuters*, 3 August 2006.

Wilson, Scott. "Israeli Head Of Military Quits after War Critique: Leadership in Conflict with Hezbollah Faulted." *Washington Post*, 17 January 2007, A10.

Xinhua News Service. "Israeli forces, Hizbollah [*sic*] clash, two Israeli soldiers feared kidnapped." 12 July 2006.

Index

NOTE: Some entries may be found in footnotes which expand on the material presented in the main text.

Divining Victory
Airpower in the 2006 Israel-Hezbollah War

Air University Press Team

Chief Editor
Jerry L. Gantt

Copy Editors
Tammi K. Long
Lula Barnes

Cover Art, Book Design, and Illustrations
L. Susan Fair

*Composition and
Prepress Production*
Vivian D. O'Neal

Quality Review
Mary J. Moore

Print Preparation
Joan Hickey

Distribution
Diane Clark

Lightning Source UK Ltd.
Milton Keynes UK
24 October 2010

161786UK00001B/14/P